POETRY
FOCUS
2015
LEAVING CERTIFICATE POEMS &
NOTES FOR ENGLISH HIGHER LEVEL

MARTIN KIERAN & FRANCES ROCKS

onomatopoeia
= use   of a word that reprents   which
imitates the   sound it represents e.g. Hiss

Gill & Macmillan

Gill & Macmillan
Hume Avenue
Park West
Dublin 12
with associated companies throughout the world
www.gillmacmillan.ie
© Martin Kieran and Frances Rocks, 2013
978 07171 5575 0

Design by Tanya M Ross, Elementinc.ie

The paper used in this book is made from the wood pulp of managed forests. For every tree felled, at least one tree is planted, thereby renewing natural resources.

Any links to external websites should not be construed as an endorsement by Gill & Macmillan of the content or view of the linked material.

For permission to reproduce photographs, the authors and publisher gratefully acknowledge the following:

© Alamy: 9, 42, 47, 61, 109, 125, 131, 137, 141, 147, 152, 161, 166, 189, 223, 233, 245, 248, 265, 286, 294, 342, 355, 395, 405, 416, 421, 430, 435, 440, 461, 478, 494, 507; © Bridgeman Art Library: 13, 93, 211, 337, 379; © Collins Agency: 361; © Corbis: 66, 205, 391; © Crawford Art Gallery, Cork: 270; © Getty Images: 4, 37, 57, 71, 77, 83, 88, 98, 104, 181, 184, 194, 199, 217, 228, 253, 259, 275, 280, 300, 315, 322, 327, 332, 348, 367, 373, 400, 426, 457, 473, 490, 512; © Imagefile: 18, 22, 27, 32, 157, 411, 452, 485; © Mary Evans Picture Library: 1; © PD Smith: 503; © RTÉ Stills Library: 311; © Saint Patrick's Cathedral: 499; © The Art Archive: 449; © Topfoto: 121, 170, 466.

The authors and publisher have made every effort to trace all copyright holders, but if any has been inadvertently overlooked we would be pleased to make the necessary arrangement at the first opportunity.

CONTENTS

Introduction

Poetry Focus is a new, modern poetry textbook for Leaving Certificate Higher Level English. It includes all the prescribed poems for 2015 as well as succinct commentaries on each one. In addition, there are sample student paragraphs on each poem, sample question plans and full graded sample essays. Well organised and easily accessible study notes provide all the necessary information to allow students to explore the poems and to develop their own individual responses.

- **Explorations** (a series of short questions) follow the text of each poem. These allow students to make initial responses before any in-depth study or analysis. Exploration questions provide a good opportunity for written and/or oral exercises.
- **Study notes** highlight the main features of the poet's subject matter and style. These discussion notes will enhance the student's own critical appreciation through focused group work and/or written exercises. Analytical skills are developed in a coherent, practical way to give students confidence in articulating their own personal responses to the poems and poets.
- **Graded sample paragraphs** aid students in fluently structuring and developing valid points and in using relevant quotations and reference in support.
- **Key quotes** encourage students to select their own individual combination of references from a poem and to write brief commentaries on specific quotations.
- **Sample essay plans** on each poet's work illustrate how to interpret a question and recognise the particular nuances of key words in examination questions. Evaluation of these essay plans increases student confidence in working out clear responses for themselves.
- **There is no single 'correct' approach** to answering the poetry question. Candidates are free to respond in any appropriate way that shows good knowledge of and engagement with the prescribed poems.
- **Full sample Leaving Certificate essays**, graded and accompanied by experienced examiners' comments, show the student exactly what is required to achieve a successful A grade in the Leaving Cert exam and to develop a real enthusiasm for English poetry. This is essential in identifying the task as required by the PCLM marking scheme.

HOW IS THE PRESCRIBED POETRY QUESTION MARKED?

Marking is done (ex. 50 marks) by reference to the PCLM criteria for assessment:

- Clarity of purpose (P): 30% of the total (i.e. 15 marks).
- Coherence of delivery (C): 30% of the total (i.e. 15 marks).
- Efficiency of language use (L): 30% of the total (i.e. 15 marks).
- Accuracy of mechanics (M): 10% of the total (i.e. 5 marks).

Each answer will be in the form of a response to a specific task requiring candidates to:

- Display a clear and purposeful engagement with the set task. (P)
- Sustain the response in an appropriate manner over the entire answer. (C)
- Manage and control language appropriate to the task. (L)
- Display levels of accuracy in spelling and grammar appropriate to the required/ chosen register. (M)

GENERAL

'Students at Higher Level will be required to study a representative selection from the work of eight poets: a representative selection would seek to reflect the range of a poet's themes and interests and exhibit his/her characteristic style and viewpoint. Normally the study of at least six poems by each poet would be expected.' (DES English Syllabus, 6.3)

The marking scheme guidelines from the State Examinations Commission state that in the case of each poet, the candidates have **freedom of choice** in relation to the poems studied. In addition, there is **not a finite list of any 'poet's themes and interests'.**

Note that in responding to the question set on any given poet, the candidates must refer to the poem(s) they have studied but are not required to refer to any specific **poem(s), nor are they expected to discuss or refer to all the poems they have chosen to study.**

In each of the questions in **Prescribed Poetry**, the underlying nature of the task is the invitation to the candidates to **engage with the poems themselves.**

EXAM ADVICE

- You are not expected to write about any **set number of poems** in the examination. You might decide to focus in detail on a small number of poems, or you could choose to write in a more general way on several poems.
- Most candidates write one or two well-developed **paragraphs** on each of the poems they have chosen for discussion. In other cases, a paragraph will focus on one specific aspect of the poet's work. When discussing recurring themes or features of style, appropriate cross-references to other poems may also be useful.
- Reflect on central **themes** and viewpoints in the poems you discuss. Comment also on the use of language and the poet's distinctive **style**. Examine imagery, tone, structure, rhythm and rhyme. Be careful not to simply list aspects of style, such as alliteration or repetition. There's little point in mentioning that a poet uses sound effects or metaphors without discussing the effectiveness of such characteristics.

- Focus on **the task** you have been given in the poetry question. Identify the key terms in the wording of the question and think of similar words for these terms. This will help you develop a relevant and coherent personal response in keeping with the PCLM marking scheme criteria.

- Always root your answers in the text of the poems. Support the points you make with **relevant reference and quotation**. Make sure your own expression is fresh and lively. Avoid awkward expressions, such as 'It says in the poem that…'. Look for alternatives: 'There is a sense of…', 'The tone seems to suggest…', 'It's evident that…', etc.

- Neat, **legible handwriting** will help to make a positive impression on examiners. Corrections should be made by simply drawing a line through the mistake. Scored-out words distract attention from the content of your work.

- Keep the emphasis on why particular poets **appeal to you**. Consider the continuing relevance or significance of a poet's work. Perhaps you have shared some of the feelings or experiences expressed in the poems. Avoid starting answers with prepared biographical sketches. Details of a poet's life are better used when discussing how the poems themselves were shaped by such experiences.

- Remember that the examination encourages **individual engagement** with the prescribed poems. Poetry can make us think and feel and imagine. It opens our minds to the wonderful possibilities of language and ideas. Your interaction with the poems is what matters most. Study notes and critical interpretations are all there to be challenged. Read the poems carefully and have confidence in expressing your own personal response.

EMILY DICKINSON

1830-86

‘Forever is composed of nows.’

Emily Dickinson was born on 10 December 1830 in Amherst, Massachusetts. Widely regarded as one of America's greatest poets, she is also known for her unusual life of self-imposed social seclusion. An enigmatic figure with a fondness for the macabre, Dickinson never married. She was a prolific letter-writer and private poet, though fewer than a dozen of her poems were published during her lifetime. It was only after her death in 1886 that her work was discovered. It is estimated that she wrote about 1,770 poems, many of which explored the nature of immortality and death, with an almost mantric quality at times. Ultimately, however, she is remembered for her distinctive style which was unique for the era in which she wrote. Her poems contain short lines, typically lack titles and often ignore the rules of grammar, syntax and punctuation, yet she expressed far-reaching ideas within compact phrases. Amidst paradox and uncertainty, her poetry has an undeniable capacity to move and provoke.

Prescribed Poems

❶ 'HOPE' IS THE THING WITH FEATHERS

'Hope' is the thing with feathers—
That perches in the soul—
And sings the tune without the words—
And never stops—at all—

And sweetest—in the Gale—is heard—   5
And sore must be the storm—
That could abash the little Bird
That kept so many warm—

I've heard it in the chillest land—
And on the strangest Sea—   10
Yet, never, in Extremity,
It asked a crumb—of Me.

'And sweetest—in the Gale—is heard—'

GLOSSARY

5   *And sweetest—in the Gale—is heard:* hope is most comforting in times of trouble.

7   *abash:* embarrass; defeat.

11 *in Extremity:* in terrible times.

EXPLORATIONS

1. What are the main characteristics of the bird admired by Dickinson? Does the image help or hinder your understanding of the meaning of hope? Refer to the poem in support of your opinions.

2. Would you consider Dickinson to be an optimist or a pessimist? How does the poem contribute to your view?

3. In your view, what is the purpose of the poem – to instruct, to explain, to express a feeling? Support your response by reference to the text.

STUDY NOTES

Few of Emily Dickinson's poems were published during her lifetime and it was not until 1955, 69 years after her death, that an accurate edition of her poems was published, with the original punctuation and words. This didactic poem explores the abstraction, hope. It is one of her 'definition' poems, wherein she likens hope to a little bird, offering comfort to all.

The dictionary definition of hope is an expectation of something desired. The Bible refers to hope, saying, 'Hope deferred maketh the heart sick', while the poet Alexander Pope (1688–1744) declares that 'Hope springs eternal in the human breast'. In **stanza one**, Dickinson explores hope by using the **metaphor of a little bird** whose qualities are similar to those of hope: non-threatening, calm and powerful. Just like the bird, hope can rise above the earth with all its troubles and desperate times. Raised in the Puritan tradition, Dickinson, although rejecting formal religion, would have been aware of the religious symbolism of the dove and its connection with divine inspiration and the Spirit or Holy Ghost, as well as the reference to doves in the story of Noah's Ark and the Flood. Hope appears against all odds and 'perches in the soul'. But this hope is not easily defined, so she refers to it as 'the thing', an inanimate object.

This silent presence is able to **communicate** beyond reason and logic and far **beyond the limitations of language**: 'sings the tune without the words'. Hope's permanence is highlighted by the unusual use of dashes in the punctuation: 'never stops—at all—'. This effective use of punctuation suggests the ongoing process of hope.

Stanza two focuses on the tangible qualities of hope (sweetness and warmth)and shows the spiritual, emotional and psychological **comfort found in hope**. The 'Gale' could refer to the inner state of confusion felt in the agony of despair. The little bird that comforts and shelters its young offers protection to 'so many'. The vigour of the word 'abash' suggests the buffeting wind of the storm against which the little bird survives. The last two lines, which run on, convey the welcoming, protective circle of the little bird's wing.

A **personal experience of hope in times of anguish** ('I've heard') is referred to in **stanza three**. Extreme circumstances are deftly sketched in the phrases 'chillest land' and 'strangest Sea'. This reclusive poet, who spent most of her life indoors in her father's house, deftly catches an alien, foreign element. She then explains that hope is not demanding in bad times; it is generous, giving rather than taking: 'Yet, never, in Extremity,/It asked a crumb—of Me.' The central paradox of hope is expressed in the metaphor of the bird, delicate and fragile, yet strong and indomitable. The tiny bird is an effective image for the first stirring of hope in a time of despair. In the solemn ending, the poet gives hope the dignified celebration it deserves.

Dickinson is a unique and original talent. She used the metre of hymns. She also uses their form of the four-line verse. Yet this is not conventional poetry, due to Dickinson's use of the dash to slow the line and make the reader pause and consider. Ordinary words like 'at all' and 'is heard' assume a tremendous importance and their position is to be considered and savoured. **Her unusual punctuation has the same effect, as it highlights the dangers ('Gale', 'Sea').** The alliteration of 's' in 'strangest Sea' and the run-on line to suggest the circling comfort of the little bird all add to the curious music of Dickinson's poems. The buoyant, self-confident tone of the poem is in direct contrast to the strict Puritanical tradition of a severe, righteous God, with which she would have been familiar in her youth and which she rejected, preferring to keep her Sabbath 'staying at home'.

ANALYSIS

'Emily Dickinson's poetry contains an intense awareness of the private, inner self.' Discuss how Dickinson gives expression to this interior world in her poetry. Support your exploration with quotations from her prescribed poems.

Sample Paragraph

Everyone has experienced the 'dark night of the soul' when it seems nothing is ever going to go right again. Dickinson, with her simple image of the bird singing in the soul, derived from psalms, provides the perfect optimistic antidote to this dark interior state of mind, '"Hope" is the thing with feathers'. She then develops this metaphor throughout the poem, comforting us with the thought that the bird/hope can communicate with us without the need for the restrictions of language, 'sings the tune without words'. There is no end to hope 'And never stops—at all'. She understands the darkness of despair, 'in the Gale', 'the strangest Sea'. The use of capitalisation by the poet seems to me to point out the terror of the individual struggling to survive. But the bird of hope provides comfort and warmth, 'And sweetest'. I like the poet's use of enjambment in the lines 'That could abash the little Bird/That kept so many warm'. It is as if the protection of hope encircles the individual, just as the wing of the little bird protects her young in the nest. This is an optimistic, buoyant poem in which Dickinson appears to be instructing the reader that one should never despair. The phrase 'perches in the soul' suggests to me that the poet regards hope as coming of its own volition, it just appears, there is a sense of otherworldliness about it. Hope, she tells us, is generous, never demanding, always giving, 'Yet, never, in Extremity,/It asked a crumb—of Me'. I think the use of the capital for 'Me' shows the heightened concern of someone for him/herself when the feeling of despair envelops.

Examiner's Comment

This response shows an awareness of the poet's style and content. It is a solid B-grade response. However, it lacks the in-depth analysis required for an A-grade answer.

CLASS/HOMEWORK EXERCISES

1. 'Dickinson is a wholly new and original poetic genius.' Do you agree or disagree with this statement? Support your response with reference to the poems on your course.

2. Copy the table below into your own notes and fill in critical comments about the last two quotations.

Key Quotes

'Hope' is the thing with feathers	The image of the bird is used to represent hope.
And sweetest—in the Gale	Hope is needed most in times of trouble.
I've heard it in the chillest land	
Yet, never, in Extremity,/It asked a crumb—of Me	

❷ THERE'S A CERTAIN SLANT OF LIGHT

There's a certain Slant of light,
Winter Afternoons—
That oppresses, like the Heft
Of Cathedral Tunes—

Heavenly Hurt, it gives us—   5
We can find no scar,
But internal difference,
Where the Meanings, are—

None may teach it—Any—
'Tis the Seal Despair—   10
An imperial affliction
Sent us of the Air—

When it comes, the Landscape listens—
Shadows—hold their breath—
When it goes, 'tis like the Distance   15
On the look of Death—

'Heavenly Hurt, it gives us'

GLOSSARY
(A-Z)

1 *Slant*: incline; fall; interpretation.
3 *oppresses*: feels heavy; overwhelms.
3 *Heft*: strength; weight.
9 *Any*: anything.

10 *Seal Despair*: sign or symbol of hopelessness.
11 *imperial affliction*: God's will for mortal
      human beings.

EXPLORATIONS

1. Describe the mood and atmosphere created by the poet in the opening stanza.

2. Comment on Dickinson's use of personification within the poem.

3. Write your own personal response to the poem, supporting your views with
   reference or quotation.

STUDY NOTES

*Dickinson was a keen observer of her environment, often dramatising her observations
in poems. In this case, a particular beam of winter light puts the poet into a mood of
depression as the slanting sunlight communicates a sense of despair. The poem typifies her
creeping fascination with mortality. But although the poet's subject matter is intricate and
disturbing, her own views are more difficult to determine. Ironically, this exploration of light
and its effects seems to suggest a great deal about Dickinson's own dark consciousness.*

From the outset, Dickinson creates an uneasy atmosphere. The setting ('Winter
Afternoons') is dreary and desultory. Throughout **stanza one**, there is an underlying
sense of time weighing heavily, especially when the light is compared to solemn
cathedral music ('Cathedral Tunes'). We usually expect church music to be
inspirational and uplifting, but in this case, its 'Heft' has a burdensome effect which
simply 'oppresses' and adds to the **downcast mood.**

In **stanza two**, the poet considers the significance of the sunlight. For her, its effects
are negative, causing pain to the world: 'Heavenly Hurt, it gives us'. The paradoxical
language appears to reflect Dickinson's ironic attitude that **human beings live in great**

fear of God's power. Is there a sense that deep down in their souls ('Where the Meanings, are'), people struggle under the weight of God's will, fearing death and judgement?

This feeling of humanity's helplessness is highlighted in **stanza three**: 'None may teach it' sums up the predicament of our limitations. Life and death can never be fully understood. Perhaps this is our tragic fate – our 'Seal Despair'. Dickinson presents **God as an all-powerful royal figure** associated with suffering and punishment ('An imperial affliction'). Is the poet's tone critical and accusatory? Or is she simply expressing the reality of human experience?

Stanza four is highly dramatic. **Dickinson personifies a terrified world** where 'the Landscape listens'. The earlier sombre light is now replaced by 'Shadows' that 'hold their breath' in the silence. The poet imagines the shocking moment of death and the mystery of time ('the Distance'). While the poem's ending is open to speculation, it seems clear that Dickinson is exploring the transition from life into eternity, a subject that is central to her writing. The only certain conclusion is an obvious one – that death is an inescapable reality beyond human understanding, as mysterious as it is natural. The poet's final tone is resigned, almost relieved. The 'Slant of light' offers no definitive answers to life's questions and the human condition is as inexplicable as death itself.

Throughout the poem, Dickinson's fragmented style is characterised by her **erratic punctuation and repeated use of capital letters**. She uses the dash at every opportunity to create suspense and drama. For the poet, the winter light is seen as an important sign from God, disturbing the inner 'Landscape' of her soul. In the end, the light (a likely metaphor for truth) causes Dickinson to experience an inner sadness and a deep sense of spiritual longing.

ANALYSIS

In your view, what is the central theme in this poem? Support the points you make with suitable reference to the text.

Sample Paragraph

I think that death is the main theme in all of Emily Dickinson's poems, including this one. The poem is very atmospheric, but the light coming through the church window can be interpreted as a symbol of God, hope for the world. However, Dickinson's language is quite negative and it could be argued that our human lives are under pressure and that fear of eternal damnation is also part of life. The phrases 'Heavenly Hurt' and 'imperial affliction' suggest that we are God's subjects, trying to avoid sin in this life in order to find salvation after death. One of the central points in the poem is the fear of dying that people have. It is outside of our control. All humans can do is 'hold their breath'. I believe that the central message of Dickinson's poem is that death comes to us all and we must accept it. The mood throughout the poem is oppressive, just like the sunlight coming in through the church window and the depressing 'Cathedral Tunes' the poet hears. The poet's distinctive punctuation, using dashes and abrupt stops and starts, is part of the tense mood of the poem. Dickinson's theme is quite distressing and the broken rhythms and disturbing images such as 'scar', 'Seal Despair' and 'Shadows' add to the uneasiness of the theme that death is unavoidable.

Examiner's Comment

A well-sustained response which attempted to stay focused throughout. In the main, references and quotations were used effectively and there were some worthwhile attempts to show how features of the poet's style enhanced the presentation of her central theme. Grade A.

CLASS/HOMEWORK EXERCISES

1. How would you describe the dominant mood of the poem? Is it positive in any way? Explain your response, supporting the points you make with suitable reference to the text.

2. Copy the table below into your own notes and fill in critical comments about the last two quotations.

Key Quotes

Winter Afternoons	The oppressive mood is reinforced through the setting itself and suggested by the use of this assonant phrase.
But internal difference	Dickinson believes that the pain of being mortal is an inner one, both psychological and spiritual.
Heavenly Hurt	
Shadows—hold their breath	

❸ I FELT A FUNERAL, IN MY BRAIN

I felt a Funeral, in my Brain,
And Mourners to and fro
Kept treading—treading—till it seemed
That Sense was breaking through—

And when they all were seated,   5
A Service, like a Drum—
Kept beating—beating—till I thought
My Mind was going numb—

And then I heard them lift a Box
And creak across my Soul   10
With those same Boots of Lead, again,
Then Space—began to toll,

As all the Heavens were a Bell,
And Being, but an Ear,
And I, and Silence, some strange Race   15
Wrecked, solitary, here—

And then a Plank in Reason, broke,
And I dropped down, and down—
And hit a World, at every plunge,
And Finished knowing—then—   20

'And then a Plank in Reason, broke'

GLOSSARY

3 *treading*: crush by walking on.
4 *Sense*: faculty of perception; the senses (seeing, hearing, touching, tasting, smelling); sound, practical judgement.

12 *toll*: ring slowly and steadily, especially to announce a death.
13 *As all*: as if all.
14 *And Being, but an Ear*: all senses, except hearing, are now useless.

EXPLORATIONS

1. Do you find the images in this poem frightening, macabre or coldly realistic? Give reasons for your answer, supported by textual reference.

2. What is the dominant tone in the poem? Where is the climax of the poem, in your opinion? Refer to the text in your answer.

3. Consider the rhyme scheme of the poem. In your view, why does the poet rhyme words like 'Drum'/'numb' and 'Soul'/'toll'? In your opinion, why does the rhyme scheme break down in the last stanza?

STUDY NOTES

This poem is thought to have been written in 1861 at a time of turbulence in Dickinson's life. She was having religious and artistic doubts and had experienced an unhappy time in a personal relationship. This interior landscape paints a dark picture of something falling apart. It is for the reader to decide whether it is a fainting spell, a mental breakdown or a funeral. That is the enigma of Dickinson.

The startling perspective of this poem in **stanza one** can be seen as the view experienced by a person in a coffin, if the poem is read as an **account of the poet imagining her death**. Alternatively, it could refer to the suffocating feeling of the breakdown of consciousness, either through fainting or a mental breakdown. Perhaps it is the dearth of artistic activity. Whichever reading is chosen, and maybe all co-exist, the **interior landscape of awareness is being explored**. The use of the personal pronoun 'I' shows that this is a unique experience, although it has relevance for all. The relentless pounding of the mourners walking is reminiscent of a blinding migraine headache. The repetition of the hard-sounding 't' in the verb 'treading—treading' evocatively describes this terrible experience. The 'I' is undergoing an intense trauma beyond understanding: 'Sense was breaking through'. This repetition and disorientation are synonymous with psychological breakdown.

Stanza two gives a first-person account of a funeral. The mourners are seated and the service has begun. Hearing ('an Ear') is the only sense able to perceive. All the verbs refer to sound: 'tread', 'beat', 'heard', 'creak', 'toll'. The passive 'I' receives the experience, hearing, not listening, which is an active process. The experience is so overwhelming that 'I' thought the 'Mind was going numb', unable to endure any more. The use of the past tense reminds the reader that the experience is over, so is the first-person narrative told from beyond the grave? Is this the voice of someone who has died? Or is it the voice of someone in the throes of a desperate personal experience? The reader must decide.

The reference to 'Soul' in stanza three suggests a spiritual dimension to the experience. The 'I' has begun to become disoriented as the line dividing an external experience and an internal one is breaking. The mourners 'creak across my Soul'. The oppressive, almost suffocating experience is captured in the onomatopoeic phrase 'Boots of Lead' and space becomes filled with the tolling bell. Existence in stanza four is reduced totally to hearing. The fearful transitory experience of crossing from awareness to unconsciousness, from life to death, is being imagined. The 'I' in stanza four is now stranded, 'Wrecked', cut off from life. The person is in a comatose state, able to comprehend but unable to communicate: 'solitary, here'. The word 'here' makes the reader feel present at this awful drama.

Finally, in stanza five, a new sensation takes over, the sense of falling uncontrollably. The 'I' has finished knowing and is now no longer aware of surroundings. Is this the descent into the hell of the angels in Paradise Lost? Is it the descent of the coffin into the grave? Or is it the descent into madness or oblivion? The 'I' has learned something, but it is not revealed. The repetition of 'And' advances the movement of the poem in an almost uncontrollable way, mimicking the final descent. The 'I' is powerless under the repetitive verbs and the incessant rhythm punctuated by the ever-present dash. This poem is extraordinary, because before the study of psychology had defined it, it is a step-by-step description of mental collapse. Here is 'the drama of process'.

ANALYSIS

'This poem is a detailed exploration of the experience of death.' Discuss this statement, using references from the text to support your views.

Sample Paragraph

When I first read Emily Dickinson's poem 'I felt a Funeral, in my Brain', I was reminded of the macabre pictures of Salvador Dali, where everything is real, but not quite right. It also reminded me of the films of Tim Burton, such as *The Nightmare Before Christmas*. All the elements are there, but nothing is totally right, it is surreal. This imagined funeral in the poem suggests to me the losing of the grip on life by the individual 'I'. The incessant noise, 'treading', 'beating', induces an almost trance-like state as the brain cannot function any more, and so becomes numb. In death, the senses are supposed to shut down, sight is one of the first to go, so I think it is very clever of the poet to suggest that being is just reduced to the one sense hearing – 'an Ear'. I also find the perspective of the poem chilling, the idea that this is the view of someone lying in the coffin observing their funeral is macabre in the extreme. But the most compelling line in the poem is 'And then a Plank in Reason, broke'. This graphically conveys the snap of reason as the 'I' finally loses a grip on consciousness and slips away, hurtling uncontrollably into another dimension. Even the punctuation, with the use of the two commas, conveys this divided reality. But the most unnerving word is yet to come, 'then'. Does the poet know now? What does the poet know, is it about the existence or non-existence of an afterlife? Where is the poet standing now – here or there, alive or dead?

Examiner's Comment

An unusual, individual reading of the poem, and generally well supported by reference to the text. There are some weaknesses in expression and the paragraph is not fully focused on the question. Overall, a B-grade response.

CLASS/HOMEWORK EXERCISES

1. 'She seems as close to touching bottom here as she ever got.' Discuss this view of Emily Dickinson with reference to the poem 'I felt a Funeral, in my Brain'.

2. Copy the table below into your own notes and fill in critical comments about the last two quotations.

Key Quotes

That Sense was breaking through	This enigmatic line could refer to the breakdown of the five senses, or that reason was collapsing or coming.
My Mind was going numb	The narrator in the poem is presented as a passive recipient who can no longer endure this traumatic experience. This is enhanced by assonance.
And creak across my Soul	
And then a Plank in Reason, broke	

4 A BIRD CAME DOWN THE WALK

A Bird came down the Walk—
He did not know I saw—
He bit an Angleworm in halves
And ate the fellow, raw,

And then he drank a Dew   5
From a convenient Grass—
And then hopped sidewise to the Wall
To let a Beetle pass—

He glanced with rapid eyes
That hurried all around—   10
They looked like frightened Beads, I thought—
He stirred his Velvet Head

Like one in danger, Cautious,
I offered him a Crumb
And he unrolled his feathers   15
And rowed him softer home—

Than Oars divide the Ocean,
Too silver for a seam—
Or Butterflies, off Banks of Noon
Leap, plashless as they swim.   20

'He glanced with rapid eyes'

GLOSSARY

3 *Angleworm*: small worm used as fish bait by anglers.
17 *the Ocean*: Dickinson compares the blue sky to the sea.

18 *silver*: the sea's surface looks like solid silver.
18 *a seam*: opening; division.
20 *plashless*: splashless; undisturbed.

EXPLORATIONS

1. In your view, what does the poem suggest about the relationship between human beings and nature?

2. What effect does Dickinson's use of humour in the poem have? Does it let you see nature in a different way? Support the points you make with reference to the text.

3. From your reading of the poem, what impression of Emily Dickinson herself is conveyed? Refer to the text in your answer.

STUDY NOTES

In this short descriptive poem, Dickinson celebrates the beauty and wonder of animals. While the bird is seen as a wild creature at times, other details present its behaviour and appearance in human terms. The poem also illustrates Dickinson's quirky sense of humour as well as offering interesting insights into nature and the exclusion of human beings from that world.

The poem begins with an everyday scene. Because the bird is unaware of the poet's presence, it behaves naturally. **Stanza one** demonstrates the **competition and danger of nature**: 'He bit an Angleworm in halves'. Although Dickinson imagines the bird within a human context, casually coming 'down the Walk' and suddenly eating 'the fellow, raw', she is amused by the uncivilised reality of the animal kingdom. The word 'raw' echoes her self-deprecating sense of shock. Despite its initial elegance, the predatory bird could hardly have been expected to cook the worm.

The poet's comic portrayal continues in **stanza two**. She gives the bird certain social qualities, drinking from a 'Grass' and politely allowing a hurrying beetle to pass. The tone is relaxed and playful. The slender vowel sounds ('convenient') and soft sibilance ('sidewise', 'pass') add to the seemingly refined atmosphere. However, the mood changes in **stanza three**, reflecting the bird's cautious fear. Dickinson observes the rapid eye movement, 'like frightened Beads'. Such **precise detail increases the drama of the moment**. The details of the bird's prim movement and beautiful texture are wonderfully accurate: 'He stirred his Velvet Head'. The simile is highly effective, suggesting the animal's natural grace.

The danger becomes more explicit in **stanza four**. Both the spectator and the observed bird are 'Cautious'. The crumb offered to the bird by the poet is rejected, highlighting the **gulf between their two separate worlds**. The description of the bird taking flight evokes the delicacy and fluidity of its movement: 'And he unrolled his feathers/And rowed him softer home'. The confident rhythm and emphatic alliteration enrich our understanding of the harmony between the creature and its natural environment. The sensual imagery captures the magnificence of the bird, compared to a rower moving with ease across placid water.

Stanza five develops the metaphorical description further, conveying the bird's poise and mystery: 'Too silver for a seam'. Not only was its flying seamless, it was smoother than that of butterflies leaping 'off Banks of Noon' and splashlessly swimming through the sky. The **breathtaking image and onomatopoeic language** remind us of Dickinson's admiration for nature in all its impressive beauty and is one of the most memorable descriptions in all of Dickinson's writing.

ANALYSIS

In your view, does Dickinson have a sense of empathy with the bird? Support your response with reference to the poem.

Sample Paragraph

It is clear from the start of the poem that Emily Dickinson is both fascinated and amused by the appearance of a small bird in her garden. She seems surprised and almost honoured that out of nowhere 'A Bird came down the Walk'. When it suddenly swallows a worm 'raw', she becomes even more interested. The fact that she admits 'He did not know I saw' tells me that she really has empathy for the bird. Her tone suggests that she feels privileged to watch and she certainly doesn't want to disturb it in its own world. The poet also finds the bird's antics funny. Although it devours the snail, it still behaves very mannerly towards the beetle. Towards the end, Dickinson shows her feelings for the bird when it becomes frightened and she notices its 'rapid eyes'. She sees that it is 'in danger'. The fact that she offered it a crumb also shows her empathy. At the very end, she shows her admiration for the beauty and agility of the bird as it flies off to freedom – to its 'softer home'. The descriptions of it like a rower or a butterfly also suggest that she admires its grace.

Examiner's Comment

Apt references and short quotations are used very well to illustrate the poet's regard for the bird. The answer ranges well over much of the poem. Some further discussion on the poet's tone would have been welcome. A good grade B.

CLASS/HOMEWORK EXERCISES

1. Comment on Dickinson's use of imagery in 'A Bird came down the Walk'. Support the points you make with the aid of suitable reference.

2. Copy the table below into your own notes and fill in critical comments about the last two quotations.

Key Quotes

He did not know I saw	Dickinson is excited at the opportunity to view the bird in its natural element.
And then he drank a Dew	The poet's comic observation recognises signs of social etiquette in the bird's behaviour.
And rowed him softer home	
plashless as they swim	

5 I HEARD A FLY BUZZ—WHEN I DIED

I heard a Fly buzz—when I died—
The Stillness in the Room
Was like the Stillness in the Air—
Between the Heaves of Storm—

The Eyes around—had wrung them dry—   5
And Breaths were gathering firm
For that last Onset—when the King
Be witnessed—in the Room—

I willed my Keepsakes—Signed away
What portion of me be   10
Assignable—and then it was
There interposed a Fly—

With Blue—uncertain stumbling Buzz—
Between the light—and me—
And then the Windows failed—and then   15
I could not see to see—

'The Stillness in the Room/Was like the Stillness in the Air—'

GLOSSARY

4 *Heaves*: lift with effort.
7 *Onset*: beginning.
7 *the King*: God.

9 *Keepsakes*: gifts treasured for the sake of the giver.
12 *interposed*: inserted between or among things.

EXPLORATIONS

1. How would you describe the atmosphere in the poem? Pick out two phrases which, in your opinion, are especially descriptive and explain why you chose them.

2. Do you think Dickinson uses contrast effectively in this poem? Discuss one contrast you found particularly striking.

3. Look at the last line of the poem. What, in your view, is the poet suggesting to us about a person's fate after death?

STUDY NOTES

Dickinson was fascinated with death. This poem examines the moment between life and death. At that time, it was common for family and friends to be present at deathbed vigils. It was thought that the way a person behaved or looked at the moment of death gave an indication of the soul's fate.

The last moment of a person's life is a solemn and often sad occasion. The perspective of the poem is that of the person dying and this significant moment is dominated by the buzzing of a fly in the room in the **first stanza**. This is **absurdly comic and strangely distorts** this moment into something grotesque. Surely the person dying should be concerned with more important matters than an insignificant fly: 'I heard a Fly buzz—when I died'. The room is still and expectant as the last breaths are drawn, a stillness like the moments before a storm. All are braced for what is to come. The word 'Heaves' suggests the force of the storm that is about to break.

The **second stanza** shows us that the mourners had now stopped crying and were holding their breath as they awaited the coming of the 'King' (God) into the room at the moment of death. The phrase 'Be witnessed' refers to the dying person and the mourners who are witnessing their faith, and it conjures up all the solemnity of a court. The word 'firm' also suggests these people's steadfast religious beliefs. The **third stanza** is concerned with putting matters right. The dying person has made a will – 'What portion of me be/Assignable' – and what is not assignable belongs to God. The person is awaiting the coming of his/her Maker, 'and then it was/There interposed a Fly' – the symbol of decay and corruption appeared. Human affairs cannot be managed; real life intervenes. The **fly comes between ('interposed') the dying person and the moment of death, which trivialises** the event.

The fractured syntax of the last stanza shows the **breakdown of the senses** at the moment of death: 'Between the light—and me'. Sight and sound are blurring. The presence of the fly is completely inappropriate, like a drunken person at a solemn ceremony, disturbing and embarrassing and interrupting proceedings. The fly is now between the dying person and the source of light. Does this suggest that the person has lost concentration on higher things, distracted by the buzzing fly? The sense of sight then fails: 'And then the Windows failed'. The moment of death had come and gone, dominated by the noisy fly. Has the fly prevented the person from reaching another dimension? Is death emptiness, just human decay, as signified by the presence of the fly, or is there something more? Do we need comic relief at overwhelming occasions? Is the poet signalling her own lack of belief in an afterlife with God? Dickinson, as usual, intrigues, **leaving the reader with more questions than answers**, so that the reader, like the dying person, is struggling to 'see to see'.

ANALYSIS

Dickinson's poems on mortality often lead to uncertainty or despair. Would you agree or disagree with this statement after reading the poem 'I heard a Fly buzz—when I died'? Discuss this statement, using references from the text to support your views.

Sample Paragraph

This first-person, reminiscent narrative takes us through a series of images, inside and outside the head, showing us confused feelings and insurmountable problems, leading to an inconclusive ending. The view of this deathbed scene is from the dying person's perspective. The problem is that when all should be focused on the last drawing of breath, all are distracted by the inappropriate arrival of a noisy fly! Life won't be managed, nor death – both are lived and experienced. Life and death are not a play, a work of art; they are messy and disorganised, which goes against the human desire for order and control: 'Signed away/What portion of me be/Assignable'. I feel that the poet may be suggesting that the dying person, distracted by the silly fly, does not reach the understanding and knowledge appropriate at this great moment, and is therefore cheated in some way. The momentous moment has passed, dominated by a buzzing fly. This was no dress rehearsal; you can only die once. Life and death happen. Are we being told that we often lose concentration at important moments, for absurd reasons, and so lose valuable insight? Dickinson is not a reassuring poet in this poem. Instead, she coldly and dispassionately draws a deathbed scene and lets us 'see to see'. Can we? Or are we, like the dying person, distracted and unable to still ourselves at the appropriate time to achieve greater wisdom? The divided voice, that of the person dying and that of the person after death, leaves us with mysteries, and so this poem of Dickinson's on mortality leaves me with bleak uncertainties about the human condition and its ability to control and order.

Examiner's Comment

This response is considered and shows a very good discursive treatment of the question. Expression is varied and fluent, and apt quotations are used effectively throughout the answer. Grade A.

CLASS/HOMEWORK EXERCISES

1. Comment on how Dickinson's style contributes to the theme or message in this poem. Quote from your prescribed poems to support your opinions.

2. Copy the table below into your own notes and fill in critical comments about the last two quotations.

Key Quotes

I heard a Fly buzz	The dying person is distracted from this significant moment by the noise made by a fly.
And Breaths were gathering firm/For that last Onset	The narrator is aware that those present are bracing themselves for the important moment of death, which for believers is associated with the coming of God.
And then the Windows failed	
and then/I could not see to see	

6 THE SOUL HAS BANDAGED MOMENTS

The Soul has Bandaged moments—
When too appalled to stir—
She feels some ghastly Fright come up
And stop to look at her—

Salute her—with long fingers—   5
Caress her freezing hair—
Sip, Goblin, from the very lips
The Lover—hovered—o'er—
Unworthy, that a thought so mean
Accost a Theme—so—fair—   10

The soul has moments of Escape—
When bursting all the doors—
She dances like a Bomb, abroad,
And swings upon the Hours,

As do the Bee—delirious borne—   15
Long Dungeoned from his Rose—
Touch Liberty—then know no more,
But Noon, and Paradise—

The Soul's retaken moments—
When, Felon led along,   20
With shackles on the plumed feet,
And staples, in the Song,

The Horror welcomes her, again,
These, are not brayed of Tongue—

'As do the Bee—delirious borne'

GLOSSARY

1 *Bandaged moments*: painful experiences.
2 *appalled*: shocked, horrified.
2 *stir*: act; retaliate.
10 *Accost*: address.
11 *Escape*: freedom.
13 *like a Bomb*: dramatically.
13 *abroad*: in unusual directions.

16 *Dungeoned*: imprisoned in the hive.
20 *Felon*: criminal.
21 *shackles*: chains, ropes.
21 *plumed*: decorated.
22 *staples*: fastenings.
24 *brayed*: inarticulate.

EXPLORATIONS

1. What details in the poem evoke the feelings of 'ghastly Fright' experienced by the soul? Support your answer with quotation or reference.

2. Choose one comparison from the poem that you find particularly effective. Explain your choice.

3. Comment on Dickinson's use of dashes in this poem, briefly explaining their effectiveness.

STUDY NOTES

Throughout much of her poetry, Dickinson focuses on the nature of consciousness and the experience of being alive. She was constantly searching for meaning, particularly of transient moments or changing moods. This search is central to 'The Soul has Bandaged moments', where the poet takes us through a series of dramatic images contrasting the extremes of the spirit and the conscious self.

Stanza one introduces the soul as being fearful and vulnerable, personified as a terrified female who 'feels some ghastly Fright', with the poem's stark opening line suggesting restriction and pain. Dickinson's language is extreme: 'Bandaged', 'appalled'. The **tone is one of helpless desperation and introspection**. Yet while the dominant mood reflects suffering and fear, the phrase 'Bandaged moments' indicates the resilient soul's ability to recover despite being wounded repeatedly.

Stanza two is unnervingly dramatic. The poet creates a mock-romantic scene between the victimised soul and the 'ghastly Fright' figure, now portrayed as a hideous goblin and her would-be lover, their encounter depicted in terms of gothic horror. The soul experiences terrifying fantasies as **the surreal sequence becomes increasingly menacing** and the goblin's long fingers 'Caress her freezing hair'. The appearance of an unidentified shadowy 'Lover' is unexpected. There is a sense of the indecisive soul being caught between two states, represented by the malevolent goblin and the deserving lover. It is unclear whether Dickinson is writing about the choices involved in romantic love or the relationship between herself and God.

The stanza ends inconclusively, juxtaposing two opposites: the 'Unworthy' or undeserving 'thought' and the 'fair' (worthy) 'Theme'. The latter might well refer to the ideal of romantic love. If so, it is confronted by erotic desire (the 'thought'). Dickinson's disjointed style, especially her frequent use of dashes within stanzas, isolates key words and intensifies the overwhelmingly **nightmarish atmosphere**.

The feeling of confused terror is replaced with ecstatic 'moments of Escape' in **stanzas three** and **four**. The soul recovers in triumph, 'bursting all the doors'. This **explosion of energy** ('She dances like a Bomb') evokes a rising mood of riotous freedom. Explosive verbs ('bursting', 'dances', 'swings') and robust rhythms add to the sense of uncontrollable excitement. Dickinson compares the soul to a 'Bee— delirious borne'. After being 'Long Dungeoned' in its hive, this bee can now enjoy the sensuous delights of 'his Rose'.

The mood is short-lived, however, and in **stanzas five** and **six**, 'The Horror' returns. The soul becomes depressed again, feeling bound and shackled, like a 'Felon led along'. **Dickinson develops this criminal metaphor** – 'With shackles on the plumed feet' – leaving us with an ultimate sense of loss as 'The Horror welcomes her, again'. Is this the soul's inevitable fate? The final line is unsettling. Whatever horrible experiences confront the soul, they are simply unspeakable: 'not brayed of Tongue'.

As always, Dickinson's poem is open to many interpretations. Critics have suggested that the poet is dramatising the turmoil of dealing with the loss of creativity. Some view the poem's central conflict as the tension between romantic love and sexual desire. Others believe that the poet was exploring the theme of depression and mental instability. In the end, readers must find their own meaning and decide for themselves.

ANALYSIS

Comment on the dramatic elements that are present in the poem, supporting the points you make with reference to the text.

Sample Paragraph

'The Soul has Bandaged moments' is built around a central conflict between two opposing forces, the 'Soul', or spirit, and its great enemy, 'Fright'. Emily Dickinson sets the dramatic scene with the Soul still recovering – presumably from the last battle. It is 'Bandaged' after the fight with its arch enemy. The descriptions of the soul's opponent are startling. Fright is 'ghastly', a 'Horror' and a sleazy 'Goblin' who is trying to seduce the innocent soul. Some of Dickinson's images add to the dramatic tension. In the seduction scene, the goblin is described as having 'long fingers'. His intended victim is seen as helpless, petrified with fear. The goblin uses its bony claws to 'Caress her freezing hair'. Both characters seem to have come out of an old black-and-white horror movie. I find the whole situation disturbing. The drama continues right to the end of the poem. The soul is compared to a 'Felon' who has just been recaptured and is being led away in 'shackles'. Such images have a distressing impact in explaining the pressures on the soul to be free. Finally, Dickinson's stop-and-start style is also unsettling. Broken rhythms and her condensed use of language increase the edgy atmosphere throughout this highly dramatic poem.

Examiner's Comment

An assured and focused A-grade response, showing a clear understanding of the poem's dramatic elements. The answer addressed both subject matter and style, using back-up illustration very effectively. Expression throughout was also impressive.

CLASS/HOMEWORK EXERCISES

1. How would you describe the dominant tone of 'The Soul has Bandaged moments'? Use reference to the text to show how the tone is effectively conveyed.

2. Copy the table below into your own notes and fill in critical comments about the last two quotations.

Key Quotes

Bandaged moments	While the adjective indicates hurt and weakness, there is also a sense of healing and recovery.
The Lover—hovered—o'er	The verb suggests menace, typical of a poem where almost every image is tinged with fear and uncertainty.
Caress her freezing hair	
The Horror welcomes her, again	

7 I COULD BRING YOU JEWELS—HAD I A MIND TO

I could bring You Jewels—had I a mind to—
But You have enough—of those—
I could bring You Odors from St. Domingo—
Colors—from Vera Cruz—

Berries of the Bahamas—have I—   5
But this little Blaze
Flickering to itself—in the Meadow—
Suits Me—more than those—

Never a Fellow matched this Topaz—
And his Emerald Swing—   10
Dower itself—for Bobadilo—
Better—Could I bring?

'Never a Fellow matched this Topaz—'

GLOSSARY

3 *Odors*: fragrances, perfumes.
3 *St. Domingo*: Santo Domingo in the Caribbean.
4 *Vera Cruz*: city on the east coast of Mexico.
5 *Bahamas*: group of islands southeast of Florida.

6 *Blaze*: strong fire or flame; very bright light.
11 *Dower*: part of her husband's estate allotted to a widow by law.
11 *Bobadilo*: braggart; someone who speaks arrogantly or boastfully.

EXPLORATIONS

1. Does the poet value exotic or homely gifts? In your opinion, which phrases suggest this contrast most effectively?

2. Slant rhyme is when words almost rhyme, as in 'those' and 'Cruz'. Identify another example of slant rhyme in the poem and suggest why, in your opinion, the poet chooses to rhyme the words in this way. (Consider emphasis, order and music.)

3. What is the tone in this poem: arrogant, humble, gentle, strident, confident? Quote in support of your opinion.

STUDY NOTES

Although described as a recluse, Dickinson had a wide circle of friends. She wrote letter-poems to them, often representing them as flowers, 'things of nature which had come with no practice at all'. This poem is one without shadows, celebratory and happy, focusing out rather than in as she concentrates on a relationship.

In the **first stanza**, the poem opens with the speaker **considering the gift she will give** her beloved, 'You'. The 'You' is very much admired, and is wealthy ('You have enough'), so the gift of jewels is dismissed. The phrase 'had I a mind to' playfully suggests that maybe the 'I' doesn't necessarily wish to present anything. There is a certain coquettish air evident here. A world of privilege and plenty is shown as, one after another, expensively exotic gifts are considered and dismissed. These include perfumes and vibrant colours from faraway locations, conjuring up images of romance and adventure: 'Odors from St. Domingo'.

The **second stanza** continues the list, with 'Berries of the Bahamas' being considered as an option for this special gift, but they are not quite right either. The tense changes to 'have I' and the laconic listing and dismissing stops. A small wildflower 'in the Meadow', 'this little Blaze', is chosen instead. This 'Suits Me'. Notice that it is not that this suits the other person. **This gift is a reflection of her own unshowy personality**. The long lines of considering exotic gifts have now given way to shorter, more decisive lines.

In the **third stanza**, the speaker has a definite note of conviction, as she confidently states that 'Never a Fellow matched' this shining gift of hers. No alluring, foreign gemstone, be it a brilliant topaz or emerald, shines as this 'little Blaze' in the meadow. The gift glows with colour; it is natural, inexpensive and accessible. The reference to a dower might suggest a gift given by a woman to a prospective husband. This **gift is suitable** for a Spanish adventurer, a 'Bobadilo'. The assured tone is clear in the word 'Never' and the jaunty rhyme 'Swing' and 'bring'. The final rhetorical question suggests that this is the best gift she could give. The poem shows that **the true value of a present cannot be measured in a material way**.

ANALYSIS

'Dickinson is fascinated by moments of change.' Discuss this statement using the poem 'I could bring You Jewels—had I a mind to' as reference.

Sample Paragraph

Unlike many of Dickinson's poems on our course, this poem turns outwards, as the speaker considers what present would be suitable to give to her 'Bobadilo'. The happy, celebratory tone continues right through the poem. This is a confident, assured woman listing and dismissing exotic gifts in a world of privilege and wealth. The 'Odors' from St. Domingo, the 'Colors' from Vera Cruz, the 'Berries' from the Bahamas are looked at and discarded by this knowing woman, 'had I a mind to'. The moment of change here is when the speaker chooses a gift that is natural and unassuming and, more importantly, which is to her liking: 'Suits Me'. It will convey something of her personality to the recipient, the swaggering 'Bobadilo'. This 'little Blaze/Flickering to itself' reflects the hidden qualities of the woman. Although it is not directly stated what this little shining gift is exactly, I think it is likely a meadow flower. It is free and easily picked, but how it shines! This is brighter than any precious stone of 'Topaz' or 'Emerald'. As the decision is reached, the long lines in which the speaker is considering her choice of gift change with her decision. Now short, crisp lines ring out with the self-belief of a woman who knows best. Even the rhyme changes from the slant rhyme where she is considering her options ('those'/'Cruz') in the first stanza to the more definite jaunty full rhyme of 'Swing' and 'bring' in the final stanza. I read that Dickinson's favourite chapter in the Book of Revelations was the description of Jerusalem as a jewel. In this poem, jewels are rejected for something more precious than material worth: beauty. I really enjoyed how Dickinson explored the very feminine trait of considering everything, and then finally deciding after humorous vacillating. This is the moment of change in the poem.

Examiner's Comment

A lucid, fluent response to the question, backed up with a convincing use of quotation, ensures a grade A. The point about the change in line length was interesting. Varied vocabulary is impressive throughout.

CLASS/HOMEWORK EXERCISES

1. 'Dickinson disrupts and transforms our accepted view of things.' What is your opinion of this statement? Refer to 'I could bring You Jewels—had I a mind to' in support of your response.

2. Copy the table below into your own notes and fill in critical comments about the last two quotations.

Key Quotes

I could bring You Jewels—had I a mind to	The speaker is confidently considering her options.
But this little Blaze/Flickering to itself	The gift chosen is simple and natural, but it is warm, vivid and beautiful, as conveyed by the lively onomatopoeia.
Dower itself	
Better—Could I bring?	

8 A NARROW FELLOW IN THE GRASS

A narrow Fellow in the Grass
Occasionally rides—
You may have met Him—did you not
His notice sudden is—

The Grass divides as with a Comb—   5
A spotted shaft is seen—
And then it closes at your feet
And opens further on—

He likes a Boggy Acre
A Floor too cool for Corn—   10
Yet when a Boy, and Barefoot—
I more than once at Noon
Have passed, I thought, a Whip lash
Unbraiding in the Sun
When stooping to secure it   15
It wrinkled, and was gone—

Several of Nature's People
I know, and they know me—
I feel for them a transport
Of cordiality—   20

But never met this Fellow
Attended, or alone
Without a tighter breathing
And Zero at the Bone—

'His notice sudden is—'

GLOSSARY

6 *a spotted shaft*: patterned skin of the darting snake.
13 *Whip lash*: sudden, violent movement.
14 *Unbraiding*: straightening out, uncoiling.

19 *transport*: heightened emotion.
20 *cordiality*: civility, welcome.
24 *Zero at the Bone*: cold terror.

EXPLORATIONS

1. Select two images from the poem that suggest evil or menace. Comment briefly on the effectiveness of each.

2. How successful is the poet in conveying the snake's erratic sense of movement? Refer to the text in your answer.

3. Outline your own feelings in response to the poem.

STUDY NOTES

In this poem, one of the few published during her lifetime, Dickinson adopts a male persona remembering an incident from his boyhood. Snakes have traditionally been seen as symbols of evil. We still use the expression 'snake in the grass' to describe someone who cannot be trusted. Central to this poem is Dickinson's own portrayal of nature – beautiful, brutal and lyrical. She seems fascinated by the endless mystery, danger and unpredictability of the natural world.

The opening lines of **stanza one** casually introduce a 'Fellow in the Grass'. (Dickinson never refers explicitly to the snake.) **The conversational tone immediately involves readers** who may already 'have met Him'. However, there is more than a hint of warning in the postscript: 'His notice sudden is'. This underlying wariness now appears foreshadowed by the menacing adjective 'narrow' and by the disjointed rhythm and slightly awkward word order.

Dickinson focuses on the volatile snake's dramatic movements in **stanza two**.

The verbs 'divide', 'closes' and 'opens' emphasise its dynamic energy. The snake suddenly emerges like a 'spotted shaft'. The poet's **comparisons are particularly effective**, suggesting a lightning bolt or a camouflaged weapon. Run-on lines, a forceful rhythm and the repetition of 'And' contribute to the vivid image of the snake as a powerful presence to be treated with caution.

Stanza three reveals even more about the snake's natural habitat: 'He likes a Boggy Acre'. It also divulges the speaker's identity – an adult male remembering his failed boyhood efforts to capture snakes. The memory conveys something of the intensity of childhood experiences, especially of dangerous encounters with nature. The boy's innocence and vulnerability ('Barefoot') contrasts with the 'Whip lash' violence of the wild snake. **Dickinson's attitude to nature is open to interpretation**. Does the threat come from the animal or the boy? Did the adult speaker regard the snake differently when he was young? The poet herself clearly appreciates the complexities found within the natural world and her precisely observed descriptions ('Unbraiding', 'It wrinkled') provide ample evidence of her interest.

From the speaker's viewpoint in **stanza four**, nature is generally benign. This positive image is conveyed by the affectionate tribute to 'Nature's People'. The familiar personification and personal tone underline the mutual 'cordiality' that exists between nature and human nature. Despite this, **divisions between the two worlds cannot be ignored**. Indeed, the focus in **stanza five** is on the sheer horror people experience when confronted by 'this Fellow'. The poet's sparse and chilling descriptions – 'tighter breathing', 'Zero at the Bone' – are startling expressions of stunned terror.

As in other poems, Dickinson attributes human characteristics to nature – the snake 'Occasionally rides', 'The Grass divides' and the bogland has a 'Floor'. One effect of this is to highlight the **variety and mystery of the natural environment**, which can only ever be glimpsed within limited human terms. The snake remains unknowable to the end, dependent on a chance encounter, a fleeting glance or a trick of light.

ANALYSIS

Comment on the effectiveness of Dickinson's use of the male persona voice in 'A narrow Fellow in the Grass'. Support the points you make with reference to the poem.

Sample Paragraph

In some of her poems, Emily Dickinson chose to substitute her own voice with that of a persona, a fictional narrator. This is the case in 'A narrow Fellow in the Grass', where she uses a country boy to tell the story of his experiences trying to catch snakes when he was young. It is obvious that he has a great love for nature, but neither is he blind to the cold fear he felt when he came face to face with the 'spotted shaft'. Dickinson's use of language emphasises his youthful terror. She lets him remember his encounter exactly as it happened. The images she uses are powerful and disturbing: 'a tighter breathing'. The boy remembers shuddering with uncontrollable fright, 'Zero at the Bone'. The description is dramatic and I found I could relate to the boy's sense of horror. The poem is all the more effective for being centred around one terrified character, the young boy. I can visualise the child in his bare feet trying to catch a frightened snake in the grass. It is only later that he realises the great danger he was in and this has taught him a lifelong lesson about nature. By using another speaker's persona, Dickinson explores the excitement and danger of nature in a wider way that allows readers to imagine it more clearly.

Examiner's Comment

Although the answer drifts at times from the central question, there is good personal engagement and a great deal of insightful discussion. Quotations are well used throughout the answer to provide a very interesting response. Grade A.

CLASS/HOMEWORK EXERCISES

1. In your opinion, how does Dickinson portray nature in 'A narrow Fellow in the Grass'? Support your points with reference to the poem.

2. Copy the table below into your own notes and fill in critical comments about the last two quotations.

Key Quotes

His notice sudden is	The awkward syntax used to describe the snake's jerky movements adds to our sense of unease.
And then it closes at your feet	Dickinson highlights the lethal unpredictability of the snake.
Nature's People	
And Zero at the Bone	

9 I TASTE A LIQUOR NEVER BREWED

I taste a liquor never brewed—
From Tankards scooped in Pearl—
Not all the Vats upon the Rhine
Yield such an Alcohol!

Inebriate of Air—am I—   5
And Debauchee of Dew—
Reeling—thro endless summer days—
From inns of Molten Blue—

When 'Landlords' turn the drunken Bee
Out of the Foxglove's door—   10
When Butterflies—renounce their 'drams'—
I shall but drink the more!

Till Seraphs swing their snowy Hats—
And Saints—to windows run—
To see the little Tippler   15
Leaning against the—Sun—

'Not all the Vats upon the Rhine/Yield such an Alcohol!'

GLOSSARY

2 *Tankards*: one-handled mugs, usually made of pewter, used for drinking beer.
3 *Vats*: large vessels used for making alcohol.
6 *Debauchee*: someone who has overindulged and neglected duty.

13 *Seraphs*: angels who are of the highest spiritual level.
15 *Tippler*: a person who drinks often, but does not get drunk.

EXPLORATIONS

1. What is the mood in this poem? Does it intensify or change? Use references from the text in your response.

2. Which stanza appeals to you? Discuss both the poet's style and content in your answer, using quotations from the poem as evidence for your views.

3. Look at the final dash in the poem. Why do you think the poet ended the poem with this punctuation? What is it suggesting about the little tippler? Does it add a sense of fun?

STUDY NOTES

This 'rapturous poem about summer' uses the metaphor of intoxication to capture the essence of this wonderful season. Dickinson's family were strict Calvinists, a religion that emphasised damnation as the consequence of sin. Her father supported an organisation that warned against the dangers of drink, the Temperance League.

This poem is written as a **joyful appreciation of this wonderful life**. The tone is playful and exaggerated from the beginning, as the poet declares this drink was never 'brewed'. The reference to 'scooped in Pearl' could refer to the great, white frothing heads of beer in the 'Tankards'. The poet certainly conveys the merriment of intoxication, as the poem reels along its happy way. The explanation for all this drunkenness is that the poet is drunk on life ('Inebriate', 'Debauchee'). The pubs are the inns of 'Molten Blue', i.e. the sky (**stanza two**). It is like a cartoon, with little drunken bees being shown the door by the pub owners as they lurch about in delirious ecstasy. The drinkers of the natural world are the bees and butterflies, but she can drink more than these: 'I shall but drink the more!' This roots the poem in reality, as drunken people always feel they can manage more.

But this has caused uproar in the heavens, as the angels and saints run to look out at this little drunk, 'the little Tippler'. She stands drunkenly leaning against the 'Sun', a celestial lamppost. The final dash suggests the crooked stance of the little drunken one. **There is no heavy moral at the end of this poem. In fact, there seems to be a slight note of envy for the freedom and happiness being experienced by the intoxicated poet**. Are the angels swinging their hats to cheer her on in her drunken rebellion? Is this poem celebrating the reckless indulgence of excess? Or is the final metaphor of the sun referring to Christ or to the poet's own arrival in heaven after she indulgently enjoys the beauty of the natural world?

Nature is seen as the spur for high jinks and good humour. The riddle of the first line starts it off: how was the alcohol 'never brewed'? The exaggerated imagery, such as the metaphor of the flower as a pub and the bee as the drunk, all add to the **fantasy-land atmosphere**. The words 'Inebriate', 'Debauchee' and 'renounce' are reminiscent of the language which those disapproving of the consumption of alcohol might use for those who do indulge. Is the poet having a sly laugh at the serious Temperance League to which her father belonged? The ridiculous costumes, 'snowy Hats', and the uproar in heaven ('swing' and 'run') all add to the impression of this land of merriment. The juxtaposition of the sacred ('Seraphs') and the profane ('Tippler') in **stanza four** also adds to the comic effect. However, it is the verbs that carry the sense of mad fun most effectively: 'scooped', 'Reeling', 'drink', 'swing', 'run' and 'Leaning'. The poem lurches and flows in an almost uncontrollable way as the ecstasy of overindulging in the delirious pleasure of nature is vividly conveyed.

There are two different types of humour present in this irrepressible poem – the broad humour of farce and the more **subversive humour of irony**. She even uses the steady metre of a hymn, with eight syllables in lines one and three and six syllables in lines two and four. Dickinson seems to be standing at a distance, smiling wryly, as she gently deflates.

ANALYSIS

'Dickinson was always wary of excess, even of joy.' Discuss this statement in relation to the above poem, using references from the text to support your answer.

Sample Paragraph

I don't agree. I think this is a funny poem and the poet is enjoying herself getting very drunk. But she is not drunk on beer. She is drunk on nature. I think it is very funny when the angels are waving their white caps, egging her on. I think this is a good poem, the best poem I ever red, as it makes me want to red more of Dickinson's poems. There is a good metaphor for drinking all through. Some of it is definately full of joy EG the bee. The part on the tippler leaning against the paling post is also joyful. I think everyone should enjoy Emily's absolutely brilliant poem as it has many good joyful images such as the drinking bee and little tippler.

Examiner's Comment

This short answer shows very little knowledge or engagement with the poem. There is no substantial referencing. The language used is repetitive, expression is flawed and there are mechanical mistakes. The over-enthusiastic ending is not convincing. A basic D-grade standard.

CLASS/HOMEWORK EXERCISES

1. 'Hypersensitivity to natural beauty produced Dickinson's poetry.' Do you agree or disagree with this statement? Refer to the poem 'I taste a liquor never brewed' in your response.

2. Copy the table below into your own notes and fill in critical comments about the last two quotations.

Key Quotes

From tankards scooped in Pearl	This line, with its use of the descriptive verb, suggests the outlining of the tankard in white, foaming beer.
Inebriate of Air—am I	The narrator in the poem is confessing to drunkenness due to an excessive indulgence in the beauty of nature.
Till Seraphs swing their snowy hats	
Leaning against the—Sun	

10   AFTER GREAT PAIN, A FORMAL FEELING COMES

After great pain, a formal feeling comes—
The Nerves sit ceremonious, like Tombs—
The stiff Heart questions was it He, that bore,
And Yesterday, or Centuries before?

The Feet, mechanical, go round—   5
Of Ground, or Air, or Ought—
A Wooden way
Regardless grown,
A Quartz contentment, like a stone—

This is the Hour of Lead—   10
Remembered, if outlived,
As Freezing persons, recollect the Snow—
First—Chill—then Stupor—then the letting go—

'First—Chill—then Stupor'

GLOSSARY

1 *formal*: serious; exact.
2 *ceremonious*: on show.
3 *He*: the stiff Heart, or possibly Christ.
3 *bore*: endure; intrude.
6 *Ought*: anything.

9 *Quartz*: basic rock mineral.
10 *Hour of Lead*: traumatic experience.
13 *Stupor*: numbness; disorientation.

EXPLORATIONS

1. Comment on the poet's use of personification in the opening stanza.

2. How does the language used in the second stanza convey the condition of the victim in pain?

3. Write your own short personal response to the poem.

STUDY NOTES

Dickinson wrote 'After great pain' in 1862, at a time when she was thought to have been experiencing severe psychological difficulties. The poet addresses the effects of isolation and anguish on the individual. Ironically, the absence of the personal pronoun 'I' gives the poem a universal significance. The 'great pain' itself is never fully explained and the final lines are ambiguous. Like so much of Dickinson's work, this dramatic poem raises many questions for consideration.

From the outset, Dickinson is concerned with the emotional numbness ('a formal feeling') that follows the experience of 'great pain'. The poet's authoritative tone in **stanza one** reflects a first-hand knowledge of trauma, with the adjective 'formal' suggesting self-conscious recovery from some earlier distress. Dickinson personifies the physical response as order returns to body and mind: 'The Nerves sit ceremonious, like Tombs'. The severe pain has also shocked the 'stiff Heart', which has become confused by the experience. Is the poet also drawing a parallel with the life and death of Jesus Christ (the Sacred Heart), crucified 'Centuries before'? The images certainly suggest timeless suffering and endurance. This **sombre sense of loss** is further enhanced by the broad vowel assonance of the opening lines.

The feeling of stunned inertia continues into **stanza two**. In reacting to intense pain, 'The Feet, mechanical, go round'. It is as if the response is unfocused and indifferent, lacking any real purpose. Dickinson uses two **analogies to emphasise the sense of pointless alienation**. The reference to the 'Wooden way' might be interpreted as a fragile bridge between reason and insanity, or this metaphor could be associated with Christ's suffering as he carried his cross to Calvary. The level of consciousness at such times is described as 'Regardless grown', or beyond caring. Dickinson's second comparison is equally innovative: 'A Quartz contentment' underpins the feeling of complete apathy that makes the victims of pain behave 'like a stone'. Is she being ironic by suggesting that the post-traumatic state is an escape, a 'contentment' of sorts?

There is a disturbing sense of resignation at the start of **stanza three**: 'This is the Hour of Lead'. The dull weight of depression is reinforced by the insistent monosyllables and solemn rhythm, but the devastating experience is not 'outlived' by everyone. Dickinson outlines the aftermath of suffering by using one final comparison: 'As Freezing persons'. This shocking simile evokes the unimaginable hopelessness of the victim stranded in a vast wasteland of snow. The poem's last line traces the tragic stages leading to oblivion: 'First—Chill—then Stupor—then the letting go—'. The inclusion of the dash at the end might indicate a possibility of relief, though whether it is through rescue or death is not revealed. In either case, **readers are left with an acute awareness of an extremely distraught voice**.

ANALYSIS

One of Dickinson's great achievements is her ability to explore the experience of deep depression. To what extent is this true of her poem 'After great pain, a formal feeling comes'? Refer closely to the text in your answer.

Sample Paragraph

'After great pain' is a very good example of Emily Dickinson's skill in addressing controversial and distressing subjects, such as mental breakdown. Although she never really explains what she means by the 'pain' referred to in the first line, she deals with the after-effects of suffering throughout the poem. The loss of a loved one can cause very great anguish. What Dickinson does very well is to explain how depression can lead to people becoming numb, beyond all emotion. I believe this is what she means by 'a formal feeling'. She uses an interesting image of a sufferer's nerves sitting quietly in a church at a funeral service. They 'sit ceremonious'. This same idea is used to describe the mourners following the hearse – 'Feet mechanical'. I get the impression that grief and mourning can destroy people's confidence and make them numb. They go beyond grief. Dickinson's images are compelling and suggest the coldness experienced by patients who have suffered depression. They are 'like a stone'. The best description is at the end, when she compares sufferers to being lost in the snow. They will slowly fade into a 'stupor' or death wish. I think Dickinson is very good at using images and moods to explore depression. She is very good at suggesting shock in this poem.

Examiner's Comment

Although the expression is awkward in places, there are a number of worthwhile points in the paragraph. There is also some good personal engagement with the poem and references are used well in support. A basic B-grade standard.

CLASS/HOMEWORK EXERCISES

1. In your opinion, what is the dominant mood in 'After great pain, a formal feeling comes'? Is it one of depression, sadness or acceptance? Refer closely to the text in your answer.

2. Copy the table below into your own notes and fill in critical comments about the last two quotations.

Key Quotes

a formal feeling comes	Dickinson states that the reaction to the experience of intense suffering is stiff and self-conscious.
A Quartz contentment, like a stone	After experiencing trauma, sufferers retreat within themselves, feeling lifeless and inhuman.
A Wooden way/Regardless grown	
First—Chill—then Stupor— then the letting go	

Has the poetry of Emily Dickinson any relevance for young people today? Support the points you make in your answer by reference to the poems by Dickinson on your course.

Marking Scheme Guidelines

Some of the following areas might be addressed:

- Interesting personal themes.
- Engaging confessional style.
- Oblique imagery is appealing.
- Unusual/eccentric punctuation.
- Experimental use of language.
- Challenging/passionate voice.

Sample Essay

(Dickinson's Relevance for Today's Youth)

1. *I feel the poetry of Emily Dickinson would recieve a very positive response from a young person today. I will discuss this with reference to the four poems:*

   Hope is a thing with Feathers

   There's a certain Slant of Light

   I Felt a Funeral in my brain

   A narrow Fellow in the Grass

   Dickinson's appeal lies not only in the content of these poems – depression, altered consciousness and death. But also in her style, how she conveys her themes.

2. *The oddness of Dickinson's poetry would, I feel, appeal to young people. It has a different slant on things, it is odd. Young people like different, eccentric things. Look at the clothes we wear, we like to be different. In the poem Slant of Light Dickinson takes an odd slant. When one thinks of light, you think of bright, warm happiness. But in this poem, Dickinson is describing light which is cold, oppressive, dying. It is the end of the year so light is dying and it is the end of the afternoon so light is fading.*

3. *In this poem she expresses religious doubts which in my opinion young people can relate to. When we were younger we looked at the concept of Heaven and God through 'rose-tinted glasses'. Anyone who dies belonging to us went to live*

with God in Heaven and everything was happy ever after. But in this poem, a portrayl of a merciless, vengeful God comes across. This is how many young people feel. 'Heavenly hurt' any young person who has lost someone close to them has felt this hurt. But there is no scar to prove this anguish. Emily uses short four line stanza's in her poems which I feel young people can definately relate to. In this fast, cosmopolitan world everyone enjoys reading a short poem. Her omission of words, articles and verbs is like a text message. Young people shorten words, leave them out in order to write a text. They therefor can relate to Emily's poetry as it is like one of the hundreds of texts they send.

4. She also has little regard for syntex, punctuation and formal grammer like young people in text messages. She uses capital letters for emphasis. 'I felt a Funeral in my Brain'. In text messages young people use capitals to emphasis something for example 'I saw JAMIE at the bus stop!'

5. Emily has two themes – Death and Nature. In her poem, 'I Felt a Funeral' she is describing the opression of her mental disorder. I feel young people can relate to this – not the mental disorder but the oppression Young people have tough lives. In Sixth year there are pre's, Leaving Cert, CAO points, the list is endless. We feel trapped, opressed like Emily. She describes the mourners as 'thudding – thudding'. This is like a bad headache. A headache students get from study and from CAO forms. The poet is lying in a coffin, she is powerless.
'And then they lifted the box
And walked across my soul'.

6. Metaphorically speaking Sixth year and all the traumas that go with it is like being powerless in a coffin. Apparently prior to writing this poem, Emily was rejected by a man. All young girls can relate to this – being rejected by the love of your life.

7. In 'Hope is a thing with Feathers' she celebrates human resillance in the face of difficulty. Students can also relate to this poem with all that is going on in their lives. She praises the power of hope to overcome the worst catastrophies, 'And hard must be the storm.' Hope lifts the human will to survive, hope is indomitable. Students can relate to this, they have to take what life throws at them. 'Yet never in extremnity, it asked a Crumb of Me'. The worst disaster imaginable leaves hope undaunted. Every young person needs hope and can relate to this poem.

8. Emily's other nature poem is 'A Narrow Fellow in the grass'. Dickinson is wary of nature in this poem. Instead of man and nature living in harmony she feels they have an acquaintance. She describes a snake 'a spotted shaft'. She is afraid of it but is curious to go after it. In my opinion, young people can relate to the curiosity in this poem. Young people are afraid to take drugs but take them out of curiosity. They would be feeling 'Zero at the bone' if they were caught but nevertheless human curiosity takes over. Like Emily going searching for the snake. She is afraid of it but intrigued by it.

9. Young people can respond to Emily Dickinson's poetry in a number of ways. The oddness of her poems entice young people to read them. They are unique. When she expresses religious doubts in her poem 'Slant of Light', in my opinion young people can relate to this. They too can harbour doubts. The compactness of her poems, her omission of words and use of capitals is like a text message which young people can definitaly relate to. Finally her themes suggesting opression relate to young people's student lives. The hardship, the studying. Her final theme of nature and curiosity can relate to young people also. The curiosity to dabble in drugs even with the fear of getting caught. (approx. 880 words)

Spellchecker

| receive | therefore | portrayal | resilience | definitely |
| extremity | syntax | grammar | oppression | emphasise |

Examiner's Comment

This is a reasonable response that tries hard to keep focused on the question. However, there is little detailed analysis of the poems themselves. For instance, although paragraph four makes a valid point about the poet's text-like style, no examples are given. The expression is awkward at times. Other distractions include spelling errors, careless punctuation and inaccurate quotations. As a convention of literary criticism, it is not usual to refer to authors by their first names.

GRADE: C2
P = 10/15
C = 10/15
L = 8/15
M = 3/5
Total = 31/50

SAMPLE LEAVING CERT QUESTIONS ON DICKINSON'S POETRY

(45/50 MINUTES)

Refer to the poems by Emily Dickinson you have studied.

1. What impact did the poetry of Emily Dickinson make on you as a reader? Your answer should deal with the following:
   • Your overall sense of the personality of the poet.
   • The poet's use of language/imagery.

2. Write about the feelings Emily Dickinson's poetry creates in you and the aspects of her poetry (content or style) that help to create those feelings. Support your points by reference to the poetry of Dickinson on your course.

3. 'Speaking of Emily Dickinson…'
   Write out the text of a public talk you might give on the poetry of Emily Dickinson. Your talk should make reference to the poetry on your course.

Sample Essay Plan (Q3)

'Speaking of Emily Dickinson…'
Write out the text of a talk you might give on the poetry of Emily Dickinson. Your talk should make reference to the poetry on your course.

- Intro: Original voice and expression of the poet has a broad appeal. Deals with the great themes.

- Point 1: 'I heard a Fly buzz' – fascination with death shown by recreation of deathbed scene.

- Point 2: '"Hope" is the thing with feathers' – a celebration of human resilience in the face of constant difficulty.

- Point 3: Style – Dickinson's fondness for capitals and dashes.

- Point 4: Impact of reclusive life on themes and style of poetry.

- Conclusion: A poet who has much to say to the anxious modern reader coping with an ever-faster world.

Sample Essay Plan (Q3)

   Develop one of the above points into a paragraph.

Sample Paragraph: Point 1

Dickinson's fascination with death is seen graphically in the poem 'I heard a Fly buzz'. She introduces a fly buzzing to the deathbed scene. She trivialises the solemn occasion as well as making it more realistic. In stanza one the 'Stillness' magnifies the sound of the buzzing fly. It is like the stillness at the centre of the storm. The storm is death, which is both powerful and destructive, just like the storm. The poet then startles us in stanza two. The reference to 'Eyes' shows the mourners who stand around the deathbed. They have stopped crying. They are waiting for the moment Death, 'King', appears. Then in stanza three we return to the narrator. She has made her last bequests and is ready to face her Maker when the fly makes its presence known. The word 'interposed' is deliberately used to show the fly interfering with the deathbed drama. The last stanza shows us the final moments of the narrator's life. Her sight goes. There is only darkness. 'And then the Windows failed'. Without the eyes and the other senses there can be no reality, as the person then has no means to perceive her surroundings. Here Dickinson is imagining her own death. She is passing comment on one of life's great moments which we must all face, yet succeeds through the introduction of the fly to show that even in the most solemn occasions there is always the trivial and unpredictable. This is what makes her poetry interesting to study.

Examiner's Comment

The paragraph includes a number of interesting observations about the chosen poem and the discussion remains well focused on the question. The absence of the register of a talk prevents the student from attaining a higher grade, as the task is not fully completed. Otherwise, a solid B grade.

LAST WORDS ""

'The Dickinson dashes are an integral part of her method and style ... and cannot be translated ... without deadening the wonderful naked voltage of the poems.'

Ted Hughes

'The Brain—is wider than the Sky—
The Brain is deeper than the sea—'

Emily Dickinson

(On her determination to hide secrets) 'The price she paid was that of appearing to posterity as perpetually unfinished and wilfully eccentric.'   *Philip Larkin*

JOHN DONNE

1572–1631

'Be thine own palace, or the world's thy jail.'

John Donne was born in London in 1572 into a prominent Roman Catholic family (his mother was a relation of the martyr, Sir Thomas More). Donne was educated at home by Catholic tutors before attending university where he trained as a lawyer. He converted to the Church of England during the 1590s.

After several appointments and trips abroad, he secretly married seventeen-year-old Ann More in 1601 and was briefly imprisoned as a result of her father's objection. The poet once wrote about the experience: 'John Donne – Ann Donne – Undone'. However, the marriage was a happy one although the family struggled financially at times. His wife died in 1617 aged thirty-three after giving birth to their twelfth child.

In 1615, Donne had been ordained as an Anglican priest and was later appointed Dean of St Paul's Cathedral where he became famous for his spellbinding sermons. He also made his name as a highly original love poet. His imagery was often passionate and sensuous. In his later years, Donne turned his talents to religious poetry, hymns and sermons.

Whatever the subject, his writing reveals the same characteristics that typified the work of the greatest metaphysical poets: dazzling wordplay (particularly conceits and paradoxes) subtle argument; surprising contrasts; intricate analysis and striking imagery selected from law, medicine, geography, science and mathematics. His most prominent themes include love – romantic and spiritual – time, and death. Donne is now considered the most outstanding of all the English metaphysical poets.

Prescribed Poems

A Note on Metaphysical Poetry

Metaphysics is usually defined as a branch of philosophy concerned with explaining the fundamental nature of existence.

Metaphysical poetry was a term used to describe a loose group of British lyric poets who lived in England between 1590 and 1680. Among them were John Donne, George Herbert, Henry Vaughan and Andrew Marvell. They did not call themselves Metaphysicals but were given this name by later writers because their poetry dealt with philosophical speculation and abstract ideas.

Their work was characterised by inventiveness of metaphor (often involving unusual and dissimilar images known as conceits). Such witty and complex poetry was influenced greatly by the changing times, new sciences and the newfound liberal behaviour of the 17th century.

Intellect and wit blending with strong feelings characterise metaphysical poetry, especially that of John Donne. Indeed, Donne represents very well the school of poetry which is still somewhat vaguely called 'Metaphysical'. He brought the whole of his experience into his poetry.

Donne's writing is full of far-fetched imagery and allusions borrowed from various branches of learning. He often makes use of ideas and experience – and the most startling connections are discovered between them. The hallmark of Donne's metaphysical poetry is passionate feeling and forceful argument.

During the 18th century, many critics believed that the metaphysical poets were too revolutionary and only wanted to show off their learning. However, their work had a significant influence on leading 20th-century poets, such as T. S. Eliot, who promoted its innovative and intellectual qualities, and helped bring the poetry of John Donne back into favour with readers.

❶ THE SUN RISING

Busy old fool, unruly sun,
   Why dost thou thus,
Through windows, and through curtains call on us?
Must to thy motions lovers' seasons run?
   Saucy pedantic wretch, go chide   5
   Late school boys and sour prentices,
  Go tell court huntsmen that the King will ride,
  Call country ants to harvest offices;
Love, all alike, no season knows nor clime,
Nor hours, days, months, which are the rags of time.   10

   Thy beams, so reverend and strong
   Why shouldst thou think?
I could eclipse and cloud them with a wink,
But that I would not lose her sight so long;
   If her eyes have not blinded thine,   15
   Look, and tomorrow late, tell me,
  Whether both th' Indias of spice and mine
  Be where thou leftst them, or lie here with me.
Ask for those kings whom thou saw'st yesterday,
And thou shalt hear, All here in one bed lay.   20

   She's all states, and all princes, I,
   Nothing else is.
Princes do but play us; compared to this,
All honour's mimic, all wealth alchemy.
   Thou, Sun, art half as happy as we,   25
   In that the world's contracted thus.
  Thine age asks ease, and since thy duties be
  To warm the world, that's done in warming us.
Shine here to us, and thou art everywhere;
This bed thy centre is, these walls thy sphere.   30

'so reverend and strong'

GLOSSARY

(A–Z)

5 *Saucy*: impertinent, brazen.
5 *pedantic*: particular, fussy.
5 *chide*: scold.
7 *court huntsmen*: opportunistic courtiers.
8 *country ants/harvest offices*: farmers, seen from the lofty point of view of the sun, busily engaged in repetitive labouring work.
9 *clime*: climate.

10 *rags*: divisions.
17 *both th' Indias*: East and West India, famous respectively for spice and gold.
23 *play*: imitate.
24 *all honour's mimic*: everything which is held in high esteem is only an impersonation of the lovers.
24 *alchemy*: false gold, pretence.

EXPLORATIONS

1. Describe Donne's attitude to the sun in the opening four lines of this poem? How is this reaction established?

2. Donne is supremely confident throughout this poem. Pick two examples of the poet's bold self-assurance.

3. The poem changes from a complaint to an invitation. In your opinion, where does the change take place in the poem? Discuss whether or not this is an impressive ending to the poem.

STUDY NOTES

'The Sun Rising' (written in 1605) is one of Donne's most charming and successful metaphysical love poems. Although the title suggests an aubade (a song sung by lovers who must part at dawn), the poet has actually written a parody making fun of such tender declarations of love. Indeed, this humorous, exuberant poem cheekily scolds the sun for waking Donne and his lover and he firmly instructs the interfering sun to go off and annoy others.

The opening lines dramatically convey the intimate scene of an irritated lover woken up too soon by a busybody sun. Donne personifies the sun and in a half-serious, petulant tone, he reprimands this 'Busy old fool' for intruding. He does not see why he and his lover should live their lives according to the dictates of the sun: 'Must to thy motion lovers' seasons run?' Throughout this **first stanza, the poet mocks the sun** ('Saucy pedantic wretch') and is highly dismissive of its power. Such lively personification of the sun gives great energy and vigour to the poem's opening. Donne goes on to abruptly instruct the sun to pester others, repeating the verb 'Go'. As far as he is concerned, lovers should define their own seasons and the sun should do fairly ordinary, trivial things like 'chide/Late school boys' and other people who have to get up early.

Donne argues that the sun would be better advised to concentrate on sycophantic courtiers and hard-working farmers who are struggling to survive. This is in contrast to the timeless world of true love which is more important than anything else. Perhaps Donne is protesting too much because he really knows that the sun reminds lovers how their blissful state may change over time. However, he concludes confidently with an emphatic rhyme ('clime' and 'time') insisting that **love transcends time**:

'Love, all alike, no season knows, nor clime,
Nor hours, days, months, which are the rags of time'

Mischievously, in **stanza two**, Donne boasts that he can shut out the power of the sun's rays 'with a wink'. He merely has to close his eyes to 'eclipse and cloud' the sun. But he does not want to be parted from his lover ('would not lose her sight so long') for even that small measure of time. In fact, he believes her beautiful eyes are so bright that they could blind the sun. **In a clever conceit, the poet shrinks the huge expanse of the world**, its exotic destinations and far-off islands of spice and minerals ('both th' Indias') and even the magnificence of the King's court into one little room. He tells the sun that the world's real treasures are contained right there in the bedroom which is now the centre of the universe, 'All here in one bed lay'. As far as Donne is concerned, his lover is worth more than anything the sun can ever find outside their bedroom. The monosyllabic phrasing asserts that their bed contains the whole world, not only for the lovers but also for the sun. Again, the forceful rhyme ('yesterday' and 'lay') emphasises how love has altered space. For lovers, the whole wide world is contracted into their own internal world: 'All here in one bed lay'.

The **third stanza** begins with Donne dramatically dismissing the external world, 'Nothing else is'. With typically playful reasoning, he exaggerates the power of love: 'She is all states, and all princes, I'. Reality is subverted as real princes are seen as mere actors pretending to be lovers, 'Princes do but play us'. Riches are dismissed as 'alchemy', a poor substitute for true feeling. The poet then realises that the sun – which is single – is only half as happy as the lovers who have created their own romantic kingdom. His **tone becomes gentle and more respectful** as he acknowledges that the sun is old, 'Thine age asks ease'. In contrast to the earlier disquiet, the mood has now become much more relaxed and assured.

Donne suggests that since the sun's function is to 'warm the world' and since the lovers encapsulate the whole world, the sun will do his duty if he shines on them. So the poet invites the sun to remain: 'Shine here to us'. **The lovers' bed is the centre of the universe**, their walls its borders. This world of love contains everything of value; it is the only one worth exploring and possessing. The final rhyme ('everywhere' and 'sphere') shows how love overcomes all boundaries with its limitless power. In the end, the sun is seen as a satellite encircling the lovers. 'The Sun Rising' demonstrates many of the qualities of metaphysical poetry. Donne's characteristic use of figurative and rhetorical techniques presents readers with a wonderfully, conversational and witty poem, celebrating love and transcending the centuries with its lively energy.

ANALYSIS

'Donne's original approach to poetry results in unique ideas and ingenious language.' Give your response to this statement in relation to the poem 'The Sun Rising'. Use references from the poem to support your views.

Sample Paragraph

It is astonishing to me how Donne in 'The Sun Rising' plays with time, space and location, almost as if he were writing a fantasy tale where none of the physical rules of the world matter. In the early 17th century, when Donne lived, the exploration and discovery of new lands was the exciting news of the day. Donne uses this contemporary image to great effect. In this unusual love poem, he asks the 'Busy old fool', the sun, to let him know if exotic places like 'both th' Indias of spice and mine' are still where they were when the sun orbited past or whether they now 'lie here with me'. The poet uses this image to show that everything of importance is now contained in the lovers' room. There is no need to go searching when everything that could be desired is here. I think this unique idea is wittily expressed by the poet's use of personification of the sun as an interfering intruder rushing here and there. He ingeniously condenses his language in his reference to the far-off Indies, famous for spices and gold. This is a delightfully original approach to poetry on Donne's part as he incorporates contemporary activities like exploration in a love poem. He is cleverly showing that love transcends the limitations of this physical world. This 17th-century poet is well worth reading in the 21st century, because Donne, like the romantic love dramatised in this poem, has transcended time.

Examiner's Comment

As part of a full essay, this is a thoughtful response that attempts to address the question directly, using reference to both content and style. There is also some good personal interaction with the poem and points are clearly expressed throughout. Grade A standard.

CLASS/HOMEWORK EXERCISES

1. The love poetry of Donne is dramatic, conversational and intimate. Is this a valid statement in relation to 'The Sun Rising?' Use quotation from the poem in your response.

2. Copy the table below into your own notes and fill in critical comments about the last two quotations.

Key Quotes

rags of time	In this effective metaphor, the divisions of hours, days and years which govern people's lives are seen as of no more worth by the poet than shreds or leftover remnants.
If her eyes have not blinded thine	Donne uses hyperbole to describe the wonderful beauty and light of his beloved's eyes which, in his opinion, will even obstruct the sun's ability to see.
Must to thy motions lovers' seasons run?	
She's all states, and all princes, I	

❷   SONG (GO, AND CATCH A FALLING STAR)

Go, and catch a falling star,
Get with child a mandrake root,
Tell me, where all past years are,
   Or who cleft the Devil's foot,
Teach me to hear mermaids singing,   5
Or to keep off envy's stinging,
     And find
     What wind
Serves to advance an honest mind.

If thou be'est born to strange sights,   10
   Things invisible to see,
Ride ten thousand days and nights,
   Till age snow white hairs on thee,
Thou, when thou return'st, wilt tell me,
All strange wonders that befell thee,   15
     And swear
     No where
Lives a woman true, and fair.

If thou find'st one, let me know,
   Such a pilgrimage were sweet,   20
Yet do not, I would not go,
   Though at next door we might meet,
Though she were true, when you met her,
And last, till you write your letter,
     Yet she   25
     Will be
False, ere I come, to two, or three.

'catch a falling star'

GLOSSARY

(A-Z)

2	*mandrake root*: a poisonous plant with a forked root.
4	*cleft*: split in two.
5	*mermaids singing*: when a traveller heard the song of the mermaids, it was an omen of disaster.

6	*envy's stinging*: jealous insults and attacks.
10	*be'est born*: are destined.
15	*that befell thee*: that you experienced.
18	*true, and fair*: honest and beautiful.

EXPLORATIONS

1. Describe the mood of the first stanza and show how the poet's use of verbs contributes to that mood.

2. 16th-century poets listed impossible tasks as a device used for emphasis in their poetry. What are the tasks Donne lists in stanza one? In your opinion, what is the connection between the list of tasks and the theme of the poem? Refer closely to the text in your answer.

3. The final line of the poem, 'False, ere I come, to two, or three', sums up Donne's argument. What is his theory? Trace the development of the poet's reasoning through the poem. Do you think he has proven his point?

STUDY NOTES

Written by Donne in his youth, when he had seen a good deal of London life (he was a 'great visitor of ladies'), 'Song: Go, And Catch A Falling Star' is a humorous example of his early work. Woman's faithlessness was a conventional subject of Elizabethan poetry, but Donne's cunning line of argument leaves us wondering. Is he mocking the standard Petrarchan love poem in which a woman is seen as an object of adoration, a goddess worthy of love when he cynically sets out to prove that it is impossible to find a really beautiful and true woman?

Stanza one includes a list of sharp commands ('Go', 'Get', 'Tell', 'Teach', 'find') as Donne demands a series of impossible tasks. The comma after 'Go' establishes the curt, almost over-bearing tone of the poet. These unachievable tasks range from the magical first line, 'Go, and catch a falling star', to the nightmarish reference to conceiving a child with a poisonous plant. He also wants to know where the past has gone and he wishes to learn how to hear the unworldly music of the 'mermaids singing'. From these fanciful tasks of the first five lines, he returns to the real world, as he seeks to find out how to change human nature so that it will not become jealous or bitter. The poet ends his wish list with another impossible request – that everyone could be totally honest. The regular line length has now shortened, highlighting his frustration. Indeed, Donne's exasperation is vigorously expressed in rhyme ('wind', 'mind') as he struggles to comprehend why life does not encourage honesty. It is typical of Donne's wry humour that his series of impossible demands will lead to his playful views on just **how hard it is to find a beautiful woman who will stay true and loyal to her husband**.

The first appearance of emphatic alliteration appears in the **second stanza** ('If thou be,est born to strange sights') as the poet introduces an imaginary traveller, one who was destined to see strange and perplexing scenes. The **disquieting world of nightmare fantasy** is continued in the vivid, dramatic details; seeing 'things invisible', riding 'ten thousand days and nights', returning with hair of snow white, telling tales of 'strange wonders'. Although great distances will have been covered and a long time will have expired, yet the poet confidently declares that 'No where/Lies a woman true, and fair'. Is Donne serious in these lines? Is he suggesting that ugly women will remain true, perhaps due to a lack of offers? Or is the tone of these lines bitter, as he now asserts that a loyal, beautiful woman does not exist?

The conditional word 'If', which began the previous stanza, is also used at the beginning of the **final stanza**. This device of supposition ('if this were the case, then this follows') is a favourite rhetorical technique used by Donne. For a brief moment, **his tone appears to become more hopeful** when he states that if such a perfect woman were discovered ('If thou find'st one, let me know'), then he would go on a 'pilgrimage', a holy journey, again referencing another aspect of Petrarchan poetry, the public adoration of a lady. He thinks this would be delightful, 'sweet'. But he soon challenges the reader with a swift change of heart as he now decides that it would be better not to know. The stanza ends with Donne petulantly declaring that he would not even go next door to meet such an exceptional woman.

Disillusionment dominates the poem's final lines. The poet asserts that even if the perfect female were found, she would have very likely been unfaithful several times before the poet could have met her. The 'pilgrimage' would have been futile. In Donne's cynical view, there is no-one to worship. All beautiful women are unreliable. He uses the recurring pattern of two lines of two words and a three-line rhyme, 'Yet she/Will be/False, ere I come, to two or three', to conclude the poem with a masculine swagger. The theory of the falseness of attractive women has been cleverly proven using the conventions of a type of love poetry which puts women on a pedestal. The heavenly body, 'falling star', has been toppled. Donne's satirical 'song' reflects the underlying theme of many of his other works in which he blames the apparent wickedness of women for his own pain and heartbreak.

ANALYSIS

'Donne's changing viewpoint and tone challenge the modern reader.' Discuss this statement in relation to the poem 'Song (Go, And Catch A Falling Star)'. Refer closely to the text in your answer.

Sample Paragraph

Donne begins 'Song (Go, And Catch A Falling Star)' by setting up in the reader expectations of romantic love poetry. At first he seems to be writing a conventional love poem, in keeping with the Petrarchan poets who looked at women with admiration and respect. He quickly undermines these expectations by the brutal image of the 'mandrake root', a poisonous plant, and now the reader is taken into a fantastic nightmarish scenario. Donne's dismissive tone seems assured as he barks out orders for a series of impossible tasks. Again the reader is caught off balance because in myths or conventional love poetry, lists of incredible challenges are used to prove a lover's devotion. The poet suddenly swaps this surreal scene and expresses his disgust for jealous people and the difficulty of finding 'an honest mind'. Donne then uses the device of the traveller, who has seen many 'strange wonders' in far-off places, not to celebrate women but to condemn them. This traveller will 'swear' that 'No where/Lives a woman true, and fair'. The reader is likely to be shocked by this extreme attack. But Donne adds further insult by suggesting that if such a woman were ever found, he would go on a 'pilgrimage'. Cruelly, he reinforces his final cynical view by stating that even if such a perfect creature was discovered, she would be unfaithful a number of times before the traveller could even write a letter informing the poet of her existence, 'False, ere I come to two, or three'. Donne uses his changing tone and viewpoint to lead the reader through several twists and turns before his final expression of disillusionment with untrustworthy women.

Examiner's Comment

A good focused attempt at addressing a challenging question. References are effectively used to illustrate some of the changing views which make up Donne's argument throughout the poem. The paragraph is also rounded off very well in the final sentence. Grade A standard.

CLASS/HOMEWORK EXERCISES

1. 'Donne's love poetry is energetic, intelligent and engaging.' Discuss this statement with reference to 'Song (Go, And Catch A Falling Star)'.

2. Copy the table below into your own notes and fill in critical comments about the last two quotations.

Key Quotes

Go, and catch a falling star	The poet is beginning his list of impossible tasks as he issues instructions to grasp a heavenly body. The tone seems to vary between good-humoured mischief and dismissive anger.
Till age snow white hairs on thee	The image refers to the traveller who has spent a lifetime seeing the wonders of the world. The use of the verb 'snow' vividly shows the effect old age has had on this man whose hair is now sprinkled with white.
No where/Lives a woman true, and fair	
Such a pilgrimage were sweet	

③ THE ANNIVERSARY

All kings, and all their favourites,
  All glory of honours, beauties, wits,
The sun itself, which makes times, as they pass,
Is elder by a year now, than it was
When thou and I first one another saw.   5
All other things to their destruction draw,
  Only our love hath no decay;
This, no tomorrow hath, nor yesterday;
Running it never runs from us away,
But truly keeps his first, last, everlasting day.   10

Two graves must hide thine and my corse;
  If one might, death were no divorce.
Alas, as well as other princes, we
(Who prince enough in one another be)
Must leave at last in death, these eyes and ears,   15
Oft fed with true oaths, and with sweet salt tears;
  But souls where nothing dwells but love
(All other thoughts being inmates) then shall prove
This, or a love increased there above,   *Sense of irony*
When bodies to their graves, souls from their graves remove. 20
    Diminish Sense of love

And then we shall be throughly blest,
  But we no more than all the rest;
Here upon earth, we're kings, and none but we *Contradiction but meaning*
    they provide each other with
Can be such kings, nor of such subjects be. *such Power.*
Who is so safe as we? where none can do   25
  Crime v. King Treason to us, except one of us two.
  True and false fears let us refrain, *Sense that they are not perfect*
    Honour
Let us love nobly, and live, and add again
Years and years unto years, till we attain
    Now
To write threescore; this is the second of our reign.   30
    or 2nd part

'Who is so safe as we?'

GLOSSARY

(A-Z)

2   *honours*: important people of prominence and distinction.

3   *makes times*: the sun controls the passing of time.

4   *Is elder*: everything in the world is older by a year.

9   *Running it never runs from us away*: ongoing love can never cease.

11 *corse*: corpse. (In Donne's time, it would have been unacceptable for an unmarried couple to be buried in the same grave.)

16 *sweet salt tears*: love can bring both joy and heartbreak.

18 *inmates*: temporary occupants.

19 *or a love increased there above*: the couple's love will be greater in heaven.

21 *throughly blest*: totally blessed.

27 *True and false fears let us refrain*: we should put aside both real and imagined misgivings.

30 *the second of our reign*: the lovers are now entering the second year of their relationship.

EXPLORATIONS

1. What expectations are set up in the opening five lines of this poem? Are they realised or refuted in the remainder of the poem? Refer to the text in your answer.

2. Do you find the ending of the poem convincing or unrealistic? Support your response with close reference to the text.

3. Write a short personal response to this poem, using reference and quotations to illustrate your views.

STUDY NOTES

'The Anniversary' is about a couple celebrating their first year together in a relationship. Royalty is the underlying conceit of the entire poem, with the speaker addressing his lover as though they were both nobles. Some critics felt that Donne should not irritate women with questions of reason and logic, but should engage their hearts. In fact, he does both. At the age of twenty-seven, he fell in love with sixteen-year-old Ann More. As he was not financially secure, they kept their love and marriage secret. When Donne

eventually told her father, he was thrown in prison, and he ended a letter to Ann with
the pun, 'John Donne- Ann Donne- Undone'. This type of clever wordplay is a recurring
feature of metaphysical poetry.

An anniversary is a useful moment to stand back and reflect. In **stanza one**, the
young lover confidently proclaims that the entire world, 'All kings, and all their
favourites … beauties, wits,/The sun itself' is a year older since he and his beloved
first met. Everyone and everything on Donne's magnificent list have been changed
over time. All splendour fades. The list is not a fanfare, but a requiem, a funeral
song. However, in contrast to this decay ('destruction'), the shared love of the
young lovers escapes: 'Only our love hath no decay'. This short line stands out
boldly in defiance of time's brutal march. The poet's clever paradox (a comparison
of opposites) illustrates how their love survives: 'Running it never runs from
us away'. This is reminiscent of a flowing river or a ticking clock's motion. The
perpetual, unbroken movement is the rhythm and pulsing beat of their constant
love. According to Donne, the lovers are at **the centre of the universe, unaffected
by time**. The beautifully balanced final line ('But truly keeps his first, last,
everlasting day') ends the opening stanza on an assertive note.

He faces up to the idea of Mortality.
He knows that they eventually will die.

However, in **stanza two**, the poet faces up to life's stark reality and the
inevitability of death. He pictures the lovers' bodies lying in separate graves,
'Two graves must hide thine and my corse'. The haunting image of burial recurs
frequently in Donne's poetry. It seems likely that he is thinking of his own personal
circumstances. His love for Ann More was still secret, so it would not have
been possible for the lovers to share a grave as they were not married. But the
couple's love is so strong that even death can not separate them on a spiritual
level. Donne develops the metaphor of royalty to emphasise how their mutual
love sets them apart: 'Who prince enough in one another be'. For a moment, the
mood is suddenly regretful at the thought of leaving behind love's 'true oaths, and
with sweet salt tears'. The argument soon twists as Donne considers how death
will free their loving souls from the prison of physical life. **The couple will then
be reunited spiritually** 'where nothing dwells but love'. Indeed, they will find in
heaven a much greater happiness, 'love increased there above'.

Love within the soul is most powerful

In the **third stanza**, Donne imagines the afterlife of the sanctified lovers when
they will be 'throughly blest'. Yet he realises that they will be no different in heaven
than all other lovers who have died – 'But we no more than all the rest'. It is ironic
that they will not be as they are on earth where they are 'kings'. During their
lives, the two of them are royalty and subjects at the same time. Their mutual

serve

We are Citizens

love is beyond deceit or treachery ('Treason'). Any harm which can happen to the couple would be self-destructive, so they can love without fear. Donne confidently dismisses whatever anxiety they might feel, whether real or imagined: 'True and false fears let us refrain'. He encourages them to 'love nobly', so they will enjoy a long life and even celebrate their sixtieth anniversary ('three score'). Once more, the royal metaphor (suggested by 'Treason', 'nobly' and 'reign') is utilised to stress the special status of true love. Donne's final tone is optimistic, with its positive message to live in the moment, to love in this world. **The couple can now look forward to celebrating the second year of their relationship**: 'the second of our reign'.

Throughout this **passionate love poem**, the inward-looking nature of young lovers in the excitement of a new romance is beautifully evoked in the conceit of royalty. Love is an exceptional state, an absorbingly complete experience, incapable of being touched by the outside world. But while there is plenty of passion in 'The Anniversary', Donne also gives readers a somewhat superior expression of romantic love. The dominant tone throughout is highly assured, 'Only our love hath no decay', yet intimate, 'Who is so safe as we?'. Characteristically, the poet's restless mind searches for far-fetched ideas and extravagant images in order to convey the quality of unconditional love. There is much metaphysical wit in Donne's poetry and he was known for his inventive wordplay, such as the oxymoron (the linking of opposite aspects) 'sweet salt tears'.

ANALYSIS

'Donne's love poetry is lively, inventive and highly compelling.' Discuss this view of the poet's work in relation to the poem, 'The Anniversary'. Quote in support of your response.

Sample Paragraph

'The Anniversary' is another of Donne's love poems, similar to 'The Sun Rising' and equally persuasive. It is the celebration of a relationship that is a year old. It has not been affected by any changes. Donne uses the extended metaphor of royalty to illustrate the special state of the young lovers. The forceful opening which begins with the glittering list, 'All kings, and all their favourites,/All glory of honours, beauties, wits,/The sun itself' is in the tradition of Petrarchan love poetry with its emphasis on courtly love. But it is the ending of the poem which is really creative as the poet reassures his loved one that they can come to no harm as he playfully asks 'Who is so safe as we?'. This is also typically imaginative as Donne suggests that they should celebrate their love while they can, 'Here upon earth we're kings'. Donne's use of language is animated and energetic, particularly in the paradox, 'Running it never runs from us away'. I thought the unusual idea of movement going nowhere was very interesting. Love is a living thing which does not fade over time. This dynamic image reminded me of a river ceaselessly flowing. The poet uses alliteration compellingly, especially the dull 'd' sound in 'destruction draw' to emphasise how everything in the world will change – except for the lovers themselves. Donne's poetry is forceful, original and convincing.

Examiner's Comment

As part of a full essay, this is a well managed paragraph which addresses the question directly and shows good personal interaction with the poem. The focus on Donne's language is clear and supported effectively with suitable reference. Expression is also confident and fluent throughout. Grade A standard.

CLASS/HOMEWORK EXERCISES

1. Trace the metaphor of royalty throughout 'The Anniversary'. What do you think this conceit adds to the poem? Quote to support your opinions.

2. Copy the table below into your own notes and fill in critical comments about the last two quotations.

Key Quotes

All other things to their destruction draw	Donne uses the insistently alliterative 't' and 'd' sounds to emphasise how everything in the world is subject to decay.
Who prince enough in one another be	The poet felt that the couple's mutual love enabled them to form a special kingdom where each was both subject and lord of the other. The image reflects the self-regarding nature of young love.
All other thoughts being inmates	
But we no more than all the rest	

[handwritten top:] Fear of Separation from death.

4 SONG (SWEETEST LOVE, I DO NOT GO)

Sweetest love, I do not go, *[hw: Sick of her]*
  For weariness of thee,
Nor in hope the world can show *[hw: Not going in search of a better form of love]*
  A fitter love for me;
    But since that I   5
Must die at last, 'tis best, *[hw: This journey away from her]*
To use myself in jest *[hw: is to see what permanent separation]*
  Thus by feigned deaths to die. *[hw: Fake]* *[hw: would be like.]*

Yesternight the sun went hence, *[hw: reassure his wife]*
  And yet is here today, *[hw: he will be back]* 10
He hath no desire nor sense, *[hw: Sun]* *[hw: Sun is not desireable to come back]*
  Nor half so short a way: *[hw: Longer journey to make.]*
    Then fear not me,
But believe that I shall make
Speedier journeys, since I take 15
  More wings and spurs than he. *[hw: bring him back quickly]*

[hw: Weak]
O how feeble is man's power,
  That if good fortune fall,
Cannot add another hour, *[hw: No power in shaping someones life]*
  Nor a lost hour recall! 20
    But come bad chance,
And we join to it our strength,
And we teach it art and length, *[hw: Try the too make the best of things]*
  Itself o'er us to advance.

[hw left: Time will pass no matter what]
[hw left: gets Sad]

When thou sigh'st, thou sigh'st not wind, *[hw: what will final departure be like?]* 25
  But sigh'st my soul away, *[hw: will not help]*
When thou weep'st, unkindly kind,
  My life's blood doth decay.
    It cannot be *[hw: If she is wasting time mourning]*
That thou lov'st me, as thou say'st, 30
If in thine my life thou waste;
  Thou art the best of me. *[hw: They merged physically + emotionally]*

[handwritten: Page 60]

Let not thy divining heart *[predict]* *[don't let your mind wonder negatively = waste of energy]*
   Forethink me any ill,
[Plan] Destiny may take thy part,   35
   And may thy fears fulfil;
   But think that we
Are but turn'd aside to sleep; *[when they want to go to sleep]*
They who one another keep
   Alive, ne'er parted be. *[• Through their Love.]*   40

'Sweetest love, I do not go, /For weariness of thee'

GLOSSARY

4 *fitter*: more appropriate.
7 *in jest*: not seriously.
8 *feigned deaths*: false deaths (preparations for the actual death which will eventually occur).
9 *hence*: from here.
16 *More wings and spurs than he*: Donne will return quicker than the sun.
21 *bad chance*: misfortune.
24 *Itself o'er us to'advance*: we focus on bad times so much that we allow them to almost overwhelm us.
25 *wind*: breath.
27 *unkindly kind*: her sorrow shows her love, but it also causes him hurt.
33 *divining*: anticipating, foretelling.
34 *Forethink me any ill*: do not imagine any harm coming to me.

EXPLORATIONS

1. Choose one image from this poem which you consider particularly powerful. Explain its effectiveness.

2. Describe the poet's tone in the first two stanzas. Refer closely to the text in your answer.

3. The final lines of the poem refer to the lovers turning on their sides to sleep. In your view, is this a happy, sad or poignant conclusion to the lovers' dilemma? Briefly explain your response.

STUDY NOTES

This song is a simple, eloquent poem on the theme of parting. It is believed that Donne wrote it for his wife before he travelled abroad in 1611. The poet argues that if two people are truly in love, then nothing – including death – can ever separate them. The poem's five stanzas hold the overwhelming emotion of the scene with its strong rhyme, which forms a pattern throughout. Donne's use of everyday language gives an air of realism to the domestic setting. The light rhythm varies from six to seven syllables, except in line 5 of each stanza, where the poet makes a more dramatic remark, such as 'It cannot be'.

Stanza one begins on a tense note, with Donne and his lover engaged in deep conversation about a journey he is planning. His affectionate address, 'Sweetest love', is tender and reassuring as he explains that he is not leaving because he is tired of her, 'For weariness of thee'. Nor does he want to look for another, 'Nor in hope the world can show/A fitter love for me'. The tone is serious and shows none of the glittering wit of Donne's other romantic poems, such as 'The Flea'. This makes it much more personal and sincere. Donne then tries to lighten the mood by arguing that **this temporary separation is merely a rehearsal** which will help both his lover and himself to become more accustomed to the inescapable parting of his actual death: 'Thus by feigned deaths to die.'

In the **second stanza**, Donne offers further assurances by comparing his travels

(handwritten margin note: when one of them dies)

to the movement of the sun across the sky. His own journey abroad will be of a much shorter duration than the sun's from dawn to dusk. He flatters his lover by focusing on her attractiveness, saying that he has much more reason than the sun to hurry back to her. **His characteristic use of hyperbole (exaggeration) emphasises just how quickly he will return**: 'I shall make/Speedier journeys'. *emphasises his desire for her.* Donne is keen to express his feelings. Being in love makes him even more powerful than the sun: 'I take/More wings and spurs than he.'

However, in the **third stanza**, the poet becomes more reflective, widening the argument to discuss how people in general deal with life's good and bad experiences. As far as Donne is concerned, 'good fortune' is taken for granted. But if we are faced with bad times ('bad chance'), we give in immediately and let it overwhelm us: 'we join to it our strength'. **He is advising his lover to fight misfortune** and resist adversity. Otherwise, disappointment will always get the better of the couple, undermining their love: 'Itself o'er us to advance'. *when things are good, we think it will last forever.*

Stanza four is almost entirely focused on Donne's lover, the repetition of 'thou' reflecting his intense feelings for her. His deeply personal tone returns as he describes how close they are. He shares every small sadness that she feels. Even the slightest sigh she makes, 'sigh'st my soul away'. When she weeps, she is not being unkind since her unhappiness also harms him: 'My life's blood doth decay'. Donne then goes so far as to apparently challenge her love for him: 'It cannot be/That thou lov'st me', as he accuses her of abandoning his life whenever she cries: 'If in thine my life thou waste'. However, **deep down he acknowledges how much he depends on her**: 'Thou art the best of me.' Such an emphatic declaration of love leaves readers feeling that an intensely personal, intimate moment is being witnessed as the two lovers struggle with their overpowering emotions.

Throughout **stanza five**, the **tone is much more tender**. Donne appeals to his lover, encouraging her not to imagine all the unfortunate things which might happen to him when he is away from her: 'Forethink me any ill'. In a more light-hearted comment, he warns her against inviting misfortune: 'Destiny may take thy part'. Instead, he coaxes her to think of a beautiful moment in their relationship and suggests that his journey is no more than the parting of a couple as they sleep ('but turn'd aside to sleep'). The poem concludes with this warm, comforting image reflecting a secure and stable relationship. *suggestion* The inference is that if his loved one can get used to this parting, then she will be able to rise above fate, death and separation. *He is consoling her*

Do not worry about the future, focus on the present

ANALYSIS

[handwritten annotations: • theme • style   • Techniques]

'Donne is a highly dramatic poet.' Discuss this statement in relation to the poem 'Song (Sweetest Love, I Do Not Go)'. Support the points you make with reference to the text.   *[handwritten: • use of Personal Pronouns "I " "we"]*

Sample Paragraph

In 'Song (Sweetest Love, I Do Not Go)', Donne plunges the reader into the turmoil of the moment as the poet tries to reassure his loved one that his journey away from her is not because he is tired of her, 'For weariness of thee'. It is a typical lovers' quarrel. Donne's urgent tone is evident when he explains that he is not going away in search of someone new, 'Nor in hope the world can show/A fitter love for me'. I can imagine the tears of his beloved as she probably is pleading for him to stay. The dramatic opening is very realistic. Donne then tries to lighten the mood as he says he might as well practise for death by short separations, 'by feigned deaths to die'. He captures the moment so well that I can almost see the grumpy shrug of his lover at this tactic. But it is the fourth stanza which is the most powerful in evoking the sheer misery of the girl who is to be left behind. He speaks of her sighing, 'When thou weep'st'. He then tries to criticise her for her grief which he says is causing him harm, 'My life's blood doth decay'. This is exactly what happens in a lovers' argument, as each tries to outwit the other by twisting and turning words. But then Donne relents and admits the truth, 'Thou art the best of me'. The short fifth line in each stanza also adds drama, particularly the line, 'Then fear not me'. He is reassuring her that he will return quickly. Finally, the commotion of the argument fades as he reminds her of their most intimate moment, 'but turn'd aside to sleep' and he suggests that this is all this little separation is, just a short night's sleep. After all the drama between the rowing lovers, there is a gentle resolution in the end.

Examiner's Comment

This A-grade paragraph addresses the question directly and explores key dramatic aspects of the poem both explicitly and implicitly. Expression is varied and well controlled and there is some good personal engagement. Effective use is also made of apt quotation and reference throughout.

CLASS/HOMEWORK EXERCISES

• relates to he and his partner (personal pronouns and first person).

1. 'John Donne's poetry is intimate and engaging.' Discuss this statement in relation to 'Song (Sweetest Love, I Do Not Go)'. Support the points you make with reference to the poem.

2. Copy the table below into your own notes and fill in critical comments about the last two quotations.

Key Quotes

But since that I/Must die at last	Donne is stating the reality that everyone must eventually die, and that the small separations in life prepare us for this inevitability.
He hath no desire nor sense,/Nor half so short a way	The poet personifies the sun and argues that he himself is so much in love that he will make an even faster journey back to his lover than the sun could ever travel. Such exaggeration is typical of Donne.
And we teach it art and length/ Itself o'er us to advance	
Thou art the best of me	

❺ A VALEDICTION: FORBIDDING MOURNING

As virtuous men pass mildly away,
   And whisper to their souls, to go,
Whilst some of their sad friends do say,
   The breath goes now, and some say, no:

So let us melt, and make no noise,   5
   No tear-floods, nor sigh-tempests move,
'Twere profanation of our joys
   To tell the laity our love.

Moving of th'earth brings harms and fears,
   Men reckon what it did and meant,   10
But trepidation of the spheres
   Though greater far, is innocent.

Dull sublunary lovers' love
   (Whose soul is sense) cannot admit
Absence, because it doth remove   15
   Those things which elemented it.

But we by a love so much refined,
   That our selves know not what it is,
Inter-assured of the mind,
   Care less, eyes, lips, and hands to miss.   20

Our two souls therefore, which are one,
   Though I must go, endure not yet
A breach, but an expansion,
   Like gold to airy thinness beat.

If they be two, they are two so   25
   As stiff twin compasses are two,
Thy soul the fixed foot, makes no show
   To move, but doth, if the other do.

And though it in the centre sit,
    Yet when the other far doth roam,   30
It leans, and hearkens after it,
    And grows erect, as that comes home.

Such wilt thou be to me, who must
    Like th' other foot, obliquely run;
Thy firmness makes my circle just,   35
    And makes me end, where I begun.

'Thy firmness makes my circle just,/And makes me end, where I begun'

GLOSSARY

The title comes from the Latin for a farewell message.

1   *As virtuous men pass mildly*: just as good men die peacefully.

5   *melt*: dissolve and blend together.

7   *profanation*: irreverence, offensive.

8   *laity*: ordinary people.

10 *reckon what it did and meant*: try to understand the significance of the turbulence.

11 *trepidation of the spheres*: movement of the planets.

13 *sublunary*: undependable.

16 *elemented*: form.

19 *Inter-assured*: trusting.

23 *breach*: separation.

26 *twin compasses*: instrument for measuring circles.

34 *obliquely*: curved.

35 *just*: exact.

> ## EXPLORATIONS

1. Trace Donne's line of argument in the poem, 'A Valediction: Forbidding Mourning'. Support your answer with suitable quotation.

2. Which comparison appeals most to you in this poem? Briefly explain why.

3. In what way does Donne see the parting of lovers as a positive move? Give reasons for your response using quotations from the poem.

> ## STUDY NOTES

'A Valediction: Forbidding Mourning' dates from 1611 when Donne embarked on a long journey to Europe and wrote this special farewell poem for his wife. The poet explores the familiar theme of separation from a loved one, and claims that the relationship between the lovers is such that physical distance cannot part them. Indeed, he argues that being apart actually strengthens their love. Characteristically, Donne breathes new life into this traditional subject by using a series of ingenious metaphors and comparisons. These provide fresh ways of looking at separation which will help the couple to avoid the mourning forbidden by the poem's title.

Stanza one opens on a reflective note as Donne considers how 'sad friends' grieve for those who are dying. The atmosphere is usually sombre but tranquil as loved ones take comfort that 'virtuous' people 'pass mildly away', confident of a spiritual life hereafter. Soft sibilant 's' sounds (such as 'whisper' and 'souls') create this untroubled mood. The separation of body and soul is so gentle that those surrounding the dying are uncertain about whether they are still alive or not. Donne uses breaks in punctuation to suggest this confusion, 'The breath goes now, and some say, no'. This gives way to a metaphor of melting in the second stanza where the poet makes a suggestion to his lover: 'So let us melt, and make no noise'. For Donne, the couple's separation is like a minor death which should also be treated in a dignified and restrained way. **He ridicules people who cannot control their feelings and resort to 'tear floods' and 'sigh-tempests'.** Such hyperbole (exaggerated figures of speech) was typical of courtly love. The poet emphasises the sacred nature of true love by asserting that it would be almost blasphemous –

a 'profanation of our joys' – to let outsiders ('the laity') know about it.

Donne introduces a further conceit in the **third stanza** when he tells his loved one that earthquakes and similar disturbances – perhaps a hint at her outpourings of grief – only bring 'harms and fears'. However, a mere earthquake is relatively unimportant compared to the movement of the planet, which ordinary people see as presenting no danger. Therefore, the geographical separation which the couple will experience should not be feared. **This astrological analogy** continues into the **fourth stanza** where the poet speaks disparagingly of 'Dull sublunary lovers' love'. Unlike the poet and his lover, other couples cannot tolerate being apart ('admit/ Absence') because their inferior type of love is dependent on physical presence. As always, Donne interlinks numerous poetic devices. The assonance of the short 'u' sounds in each word of the first line reinforces the concept of dreariness which he associates with shallow relationships. The term, 'sublunary' (literally meaning 'under the moon') suggests that all these other lovers are changeable and unreliable just like the variable moon.

Stanza five continues to focus on the superiority of the couple's shared love. This is the reason why Donne forbade mourning in the poem's title. In his confident view, their relationship is purified like precious metal. They both know that each is loyal to the other, 'Inter-assured of the mind', because they share this special love. In contrast to ordinary couples, they are not dependent on the physical presence of the loved one, making each of them 'Care less, eyes, lips and hands to kiss'. **Their love is more a union of souls which transcends the physical**. Geographical separation means nothing to two united spirits. The poet's forceful, rhetorical tone is developed in **stanza six**. Donne argues that since their two souls are 'one', they are not really faced with any 'breach' or division. Indeed, they are experiencing an 'expansion' in much the same way as gold can be stretched to the slender thickness of paper if it is beaten to 'airy thinness'. Since gold is always associated with beauty and value, this typically inventive simile flatters Donne's lover and celebrates the couple's love.

The final reason for refusing to mourn being separated is presented in **stanzas seven** and **eight** when Donne uses a compass as a metaphor to describe the couple's unity. Although lovers retain their souls, they are divided into two parts. When the compass draws a circle, one point remains stationary in the centre, at a fixed point, which allows the other to complete its circuit. Similarly, if one of the lovers remains at home, it ensures the return of the other. A perfect circle is a symbol of infinity, as there is no apparent beginning or end. This ingenious conceit aptly sums up the couple's spiritual relationship which is also balanced and mutual. In the **final stanzas**, their heightened love is seen as serious and beautiful in its polished simplicity. Yet, there is still a human dimension, the fixed foot 'hearkens after' the moving foot. The loved one will always yearn for the one who has gone. Overall, the **poem tenderly comforts both lovers** at this moment of uneasy parting. Donne concludes by offering a firm assurance that the traveller eventually 'comes home'.

ANALYSIS

'Donne's poetry rarely tells us anything new; rather it reminds us of what we know already.' To what extent is this true of 'A Valediction: Forbidding Mourning'? Support your answer with relevant quotation.

Sample Paragraph

I agree with this view. Donne addresses conventional and familiar themes, particularly in his love poetry whether it is celebrating an anniversary or dealing with a parting from a loved one. However, it is how Donne communicates his message, his own unique approach, which makes him an exciting and original poet. He dares to go against conventions of his own time and he appeals not only to a woman's emotions, but to her intellect through clever comparisons. The opening of 'A Valediction: Forbidding Mourning' presents the reader with a calm, sad scene of dying men accepting death, 'pass mildly away'. The poet is suggesting that this attitude – 'make no noise'– is how he would like himself and his loved one to part, 'So let us melt'. He regards their love as so extraordinary, 'refined', that their parting will be an 'expansion'. Just as gold expands to 'airy thinness', so their love will bridge the gap of their separation. Finally, in a striking, daring comparison, Donne compares these two lovers to a mathematical compass, free to move, yet always connected and secure. So the treatment of an ordinary theme – separation – is raised to a new level as readers are stretched to follow the poet's thought-provoking logic. Donne may not explore any new ideas, but he does offer original perspectives on well-known themes. I particularly liked the tenderness of the steady foot being rewarded by the return of the moving foot which always 'comes home'.

Examiner's Comment

This is a confidently written response to the question and addresses some of Donne's prominent ideas directly. Several suitable references are used effectively to discuss the poet's treatment of recurring themes. Expression is controlled throughout and there is some interesting personal engagement. Grade A.

CLASS/HOMEWORK EXERCISES

1. 'Donne is a memorable, original poet.' Discuss this statement in relation to the poem, 'A Valediction: Forbidding Mourning'. Use evidence from the poem to support your response.

2. Copy the table below into your own notes and fill in critical comments about the last two quotations.

Key Quotes

So let us melt	The poet wishes his loved one to adapt the attitude of the dying person, serenely accepting the separation.
Dull sublunary lovers' love	Donne's tone is highly judgmental as he criticises ordinary lovers. The alliterative 'l' emphasises his dismissive attitude.
Thy soul the fixed foot	
It leans, and hearkens after it	

6   THE DREAM

Dear love, for nothing less than thee
Would I have broke this happy dream,
      It was a theme
For reason, much too strong for fantasy.
Therefore thou waked'st me wisely; yet   5
My dream thou brok'st not, but continued'st it.
Thou art so true that thoughts of thee suffice
To make dreams truths, and fables histories;
Enter these arms, for since thou thought'st it best,
Not to dream all my dream, let's act the rest.   10

As lightning, or a taper's light,
Thine eyes, and not thy noise waked me;
      Yet I thought thee
(For thou lovest truth) an angel, at first sight,
But when I saw thou saw'st my heart,   15
And knew'st my thoughts, beyond an angel's art,
When thou knew'st what I dreamt, when thou knew'st when
Excess of joy would wake me, and cam'st then,
I must confess, it could not choose but be
Profane, to think thee anything but thee.   20

Coming and staying showed thee, thee,
But rising makes me doubt, that now,
      Thou art not thou.
That love is weak where fear's as strong as he;
'Tis not all spirit, pure and brave,   25
If mixture it of fear, shame, honour have;
Perchance as torches which must ready be,
Men light and put out, so thou deal'st with me,
Thou cam'st to kindle, goest to come; then I
Will dream that hope again, but else would die.   30

'Thou art so true that thoughts of thee suffice,/To make dreams truths, and fables histories'

GLOSSARY

7   *suffice*: are enough to.
8   *fables histories*: stories become true.
11   *taper's light*: bright candlelight.
16   *beyond an angel's art*: more than an angel.
19   *it could not choose but be*: there was no other option
20   *Profane*: disrespectful.

21   *showed thee, thee*: revealed your true self.
27   *Perchance as torches which must ready be*: worn torches light up more quickly than new ones.
29   *kindle*: re-ignite; awaken.
29   *goest to come*: you leave in order to return again.

EXPLORATIONS

1. In your own words, describe Donne's attitude to his lover in the opening stanza.

2. Choose one image from the poem which you consider particularly effective. Briefly explain your choice.

3. Although John Donne enjoys arguing in his love poetry, he treats women as his intellectual equals. Where is this evident in 'The Dream'? Quote in support of your response.

STUDY NOTES

John Donne's love poetry reacted against the courtly love tradition of his time. He did not believe in worshipping an aloof, inaccessible figure. Instead, he wanted a real connection with his loved one. This can be clearly seen in 'The Dream', a sensual love poem which plays with ideas of dreams, desire and truth. Like love itself, the woman Donne addresses is praised in hyperbolic terms and acclaimed as someone who is even above the level of angels.

At the start of **stanza one**, Donne is clearly delighted to have been awoken by the same person he was dreaming about. The poet's engaging tone is evident as he sleepily declares, 'Dear love, for nothing less than thee/Would I have broke this happy dream'. There is an unexpected gentleness in these lines. The rhythm is intricate, with the stress firmly placed on the words, 'Dear', 'Nothing', 'thee', 'broke' and 'dream'. Using this playfully intimate mood, Donne explains that reality (his lover's physical presence) is stronger than fantasy, 'It was a theme/For reason, much too strong for fantasy'. The poet congratulates his beloved on waking him, 'Therefore thou waked'st me wisely'. He even suggests that she can alter history, 'Thou art so true, that thoughts of thee suffice,/To make dreams truths'. Donne is implying that women have remarkable power over the perception of reality. **This subtle poem blends dream and reality seamlessly** as the poet declares that his loved one did not ruin his dream, 'My dream thou brok'st not', but by her actual presence, she is continuing it, and so he invites her to 'Enter these arms ... let's act the rest'. Donne is clearly not satisfied with any distant adoration of a loved one. Instead, he desires an urgent, passionate connection, 'Not to dream all my dream', but to make his dream come true.

Stanza two begins with a flattering analogy. Donne compares the woman's eyes to a soft light, 'As lightning, or a taper's light,/Thine eyes'. Such characteristic wordplay emphasises her beauty and more than compensates for any interruption which may have disturbed him, 'not thy noise wak'd me'. For a brief moment, he thought she was an angel, but the bracketed afterthought, '(For thou lovest truth)', removes this romantic poem from the conventional style of Donne's time and gives it a more personal significance. There is no denying the poet's emotional vulnerability. He suddenly realises that his lover 'knew'st my thoughts' – something that makes her more special than any heavenly angel. He imagines that she knew he was dreaming of her and wanted to play out the dream in reality so that they could share the 'Excess of joy'. The **complicated and challenging argument** continues as Donne confesses that it would be 'Profane' or blasphemous to regard his loved one as anyone but herself. From the poet's viewpoint, their relationship is based on mutual empathy, a sharing of thoughts. Religious references, such as 'angel' and 'Profane', emphasise how exceptional this love is.

Donne continues to applaud his lover in the opening lines of **stanza three**. By 'Coming and staying', she has revealed her real character, 'showed thee, thee'. He maintains that when she is with him, she is most like her true self. However, there is an abrupt change of mood as she attempts to leave, 'rising makes me doubt'. Donne suddenly criticises his companion for not being truly in love with him, 'that now,/Thou art not thou'. He challenges her feelings towards him in a finely balanced argument, 'love is weak, where fear's as strong as he'. The personification suggests that her fear becomes stronger as her love weakens. The poet claims that the woman's reluctance to express her love physically is because of various social pressures, especially 'fear, shame, honour'. He bitterly accuses her of taking him for granted, like an old torch. Up until this moment, Donne had been hoping she had come to ignite their love, 'Thou cam'st to kindle'. However, in another startling turn, he uses an oxymoron (a contradictory expression) to reassure himself that his companion only leaves him in order to return, 'goest to come'. She will revisit him and inflame his desires for her even further, just as torches, once lit, are easier to ignite a second time. **The poem ends on an enthusiastic note of expectation**. Donne will 'dream that hope again'. Meantime, he leaves his lover with a parting shot that he 'but else would die' if she does not return to him. Clearly, without the woman of his dreams, he cannot achieve satisfaction.

ANALYSIS

'John Donne pursues his themes by means of vigorous and surprising arguments.' Discuss this statement in relation to 'The Dream'. Use close reference to the text to support your points.

Sample Paragraph

With an intimate glimpse of the poet in the unguarded moments between sleep and wakefulness, Donne opens the poem, 'The Dream'. He wakes to find his loved one, of whom he has been dreaming, at his side. In an intensely enthusiastic tone, he aims to pursue in real life what he has been dreaming of. He begins with compliments, telling her that she is so real that her very presence turns his imaginings to fact, 'Thou art so true'. He lavishes endearments, 'Dear love'. Uniquely, for his time he does not simplify his arguments because she is a woman, but treats her to the full force of his intellectual rigour. The poet felt her presence so vividly in his dream that he does not feel that the spell is broken when he wakes, 'My dream thou brok'st not'. In reality, he feels the dream continuing. His reasoning moves to unforeseen areas, as particularly in the last stanza, he abruptly changes course because she is leaving, accusing her that 'love is weak'. Because his lover is afraid to stay with him, her fear is as 'strong as he'. Unexpectedly, the logic of the poem takes a different direction as he consoles himself that she 'cam'st to kindle' and she is only going so that she can come again, 'goest to come'. His argument, therefore, ends optimistically, that he 'Will dream that hope again' – as a result of his dependency on her. So John Donne rejects the conventional treatment of women in love poetry as delicate and submissive creatures and instead subjects them and us, the readers, to a robust series of remarkable arguments.

Examiner's Comment

This is a well sustained response to a challenging question. There is good engagement with the development of thought in the poem, and useful reference to the changes in Donne's line of argument. Expression is assured throughout and effective use is made of suitable quotation. Grade A.

CLASS/HOMEWORK EXERCISES

1. What type of relationship is revealed in the poem, 'The Dream'? Refer closely to the poem in your response.

2. Copy the table below into your own notes and fill in critical comments about the last two quotations.

Key Quotes

It was a theme/For reason, much too strong for fantasy	Donne's confident tone emphasises his view that the content of his dream was better suited to reality rather than sleeping imagination.
so true, that thoughts of thee suffice/To make dreams truths	The poet argues that his lover is the very essence of truth itself, so that even a thought of her changes dreams and fantasies into true histories. Such exaggeration is a common feature of metaphysical poetry.
For thou lovest truth	
as torches which must ready be, Men light and put out	

7 # THE FLEA

Conceit - uses "Flea" to discuss the relationship. It is an analogy or a symbol.

Mark but this flea, and mark in this, *take note*
How little that which thou deny'st me is;
Me it suck'd first, and now sucks thee, *· Flea has combined them.*
And in this flea, our two bloods mingled be;
Thou know'st that this cannot be said   5
A sin, nor shame, nor loss of maidenhead,
  Yet this enjoys before it woo,   *The flea has brought them closer*
  And pampered swells with one blood made of two,
  And this, alas, is more than we would do. *They are not at that stage also.*

O stay, three lives in one flea spare,   10
Where we almost, yea more than married are.   *He doesn't want her to destroy the flea*
This flea is you and I, and this
Our marriage bed, and marriage temple is;   *Sacred*   *Humour about Flea*
Though parents grudge, and you, w'ere met,   *difficulty*   *Through that intermingling of blood they are almost marry*
And cloistered in these living walls of jet.   *Protection*   15
  Though use make you apt to kill me,
  Let not to that self-murder added be,   *Kill flea = Kills herself*
  And sacrilege, three sins in killing three.   *inadvertant = Simply occured (Flea brought them together*

She crushes it Cruel and sudden, hast thou since   *she has disobeyed.*
Purpled thy nail, in blood of innocence?   20
Wherein could this flea guilty be,   *Maybe he deserves to be killed?*
Except in that drop which it sucked from thee?
Yet thou triumph'st, and say'st that thou
Find'st not thy self, nor me the weaker now.
  'Tis true, then learn how false, fears be;   25
  Just so much honour, when thou yield'st to me,   *She would suffer no more*
  Will waste, as this flea's death took life from thee.

'Me is suck'd first, and now sucks thee'

GLOSSARY (A-Z)

1   *Mark*: note.
4   *our two bloods mingled be*: intimacy between lovers was believed to result in the mingling together of each partner's blood.
6   *maidenhead*: virginity.
7   *this enjoys before it woo*: the flea achieves what the poet desires, without the trouble of courtship.

15   *cloistered*: enclosed.
15   *jet*: shiny black.
16   *apt*: ready.
18   *sacrilege*: destruction of something holy.
19   *sudden*: without warning.
20   *Purpled*: stained with the blood of the flea.
23   *Yet thou triumph'st*: Donne declares that the woman believes she has defeated his argument.

EXPLORATIONS

1. In your opinion, what is Donne's attitude to love in this poem? Support your answer by close reference to the text.

2. Choose two lines or phrases which you think would have surprised or shocked Donne's audience in the 1600s. Briefly explain your choice in each case.

3. Write your own personal response to the poem, highlighting its impact on you.

STUDY NOTES

Donne's humorous and sensual poem makes use of the conceit (extended image) of a flea to explore his relationship with the woman he loves. However, in associating romantic love with a bloodsucking parasite – rather than something of beauty – the poet expresses his own desire for intimacy in an unexpected way. While many of Donne's poems deal with spiritual love between couples, here it is purely physical.

Readers are immediately plunged into a turbulent scene between two lovers in **stanza one**. The poet addresses an unnamed woman, insisting that she pays close attention to what he is saying. She is denying him something he craves, which is as yet unspecified, but – according to Donne – is trivial, 'How little that which thou deny'st me is'. He then comments on the actions of the flea, 'It suck'd me first, and now sucks thee'. The poet even uses religious imagery ('sin', 'shame') to add weight to his argument that an intimate, physical relationship is not wrong. He complains that **the flea has already enjoyed more intimacy than himself with this woman**, even though it has not had to go through the ritual of courtship.

Unlike Donne, the flea 's 'pampered' and satisfied. The monosyllabic verb, 'swells', dramatically describes the bloating of the insect with its consumption of the couple's blood. The peevish complaint, 'Yet this enjoys before it woo', highlights just how frustrated Donne feels. **Although he has played the game of love by the rules**, he is a miserable failure. The punctuation breaks before and after 'alas' emphasise how cruelly he believes he is being treated. Is the tone here mock-dramatic, with the use of the regretful, 'alas'? If so, the reader can react with amusement. Or, is the tone emotional, verging on petulant blackmail? Then, the reader might feel anger at the poet's whining, adolescent behaviour.

In **stanza two**, Donne's argument switches as he asks the woman to respect the flea and what it represents. His pleading tone is evident when he begs for its life to be spared, 'Oh, stay'. Such flamboyant exaggeration strikes a note of humour. The poet presents an elaborate explanation outlining why the flea should be allowed to live. If killed, it will not only result in the insect's death, but also the symbolic death of the couple, as their bloods are mingled in the body of the flea, 'three lives in one flea spare'. Donne maintains that he and his lover are even closer than if they were joined together in marriage ('yea, more than married are') since their bloods have mingled. To the poet, this represents a relationship that is blessed in heaven. He argues that even though there are objections to this sacred union from both his loved one herself and her family, 'Though parents grudge, and you', yet the fact remains that **the lovers are already joined together**, 'cloistered in these living walls of jet'. This striking religious image is typical of Donne who exaggerates how the flea's glossy, black body contains the couple's unified blood.

Donne develops his argument by referring to a major difficulty in their relationship – the woman's coldness towards him. As far as he is concerned, she takes him for granted, 'Though use make you apt to kill me'. **The tone changes from an almost contemplative voice to a more impatient one** in this stanza. But he continues to persuade the woman, urging her to spare the fly and show her love for him. The 'three lives in one' of the flea (her blood, his and its) is a clear reference to the Christian idea of the Trinity. The flea is seen as their marriage 'temple', which would be 'sacrilege' to destroy. It's interesting that Donne never lets the reader hear the woman speak, yet from the various twists and turns of his argument, there is a real sense of the woman's presence, and the reader is left in no doubt of her negative reaction to the poet's persistent pleas.

The tone becomes increasingly accusatory in **stanza three** as Donne reacts to his companion's impulsive killing of the flea, 'Cruel and sudden'. But it is clear that his real resentment is almost certainly due to the woman's forceful rejection of his advances. Like the unfortunate fly, **he sees himself as a victim of her callous behaviour**. The vivid, colloquial language ('hast thou since/Purpl'd thy nail, in blood of innocence?') seems to have a timeless resonance. For a moment, Donne appears to admit defeat ('Yet thou triumph'st') – but is he lulling his lover into a false sense of security before coming up with yet another argument?

In a final flourish, **the poet insists on having the last word by turning the woman's own resistance against her**. He admits that, of course, she is completely right, ''Tis true'. Neither she nor Donne have lost anything by the flea's death, 'not thyself, nor me the weaker now'. Once again, as in the poem's opening lines, he issues instructions to this alluring woman – 'then learn'. What he wants her to believe is that she will lose almost nothing in yielding to his sexual advances. But readers are still left with an unresolved situation. Will the poet ever convince his beloved to put aside her 'fears'? Or will he be forced to accept that he cannot always get what he desires? What is certain, however, is that during the course of this unusual love poem, Donne's dazzling argument has ingeniously explored some of the age-old questions about the games lovers play.

ANALYSIS

'John Donne's poems can be described as intimate dramas.' Discuss this statement in relation to 'The Flea', using quotations from the text to support your answer.

Sample Paragraph

Donne's erotic poem opens with a stabbing repetition as he instructs his lover to pay more attention to him – 'How little that which thou deny'st me is'. The reader is immediately involved in an intimate argument taking place between the couple. The seduction scene is highly charged as they disagree about committing to a full sexual relationship. Donne uses the flea – which has bitten both himself and his lady friend – as a symbol of physical union. The conflict between the two characters increases in intensity in the second stanza when the poet begs her not to kill the flea – 'Oh, stay'. Detailed, probing argument is used as Donne points out that this flea 'is you and I', since it contains their mixed blood. His frustration is evident in the reference to her parents who hold a 'grudge' against the couple's romance. The bitter tone is highly convincing. The poet's annoyance is suggested in the melodramatic third stanza as he calls his beloved 'Cruel and sudden' because she has killed the insect. The lovers' drama reaches a high point when he eventually tricks her by suddenly agreeing with her cruel decision to refuse him – 'Yet thou triumph'st'. He ends by then reminding her how little she will have lost if she gives in to his physical advances. The poem is typical of Donne's exaggerated domestic dramas, filled with striking imagery and characteristic playfulness.

Examiner's Comment

This is a confident A-grade response which addresses the question directly and includes good engagement with the poem. Suitable quotations illustrate key points, highlighting the various references to drama. Expression is varied, fluent and very well controlled throughout.

CLASS/HOMEWORK EXERCISES

1. Comment on the effectiveness of Donne's use of imagery in his poem, 'The Flea'. Support your answer with suitable reference and quotation.

2. Copy the table below into your own notes and fill in critical comments about the last two quotations.

Key Quotes

And this, alas, is more than we would do	The poet is complaining bitterly that the flea has achieved more success than the couple, since the woman is refusing the poet's advances. The self-pitying tone is suggested by 'alas'.
learn how false, fears be	Donne's companion is being assured that she has nothing to worry about if she gives in to the poet's request that they become lovers. The alliterative 'f' adds emphasis to the poet's didactic tone.
three lives in one flea spare	
cloistered in these living walls of jet	

8   AT THE ROUND EARTH'S IMAGINED CORNERS

At the round earth's imagined corners, blow
Your trumpets, angels, and arise, arise
From death, you numberless infinities
Of souls, and to your scattered bodies go,
All whom the flood did, and fire shall, o'erthrow,   5
All whom war, dearth, age, agues, tyrannies,
Despair, law, chance, hath slain, and you whose eyes
Shall behold God, and never taste death's woe.
But let them sleep, Lord, and me mourn a space;
For, if above all these, my sins abound,   10
'Tis late to ask abundance of thy grace,
When we are there. Here on this lowly ground,
Teach me how to repent; for that's as good
As if thou hadst sealed my pardon, with thy blood.

'the round earth's imagined corners'

GLOSSARY

1   *the round earth's imagined corners*: the Biblical idea of the four corners of the earth.

2   *Your trumpets*: old maps include illustrations of angels blowing trumpets in four directions, North, South, East and West.

5   *All whom the flood did, and fire shall o'erthrow*: God drowned the world in a great flood because He felt humanity had forgotten about Him. Fire will destroy the world in the end.

6   *dearth*: scarcity, poverty, famine.

6   *agues*: sickness, disease.

8   *Shall behold God, and never taste death's woe*: those people who are still alive on the Last Day will not be consumed by the end of the world fires, but will go straight to judgement.

9   *But let them sleep*: Donne asks God to postpone Judgement Day.

9   *a space*: for a moment.

11 *abundance of thy grace*: God's forgiveness.

12 *lowly ground*: here on earth where Donne is praying.

13 *repent*: ask for God's mercy.

14 *As if thou hadst sealed my pardon*: According to Christian teaching, Jesus died for people's sins and his blood sacrifice guarantees forgiveness.

EXPLORATIONS

1. What picture of the Last Judgement is given in the poem's opening eight lines? Refer to the text in your answer.

2. The poem changes direction in line 9. Describe this change and explain why you think the poet has switched his line of thought. Refer closely to the text in your answer.

3. In your opinion, is Donne fascinated by death? Choose two lines or phrases from the poem which support your view and discuss their effect on you.

STUDY NOTES

John Donne's famous Holy Sonnet, 'At the Round Earth's Imagined Corners', is set against the dramatic backdrop of the Apocalypse, the final destruction of the world, described in the Bible's Book of Revelations. The poem is divided into two parts: the noisy tumult of Judgement Day in the octet and the quieter, more meditative sestet. What gives this powerful poem its universal significance is that Donne confronts the certainty of death which all humans face.

Donne presents the reader with a tantalisingly surreal paradox in line 1. Using the traditional expression, 'the round earth's imagined corners', he visualises what will happen when the dead are resurrected and reunited with their spirits. Broad vowel assonance adds to the **magnificent tension of this imagined scene**. The poet's powerful, visual language has cleverly captured a sense of huge expanse. He quickly introduces an urgent tone with the monosyllabic verb 'blow' which teeters at the end of the opening line. Donne is demanding that the angels signal Judgement Day, almost as if it were a race. He imagines them with bright trumpets sounding a triumphant call, just as a fanfare announces the arrival of a king. The sound is so loud and resonant that it immediately wakens the dead. Is this the reverberation of triumph over death? Donne heightens the drama as he repeats, 'arise, arise', insisting that all the dead souls 'go' to their bodies. The run-on lines (enjambment) accelerate with breathless energy as confusion reigns. Spirits rush around trying to find their 'scattered' bodies. Throughout this **first quatrain**, the forceful end-of-line verbs ('blow', 'arise', 'go') clearly emphasise this momentous occasion. With characteristic hyperbole, Donne speaks of 'numberless infinities', successfully reinforcing the scale of the overwhelming numbers involved in this frenzy.

In the **second quatrain**, Donne reflects on how all these people died. The repetition of the phrase, 'All whom', with its monosyllabic broad vowels, signifies the enormity of these events. Ranging over time, the poet considers great natural disasters, 'All whom the flood did' (a reference to the Great Flood described in the Bible), and then imagines the future, 'and fire shall o'erthrow' (another Biblical prophecy about the destruction of the world by fire). Donne sweeps at breathtaking pace through possible causes of death, such as 'war, dearth, age, agues, tyrannies'. His **pounding rhythm is relentless** as he rushes on through his solemn list: 'Despair, law, chance'. The poet then thinks about everyone who will be still alive on the Last Day, those who will 'never taste death's woe'. For Donne, these are the fortunate ones who will go straight to God's judgement, having been spared the ordeal of death. The noisy, forceful eight lines with their purposeful, regular rhyme form one overwhelming sentence, concluding with triumph over death.

There is a sudden change of tone in **line 9**. This dramatic turn (volta) diverts the poem from Donne's insistent demand that the world should end now, and allows the reader to catch breath and realise that the apocalypse has not yet happened.

Indeed, the poet has been imagining the whole panoramic scene. His enthusiasm for the end of the world evaporates and the earlier impassioned conviction gives way to **a mood of self-doubt and contrition**. But as Donne focuses on his own personal relationship with God, the reader is left wondering whether his apparent concern for the dead is an act of compassion, or just a selfish request for his own spiritual salvation. At any rate, he realises that he needs time to atone for his own sins, 'and me mourn a space'. Donne becomes acutely aware that he was hasty in calling for the Day of Judgement, before knowing if he himself had been forgiven. Now he pleads for more time, begging God to be taught 'how to repent'. He realises that it will be too late to ask for forgiveness on Judgement Day, ''Tis late to ask abundance of thy grace/When we are there'. His submissive tone is plainly evident in the poignant phrase, 'Here on this lowly ground'.

The sonnet's final lines confirm Donne's belief that Christ's death on the cross brought salvation to the world. This paradox shows that although human beings as a group were redeemed, individuals cannot be saved unless they recognise this sacrifice of 'blood'. A complete individual act of faith is required. Donne's language is dense and legalistic. This conclusion is a plea for 'pardon', a reprieve. The word 'sealed' reminds the reader of a waxed seal which stamps and finalises a legal document. Christ's blood is the seal on the poet's 'pardon'. This poem has moved on considerably from the octet, where Donne confidently urged the angels and the dead to prepare for the end of the world. In the sestet, **he has become unsettled, afraid of the consequences of the Apocalypse for himself**. However, the **concluding couplet** represents a resolution, since the poet now puts his trust in Christ's salvation. Readers are left with their own questions. Is the poem merely a display of arrogant presumption which ends with a cringing plea for forgiveness? Or is it a genuine act of repentance?

ANALYSIS

Donne's sonnet, 'At the Round Earth's Imagined Corners', is a private, personal religious meditation which alienates the modern reader. Discuss this view, supporting your answer with reference to the poem.

Sample Paragraph

All human beings face death as well as sickness and natural disasters. So I do not think Donne's poem 'At the round earth's imagined corners' is all that remote from people today. We see floods, famine and man-made 'tyrannies' nightly on TV. The difference between the modern reader and Donne is found in the outdated language and references used. Many of the Biblical references wouldn't be as familiar to today's readers as they would have been to Donne. These references which describe the angels blowing their loud trumpets at the end of the world would not be very widely known. Similarly, the reference to a seal would seem dated as the practice of signing something with wax and a stamp would not be widely used nowadays. However, I think the brash tone in the first eight lines would appeal to the modern reader as the poet shouts 'blow', 'arise', 'go'. I don't think Donne's humble personal tone in the sestet, 'on this lowly ground', would be familiar today. In some ways, I can relate to Donne's fear of death – which is still the one great unknown. At times of trouble, believers often light candles in hope. Donne's personal hope was for salvation bought by the death of Christ, 'with thy blood'. There is a longing for something else, a spirituality of some sort which still remains down the centuries.

Examiner's Comment

This is an uneven attempt at a challenging question. While the paragraph touches on some noteworthy points about the poem's archaic expressions and references which might alienate modern readers, it lacks in-depth discussion of Donne's central concern – his own relationship with God. Grade C standard.

CLASS/HOMEWORK EXERCISES

1. 'A feature of Donne's poetry is that his vocabulary is easy to understand, but his ideas are difficult to follow.' Discuss this statement in relation to the poem, 'At the Round Earth's Imagined Corners', quoting in support of your response.

2. Copy the table below into your own notes and fill in critical comments about the last two quotations.

Key Quotes

At the round earth's imagined corners	This vivid paradox comes from the Book of Revelations which states, 'After this I saw four angels standing at the four corners of the earth, holding back the four winds of the earth'.
blow/Your trumpets	Donne addresses the angels who will blow their trumpets to signal the end of time and the final judgement of all souls. The run-on line adds urgency to the rhythm.
and me mourn a space	
Teach me how to repent	

Bleak Poem

9 THOU HAST MADE ME, AND SHALL THY WORK DECAY?

Thou hast made me, and shall thy work decay?
Repair me now, for now mine end doth haste,
I run to death, and death meets me as fast,
And all my pleasures are like yesterday;
I dare not move my dim eyes any way,
Despair behind, and death before doth cast
Such terror, and my feeble flesh doth waste
By sin in it, which it towards hell doth weigh.
Only thou art above, and when towards thee
By thy leave I can look, I rise again;
But our old subtle foe so tempteth me,
That not one hour myself I can sustain;
Thy grace may wing me to prevent his art,
And thou like adamant draw mine iron heart.

Handwritten annotations:
- All aspects of 5 seem to be in the past
- All he can see in the future is death
- Makes him fearful.
- 10 Casts fear across him.
- Not capable of remaining on the positive path.
- Body decomposes when dead = Sin
- body weak
- drifting towards hell
- with your help
- reinvigorated by god
- hidden enemy
- keep up
- gods forgiveness allows him to move away
- Magnetic power of god
- Magnet keeps him on right track.

'And thou like adamant draw mine iron heart'

GLOSSARY

(A-Z)

2   *Repair*: renew, rescue.
2   *doth*: does.
5   *dim*: blurred, unseeing.
7   *feeble*: weak.
8   *weigh*: pull down.

11   *old subtle foe*: Satan, the old enemy.
14   *adamant*: a naturally occurring magnet or lodestone.
14   *iron*: hard, uncompromising.

EXPLORATIONS

1. How would you describe Donne's tone in the first four lines of the poem?

2. Comment on the effectiveness of the phrase, 'old subtle foe'.

3. In your opinion, is the conclusion of the poem optimistic or pessimistic? Refer closely to the text in your response.

STUDY NOTES

The religious poems of John Donne explore the intense spiritual struggle which preoccupied his mind and soul. Sonnets, such as 'Thou Hast Made Me, and Shall Thy Work Decay?' are personal discourses or 'conversations' which show his passionate relationship with God as he privately meditates on the reality of life and death.

14 Line poem is a sonnet

Donne begins this poem in a similar way to his love poetry, in mid-action, addressing God directly. His bold question ('Thou hast made me, and shalt thy work decay?') manipulatively suggests that God will be unsuccessful in his great work on behalf of sinners if he does not redeem the poet. **Donne's lifelong search for truth is channelled into this simple, dramatic confrontation**. He regards it as a priority that God should forgive him without delay, 'Repair me now', as he is facing imminent death, 'for now mine end doth haste'. Throughout this first quatrain, the poet bluntly admits his spiritual distress. Ironically, while Donne accepts his dependence on God, he uses an authoritative tone in demanding God's immediate help. The urgency of this impatient request is evident in the personification of death as a familiar figure hurrying towards him, 'I run to death, and death meets me as fast'. Powerfully monosyllabic language emphasises the surging movement of this crucial encounter, which is further underlined by the mid-line repetition of 'death'. This daring image evokes the running action of two lovers as they rush to meet each other. There is a sense of both intimacy and inevitability as Donne now accepts the chilling realisation that the many [*diminishing*] sensual delights he once enjoyed are gone: 'And all my pleasures are like yesterday'. Is the remorse of an indulgently sinful life flashing before the eyes of this vulnerable man who is about to die?

In the **second quatrain**, Donne appears to be haunted by this intense realisation: 'I dare not move my dim eyes any way'. Terrified of looking back at a past that is full of sin, he is equally petrified by the future of certain death and possible damnation. The fragility of his human condition is shown in the adjective, 'dim'. He is horrified by the shocking prospect of his decaying body, putrefying with sin: 'my feeble flesh doth waste'. An increasing **sense of hopelessness dominates his restless mind**, as Donne imagines his doomed soul being dragged into eternal punishment, 'towards hell doth weigh'. The mood throughout is fearful and guilt-ridden, focusing on a negative view of man's mortal condition: 'decay', 'dim', 'terror', 'hell'.

However, the **sestet** signals a change of direction, an acknowledgment that the only hope of salvation is the complete surrender of the poet's strong individual will to the will of God, **an act of submission**. [*The only way to help his anxiety is god.*] Donne's humble tone is liberating. He asks permission to raise his eyes to God, 'By thy leave I can look'. Now there is a real possibility of redemption, 'I rise again'. If the poet accepts God's power to forgive, he 'can look' again and focus his 'dim' eyes. The weight of all Donne's sinfulness – which seemed so heavy in the octet – now dissolves as he takes a leap of faith towards his Creator. For a moment, the downward spiral of the poem's opening is reversed into an upward movement towards God. Nevertheless, the poet is not quite completely free – since he is so easily tempted by the Devil, the 'old subtle foe'. Donne's use of 'our' suggests his closeness to God, in their common struggle against Satan. In eventually coming to terms with his own weakness and constant dependence on God's grace, the poet has finally found a way to 'sustain' himself. The **rhyming couplet** sums up Donne's continuing need of divine power against the Devil's scheming, 'to prevent his art'. God must act on his behalf, so that 'Thy Grace may wing me'. It is **God's choice whether Donne is saved or not**. The vision of his immortal soul soaring upwards is captured in the verb, 'wing'. The sonnet concludes with a typical metaphysical image drawn from science. God is compared to 'adamant', a magnetic stone which can guide ('draw') iron, a symbol of the poet's sinful heart. To his relief, Donne's newly-confident faith

[marginal notes: Trust in god. What is this redemption? Heaven.]

reassures him that God has the ability to secure his soul with ease. The poet's appealing tone is clearly seen in his reserved form of address to God. This is in sharp contrast to the curt opening question. Throughout these final lines, the recurrence of personal pronouns underlines the intimate intensity of the poet's all-consuming relationship with God. — *Replace Names e.g. "Thy"*

Donne has adapted two sonnet forms for his poem. The basic structure is Petrarchan, divided into the despairing octet followed by a more hopeful sestet. However, he also uses the compact rhyme scheme of the Shakespearean sonnet, a highly disciplined form which effectively accommodates his central theme of dependence on God. *• first eight lines are more depressing.*

ANALYSIS

Forceful   softer respectful   V. Careful • Language • Know what words mean

'The language of Donne's poetry ranges from violence to tenderness, and from the unconventional to the paradoxical.' Using close reference to the text, discuss this view in relation to the sonnet, 'Thou Hast Made Me, and Shall Thy Work Decay?'. *• 2 halves of poem are different*

unusual use of Conceit

Sample Paragraph

Donne's religious poem, 'Thou Hast Made Me, and Shall Thy Work Decay?' contains both forceful and gentle expressions as he puts forward his unusual and often contradictory concerns. I was immediately aware of the poet's sharp voice in the calculating opening line where he demands to know if God is going to squander his creation of Donne's soul. He urgently insists, 'Repair me now'. There is no time to lose, 'for now mine end doth haste'. An unexpected image of two lovers rushing to meet unusually describes the terrifying end of life, 'I run to death, and death meets me at last'. This original conceit captures the inevitability of every person's appointment with death. The genuine agony of his position is clear in the line, 'I dare not move my dim eyes any way'. He stands, seemingly paralysed with fear, 'Despair behind', 'death before doth cast/Such terror'. His eyes are 'dim', stupidly closed by sin. He paradoxically links God's conflict with the Devil to his own battle with sin by the use of the word, 'our'. Donne suggests that God, who is all-powerful, also has problems with this 'subtle old foe'. For me, the sestet shows a gentler voice as the poet realises that God's grace alone can save him. His tone is softly submissive, 'By thy leave I can look'. The warm, effortless language speaks of the possibility of his saved soul which 'may wing' its way to heaven with the power of God. Donne chooses an odd image from science, 'adamant' – a lodestone to show the magnetic power of God gathering the stubborn soul, 'iron heart' to eternal happiness. All through this poem, I was impressed by Donne's turbulent yet sensitive expressions which explored a highly enigmatic exchange between himself and God.

Examiner's Comment

This is an effective and well written response which focuses firmly on the poet's style. Effective use is made of a great many accurate quotations to illustrate the variation in tone and range of language evident in the poem. There is also some good personal interaction with the text. Grade A.

CLASS/HOMEWORK EXERCISES

1. 'Donne's religious poetry is both stimulating and challenging.' Discuss this statement in relation to 'Thou hast made me, and shall thy work decay?' Refer to the poem in your response.

   Makes you think about death
   Consider our own sense of Mortality in Life
   techniques, dealing with death

2. Copy the table below into your own notes and fill in critical comments about the last two quotations.

Key Quotes

Repair me now, for now mine end doth haste	Repetition of 'now' and a robust rhythm add urgency to the poet's insistence that God's help is essential.
my feeble flesh doth waste/By sin in it	The poet is candidly confessing that he is weak, not only because of age, but also to due to sin. The alliterative 'f' sound emphasises the frailty of his condition.
Despair behind, and death before	
our old subtle foe	

Serious view on what is right and what is wrong — (handwritten)

He talks in a very strict sense — (handwritten)

(Beat)

10 BATTER MY HEART, THREE-PERSONED GOD

Wants God to break into his heart. Conflict — (handwritten)

Batter my heart, three-personed God; for, you

As yet but knock, breathe, shine, and seek to mend;

take control of him — (handwritten)

That I may rise, and stand, o'erthrow me and bend

He is passive. He has no control — (handwritten)

Your force, to break, blow, burn, and make me new.

Forgiveness? Wants to be reinvigorated — (handwritten)

Talking to God about his relationship with God. The nature of it. — (handwritten)

Simile — (handwritten)

I, like an usurped town, to another due,   5

Labour to admit you, but oh, to no end,

Reason your viceroy in me, me should defend,

He wants God's representative to come — (handwritten)

God played a major role in his life — (handwritten)

But is captived, and proves weak or untrue,

Yet dearly I love you, and would be loved fain,

Promise — (handwritten)

But am betrothed unto your enemy,   10

Divorce me, untie, or break that knot again,

No way he can drift from God again. For him to be truly good he has to be in the presence of God — (handwritten)

Take me to you, imprison me, for I

Captivated — (handwritten)

Except you enthrall me, never shall be free,

Loyal — (handwritten)

Complex relationship. — (handwritten)

Nor ever chaste, except you ravish me.

Sexual experience — (handwritten)

innocent, pure when he is with God. — (handwritten)

Contradiction: He can only be free when he is in prison — (handwritten)

Last 3 lines Sum up poem. — (handwritten)

'Batter my heart, three-personed God'

GLOSSARY

(A–Z)

1   *Batter*: strike, knock down. (Donne wants God to attack his heart as if it were the gates of a fortress town.)
1   *three-personed God*: Christianity teaches that God is three separate beings, God the Father, Jesus Christ the Son, and the Holy Ghost.
5   *usurped*: occupied, taken over.
7   *viceroy*: ruler on God's behalf.

9   *fain*: willingly, readily.
10 *betrothed*: engaged to be married.
11 *break that knot again*: dissolve that marriage union.
13 *enthrall*: enslave.
14 *Nor ever chaste, except you ravish me*: the central paradox of the poem asserts that true freedom can only be achieved in surrendering.

EXPLORATIONS

1. Would you consider this an unusual prayer to God? Consider the poet's use of language and imagery in your response.

2. 'Donne unashamedly thinks of no-one but himself.' In your opinion, is this the case in 'Batter My Heart, Three-Personed God'? Give reasons quoting closely from the poem.

3. 'This sonnet shows a troubled mind in a continuous search for certainty.' To what extent would you agree with this assessment? Refer to the text in your answer.

STUDY NOTES

Donne is a poet deeply divided between religious spirituality and a sensual lust for life. In 'Batter My Heart, Three-Personed God', he dares to introduce the powerful sensuous language of secular love poetry into his treatment of a profoundly religious theme. He claims that he can only overcome his sinful nature if he is forced by God in the most violent ways imaginable.

Characteristically of Donne, this sonnet begins with a dramatic exclamation: 'Batter my heart, three-personed God'. The force of this powerful opening line sets a determined tone that is maintained all through the poem. **In this daring image,**

the poet wants God to attack his heart as if it were the gates of a fortress town. The fearsome knocking of a battering ram echoes from the heavily stressed verb and pounding rhythm. Although this was a common metaphor in courtly love poetry to suggest the reluctance of a woman to yield to a lover's advances, it is a shocking – almost bizarre – conceit when presented in this religious context. Such exaggeration is also a recurring feature in Donne's work and is used here to highlight how the poet is challenging God to enter his heart aggressively, not gently.

However, this initial commanding tone of the verb 'Batter' with its explosive 'B' sound gives way to a bitter complaint against God's considerate behaviour. In **line 2**, the poet describes God as a careful craftsman, carrying out superficial repairs to 'mend' Donne's sinful soul. The pace is steady, reflecting such painstaking work. But this is quickly shattered by a distinctive paradox. Because he is so desperate to 'rise, and stand', **Donne requires God to 'o'erthrow' his wickedness in order to rebuild him spiritually**. The poet seems to show neither respect nor humility. Instead, throughout this **first quatrain**, he is busily putting up a challenge to God. The underlying sense of entitlement is insidious. Donne is convinced that he deserves all God's attention. The tender approach, where the Father knocks, the Son shines and the Holy Ghost breathes is not sufficient. Echoing the intense feeling, a dense accumulation of strongly accented verbs ('break', 'blow', 'burn') vividly conveys the energetic emotional conviction behind Donne's rhetoric. He is pinning all his hopes on divine intervention to rid him of sin ('make me new').

The **second quatrain** is dominated by the symbol of a besieged town. Donne sees his helpless soul as 'usurped' from God, its rightful ruler. His greatest wish now is that God will reclaim what is rightfully his. But who is the real enemy – Satan or Donne himself? **The poet's tone becomes less imperative and more apologetic** as he admits his longing to find God's grace – 'Labour to admit you'. Unfortunately, the poet's own conscience lacks willpower and strength ('Reason' is proving 'weak or untrue') and therefore his sinful soul remains at risk. Ironically, Donne uses the language of unrequited love to express his personal dilemma, caught between life's temptations and spiritual renewal.

The poet's candid admission ('Yet dearly I love you') at the start of the sestet marks a crucial turning-point. Donne exchanges the clever metaphysical comparisons for **a more direct, personal approach**. His open declaration of love for God is reminiscent of the courtly language of romantic poetry as he wistfully requests: 'And would be loved fain'. But the change of tone is short-lived and

Donne immediately introduces a new metaphor. He assumes the persona of a 'betrothed' woman, engaged to be married 'unto your enemy' (Satan). The horrifying reality of facing eternal damnation leads him back to the earlier intensity of the poem's opening lines and the frantic demand that God should do whatever it takes ('Divorce me, untie, or break that knot') in order to rescue his immortal soul. In the midst of this panic, the castle siege metaphor reappears as Donne insists that God 'imprison' him. As in many of these Holy Sonnets, the initial problem established in the octave is drawing to a solution.

The **final rhyming couplet** contains a fascinating double paradox. Firstly, Donne states that unless God entices him ('enthrall me'), he will never be free. The second dramatic paradox is even more shocking as he asserts that he can never be perfect ('chaste') unless God 'ravish' him. He acknowledges his absolute dependence on God to forcibly save him from his own human weakness. Although the word 'ravish' has an obvious violent intent, the tone is soft, almost a whisper, as though Donne deeply relishes the idea of spiritual unity with God. The poet is almost like a distracted lover speaking intimately to his God. Although he is struggling to define a sacred, spiritual relationship, the language he chooses is the metaphor of brutal, physical love. However, Donne's agonised perseverance ensures that the reader is left in no doubt of the poem's central message: **sinners must first be broken before being made whole again in God's love.**

ANALYSIS

'Donne is a poet who is full of contradictions.' Discuss this statement in relation to the poem, 'Batter My Heart, Three-Personed God'. Quote in support of your opinions.

Sample Paragraph

What does Donne want exactly? He actually wants God to save him from himself as if God was somehow physically present. This is the contradiction at the centre of the poem. Donne wants God to physically 'Batter' the poet into a state of grace. Another inconsistency is that he actually dismisses the gentle God who is attempting to 'mend', him and insists that a more forceful approach be taken. This is seen in the alliterative verbs, 'break', 'burn', 'blow'. He is seriously looking to be saved, yet he is instructing this powerful being how this must be done. For me, the most intriguing paradox is that the poet must be crushed, conquered, overthrown in order to be made 'new'. Donne complains that 'reason' – his own common sense – is actually behaving irrationally. Not saving him. This is what 'reason' should be doing – 'me defend'. Yet it has proved 'weak and untrue'. The opposing views expressed in this poem are breathtaking. Donne even wants to be freed from sin so he can be imprisoned in God's forgiveness. The contradictions actually make sense to me. Donne wants to be ravished by God so that he can be spiritually pure. The poet struggles with the dilemma in which he finds himself 'just like a usurped town'. Donne likes the idea of God taking responsibility. Doing all the soul-saving. He actually orders God to 'break the knot again'. As usual, the focus is all about Donne – 'me, me'. This is a contradictory poem, but it has a strong argument which attempts to force God to accept the poet's point of view, even though he is the one who actually needs the favour, and to deliver the poet's solution. Not God's.

Examiner's Comment

This lively response touches on interesting aspects of Donne's contradictory views of his complex relationship with God. The discussion is aptly illustrated and includes some good personal engagement. However, expression is note-like and awkward at times (with overuse of 'actually') and there are some inaccurate quotations. A good grade C.   *Not put together well*

CLASS/HOMEWORK EXERCISES

1. In your view, is 'Batter My Heart, Three-Personed God' a good example of metaphysical poetry? Refer to both content and style in your response, using evidence from the poem to support your opinions.

2. Copy the table below into your own notes and fill in critical comments about the last two quotations.

   - Relationship with God
   - Complexity
   - Paradox
   - Conceit

Key Quotes

That I may rise, and stand	Donne's pleading tone highlights his longing to be saved. The reference here could also be to the rising of all souls on the Last Day as they stand before God to be judged.
like an usurped town	The poet uses the simile of a captured town to describe his dilemma. His soul truly belongs to God, but is temporarily being controlled by the Devil.
Reason your viceroy in me	
imprison me	

LEAVING CERT SAMPLE ESSAY

'John Donne's intense experiences of love are always expressed in a highly distinctive style of writing.' To what extent, do you agree with this assessment of Donne's poetry? Support the points you make with the aid of suitable reference to the poems on your course.

Marking Scheme Guidelines

Candidates are free to agree and/or disagree with the statement. Expect discussion (though not necessarily equal) on both the intense experiences of love in Donne's poetry and on the poet's distinctive style. Evidence of genuine engagement with the poetry should be rewarded.

Material might be drawn from the following:

- Unusual views on romantic love.
- Revealing dramatic techniques.
- Eccentric approach to spiritual love.
- Controversial arguments, logic and reason.
- Inventive metaphysical wit – striking images, paradoxes, etc.

Sample Essay

(Donne's intense love expressed in a distinctive style)

1. *Many of John Donne's poems explore aspects of love – either for another person or for God. What really defines this famous metaphysical poet, of course, is his unique style of writing. Donne clearly delights in language, using imaginative arguments, dramatic settings, memorable imagery and a wide variety of tones to convey his views on the universal theme of love.*

2. *In 'The Anniversary', Donne celebrates the timelessness of true love. The poem is dramatic from the start – similar to 'The Sun Rising' and 'The Dream'. Donne creates a mood of excitement as he reviews the relationship between himself and his lover on their first anniversary. The exaggerated flattery he uses reflects his intense feelings. Always sincere. He contrasts the couple's enduring love with all the changes going on around him – even the sun – and then proudly declares: 'Only our love hath no decay'. The confident tone is found in the strong rhythms and the use of appealing paradoxes which express the strength and faithfulness of the couple's relationship – 'Running it never runs from us away'. The poet is so positive about love that he sees it surviving death when 'souls from their graves remove'. He ends on a highly optimistic note, glorifying the couple's 'blessed' love – which raises them to the level of royalty – 'Here upon earth, we're kings'. This conceit runs through the entire poem which ends with Donne boldly looking ahead to many more years of their 'reign'.*

3. *Donne's 'Song (Sweetest Love, I Do Not Go)' is equally complimentary. The poet is involved in a sensitive conversation about having to leave his wife for a short time. He uses the occasion to be reassuring, addressing her affectionately – 'Sweetest love'. In typical metaphysical style, Donne produces a series of clever arguments. These show how strongly he feels. He suggests that their parting will be a good preparation for the inevitable separation of death. Such persuasive arguments are common in his poems. He comforts his wife by reminding her of how the sun always returns every morning and – in a similar way – he can also be relied on to make even 'Speedier journeys'. In the final lines, Donne pleads with her to trust him. He ends with a simple but memorable request that his wife 'think that we/Are but turned aside to sleep'. Once again, I don't think there is any denying the sincerity of Donne's plea. His deep commitment to his wife is unmistakably evident in this final intimate image honouring a truly loving couple which can 'ne'er parted be'.*

4. There are surprising similarities between Donne's romantic poems and his Holy Sonnets. If anything, his religious poetry is more dramatic and passionate than the romantic poems. 'Thou Hast Made Me' is a good example of his obsessive relationship with God. It begins with a challenge – 'Repair me now'. Donne's domineering tone is very obviously ironic. This is a recurring feature of the poet's apparently disrespectful attitude to God. In 'At the Round Earth's Imagined Corners', he orders God to 'Teach me how to repent'. At first, I thought Donne was being irreverent, but it soon became clear that he is desperate for God's forgiveness. The poet seems to dread death and the terror of dying in sin. He admits his weakness – 'my feeble flesh' – and his inability to resist the Devil – 'our old subtle foe'. Donne's tone is heartfelt. Even vulnerable. But the ending is hopeful when his spirits are raised to heaven in the same way as a lodestone attracts iron – 'And thou like adamant draw mine iron heart'. The scientific image is characteristic of Donne, in this case highlighting his essential relationship and dependence on God.

5. The same sense of urgency is present in 'Batter My Heart' where the poet confronts God and demands to be liberated from sin. Once again, he uses a series of energetic verbs – 'knock, breathe, shine' – to force God to rescue his soul from sin. The tone is insistent as Donne makes his dramatic demand. Alliterative 'b' sounds add force to his persuasive tone – 'break, blow, burn, and make me new'. As always, his tone can suddenly change from anguish to a gentler pleading – 'Yet dearly I love you and would be loved fain', portraying a more dependent side of Donne's character, the frightened sinner. He introduces various conceits, seeing himself as a captured town controlled by the 'enemy' Satan. The poem's final image, seeing himself as a woman who wishes to be violently assaulted struck me as inappropriate at first, but the poet genuinely seems to be focusing on the need to submit his sinful soul to God's love by any means. Donne ends with a startling paradox. His soul will never be free until God enslaves and purifies it – 'Nor ever chaste, unless you ravish me'.

6. I have not studied any other poets who express their love in quite such an intense and compelling way as John Donne. His inventive use of language adds power and intimacy to the feelings he expresses – both in dealing with romantic and spiritual love. For me, Donne is a unique and passionate voice who is sometimes controversial but always genuine.

(approx. 870 words)

Examiner's Comment

This is a focused and well-sustained response. Points are made clearly, using cross-reference and displaying a close understanding of specific poems. The overall expression is fluent, although a little disjointed occasionally. All the quotations are accurate and integrated effectively into the general commentary. There is also some good engagement with Donne's writing. Grade A.

GRADE: A1
P = 15/15
C = 13/15
L = 12/15
M = 5/5
Total = 45/50

SAMPLE LEAVING CERT QUESTIONS ON DONNE'S POETRY

(45/50 MINUTES)

1. 'John Donne – a unique poetic voice.'
   Using the above title, write the text of a talk you would give to a group of Leaving Certificate students. You should focus on the poet's prominent themes and stylistic features. Support the points you make with reference to the poetry on your course.

2. 'Donne's mood ranges from hope to hopelessness in his poetry.' To what extent would you agree with this view? In your response, refer to the poems by Donne that you have studied.

3. 'John Donne's poetry has continuing appeal and meaning for today's reader.' Discuss this statement, supporting your points with reference to the poems by Donne on your course.

Sample Essay Plan (Q1)

'John Donne – a unique poetic voice.'
Using the above title, write the text of a talk you would give to a group of Leaving Certificate students. You should focus on the poet's prominent themes and stylistic features. Support the points you make with reference to the poetry on your course.

- Intro: Donne widely regarded as a fresh poetic voice defining 17th-century poetry. Individual and inventive use of language, imaginative arguments, often expressing deep emotion. Controversial approach to conventional themes, especially the daring Holy Sonnets.

- Point 1: 'The Sun Rising' – intimate, dramatic scene has a sense of immediacy. Powerful central image of the enclosed lovers' world. Characteristic use of playful argument.

- Point 2: Donne's metaphysical style – dramatic settings, conceits, paradoxes, visual and aural effects, wit, puns, etc. All illustrated in 'A Valediction: Forbidding Mourning'.

- Point 3: Original love poetry, sometimes daring and erotic. 'The Flea' – effective impact of exaggeration and extended metaphor expressing sexual desire.

- Point 4: 'At the Round Earth's Imagined Corners' – Petrarchan sonnet. The contrasting octet and sestet explore the poet's intense relationship with God. Typically dramatic imagery, rhetorical style, lists, sound effects, etc.

- Conclusion: Readers can relate to Donne's enduring themes and highly individualistic use of language. Memorable scenes, unusual images and passionate arguments define this great English poet.

Sample Essay Plan (Q1)

Develop one of the above points into a paragraph.

Sample Paragraph: Point 2

Donne is widely considered a master of the metaphysical conceit, an extended metaphor that combines two very different ideas into a single image. Donne avoided clichéd comparisons between closely related objects (such as a rose and love). This is one of the most appealing aspects of his poetry. He often took chances by linking two completely unlike objects. One of the most famous of his conceits is found in 'A Valediction: Forbidding Mourning' where he compares his wife and himself to the two legs of a compass: 'As stiff twin compasses are two'. Metaphysical poets liked to display their scientific learning and this distinguishes Donne who also showed his remarkable wit through paradoxes, puns, and subtle analogies. To convince his grieving wife that he will soon return to her, Donne uses several inspired metaphors. He demands 'no tear-floods, nor sigh-tempests', suggesting that their separation isn't some great natural disaster. His tone is slightly humorous as he tenderly encourages her to be brave. He also refers to astronomy, contrasting the couple's strong relationship with 'Dull sublunary lovers' love'. As always, the poet expresses his feelings passionately, ending with a powerful plea that true love will survive short separations. I liked the final compass conceit which really showed how closely connected he and his wife were: 'Thy firmness makes my circle just'.

Examiner's Comment

As part of a full essay, this is a competent and engaging response which illustrates some of Donne's recurring stylistic features. Good general comments on the poet's use of conceits are effectively illustrated with quotations. Well-controlled expression throughout. Grade A standard.

LAST WORDS

'No man is an island.'

John Donne

'Poetry is not a turning loose of emotion, but an escape from emotion; it is not the expression of personality, but an escape from personality. But, of course, only those who have personality and emotions know what it means to want to escape from these things.'

T. S. Eliot

'Rave on, John Donne.'

Van Morrison

ROBERT FROST

1874–1963

‘A poem begins in delight and ends in wisdom.’

One of the great 20th-century poets, Robert Frost is highly regarded for his realistic depictions of rural life and his command of American colloquial speech. His work frequently explores themes from early 1900s country life in New England, often using the setting to examine complex social and philosophical ideas. Nature is central to his writing. While his poems seem simple at first, they often transcend the boundaries of time and place with metaphysical significance and a deeper appreciation of human nature in all its beauty and contradictions. Despite many personal tragedies, he had a very successful public life. It is ironic that such a calm, stoical voice emerged from his difficult background. At times bittersweet, sometimes ironic, or often marvelling at his surroundings, Frost continues to be a popular and often-quoted poet. He was honoured frequently during his lifetime, receiving four Pulitzer Prizes.

Prescribed Poems

Note that Frost uses American spellings in his work.

❶ THE TUFT OF FLOWERS

I went to turn the grass once after one
Who mowed it in the dew before the sun.

The dew was gone that made his blade so keen
Before I came to view the levelled scene.

I looked for him behind an isle of trees;   5
I listened for his whetstone on the breeze.

But he had gone his way, the grass all mown,
And I must be, as he had been,–alone,

'As all must be,' I said within my heart,
'Whether they work together or apart.'   10

But as I said it, swift there passed me by
On noiseless wing a bewildered butterfly,

Seeking with memories grown dim o'er night
Some resting flower of yesterday's delight.

And once I marked his flight go round and round,   15
As where some flower lay withering on the ground.

And then he flew as far as eye could see,
And then on tremulous wing came back to me.

I thought of questions that have no reply,
And would have turned to toss the grass to dry;   20

But he turned first, and led my eye to look
At a tall tuft of flowers beside a brook,

A leaping tongue of bloom the scythe had spared
Beside a reedy brook the scythe had bared.

The mower in the dew had loved them thus,   25
By leaving them to flourish, not for us,

Nor yet to draw one thought of ours to him,
But from sheer morning gladness at the brim.

The butterfly and I had lit upon,
Nevertheless, a message from the dawn,   30

That made me hear the wakening birds around,
And hear his long scythe whispering to the ground,

And feel a spirit kindred to my own;
So that henceforth I worked no more alone;

But glad with him, I worked as with his aid,   35
And weary, sought at noon with him the shade;

And dreaming, as it were, held brotherly speech
With one whose thought I had not hoped to reach.

'Men work together,' I told him from the heart,
'Whether they work together or apart.'   40

'his long scythe whispering'

GLOSSARY

Tuft: cluster, bunch.

1   *turn*: upturn; toss grass to dry it out.

3   *keen*: sharp; effective.

6   *whetstone*: stone used for sharpening scythes.

18   *tremulous*: trembling.

22   *brook*: stream.

23   *scythe*: implement used for cutting grass or hay.

29   *lit upon*: discovered.

33   *kindred*: closely related to.

EXPLORATIONS

1. Describe the dominant mood in lines 1–10 of the poem.

2. Choose two images from the poem that you found particularly interesting and effective. Briefly explain your choice in both cases.

3. Would you describe the poem as uplifting? Give reasons for your answer.

STUDY NOTES

The poem describes how a simple, uncut clump of wild flowers can unite two separate people. It is one of Frost's best-loved works and typifies his technique of bringing readers through an everyday rustic experience to reveal a universal truth – in this case about alienation, friendship and communication. The poem consists of 20 rhymed couplets written in strict verse. Frost once remarked that 'writing without structure is like playing tennis without a net'.

The narrative voice in the **opening section** of the poem is relaxed, in keeping with the unhurried rhythm. Frost's initial tone is low-key and noncommittal. The speaker has gone out to turn the grass so that it can dry. Someone else had mowed it earlier 'in the dew before the sun'. **Lines 5–6** reveal the speaker's sense of solitude and isolation; the unnamed mower has 'gone his way'. This leads him to consider **the loneliness of the scene and of human experience**. The introspective mood becomes more depressed as the poet searches for his fellow worker. Figurative descriptions of the 'leveled scene' and 'an isle of trees' add to the atmosphere of pessimism as the speaker implies that he must also be 'alone'. For Frost, this is the essential human experience for all, 'Whether they work together or apart'.

The poem's **second section** is marked by the sudden appearance of a 'bewildered butterfly'. After fluttering 'round and round' looking for the 'resting flower' that gave it such delight the day before, it then flies close to the speaker: 'on tremulous wing came back to me'. The adjective 'tremulous' suggests fragility and a **new sense of excited anticipation in the air**. The butterfly seems to reflect the speaker's 'questions that have no reply'. Perhaps they have both enjoyed great happiness in the past. The butterfly eventually turns and leads the speaker to a 'tall tuft of flowers beside a brook' that have escaped the mower's scythe – not by accident, but because 'he had loved them' and left them to flourish out of 'sheer morning gladness'.

The significance of the meadow flowers and the brook cannot be overlooked, because here the **mood suddenly changes to optimism**. The presence of the mysterious butterfly establishes communication between the early-morning mower and the narrator. Frost suggests this connection with his vivid description of the spared flowers as 'a leaping tongue of bloom'. In the **final section**, the speaker and the butterfly 'lit upon,/Nevertheless, a message from the dawn'. With images such as the 'wakening birds around' and a 'spirit kindred to my own', we might assume that this 'message' could indeed be one of human friendship and communal love.

The ending is paradoxical: 'Men work together ... Whether they work together or apart'. However, **Frost believed in spiritual presence and was inspired by an overwhelming sense of fellowship**. Although apart, the speaker and the absent mower are working with a shared appreciation of nature's beauty and a common commitment to a better world. The poem could also be interpreted biographically, since Frost had lost several of his loved ones and may well have written it as an emotional outlet. Even though his family members were deceased, he remains close to them in spirit. Whatever the poet's intention, readers should draw their own conclusions from the poem.

ANALYSIS

In your view, is 'The Tuft of Flowers' a dramatic poem? Refer closely to the text in your answer.

Sample Paragraph

I liked Frost's poem 'The Tuft of Flowers' for many reasons – one of which was its dramatic storyline. It has been described as a lyrical soliloquy. The narrative element is there from the start. The first mower mentioned seems a mysterious character who got me wondering. The central character (poet) is obviously close to nature as he goes about his work turning the grass. His inner drama interests me most, as his attitude changes from loneliness at the beginning to happiness and companionship. The two moods contrast dramatically. First, the sadness of 'I looked for him', 'I listened for his whetstone' and 'brotherly speech' and then the more sociable 'Men work together'. The clear, vivid imagery is also dramatic, especially the butterfly's flight – 'On noiseless wing' – and the description of the small outcrop of flowers – 'a leaping tongue of bloom'. Frost sets his poems in the secluded New England landscape and this provides a beautiful setting for what are deep meditations about the important questions in life – 'questions that have no reply'. The rhythm or movement of the poem quickens in the final lines as the poet expresses his positive view of life – 'Men work together'. I thought this was the ideal way to round off this quietly dramatic poem.

Examiner's Comment

A very well controlled answer, focusing on some key elements of drama and demonstrating a close understanding of the poem. Good personal interaction and commentary also. References were handled effectively and points were clearly presented throughout. Grade A.

CLASS/HOMEWORK EXERCISES

1. In your opinion, what is Frost's main theme or message in 'The Tuft of Flowers'? Refer closely to the text of the poem in your answer.

2. Copy the table below into your own notes and fill in critical comments about the last two quotations.

Key Quotes

I went to turn the grass once	Frost's personal narrative voice uses the language of ordinary day-to-day speech.
And I must be, as he had been,–alone	Solitude (leading to a revelation or epiphany) is one of the poem's central themes.
I thought of questions that have no reply	
a message from the dawn	

2 MENDING WALL

IMAGES

Freeze thaw action

Something there is that doesn't love a wall,
That sends the frozen-ground-swell under it, *Freeze thaw action*
And spills the upper boulders in the sun; *heat*
And makes gaps even two can pass abreast.
The work of hunters is another thing: 5
Hunt's jumping wall and dogs I have come after them and made repair *Hunts*
Where they have left not one stone on a stone,
But they would have the rabbit out of hiding,
To please the yelping dogs. The gaps I mean,
No one has seen them made or heard them made,   10
But at spring mending-time we find them there.
I let my neighbor know beyond the hill;
Check wall Together in Spring And on a day we meet to walk the line
And set the wall between us once again.
We keep the wall between us as we go.   15
To each the boulders that have fallen to each.
And some are loaves and some so nearly balls
Rocks fall when they turn around. We have to use a spell to make them balance:
'Stay where you are until our backs are turned!' ← *Talking to stones*
We wear our fingers rough with handling them.   20
Oh, just another kind of outdoor game, ← *Takes away Seriousness*
One on a side. It comes to little more:
Pine Trees and There where it is we do not need the wall:
Apple Trees He is all pine and I am apple orchard. *Personifies Apple tree*
no for fence My apple trees will never get across   25
Separated. And eat the cones under his pines, I tell him. *Humour*
He only says, 'Good fences make good neighbors.'
Spring is the mischief in me, and I wonder
If I could put a notion in his head:
'Why do they make good neighbors? Isn't it   30
Where there are cows? But here there are no cows.
Before I built a wall I'd ask to know
What I was walling in or walling out,
And to whom I was like to give offense.
Something there is that doesn't love a wall,   35
That wants it down.' I could say 'Elves' to him,
But it's not elves exactly, and I'd rather
He said it for himself. I see him there,

Bringing a stone grasped firmly by the top
In each hand, like an old-stone savage armed.   40
He moves in darkness as it seems to me,
Not of woods only and the shade of trees.
He will not go behind his father's saying,
And he likes having thought of it so well
He says again, 'Good fences make good neighbors.'   45

[handwritten note: Neighbour not changing his ways and builds up Wall]

[handwritten note: Separation]

'Something there is that doesn't love a wall'

GLOSSARY

1 *Something there is that doesn't love a wall*: ice and frost dislocate walls (also a pun on the poet's name).

4 *abreast*: side by side.

27 *Good fences make good neighbors*: one reading is that a strong fence protects by keeping people apart.

36 *Elves*: small supernatural beings, often malevolent.

EXPLORATIONS

1. In your opinion, what is it that doesn't love a wall? Support your answer with reference to the poem.

2. There are two speakers in the poem. Which one is the wiser, in your view? Refer to the text in your answer.

3. Point out two examples of humour in the poem and comment on how effective they are in adding to the message of 'Mending Wall'.

STUDY NOTES

This popular poem of Robert Frost's was written in 1913 and appears first in his second collection, 'North of Boston'. When the land was being cleared for agriculture, the stones gathered were made into walls. Frost said this poem 'contrasts two types of people'. President John F. Kennedy asked Frost to read this poem to Khrushchev, Russia's leader at the time of the Cuban Missile Crisis, when there was a possibility of another world war. The Berlin Wall was a symbol of the cold relations between Russia and the US. Imagine the leaders listening to the line 'I'd ask to know/What I was walling in or walling out'.

'Mending Wall' was responsible for building a picture of Frost as an ordinary New England farmer who wrote about normal events and recognisable settings in simple language. **Line 1** is mysterious: 'Something there is that doesn't love a wall'. **A force is at work to pull down the barriers** people insist on erecting. The speaker repairs the holes in the wall left by hunters: 'I have come after them and made repair'. But there are other holes in the wall, though 'No one has seen them made or heard them made'. In a yearly ritual, 'at spring mending-time', the poet and his neighbour meet to carry out repairs. Each looks after his own property as they walk along: 'To each the boulders that have fallen to each'. But a tone of coldness creeps into the poem amid this neighbourly task, with the repetition of how the wall has separated them at all times: 'set the wall between us', 'keep the wall between us'.

It is a difficult task, as the stones fall off as quickly as they are placed: 'Stay where you are until our backs are turned!' The **good-humoured banter** of the workers comes alive in the humorous remark, and readers feel as if they are there in New England watching the wall being repaired. The light-hearted mood is continued in **line 21** as the poet describes the activity as an 'outdoor game'. Then he comments that they don't even really need the wall where it is: 'He is all pine and I am apple orchard'. The poet jokes that his apple trees cannot go over and eat his neighbour's pine cones. His neighbour then speaks: 'Good fences make good neighbors'. He comes across as a serious type, quoting old sayings, in **contrast** to the mischievous poet: 'Spring is the mischief in me'. Frost is allying himself with the turbulent force that is pushing through the land, creating growth and pulling down walls. The neighbour is shown as one who has accepted what has been said without question, one who upholds the status quo.

In **line 31**, the poet poses questions to himself and wishes he could say to his neighbour, 'Why do they make good neighbors?' **He then wonders what a wall is keeping in and keeping out**. He also wonders what is pulling down the wall. He mockingly suggests 'Elves', then discounts that. Frost presents his rather uncommunicative neighbour in a series of unflattering images: 'an old-stone savage armed', 'He moves in darkness'. Is the poet saying that we must question received wisdom and not blindly follow what we are told? The neighbor, who accepts, is presented as a figure of repression who 'moves in darkness'. He just repeats 'Good fences make good neighbors' like a mantra. Is the poet suggesting that there are some people who derive comfort from just remaining the same, who do not welcome change ('He will not go behind his father's saying')?

The tone of the poem changes as the easy, neighbourly sociability of a shared task is replaced by a **feeling of tension**, first in the effort to keep the tumbling wall upright, and then in the opposite attitudes of the two neighbours – the mischievous, questioning poet and the taciturn, unquestioning neighbour 'like an old-stone savage'. The desire for human co-operation is often stopped, not by outside circumstances, but by a lack of desire on the part of the people involved. This is the poet commenting on human dilemmas. The easy-going, almost ruminative tone of someone musing to himself is written in blank verse, unrhymed iambic pentameter. The colloquial conversational phrases are all tightly controlled throughout this thought-provoking poem.

ANALYSIS

Frost examines the distances between people in his work. In your opinion, how successfully is this done in the poem 'Mending Wall'?

Sample Paragraph

I think Frost has very successfully given us a picture of two opposite personalities in this poem. The moody neighbour who doggedly walks on his side of the wall, 'We keep the wall between us both as we go', is vividly described. Here is a person who accepts what was told to him without question 'Good fences make good neighbors'. It is as if he is reciting the two-times tables. This is fact. There is no need to question. He is comfortable and secure in his traditional mindset. 'He will not go behind his father's saying'. He almost mindlessly repeats it. The poet describes him in unflattering terms, referring to him as 'an old stone-armed savage'. He also states that he was one who moved 'in darkness'. Frost does not agree with this unquestioning attitude of his neighbour's. It is not only a wall which divides these two, there is a completely different mindset. The poet has a lively personality, making jokes as they work, 'Stay where you are until our backs are turned', regarding the work as a game. However, he is not lightweight, as he asks the fundamental question about any boundary, 'I'd ask to know/What I was walling in or out'. He also asks the rather sensitive question about who he was likely to give offence to, with his wall. The neighbour has no such finer feeling, and is portrayed as someone who keeps on going in the same route as always. This apparently simple poem, written in blank verse, sticks in the reader's mind long after the reading. Frost has written a poem which is hard to get rid of. We are left wondering, are walls natural or necessary? Must we break down barriers to live as good neighbours? What if we are over-run?

Examiner's Comment

A solid response. The poem is examined in some detail. The questions at the conclusion are lively and show engagement with the poem. Some quotations are inaccurate and this reduces the overall standard. Grade B.

> ## CLASS/HOMEWORK EXERCISES

1. Comment on Frost's use of imagery. Do you find it effective? Refer closely to the text in your answer.

2. Copy the table below into your own notes and fill in critical comments about the last two quotations.

Key Quotes

Something there is that doesn't love a wall	The unnatural barriers erected by people are often pushed aside by nature.
We keep the wall between us as we go	The two neighbours walk on their own side of the wall as they carry out repair work. The wall also acts as a metaphor for the barriers erected by people between themselves.
He moves in darkness as it seems to me	
'Good fences make good neighbors'	

❸ AFTER APPLE-PICKING

My long two-pointed ladder's sticking through a tree
Toward heaven still,
And there's a barrel that I didn't fill
Beside it, and there may be two or three
Apples I didn't pick upon some bough.   5
But I am done with apple-picking now.
Essence of winter sleep is on the night,
The scent of apples: I am drowsing off.
I cannot rub the strangeness from my sight
I got from looking through a pane of glass   10
I skimmed this morning from the drinking trough
And held against the world of hoary grass.
It melted, and I let it fall and break.
But I was well
Upon my way to sleep before it fell,   15
And I could tell
What form my dreaming was about to take.
Magnified apples appear and disappear,
Stem end and blossom end,
And every fleck of russet showing clear.   20
My instep arch not only keeps the ache,
It keeps the pressure of a ladder-round.
I feel the ladder sway as the boughs bend.
And I keep hearing from the cellar bin
The rumbling sound   25
Of load on load of apples coming in.
For I have had too much
Of apple-picking: I am overtired
Of the great harvest I myself desired.
There were ten thousand thousand fruit to touch,   30
Cherish in hand, lift down, and not let fall.
For all
That struck the earth,
No matter if not bruised or spiked with stubble,
Went surely to the cider-apple heap   35
As of no worth.
One can see what will trouble
This sleep of mine, whatever sleep it is.

Were he not gone,
The woodchuck could say whether it's like his   40
Long sleep, as I describe its coming on,
Or just some human sleep.

'Toward heaven still'

GLOSSARY

7   *Essence*: scent.
10 *glass*: ice.
12 *hoary*: covered in frost.
20 *russet*: reddish-brown.
22 *ladder-round*: a rung or support on a ladder.

34 *stubble*: remnant stalks left after harvesting.
40 *woodchuck*: groundhog, a native American burrowing animal.

EXPLORATIONS

1. Select one image that evokes the hard, physical work of apple-picking. Comment on its effectiveness.

2. What do you understand lines 27–29 to mean?

3. Write a short personal response to this poem.

STUDY NOTES

The poem is a lyrical evocation of apple harvesting in New England. Frost takes an ordinary experience and transforms it into a meditative moment. Harvesting fruit soon becomes a consideration of how life has been experienced fully but with some regrets and mistakes. Frost chose not to experiment but to use traditional patterns, or as he said, he preferred 'the old-fashioned way to be new'. 'After Apple-Picking' is not free verse, but it is among Frost's least formal works, containing 42 lines varying in length, a rhyme scheme that is also highly irregular and no stanza breaks.

The speaker in the poem (either Frost himself or the farmer persona he often adopted) feels himself drifting off to sleep with the scent of apples in the air. He thinks of the ladder he has left in the orchard still pointing to 'heaven'. Is the poet suggesting that his work has brought him closer to God? The slow-moving rhythm and broad vowel sounds ('two-pointed', 'bough', 'drowsing') in the **opening lines** reflect his **lethargic mood**. Although he seems close to exhaustion, he is pleased that the harvest is complete: 'But I am done with apple-picking now'. Ironically, his mind is filled with random thoughts about the day's work. The drowsy atmosphere is effectively communicated by the poet's mesmerising description: 'Essence of winter sleep is on the night'.

This dream-like state releases Frost's imagination and he remembers the odd sensation he felt while looking through a sheet of ice he had removed earlier from a drinking trough. While the memory is rooted in reality, it appears that he has experienced the world differently: 'I cannot rub the strangeness from my sight'. As he is falling asleep, he is conscious that his dreaming will be associated with **exaggerated images of harvesting**: 'Magnified apples appear and disappear' (**line 18**). The poet emphasises the sensuousness of what is happening. The vivid apples display 'every fleck of russet' and he can feel the pressure of the 'ladder-round' against his foot. He hears the 'rumbling sound' of the fruit being unloaded. The images suggest abundance: 'load on load of apples', 'ten thousand thousand'. Frost's use of repetition, both of evocative sounds and key words, is a prominent feature of the poem that enhances our appreciation of his intense dream.

Physically and mentally tired, the poet also relives the anxiety he had felt about the need to save the crop from being 'bruised or spiked with stubble', and not to lose them to 'the cider-apple heap'. In the poem's **closing lines**, which seem deliberately vague and distorted, Frost wonders again about the nature of consciousness: 'This sleep of mine, whatever sleep it is'. Like so many of his statements, the line is rich in possible interpretations. For some critics, the poem appears to be exploring the art and craft of writing. Others take a broader view, seeing it as a metaphor for how human beings live their lives. The poet's own final thoughts are of the woodchuck's winter retreat, before he eventually surrenders to his own mysterious 'sleep'.

'After Apple-Picking' is typical of Frost's work. Despite the apparent cheerfulness of much of the writing, it has **undertones of a more sober vision of life**. As always, there is a thoughtful quality to the poem. The reference to the approach of winter hints at the constant presence of mortality. Frost's question about what kind of sleep to anticipate suggests untroubled oblivion or possibly some kind of renewal, just as the woodchuck reawakens in the springtime after its long hibernation.

ANALYSIS

How would you describe the dominant mood in 'After Apple-Picking'? Refer closely to the poem in your answer.

Sample Paragraph

In his famous dramatic monologue, 'After Apple-Picking', Robert Frost creates a mood of otherworldliness. At the start, his accurate description of the orchard is realistic. But some of the poem seems symbolic – such as the mention of the ladder pointing to heaven which might suggest Frost's religious feelings. The setting is calm and the poet feels tired but satisfied after his demanding physical work – 'there's a barrel that I didn't fill'. But his tiredness soon makes his mood more dreamy – 'Essence of winter sleep is on the night'. The sibilance and slender vowels add to this languid atmosphere. I could trace a growing surreal quality to the poem as Frost drifts in and out of consciousness, remembering flashes of his work picking the apples – 'The scent of apples: I am drowsing off'. He mentions 'sleep' repeatedly, reflecting his deep weariness. The rhythm is slow and irregular, just like his confused thoughts about the apples he harvested or damaged. At times he is troubled, recalling his worries that some of the fruit would be 'bruised'. By the end of the poem, he is in a dream-like state, equally obsessed with apple-picking and his own need for sleep. He even wonders about 'whatever sleep it is'. As he drifts off, he thinks of the animals that sleep through the winter and compares himself to the woodchuck. I think this kind of whimsical mood reflects his great interest in nature and is a characteristic of this great American poet.

Examiner's Comment

This is an accomplished answer that ranges widely and shows some good personal engagement with the poem. There is an assured sense of the central mood and this is supported well with apt quotations. The references to Frost's style are also worthwhile. Grade A.

CLASS/HOMEWORK EXERCISES

1. Comment on the effectiveness of the poem's imagery in appealing to the senses. Refer closely to the text in your answer.

2. Copy the table below into your own notes and fill in critical comments about the last two quotations.

Key Quotes

But I am done with apple-picking now	It is ironic that although the harvesting itself has ended, its significance for Frost is just beginning.
I cannot rub the strangeness from my sight	Exhaustion has caused the poet's confusion. The strong sibilant effect adds emphasis to the mood.
Magnified apples appear and disappear	
I feel the ladder sway as the boughs bend	

4   THE ROAD NOT TAKEN

Choice

Two roads diverged in a yellow wood,
And sorry I could not travel both   *Dilemma*
And be one traveler, long I stood
And looked down one as far as I could   *Aware it's an important decision*
To where it bent in the undergrowth;   5

Then took the other, as just as fair,
And having perhaps the better claim,
Because it was grassy and wanted wear;   *unknown   Don't follow blindly*
Though as for that, the passing there
Had worn them really about the same,   10

And both that morning equally lay   *Autumn*
In leaves no step had trodden black.
Oh, I kept the first for another day!
Yet knowing how way leads on to way,
I doubted if I should ever come back.   *He's a realist*   15

I shall be telling this with a sigh
Somewhere ages and ages hence:
Two roads diverged in a wood, and I—
I took the one less traveled by,
And that has made all the difference.   20

Make your decision carefully   positive or negative difference

'where it bent in the undergrowth'

GLOSSARY

1   *diverged*: separate and go in different directions.
5   *undergrowth*: small trees and bushes growing beneath larger trees in a wood.

7   *claim*: attraction, entitlement.

EXPLORATIONS

1. In your opinion, is this a simple poem or does it have a more profound meaning? Outline your views, supporting them with relevant quotation.

2. Select one image from the poem that you consider particularly effective or interesting. Briefly justify your choice.

3. Frost has been described as someone who 'broods and comments on familiar country things … catching a truth in it'. In your view, what is the tone of this poem? Does it change or remain the same?

STUDY NOTES

One of Frost's most popular poems, it was the first published in the collection 'Mountain Interval' (1916). It was inspired by his friend, the poet Edward Thomas. Frost told Thomas, 'No matter which road you take, you'll always sigh, and wish you'd taken another'. Frost also said he was influenced by an event which happened to him at a crossroads after a winter snowstorm in 1912. He met a figure, 'my own image', who passed silently by him. Frost wondered at 'this other self'. The poem dramatises the choices we make in life and their consequences.

Huge themes are summarised in a simple narrative in this poem. In the **first stanza**, the speaker stands in a wood in autumn where two roads run off in different directions. He has to make a decision – which one will he take? The roads are 'about the same', so the emphasis is not on the decision, but on the **process of decision-making and its consequences**. The speaker decides that he cannot see where the first road is leading ('it bent in the undergrowth'), so he chooses the other one, though it is unclear why. The reference to the 'yellow wood' suggests [Maturity] that the poet is mature enough to realise the consequences of his decision. He [chied] won't have this opportunity again: 'I doubted if I should ever come back.' The beautiful image of the 'yellow wood' conjures up a picture of the autumn in New England, but it also has a deeper meaning and is tinged with regret. A person can't do everything in life; choice is part of the human condition.

Frost has said, 'I'm not a nature poet. There's always something else in my poetry.' Here, in this simple act, he is **exploring what it means to be human** and dramatises the decision-making process. There is the human desire to avoid making a decision ('sorry I could not travel both') and the consideration of the possible choices ('long I stood/And looked down one as far as I could'). The **regular rhyme scheme** mirrors the poet looking this way and that as he tries to decide which to choose (abaab, cdccd, efeef, ghggh). The unusual rhyme also underlines the unusual choice made. Frost felt that 'the most important thing about a poem … is how wilfully, gracefully, naturally entertainingly and beautifully its rhymes are'.

Then, in **stanza two**, **he makes the decision**: he 'took the other one'. Why? Was it because it 'was grassy and wanted wear'? Is this someone who is individualistic and likes to do something different to the crowd? Does this suggest a desire for adventure? Then the poet becomes increasingly mischievous. When he sent the poem to his friend, Edward Thomas, Frost wrote: 'I don't know if you can get anyone to see the fun of the thing without showing them.' After pointing out the difference between the two roads, he now declares that they were not so different: 'the passing there/Had worn them really about the same'.

In the **third stanza**, he continues to **point out the similarity of the two roads**, which 'equally lay'. So is the idea that if you choose the less conventional route in life, you may not end up having adventures? The reader is now as confused as the poet was when trying to decide what to do. The second great truth is then revealed: no matter what we get, we always want what we don't have. The regret is palpable in the emphatic 'Oh, I kept the first for another day!' But there won't be [only way is forward] another day, because time marches on and we cannot return to the past; we can only go on, as 'way leads on to way'.

In **stanza four**, the poet realises in **hindsight** that he will tell of this day in the future, 'ages and ages hence', though why 'with a sigh'? Has his choice resulted in suffering? Frost's own personal life was littered with suffering and tragedy. Does the repetition of 'I' and the inclusion of the dash suggest that the poet is asserting

The Sigh is inconclusive

his maverick individuality as he resolutely declares: 'I took the one less traveled by,/And that has made all the difference'? Do you think he feels he made the right choice for himself? This common experience of choice and decision-making is caught succinctly in this simple narrative. It sounds like a person thinking aloud; the language seems ordinary. Yet upon closer examination, we become aware of the **musical sound effects**. The repeated 'e' sound, coupled with the sibilant 's' sounds ('it was grassy') and alliteration ('wanted wear') convey a calm, deliberating voice. Here is Frost's 'sound of sense'. This poem is inclusive rather than exclusive, as it invites the reader to share in the poet's decision-making.

ANALYSIS

'Frost uses traditional form not in an experimental way, but adapted to his purpose.' Discuss this statement with reference to 'The Road Not Taken'. Quote in support of your answer.

Sample Paragraph

Frost takes traditional subject matter similar to the Romantics, nature and man's relationship with nature, and tells us, 'There's plenty to be dark about, you know. It's full of darkness.' He forms his poems not in an experimental way, but in a deliberate way which suits his purpose. He uses iambic pentameter, a traditional metre used by Shakespeare, as it most closely resembles the English speaking voice, and it is an ironic, sceptical voice, 'yet knowing how way leads on to way', which resonates in 'The Road Not Taken'. The structure of the poem follows the deliberating process, as first the speaker tries to avoid making a choice, then considers the alternatives, 'long I stood'. The decision is made and almost immediately there is a sense of regret: 'Oh, I kept the first for another day'. The use of an unusual rhyme scheme adds to the excluded feel of the speaker. This is someone to whom individuality and self-sufficiency matters: 'I took the one less traveled by,/And that has made all the difference'. The rhyme scheme of the first stanza is abaab. The unusual rhyme scheme mirrors the unusual choice the poet made. Frost believed in the 'sound of sense', as he tells us that we can know what is going on even through a closed door by the sound, not necessarily the meaning of words. Consider the line, 'Because it was grassy and wanted wear'. The alliteration and the sibilance suggest an almost idyllic wilderness. So Frost structures the form of his poems for a purpose. In this poem the rhyme scheme mimics the glancing this way and that as the speaker tries to decide what route to take. These are some of the ways Frost uses form for a purpose, rather than experimenting just for its own sake.

Examiner's Comment

This thoroughly developed answer shows a deep sense of engagement with both the poem and poet. The well-sustained focus and integrated quoting ensure that the paragraph reached an impressive A-grade standard.

CLASS/HOMEWORK EXERCISES

1. Frost's ambition was to 'write a few poems it will be hard to get rid of'. Do you think he succeeded? Refer to the poem 'The Road Not Taken' in your response.

2. Copy the table below into your own notes and fill in critical comments about the last two quotations.

Key Quotes

And sorry I could not travel both/ And be one traveler	Frost expresses a universal sorrow that it is not possible to be everyone and do everything.
the passing there/Had worn them	The poet is admitting that there was little difference between the roads.
I shall be telling this with a sigh	
I took the one less traveled by,/And that has made all the difference	

5   BIRCHES

When I see birches bend to left and right
Across the lines of straighter darker trees,
I like to think some boy's been swinging them.
But swinging doesn't bend them down to stay
As ice storms do. Often you must have seen them   5
Loaded with ice a sunny winter morning
After a rain. They click upon themselves
As the breeze rises, and turn many-colored
As the stir cracks and crazes their enamel.
Soon the sun's warmth makes them shed crystal shells   10
Shattering and avalanching on the snow crust—
Such heaps of broken glass to sweep away
You'd think the inner dome of heaven had fallen.
They are dragged to the withered bracken by the load,
And they seem not to break; though once they are bowed   15
So low for long, they never right themselves:
You may see their trunks arching in the woods
Years afterwards, trailing their leaves on the ground
Like girls on hands and knees that throw their hair
Before them over their heads to dry in the sun.   20
But I was going to say when Truth broke in
With all her matter-of-fact about the ice-storm
I should prefer to have some boy bend them
As he went out and in to fetch the cows—
Some boy too far from town to learn baseball,   25
Whose only play was what he found himself,
Summer or winter, and could play alone.
One by one he subdued his father's trees
By riding them down over and over again
Until he took the stiffness out of them,   30
And not one but hung limp, not one was left
For him to conquer. He learned all there was
To learn about not launching out too soon
And so not carrying the tree away
Clear to the ground. He always kept his poise   35
To the top branches, climbing carefully
With the same pains you use to fill a cup
Up to the brim, and even above the brim.

Then he flung outward, feet first, with a swish,
Kicking his way down through the air to the ground.   40
So was I once myself a swinger of birches.
And so I dream of going back to be.
It's when I'm weary of considerations,
And life is too much like a pathless wood
Where your face burns and tickles with the cobwebs   45
Broken across it, and one eye is weeping
From a twig's having lashed across it open.

Word shows complexity of the world

I'd like to get away from earth awhile
And then come back to it and begin over.
May no fate willfully misunderstand me   50
And half grant what I wish and snatch me away
Not to return. Earth's the right place for love:
I don't know where it's likely to go better.
I'd like to go by climbing a birch tree,
And climb black branches up a snow-white trunk   55
Toward heaven, till the tree could bear no more,
But dipped its top and set me down again.
That would be good both going and coming back.
One could do worse than be a swinger of birches.

'birches bend to left and right'

GLOSSARY

1   *birches*: deciduous trees with smooth, white bark.
7   *click*: tapping sound made by the branches when they touch.
9   *crazes their enamel*: cracks the ice on the trees.

10 *crystal shells*: drops of melting ice on branches.
11 *avalanching*: collapsing.
14 *bracken*: fern leaves.
31 *limp*: loose; wilted.
39 *swish*: whoosh.
50 *willfully*: deliberately.

EXPLORATIONS

1. Choose one image from the poem that you found particularly interesting or effective. Briefly explain your choice.

2. Comment on Frost's use of contrast in the poem.

3. Do you find the poet's overall outlook optimistic or pessimistic? Refer to the text in your answer.

STUDY NOTES

'Birches' was published in 1915, and like so much of Robert Frost's popular work, there is far more happening within the poem than first appears. The poem has been viewed as an important expression of his philosophical outlook on life. With its formal perfection, its opposition of the internal and external worlds and its occasional dry wit, it is one of the best examples of everything that is interesting and engaging about Frost's poetry.

The opening description of the leaning birches is interesting, as Frost compares them to the 'straighter darker trees'. The scene immediately brings him back to his childhood and he likes to think that 'some boy's been swinging them'. This tension between what has actually happened and what the poet would like to have happened – between the real world and the world of the imagination – runs through much of the poem. Throughout **lines 1–20**, he wonders why the birches are bent 'to left and right'. He accepts that the true reason is because of the ice weighing them down. The poet's **precise, onomatopoeic language** – particularly the sharp 'c' effect in 'cracks and crazes their enamel' – echoes the tapping sound of the frozen branches. Vivid, sensual imagery brings the wintry scene to life: 'crystal shells', 'snow crust', 'withered bracken'. Frost's conversational tone is engaging: 'You'd think the inner dome of heaven had fallen'. Characteristically, he adds a beautiful simile, comparing the bent branches 'trailing their leaves on the ground' to girls who are drying their cascading hair in the sunshine.

In the poem's second section (**lines 21–40**), Frost resists the accurate explanation ('Truth') for the bent trees, preferring to interpret the scene imaginatively. He visualises a lonely boy ('too far from town to learn baseball') who has learned to amuse himself among the forest birches. In simple, factual terms, the poet describes the boy as he 'subdued his father's trees'. We are given a sense of his youthful determination to 'conquer' them all until 'not one was left'. His persistence teaches him valuable lessons for later life. Swinging skilfully on the trees, the boy learns 'about not launching out too soon'. Readers are left in no doubt about the rich **metaphorical significance of the birches**. In highlighting the importance of 'poise' and 'climbing carefully', Frost reveals his belief in discipline and artistry as the important elements of a successful life ('to fill a cup/Up to the brim'). Such symbolism is a common feature of his writing.

Lines **41–59** are more nostalgic in tone. Frost recalls that he himself was once 'a swinger of birches' and extends the metaphor of retreating into the world of imagination and poetry. The similarities between climbing birches and writing poetry becomes more explicit: 'I'd like to get away from earth'. However, he stresses that he does not wish for a permanent escape because 'Earth's the right place for love'. Is this what poets do when they withdraw into their imaginations and reflect on reality in an attempt to explore the beauty and mystery of life? They are dreamers, idealists. The birch trees are similarly grounded, but they also reach '*Toward* heaven'. The emphatic image (the italics are Frost's) suggests his continuing aspiration for **spiritual fulfilment through the poetic imagination**: 'That would be good both going and coming back'. Frost ends his poem by stating his satisfaction with overcoming challenges and benefiting from the desire to achieve by writing: 'One could do worse than be a swinger of birches'.

ANALYSIS

Based on your study of 'Birches', comment on the poet's use of detailed description. Refer closely to the text in your answer.

Sample Paragraph

Frost's detailed use of language makes 'Birches' one of the poet's most accessible poems. The simple images and colloquial expression create a natural connection between the poet and his readers. I very much liked the closely observed descriptions of the ice-covered branches: 'the sun's warmth makes them shed crystal shells'. The sibilance here adds to the beauty of the language. There are so many impressive images in the poem. Using onomatopoeia, Frost captures the subtle sounds of the forest in the bitter weather. The trees 'click upon themselves'. The poet obviously loved nature and had a keen eye for its beauty. I also liked his comparison of the trail of leaves to the 'girls on hands and knees that throw their hair'. It was dramatic, fresh and unusual. The boy's movement playing on the trees is dynamic: 'Then he flung outward, feet first, with a swish'. Near the end of the poem, Frost describes a harsher side of the forest when 'your face burns and tickles with the cobwebs'. As someone who spent my childhood in the country, I could relate to this tactile image. For me, Frost is a wonderful writer whose poems give a clear sense of the New England landscape. 'Birches' is a very successful piece of description, mainly due to the poet's precise choice of words and the vivid imagery.

Examiner's Comment

This paragraph showed a good knowledge of the text and a clear appreciation of Frost's writing skills. There was a strong sense of personal engagement with the poem and the comments on imagery were very convincing. Grade A.

CLASS/HOMEWORK EXERCISES

1. In your opinion, what is the central theme or message in 'Birches'? Support your answer with reference to the text.

2. Copy the table below into your own notes and fill in critical comments about the last two quotations.

Key Quotes

the stir cracks and crazes their enamel	Onomatopoeia and alliteration combine to echo the wintry atmosphere and bitter, sharp frost.
You'd think the inner dome of heaven had fallen	Colloquial and metaphorical language are used to suggest that the picturesque scene has been destroyed.
Shattering and avalanching on the snow crust	
Where your face burns and tickles with the cobwebs	

graphic depiction of a boys death

6 'OUT, OUT—'

Personification *onomatopoeia*

The buzz saw snarled and rattled in the yard
And made dust and dropped stove-length sticks of wood,
Sweet-scented stuff when the breeze drew across it.
And from there those that lifted eyes could count *can't look up*
Five mountain ranges one behind the other   5
Under the sunset far into Vermont.
And the saw snarled and rattled, snarled and rattled, *Repition*
As it ran light, or had to bear a load.
And nothing happened: day was all but done. *routine*
Call it a day, I wish they might have said   10
To please the boy by giving him the half hour
That a boy counts so much when saved from work.
His sister stood beside them in her apron
To tell them 'Supper.' At the word, the saw,
As if to prove that saws knew what supper meant,   15
Leaped out at the boy's hand, or seemed to leap— *Personification*
He must have given the hand. However it was,
Neither refused the meeting. But the hand!
The boy's first outcry was a rueful laugh, *regretful /nervous*
As he swung toward them holding up the hand,   20
Half in appeal, but half as if to keep *Cut /wound*
The life from spilling. Then the boy saw all—
Since he was old enough to know, big boy
Doing a man's work, though a child at heart—
He saw all spoiled. 'Don't let him cut my hand off— *Child comment*   25
The doctor, when he comes. Don't let him, sister!'
So. But the hand was gone already.
The doctor put him in the dark of ether. *an aesthetic*
He lay and puffed his lips out with his breath.
And then—the watcher at his pulse took fright.   30
No one believed. They listened at his heart.
Little—less—nothing!—and that ended it.
No more to build on there. And they, since they *Blunt No Compassion*
Were not the one dead, turned to their affairs. *Continued on with Life*

'Sweet-scented stuff when the breeze drew across it'

Rural

Social Commentary

Contrast between
surrounding
and incident

GLOSSARY (A–Z)

'Out, Out—': phrase from a speech which
Macbeth, King of Scotland, made on
hearing of the death of his wife and when
he was surrounded by enemies. He was
commenting on the brevity and fragility
of life: 'Out, out brief candle. Life's but a
walking shadow' (Shakespeare).

4 **lifted eyes**: reference to Psalm 21 – 'I will
lift up mine eyes unto the hills' – but the
people here don't. The sunset is ignored.

6 **Vermont**: a state in New England, America.

28 **ether**: form of anaesthetic.

Contrast

EXPLORATIONS

1. What kind of world is shown in the poem? Consider the roles of adults and children. Refer to the text in your response.

2. In your opinion, why does the poet tell the story in chronological order? How does it affect your understanding of the story?

3. Comment on the use of colloquial language in the poem. Refer closely to the text in your answer.

STUDY NOTES

Based on an actual event that occurred in 1910, the poem refers to a tragic accident when the son of a neighbour of Frost's was killed on his father's farm. By chance, he had hit the loose pulley of the sawing machine and his hand was badly cut. He died from heart failure due to shock. The event was reported in a local paper.

This **horrifying subject matter**, the early violent death of a young boy, was, in Frost's opinion, 'too cruel' to include in his poetry readings. The title, which is a reference to a speech from Shakespeare's Macbeth, is a telling comment on how tenuous our hold on life is. The scene is set on a busy timber yard: 'a world of actual hard, rattling, buzz saw, snarling action' (Seamus Heaney). **In line 1**, Frost's rasping onomatopoeic sounds give a vivid sound picture of the noisy, dangerous yard. The **long, flowing, descriptive lines** paint a picture of a place full of menace and physical reality where work has to be done. But there is beauty in the midst

Contradictions of life

of this raw power: 'Sweet-scented stuff when the breeze drew across it'. The soft sibilant 's', the assonance of the long 'e' and the compound word 'Sweet-scented stuff' all go to show the surprising beauty to be found in the midst of the practical 'stove-length sticks of wood'.

The **surroundings are also beautiful**, if only the people would look up. But they, unlike the poet, are unaware of 'Five mountain ranges one behind the other/Under the sunset far into Vermont', as their focus is on the work. The repetition of the verbs 'snarled and rattled, snarled and rattled' mimic the action of the repeated sawing. The detail 'As it ran light, or had to bear a load' shows how the saw pushed through the wood to get it cut, then lightly ran back through the cut. Line 9 tells us that the day was 'all but done'. A foreshadowing of the impending tragedy is given in 'I wish they might have said'. This is the only time in the whole poem when the personal pronoun 'I' is used. The poet's compassionate understanding for the young boy is evident as he explains how much it matters to a boy to be given precious time off from such hard work: 'That a boy counts so much'. The colloquial language in **line 10**, 'Call it a day', brings the reader right into this rural scene, rooting the poem in ordinary day-to-day life. The irony shimmers from the line, for soon there will be no more days for the boy.

A domestic detail adds to the reality of this scene as the boy's sister appears 'in her apron/To tell them "Supper."' In this central episode in **line 14**, the saw suddenly becomes personified, as if it too 'knew what supper meant'. The **jagged language**, 'Leaped out at the boy's hand, or seemed to leap—', reminds us of the jagged teeth of the saw as it seeks its prey. The mystifying accident is referenced in 'seemed to'. How could it have happened? 'He must have given the hand.' The helplessness of the victim, the boy, is shown: 'Neither refused the meeting'. We are reminded of someone almost paralysed into inaction at the split second of a horrific accident. Was this destiny? Is the poet adversely commenting on the mechanisation of farming, or on the practice of getting a boy to do a man's job? **All the attention is now focused on the hand**: 'But the hand!' The pity of the event is palpable in this climactic phrase.

The boy's reaction is chilling and poignant. He holds up the hand, 'spilling' its life blood. He pathetically asks for help, begging his sister not to let the doctor amputate his hand: 'Don't let him'. Now the poet interjects: 'So.' What more is to be said? It is like a drawn-out breath after the tension of the awful accident. The harsh reality is there for all to see: 'the hand was gone already'. The boy realised this when he 'saw all'. Without the use of his hands, there would be no man's work for him any more: 'He saw all spoiled'.

The closing section in lines **27–31** shows the details of the medical help: the 'dark of ether', the boy's breath 'puffed'. Now **the lines break up into fragments** as the terrible final act of the tragedy unfolds: 'No one believed'. The heartbeats ebbed away: 'Little—less—nothing!' There are echoes of the Macbeth speech when Macbeth says, 'It is a tale told by an idiot … signifying nothing'. The **sober reality hits home**: 'and that ended it'. The realisation that there is now no future for the boy is grasped: 'No more to build on there'. Frost has said that the reality of life is that 'it goes on'. And so the people there, because they were not the one dead, 'turned to their affairs'. No matter what horror happens in life, a new day comes. Neither the people nor the poet are being callous and unfeeling. Seamus Heaney calls it the 'grim accuracy' of the poem's end. The long line length also signals the return to normality.

The tone in this narrative poem shades from the anger and menace of the saw, to the calm of the beautiful rural countryside, to the wistful wishes of the poet and on to the fear and horror of the accident. In the end, Frost's ironic tone gives way to the cold fear of the finality of death, when all is changed forever.

> ## ANALYSIS

Seamus Heaney commented, 'Here was a poet who touched things as they are, somehow.' Discuss this statement with reference to the poem 'Out, Out—'.

Sample Paragraph

This poem touched me deeply, as it reminded me of the Elton John song 'A Candle in the Wind', which he wrote for another young person whose life was cruelly snuffed out in a terrible accident, just like this young boy. Many people are horrified at the poet and the people at the end of the poem, as they 'turned to their affairs'. Yet this is what life is like; after an accident, people put the kettle on. This does not mean they don't care, it means that the reality of life is, as Frost once said, 'It goes on'. I think it was very brave of the poet to just say things as they are, rather than pretending that life is not dark sometimes. I also felt as if I were actually in the timber yard as the saw 'snarled and rattled' in Vermont. The detail of sound and smell, 'Sweet-scented stuff', brought me there. It reminded me of Kavanagh, our Irish poet, who could see beauty in the most ordinary places. Frost, it seems to me, is also commenting negatively on the practice of having a young boy perform a man's job. The wistful 'I wish they might have said' condemns those who insisted on getting the job finished at the expense of the boy. It was too much to ask of a 'big boy', a 'child at heart'. The reality of the boy's life fading away was vividly captured by the poet in the line 'Little—less—nothing!' The punctuation adds to the effect of the heartbeat becoming weaker and finally stopping. This poet dared to say what life is like. He 'touched things as they are'. He achieved this by his craftsmanship as a poet, and his compassionate eye as a human being.

Examiner's Comment

A thoughtful, personal exploration of the poem, using quotations that are well integrated into the answer, which results in an A grade. Contemporary references illustrate the continuing relevance of Frost as a realistic voice.

CLASS/HOMEWORK EXERCISES

1. It has been said that Frost's poems are 'little voyages of discovery'. Write a personal response to this poem, using quotations from the poem to support your answer.

2. Copy the table below into your own notes and fill in critical comments about the last two quotations.

Key Quotes

The buzz saw snarled and rattled in the yard	The harsh reality of farm life is graphically portrayed in this onomatopoeic line.
the saw,/As if to prove saws knew what supper meant	Personification adds to the horror of the accident. It is as though the saw is a predatory animal.
No one believed	
And they, since they/Were not the one dead, turned to their affairs	

7   SPRING POOLS

These pools that, though in forests, still reflect
The total sky almost without defect,
And like the flowers beside them, chill and shiver,
Will like the flowers beside them soon be gone,
And yet not out by any brook or river,   5
But up by roots to bring dark foliage on.

The trees that have it in their pent-up buds
To darken nature and be summer woods—
Let them think twice before they use their powers
To blot out and drink up and sweep away   10
These flowery waters and these watery flowers
From snow that melted only yesterday.

'darken nature'

GLOSSARY

2   *defect*: blemish; flaw.
5   *brook*: small stream.

6   *foliage*: plants; undergrowth.

EXPLORATIONS

1. What aspects of the spring pools are conveyed in the first stanza? Refer to the text in your answer.

2. Choose one image from the poem that you found particularly striking. Briefly explain your choice.

3. Write your own personal response to the poem.

STUDY NOTES

'Spring Pools' captures a moment at the end of winter during which the poet reflects on the natural cycle of growth, decay and renewal. Rain falls from the sky, settles in pools and is then drawn up into the trees. In recalling the origins of this beautiful lyric poem, Frost commented, 'One night I sat alone by my open fireplace and wrote "Spring Pools". It was a very pleasant experience, and I remember it clearly, although I don't remember the writing of many of my other poems.'

The poem's title seems to celebrate new growth and regeneration. Ironically, **stanza one** focuses mainly on the fragility of nature. As always, Frost's **close observation of the natural world is evident** from the start. The clear pool water mirrors the overhead sky 'almost without defect'. While the simple images of the forest and flowers are peaceful, there is no escaping the underlying severity of 'chill and shiver'. The entire stanza of six lines is one long sentence. Its slow-moving pace, repetition and assonant vowels ('pools', 'brook', 'roots') enhance the sombre mood. Pool water will be absorbed by the tree roots to enrich the leaves and create 'dark foliage' and water and flowers will all 'soon be gone'. Frost pays most attention to the interdependence within the natural world and the transience of the beauty around him.

In **stanza two**, the poet addresses the trees directly, warning them to 'think twice before they use their powers'. He personifies them as an intimidating presence, associating them with dark destructiveness and 'pent-up' energy to 'blot out and drink up and sweep away'. Such forceful language combines with a resurgent rhythm to emphasise the power of the trees. The **tone becomes**

increasingly regretful in the final lines. We are left with another evocative image of how nature's beauty is subject to constant change: 'snow that melted only yesterday'.

Frost's **poem is typically thought provoking**, touching on familiar themes regarding the mysteries of nature and the passing of time. Some critics interpret 'Spring Pools' as a metaphor for the creative process – water has long been a symbol of inspiration. Frost's own writing is wonderfully controlled, in keeping with the sense of order within the natural world that he describes. Both stanzas mirror each other perfectly and the aabcbc rhyme scheme completes the fluency of the lines.

ANALYSIS

How would you describe the dominant mood or atmosphere in 'Spring Pools'?

Sample Paragraph

There is a deep sense of loss going through much of Frost's poem 'Spring Pools'. It struck me first in the negative language of the opening stanza. Frost refers to the perfect sky 'without defect', implying that something might soon destroy the perfection. The peaceful setting of the winter flowers beside the pools is also spoiled when the poet points out that they 'chill and shiver'. The mood is downbeat – everything in nature will end inevitably and 'soon be gone'. The image of the trees ('dark foliage') adds to my sense of this depressing feeling. In the second part of the poem, Frost points out the irony of springtime as a season of decay just as much as of growth. To some degree, I think this is a realistic view, but it does take away from the joy of spring. The mood deteriorates as the poem continues. The trees are seen as agents of destruction, drying up the water from the pools and removing the flowers. They 'darken nature' – a dramatic way of summing up the overall mood of this poem.

Examiner's Comment

This focused paragraph uses quotations very effectively to communicate the central mood of the poem. Some further discussion of style, particularly tone and rhythm, would have helped the answer. Overall, a basic B grade.

CLASS/HOMEWORK EXERCISES

1. In your view, what is the central theme or message of 'Spring Pools'? Refer closely to the poem in your answer.

2. Copy the table below into your own notes and fill in critical comments about the last two quotations.

Key Quotes

The total sky almost without defect	At the start of the poem, the setting is still and tranquil.
And like the flowers beside them, chill and shiver	Frost introduces a more disturbing element – the vulnerability of nature, as personified by the verbs.
dark foliage	
These flowery waters and these watery flowers	

[handwritten annotation: Disconnection with people or the world.]

⑧ ACQUAINTED WITH THE NIGHT

[handwritten annotation: Repitition of rain → ever presence of the rain.]

[handwritten annotation: to be in touch or in contact with]
I have been one acquainted with the night.
[handwritten annotation: constant]
I have walked out in rain—and back in rain.
I have outwalked the furthest city light. *[handwritten annotation: into the darkness]*

[handwritten annotation: Supperlatives → he couldn't be any worse.]
I have looked down the saddest city lane.
[handwritten annotation: Patrol]
I have passed by the watchman on his beat   5
And dropped my eyes, unwilling to explain. *[handwritten annotation: tries to ignore watchman. Wants to remain isolated. Afraid to reveal himself to stranger]*

I have stood still and stopped the sound of feet
When far away an interrupted cry
Came over houses from another street,

But not to call me back or say good-by;   10
And further still at an unearthly height   *[handwritten annotation: Depression]*
[handwritten annotation: Positivity]
One luminary clock against the sky
[handwritten annotation: glimmer of hope]

Proclaimed the time was neither wrong nor right.
I have been one acquainted with the night.

'I have looked down the saddest city lane'

GLOSSARY

A-Z

12 *luminary clock*: moon; a real clock shining with reflected light; simply passing time.
13 *Proclaimed ... wrong nor right*: this ambiguous message that the clock brings leaves us with more questions than answers. Why is the time neither wrong nor right? For whom is it so? For what is the time neither right nor wrong?

EXPLORATIONS

1. Does the shape of the poem add to or subtract from the poem's message? Comment on how the stanzas are arranged. Refer to the text in your answer.

2. Is there a sense of climax or anticlimax in this poem? Look at the rhyme scheme, the prevalence of end-stopped lines and the repetition. Refer to the text in your answer.

3. Write your own personal response to the poem.

STUDY NOTES

'Acquainted with the Night' is a sonnet from Frost's collection of poetry called 'West-Ring Brook' (1928). Unusually for Frost, it is set in a bleak city rather than the countryside. This is one of Frost's darkest poems and portrays a solitary, isolated figure filled with despair. It is reminiscent of the Modernist poets, such as T. S. Eliot, or the American artist Edward Hopper, whose paintings frequently showed a solitary individual.

The 20th century was a time of huge social upheaval and warfare, and was primarily focused on material progress rather than spiritual awareness. It was the century of the individual, rather than the community. Many people became alienated, lonely and confused. The certainty that institutions bring was lost, moral codes were abandoned and the traditional comforts of extended family and community began to disappear. The poem begins with a declaration: 'I have been one acquainted with the night'. It is a frank statement, rather like the declarations made at an AA meeting. It is also reminiscent of the Old Testament reference to **one who was despised and rejected by men**, a man of sorrows 'acquainted with grief'. The second line in this **first stanza** shows the direction that the poem will take. There are two journeys: the body travels outwards towards the edge of the city ('I have walked out in rain') while the mind travels inwards to the edge of the psyche ('and back in rain').

This **alienation is echoed in the form of the poem**, which is not a conventional 14-line sonnet (either three quatrains and a rhyming couplet, or an octet and sestet); here there is a terza rima format. The poet uses a three-line rhyming stanza, concluding with a rhyming couplet (aba, bcb, cdc, ded, ff). The terza rima was used by the great Italian poet Dante in his famous poem 'The Divine Comedy' to describe the descent into hell. Is Frost using this structure in his poem because he is describing his own descent into his own private hell? (His own life had included many personal tragedies.) Is he using this format because nothing is conventional any more? This is a highly personal poem, as it uses 'I' at the beginning of seven of its fourteen lines. The rhythm imitates a slow walking movement: 'I have outwalked the furthest city light'. The poet has now gone beyond the last visible sign of civilisation. The use of iambic pentameter is the metre closest to the speaking voice in English, and the measured flow underlines the poet's melancholy mood.

The **solemn, sombre mood** of overwhelming anxiety is shown in the long vowel sounds of the **second stanza**: 'I have looked down the saddest city lane'. The broad vowels 'a' and 'o' lengthen the line and show the world-weariness of one who has seen and experienced too much. Although it is set at night, the traditional time for romance and lovers, we are presented with never-ending rain and gloom. A listless mood is created by the repetition of 'I have'. The run-on line suggests the ongoing trudging of this weary man who is too caught up in his own dark thoughts to even bother communicating with the 'watchman'. He is 'unwilling to explain' and is jealously guarding his privacy. Is this walk symptomatic of his inner state? Can nothing penetrate this extreme loneliness?

The use of the run-on line continues in the **third stanza**. Frost comes to an abrupt stop on his journey as an 'interrupted cry' rings out across the **desolate urban landscape**. Who cried? Why? And why was the cry 'interrupted'? Is something awful happening to someone? We, and the poet, don't know. Can anything be done about it? No. The poet just remarks in the next stanza that it has nothing to do with him, 'not to call me back or say good-by'. This is the chilling aspect of living in a big city: the sense of just being another person nobody cares about. These others have no substance, being reduced to the 'sound of feet' or a 'cry'.

In the **fourth stanza**, the poet speaks of a 'luminary clock'. This could be the moon or a real clock that is reflecting light. Is it symbolic of time passing relentlessly? Why is it at an 'unearthly height'? Is it because time rules the human world and nothing can change this? The **final couplet** proclaims that the 'time was neither wrong nor right'. We are left wondering what the time was neither right nor wrong for – what was supposed to happen? There is a real **sense of confusion** here, and echoes of Hamlet's declaration that 'the time is out of joint'. The poem ends as it begins: 'I have been one acquainted with the night'. We have come full circle, though **nothing has been achieved**. We have experienced the darkness with the poet. There is no sense of comfort or guidance, only the realisation of a hostile world.

ANALYSIS

This poem has been described as a 'dramatic lyric of homelessness'. Do you agree or disagree with this statement? Support your view with references from the text.

Sample Paragraph

The sense of homelessness is palpable in this unconventional sonnet of Robert Frost's. The individual in the poem seems to be always on his own, not connected either with family, friend or acquaintance, a real loner in a big anonymous city. The form of the poem mirrors this individualism. It is a maverick sonnet, just like in the great American tradition of cowboy films or gangster movies: the hero is the loner who never quite fits in. There is no network to comfort this man, no community to offer help and encouragement. This emphasis on self comes at a price. The hero does not want to engage, 'And dropped my eyes'. He wanders through town like the tumbleweed of old, with no roots to hold it still. The poem is like a mini drama as the main character plays out his exterior action: 'I have walked out in rain', and his interior journey, 'unwilling to explain'. The verbs carry the action of this sad man: 'outwalked', 'looked', 'passed by', 'stood', 'stopped'. This man is going nowhere. The setting is vividly realised as the bleak urban landscape is drawn with its endless rain and strange noises. So there is character, action, setting and mood. The music of this lyrical poem is the rhythm of a slow walk as the steady iambic pentameter tempo steps out a hypnotic beat: 'I have outwalked the furthest city light.' The broad vowels add to this sombre music as the poem grinds on relentlessly: 'I have looked down the saddest city lane'. This is indeed dark mood music, as the drawn-out vowel sounds 'lane', 'explain', 'beat' and 'feet' tap out the despair of this lonely man. So, in conclusion, I do agree with the statement that 'Acquainted with the Night' is indeed a dramatic lyric of homelessness.

Examiner's Comment

This paragraph addresses the three elements of the question (homelessness, dramatic and lyric). It shows a real appreciation of poetic technique, as the terms are not only explained, but are examined well in relation to the poem. Grade A.

CLASS/HOMEWORK EXERCISES

1. Seamus Heaney describes this poem as 'dark'. What type of darkness is there? Is it literal or metaphorical or both? Refer to the text in your answer.

2. Copy the table below into your own notes and fill in critical comments about the last two quotations.

Key Quotes

I have been one acquainted with the night	Frost tells us that he has known bad times – in an almost biblical fashion. But we are left with a mystery: what were those bad times?
I have outwalked the furthest city light	There are now no signs of civilisation. The poet has reached a place where there is no guiding light.
But not to call me back or say good-by	
Proclaimed the time was neither wrong nor right	

9 DESIGN

I found a dimpled spider, fat and white,
On a white heal-all, holding up a moth
Like a white piece of rigid satin cloth—
Assorted characters of death and blight
Mixed ready to begin the morning right,   5
Like the ingredients of a witches' broth—
A snow-drop spider, a flower like a froth,
And dead wings carried like a paper kite.

What had that flower to do with being white,
The wayside blue and innocent heal-all?   10
What brought the kindred spider to that height,
Then steered the white moth thither in the night?
What but design of darkness to appall?—
If design govern in a thing so small.

'a dimpled spider, fat and white'

GLOSSARY

The poem's title refers to the argument that the natural design of the universe is proof of God's existence.

1   *dimpled*: indented.

2   *heal-all*: plant (once used as a medicine).

4   *blight*: disease in plants; evil influence.

6   *witches' broth*: revolting recipes used to cast spells.

12   *thither*: to there, to that place.

13   *appall*: horrify (to make pale, literally).

EXPLORATIONS

1. How important a part does the colour white play in this poem? Refer to the text in your answer.

2. Select one comparison from the poem that you consider particularly effective. Briefly explain your choice.

3. Describe the poet's tone in the octave. How does it compare with the tone in the sestet?

STUDY NOTES

'Design' explores our attempts to see order in the universe – and our failure to recognise the order that is present in nature. Frost's sonnet raises several profound questions. Is there a design to life? Is there an explanation for the evil in the world? The poet was fascinated by nature from a philosophical point of view. His choice of the traditional sonnet form allows him to address such an important theme in a controlled way.

In the **opening line**, Frost describes how he finds a 'dimpled spider, fat and white' on a flower, 'holding up a moth' it has captured. The adjective 'dimpled' usually has harmless connotations far removed from the world of arachnids, but in this context, and combined with the word 'fat', it suggests an unattractive image of venomous engorgement. The colour white (used four more times in this short poem) also tends to have positive overtones of innocence and goodness. But most spiders are brown or black, and purity here quickly gives way to pale ghastliness.

Indeed, the **tone becomes increasingly menacing** as the octave proceeds. The unwary moth has been lured to its grizzly death on the 'white heal-all' flower, which makes the situation even more deceitful.

Frost's chilling similes reflect the deathly atmosphere. The hapless moth is held 'Like a white piece of rigid satin cloth'. The 'characters of death' in this grim drama are compared to the 'ingredients of a witches' broth'. **Lines 7–8** are particularly ironic. Frost then revises his view of the grotesque scene, seeing the **tragic coincidence** involving the 'snow-drop spider' and 'a flower like a froth'. While the images appear attractive, there is a lingering suggestion of gloom and ferocity.

The focus changes in the **sestet** as the tone grows passionately angry. Frost uses a series of **rhetorical questions demanding an explanation** for what he has witnessed: 'What had that flower to do with being white'? Is this implying that nature isn't so innocent after all? He reruns the sequence of events and wonders what 'steered the white moth thither in the night'. The possibility that such a catastrophic event might be part of a great 'design of darkness' appalls the poet. However, the poem's final line ('If design govern in a thing so small') is the most intriguing of all. The word 'if' leaves the possibility that there is no grand plan for the universe, that it is all accidental. Whether predestination or chance is the more terrifying reality is left for readers to consider.

ANALYSIS

In your view, what image of nature does Frost present in his poem 'Design'? Refer closely to the text in your response.

Sample Paragraph

In his poem 'Design', Robert Frost takes an ironic approach to nature. Unlike other poems (e.g. 'The Tuft of Flowers'), where he ends up being reassured by the beauty and mystery of his natural environment, 'Design' is decidedly disquieting. The first few lines describe a repulsive side of nature's basic law – kill or be killed. I found the image of the bloated spider quite revolting: 'fat and white'. The poet cleverly conveys a strong sense of the violence and death that takes place when nature begins 'the morning right'. Dead moths are routine – often in beautiful settings. Nature is full of such contradictions. The image of the moth like a 'white piece of rigid satin cloth' suggested the lining of a coffin and reminded me that we see signs of our own mortality all around us. At the same time, Frost seems to be realistic about nature. Even in violent situations, there are beautiful creatures. The 'dead wings' are compared to a graceful 'paper kite'. Under different circumstances, I could imagine a more attractive 'snow-drop' or the 'wayside blue' of a wild flower. Overall, I think the poet probably shows a less attractive side to nature in the poem, but it is not altogether bleak or depressing. I found his ideas interesting and liked the way he managed simple language to raise deep and disturbing questions about our natural world.

Examiner's Comment

The paragraph addressed the question very well. The response was balanced but clear, demonstrating a good understanding of the poem. References and quotations were carefully chosen and used effectively. Varied, confident expression throughout. Grade A.

CLASS/HOMEWORK EXERCISES

1. Sonnets often move from description to reflection ('sight to insight'). To what extent is this true of 'Design'? Refer closely to the poem in your answer.

2. Copy the table below into your own notes and fill in critical comments about the last two quotations.

Key Quotes

I found a dimpled spider, fat and white	Frost takes a matter-of-fact, narrative approach, using his characteristic colloquial diction.
And dead wings carried like a paper kite	The juxtaposition of a disturbing image alongside a childlike simile is a common feature of this poem's ambivalence.
Assorted characters of death and blight	
design of darkness	

⑩ PROVIDE, PROVIDE

The witch that came (the withered hag)
To wash the steps with pail and rag
Was once the beauty Abishag,

The picture pride of Hollywood.
Too many fall from great and good   5
For you to doubt the likelihood.

Die early and avoid the fate.
Or if predestined to die late,
Make up your mind to die in state.

Make the whole stock exchange your own!   10
If need be occupy a throne,
Where nobody can call *you* crone.

Some have relied on what they knew,
Others on being simply true.
What worked for them might work for you.   15

No memory of having starred
Atones for later disregard
Or keeps the end from being hard.

Better to go down dignified
With boughten friendship at your side   20
Than none at all. Provide, provide!

'once the beauty Abishag'

GLOSSARY

3 *Abishag*: beautiful young woman who comforted King David in his old age.

12 *crone*: witchlike; old, withered woman.

17 *Atones*: makes amends (for sin or wrongdoing).

20 *boughten*: bought.

EXPLORATIONS

1. Is the advice given in the poem to be taken seriously or humorously, or a mixture of both? Discuss, using reference from the poem to support your answer.

2. What elements in the poem resemble a fairytale or fable? Pick your favourite element and explain why you like it.

3. What conclusion, if any, does the poem come to? Do you agree or disagree with the view expressed? Refer to the text to support your view.

STUDY NOTES

This poem was written at the height of Frost's fame, in a collection called 'A Further Rage' (1936). It was based on a real woman he had seen cleaning steps. The poem contrasts with most of Frost's work, as the tone is bitter and the emphasis is on material success. The Great Depression, a time of mass unemployment in America, was taking place. Is Frost suggesting that self-sufficiency is the answer?

The **first stanza** advises us to **plan for the future**. Why? A cold, bleak scene of a withered old woman doing a menial job of washing steps is given as a salutary picture of what happens if you don't provide. This is what happened to Abishag. The reference to the biblical character adds a timeless element – this is a truth for all generations. We don't know what is to be. In this poem, old age equals diminishing beauty and success.

In **stanza two**, the destructive element of time is stressed as the poem comes to the present, 'Hollywood'. Even in the dream factory, beauty does not last. The tone of the poem is one of **addressing a public audience**, as if at an evangelical rally:

'For you to doubt the likelihood'. Fortune is fickle, as we all know.

The poem now offers **mock advice: the only solution is to die young** ('Die early'). Images of icons hover in our minds of tragic, famous deaths of the young and beautiful, such as James Dean and Marilyn Monroe. In the **third stanza, the only other solution is to become wealthy** and 'die in state'. An imperative verb, 'Make', in the **fourth stanza** shouts at us to grab material success: 'Make the whole stock exchange your own!' The exclamation mark captures the mood of exhortation that pervades this unusual poem of Frost's. The quaint image of the throne adds to the timeless element of this poem, as it is a universal symbol of power and wealth. Only political power, privilege and riches provide protection against the harsh reality of ageing. If 'you' don't want the same fate as Abishag, 'you' must be alert.

Independence was very important to Frost. Now, in **stanza six**, the poem cautions us that even if our early lives were wonderful, 'having starred', that memory is not a safeguard against the misfortune that might happen later in life. Black humour in the **final stanza** suggests, with wry, unsentimental honesty, that it is better to **buy friendship** ('boughten') than suffer loneliness at the end of life. Is this cynical view that bought friends are better than none realistic? The poem concludes with great urgency: 'Provide, provide!' Frost did not believe in a benevolent God ruling the universe, but rather takes the view that there is an indifferent God and we are subject to random darkness. This is not an affirmative poem.

Frost favoured **traditional poetic structures**, declaring that he was 'one of the notable craftsmen of this time'. Here the full rhyme of aaa, bbb, ccc, ddd, etc. does not seem strained. We hardly notice it in this carefully crafted poem of seven triplets. The rhythmic pattern of blank verse, i.e. four short–long beats, set against the irregular variations of colloquial speech gives this poem its energy. The use of the imperative for the verbs, especially 'Provide, provide', demands that the reader take this message on board. Frost presents **painful ideas** – in this instance a cynical view of fame and success – **in a controlled form**. He has said, 'The poems I make are little bits of order.'

> ## ANALYSIS

'Poetry is a momentary stay against confusion.' Discuss this statement in relation to the poem 'Provide, Provide'. Use references from the text to support your views.

Sample Paragraph

The bleak, cold situation painted by Frost is very different from his other poems where a quiet, sensible speaking voice alerts us to the beauties of nature. Here the focus is on 'look out for your old age, as no one is going to want you'. I wonder if Frost was uncomfortable about his decision to commit himself to being famous? Did he, like so many contemporary stars today, find the whole fame business tacky and shallow? When he read this poem in public, he usually added a line, 'Or somebody else'll provide for you!/And how'll you like that?' He is condemning those who take 'handouts', social benefits. The poem is stating that change is the only certainty and vehemently exhorts us to get ourselves in order if we don't want to have a miserable time when looks and youth are gone. I like the mock serious tone in which this message is delivered: 'If need be occupy a throne,/Where nobody can call you crone'. I think this wry, dry, cynical tone appeals especially to today's reader who is saturated with this 'fame' issue. I also think that humour is very effective in delivering a message, particularly one as unpalatable as this. The airbrushed perfection of the groomed Hollywood stars is captured perfectly in the alliterative phrase: 'The picture pride of Hollywood'. Frost has arranged this line as carefully as the lighting technician has arranged the lighting of a star, so that all seems picture perfect. But the poet knew that this is not how it is – 'the end' is 'hard'. Frost said, 'If you suffer any sense of confusion in life, the best thing you can do is make little poems.' Here is the human's need for order in a terrifying universe.

Examiner's Comment

This response (to a very challenging question) has taken a ruminative view of Frost's poetry, connecting his views on poetry and life as well as his own personal circumstances into the discussion. However, it over-relies on biographical references and is not sufficiently rooted in the text. B grade.

CLASS/HOMEWORK EXERCISES

1. 'A poem begins in delight and ends in wisdom.' Is this a valid statement in relation to the poem 'Provide, Provide'? Use quotation from the poem in your explorations.

2. Copy the table below into your own notes and fill in critical comments about the last two quotations.

Key Quotes

The witch that came	This is a reference to an old washing woman Frost saw at Harvard University.
Die early and avoid the fate	Mock serious advice given in the poem. Note the imperative tone.
No memory of having starred/ Atones for later disregard	
Better to go down dignified/With boughten friendship at your side/ Than none at all	

LEAVING CERT SAMPLE ESSAY

'We enjoy poetry for its ideas and language.'
Using the above statement as your title, write an essay on the poetry of Robert Frost.
Support the points by reference to the poetry of Robert Frost on your course.

Marking Scheme Guidelines

Expect candidates to deal with both elements of the question – ideas and language – but not necessarily separately. Take 'ideas' to mean themes, subjects, attitudes, issues and so on. Take 'language' to mean style, manner, phraseology, appropriate vocabulary, imagery, etc. The level of engagement with the poetry will serve as an implicit treatment of what 'we enjoy' in the poetry of Robert Frost.

Some of the following areas might provide material for candidates:

- Poet's views on life/experience.
- Habitual concerns in the poems.
- Elegant plainness of his expression.
- Typical patterns of imagery/language.
- Variety of registers in the texts, etc.

Sample Essay

(We enjoy Frost's poetry for its ideas and language)

1. *How could you not enjoy the work of a man whose favourite book was Robinson Crusoe? Here is a quiet, sensible speaking voice dealing with human suffering, isolation, loneliness and our relations with the world around us. No wonder his poems were sent to inspire soldiers in the Second World War, or that he was chosen to speak at the inauguration of JFK. 'Mending Wall' deals with an annual event where two neighbours check and mend their boundary wall ritualistically each spring. The communal activity joins people, but this poem is also about gaps in understanding between people. The speaker delights in mischief, in contrast to his neighbour, who 'walks in darkness' because he is traditional and is content to repeat received wisdom from previous generations without question: 'Good walls make good neighbors'.*

2. *Civilisation needs boundaries and order. Respecting rules is necessary in society, otherwise there is chaos. We must respect equality, but also difference. Each remains on his own land, 'One on a side'. So Frost's single event contains a complex issue: boundaries connect and divide. The two neighbours can also be seen as reflecting the two contrasting facets of Frost – the wall toppler who delights in wildness, breaking rules, being disruptive; and the builder who abides by strict rules, form, grammar and the traditional structure of poems. Such insights are what attracts me to Frost's work.*

3. *I also enjoyed the idea that there is a force in nature that does not like the way men construct boundaries. When I think of the Native Americans who did not believe in land ownership but rather guardianship and care of Mother Earth, I agree that 'Something there is that doesn't love a wall'. I think it was a good poem to read to President Khrushchev, particularly at a time of the Cold War and the Iron Curtain: 'I'd ask to know what I was walling in or walling out'. The Romantic influence can be seen in the subject matter of 'The Road Not Taken'. Nature is the stimulus for an insight. This poem deals with decisions taken when young. We are all facing tough decisions*

now regarding study, points and careers and will we be like Frost's friend who inspired this poem, and regret decisions we have made? Will we be thinking of things that might have been: 'I shall be telling this with a sigh'? When we look at our classmates and know that we will all take different roads and may not meet again for quite some time, don't the lines 'Yet knowing how way leads on to way, I doubted if I ever should come back' ring very true?

4. Nature provides a beautiful but passive background to the horrific event in 'Out, Out—'. Frost never read this poem at his readings as he regarded it as too cruel. It was inspired by a newspaper account about a young boy whose hand was amputated by a saw as he was doing a man's job and who subsequently died. This reminded me of how Bob Geldof created Live Aid from an item of TV news. Like the Victorians, Frost believed that there was no benevolent God compassionately caring for the world. Terrible things happen. For me, the most shocking thing in this poem was not the chainsaw as it became an animal and devoured the boy's hand; rather it was how the onlookers who 'since they were not the one dead, turned to their affairs'. This is chilling. But Frost believed one thing about life: 'It goes on'. When I consider the tragic life Frost lived, I can see how he understood the importance of endurance, however cold it may seem.

5. Frost's simple subject matter covers complex issues: 'There's always something else in my poetry.' His language allows us access to them. He did not follow the fashion of the time. Instead, he adopted the persona of the New England farmer inspired by natural events. But underpinning the colloquial language is a strict adherence to traditional forms and patterning. To him, free verse was like 'playing tennis without a net'. He used blank verse and iambic pentameter, which has rhythm but not rhyme: 'Something there is that doesn't love a wall'. There is a tension between the ordinary subject matter and the colloquial voice, as it is constrained by poetic patterning.

6. Frost believed in the sound of a poem; he said poems rather than read them, believing the sound carried the meaning. I see this clearly in 'The buzz saw snarled and rattled in the yard'. The sound of this line suggests a menacing element in the midst of beauty. The dust is beautifully described as 'sweet-scented stuff when the breeze blew across it'. The gentle 's' sound conveys the harmony in the timber yard, in contrast to the strident sound of the saw. I also enjoyed Frost's use of drama in his poetry, the moment of decision in 'The Road Not Taken' when he wrote: 'Two roads converged in

a yellow wood' and the strange 'interrupted cry' in 'Acquainted with the Night' which left me wondering who had cried and why. No wonder I am just one of millions who enjoy Frost's poetic ideas and language.

(approx. 870 words)

Examiner's Comment

A detailed exploration of the question and well-developed points on both subject matter and style supported by succinct quotations. The essay ranged widely and showed very good personal engagement with the poetry. Expression was varied and confidently managed throughout. A very assured response.

GRADE: A1

P = 15/15

C = 15/15

L = 15/15

M = 5/5

Total = 50/50

SAMPLE LEAVING CERT QUESTIONS ON FROST'S POETRY

(45/50 MINUTES)

1. 'The appeal of Robert Frost's poetry for a young audience.' Write an essay on this statement, focusing particular attention on his themes and how he expresses them. Support the points you make by reference to the poetry of Robert Frost on your course.

2. What impact did the poetry of Robert Frost make on you as a reader? In shaping your answer, you might like to consider the following:

• Your overall sense or outlook of the poet.

• The poet's use of language and imagery.

• Your favourite poem or poems.

3. 'Life by the throat' is a phrase often associated with the poetry of Robert Frost. How does the poetry catch life by the throat? Discuss, referring both to the content and style of the poems by Frost on your course.

Sample Essay Plan (Q2)

What impact did the poetry of Robert Frost make on you as a reader? In shaping your answer, you might like to consider the following:

- Your overall sense or outlook of the poet.
- The poet's use of language and imagery.
- Your favourite poem or poems.

- Intro: Interesting themes, individualistic style. His fascination with nature and human nature. Favourite poem – 'The Road Not Taken'.

- Point 1: Family – background tragic, yet it is the still, calm voice which sounds from the poem. He extends the invitation, 'you come too', as he explores man's relationship with nature.

- Point 2: 'Sound of sense' – 'Writing with your ear to the voice'. Use of first person in 'Out, Out—'. Use of first person pronoun in 'The Road Not Taken'.

- Point 3: Formal rhyme – traditionalist, good craftsman, art deceptive, rhyme scheme in 'The Road Not Taken'. Terza rima in 'Acquainted with the Night'.

- Point 4: Metaphors – Doesn't force, allows the metaphors to speak for themselves, e.g. road is a metaphor for a journey in 'The Road Not Taken'.

- Point 5: Other themes – natural world, endurance, ordinary life, etc.

- Conclusion: Wrote about ordinary people living ordinary lives. View of nature bleak. Aware of time and effect on human beings.

Sample Essay Plan (Q2)

Develop one of the above points into a paragraph.

Sample Paragraph: Point 5

The subject matter of Frost's poetry is rooted in the natural world. He believed that 'man has need of nature, but nature has no need of man'. But it was nature which was thought-provoking, a stimulus for the poet, leading to insight and revelation: 'A poem begins in delight and ends in wisdom.' This was in keeping with the Romantic poets, such as Wordsworth, and was in contrast to the Modernist movement that was in vogue at this time. They were urban poets who used classical references and were often obscure. Frost was and is accessible. He was influenced by current events – just like Geldof was inspired by a news item to create Live Aid, so Frost was inspired by a newspaper article to write the chilling poem of injured innocence, 'Out, Out—'. Frost believed in endurance: 'In three words I can sum up everything I've learned about life – it goes on.' He was influenced also by the Victorian poets like Hardy who did not believe in a world ruled by a benevolent God. Darkness erupts in a random manner with tragic consequences, as in 'Out, Out—'. He wrote about ordinary people living ordinary lives. But his view of the human condition was bleak and cold. He was aware of time and its effect on human beings.

Examiner's Comment

As part of a full essay answer, the student has written a general exploration that shows a real understanding of Frost's aims. The paragraph focuses on the insight to be gained from a mature perception of nature. Grade A.

LAST WORDS

'Like a piece of ice on a hot stove, the poem must ride on its own melting.'

Robert Frost

'Robert Frost: the icon of the Yankee values, the smell of wood smoke, the sparkle of dew, the reality of farm-house dung, the jocular honesty of an uncle.'

Derek Walcott

'I'll say that again, in case you missed it first time round.'

Robert Frost

THOMAS HARDY

1840–1928

'Human beings are of no matter or appreciable value in this nonchalant universe.'

English writer Thomas Hardy is best known for his novels *Far From the Madding Crowd* (1874) and *Tess of the d'Urbervilles* (1891). He spent most of his life in rural Dorset, which provided a background for his fiction. Hardy trained as an architect and spent five years in London at that profession before finding success as a novelist in the 1870s. He published several popular books over the next twenty years, but harsh criticism of *Tess of the d'Urbervilles* and *Jude the Obscure* – both of which were called vulgar and pessimistic, but sold well – turned him from writing novels to writing poetry. These were first published when he was in his fifties and many of them deal with themes of disappointment in love and life. Hardy was married twice; his first marriage in 1874, long and mostly unhappy, was to Emma Gifford. Emma died in 1912, and in 1914, Hardy married his secretary, Florence Dugdale, who later became his biographer. Throughout his life, Hardy displayed a deeply-felt love of the natural world and took a firm stance against animal cruelty. He died in 1928 and his heart was interred at Dorset's Stinson Church, but his remains (he was cremated) were interred in the Poets' Corner at Westminster Abbey. Although his poems were not initially well received, Hardy is now widely recognised as one of the greatest poets of the 20th century.

Prescribed Poems   HIGHER LEVEL

awaits those who glorify material objects. Here, the poet does not mourn the dead, but concentrates instead on the encounter between ship and iceberg.

① DRUMMER HODGE

They throw in Drummer Hodge, to rest
    Uncoffined – just as found:
His landmark is a kopje-crest
    That breaks the veldt around;
And foreign constellations west   5
    Each night above his mound.

Young Hodge the Drummer never knew –
    Fresh from his Wessex home –
The meaning of the broad Karoo,
    The Bush, the dusty loam,   10
And why uprose to nightly view
    Strange stars amid the gloam.

Yet portion of that unknown plain
    Will Hodge for ever be;
His homely Northern breast and brain   15
    Grow to some Southern tree,
And strange-eyed constellations reign
    His stars eternally.

'His landmark is a kopje-crest/That breaks the veldt around'

GLOSSARY

1. **Hodge**: nickname given to country boys who were often regarded as slow and unsophisticated by military officers.
2. **Uncoffined**: the young soldier was not even given a proper burial.
3. **kopje**: hill, headland (Afrikaans, language spoken in South Africa).
4. **veldt**: extensive grassland.
5. **west**: set in the west.
8. **Wessex**: Hardy used the old Saxon name for Dorset.
9. **Karoo**: high dry plain in South Africa.
10. **The Bush**: land covered in brushwood.
10. **loam**: dark soil.
12. **gloam**: twilight.
15. **homely**: ordinary.
17. **strange-eyed constellations**: unfamiliar star clusters.

EXPLORATIONS

1. Why, in your opinion, did Hardy change the original title of the poem, 'The Dead Drummer', to 'Drummer Hodge'? Which title do you prefer? Briefly explain your choice.

2. How does the poet show the strangeness of the foreign land where Hodge is killed? Refer to the imagery and use of Afrikaans vocabulary in your response.

3. Would you consider 'Drummer Hodge' an effective anti-war poem? Refer closely to the text in your response.

STUDY NOTES

'Drummer Hodge' (originally titled 'The Dead Drummer') was written during the Boer War of 1899–1902 when Britain fought against a number of Afrikaner republics. The Boers were South Africans of Dutch descent, many of whom made their living from farming. Hardy's poem shows the pointless waste of war. His tragic vision suggests the futility of one young soldier's sacrifice for a land he hardly knew. In times of battle, the drummer's role was a very important one. The drum was used as a battlefield communication device, signalling when to advance, retreat and regroup. Hodge was not the actual name of the young victim, but a derogatory term for a country person.

From the outset, Hardy's tone is knowingly critical. He immediately exposes the cold reality of war where every ordinary soldier is expendable. The dead drummer's corpse is flung into a makeshift grave. He is accorded no dignity as a human being, but treated like a dead animal. The monosyllabic pronoun, 'They', refers anonymously to Hodge's brutalised comrades. In this hurly-burly theatre of conflict, there is no time for religious rites or military honours. Throughout **stanza one, the poet lets readers keenly feel the lack of respect for the young boy** as the opening line runs on, 'to rest/Uncoffined'. In Hardy's works of fiction, the churchyard was a place of importance where the dead are duly honoured. But Hodge is buried 'just as found'. There is further indignity as his grave is lacking a headstone. Ironically, the deceased soldier is now honoured by this foreign place which is defined by the 'kopje-crest'. But will he 'rest' peacefully?

The poet's restrained, sympathetic tone continues into **stanza two** which focuses on the contrast between Hodges's rural English background, 'Fresh from his Wessex home' and his remote burial place. Hardy uses the Afrikaans expressions, 'Karoo' and 'Bush' to emphasise the disconnection. These **enduring landscapes are permanent natural forces which underline the fragility of human existence**. Adjectives such as 'Young' and 'Fresh' add pathos to the offensive circumstances of the soldier's death. Hodge was vulnerable and innocent – and 'never knew' what lay ahead of him. He was ignorant of 'the broad Karoo', this alien land for which he laid down his life. Hardy draws a contrast between the old English word, 'gloam' (meaning twilight) and South Africa's 'Strange stars' which will form a continuous guard over Hodge's burial place.

The word 'Yet' to introduce the **third stanza** suggests a new way of looking at the young drummer's pitiful experience. It is ironic that Hodge will 'forever be' part of the South African veldt. His earthly remains ('His homely Northern breast and brain') will nourish 'some Southern tree'. Hardy believed in the mysterious power of nature, and the compound word, 'strange-eyed', graphically personifies the foreign stars as they rule ('reign') over the lonely grave. The tight structure of regular stanzas and set line lengths coupled with the use of formal imagery and regular rhyme add dignity to the pathetic situation that the young boy will remain away from home forever. Hardy's controlled description of Hodge's burial increases its poignancy. The poem is non-political; there is no specific criticism of the Boer War. Instead, **the timeless central theme is the routine waste of innocent life during warfare**. Indeed, the concluding lines are hopeful and harmonious. In death, the fallen soldier has become integrated with the landscape in a way that he did not when he was alive. But does the poem itself stand as a memorial to Drummer Hodge? Or is he already forgotten, a routine casualty of another war?

ANALYSIS

'The natural world provides a permanent unchanging backdrop for humanity's brief tragic transience.' To what extent is this true of 'Drummer Hodge'? Refer to the poem in your response.

Sample Paragraph

Hardy's strikingly individual vocabulary depicts a huge South African sky, 'strange-eyed constellations', under which the young drummer, 'Fresh from his Wessex home' died. These stars would have been foreign to young Hodge who came from England where dusk was called the 'gloam'. The alien landscape is illustrated using Afrikaans vocabulary, 'kopje-crest', 'Karoo'. Hodge did not belong here and his young life was ended unceremoniously as he was dumped in an unmarked grave by an uncaring military. The poet observes this travesty with the eye of a detached observer, 'They throw'. The boy's brief life is contrasted with the power of nature which treats the body with more dignity than Hodge's companions did. It is an irony that the kopje-crest becomes his 'landmark' or headstone. The stars keep an eternal vigil over the young war victim. This permanent natural world now embraces the tragic boy who is so far from home. Nature quietly absorbs him to nourish a 'Southern tree'. I found that Hardy's short poem really conveyed the insignificance of human life – especially in times of war. Nature can renew, man cannot. Hodge's short tragic life is over. His human fragility is clearly silhouetted against the robust South African landscape just as the 'aged thrush, frail, gaunt, and small' is contrasted with the enveloping 'growing gloom' of the countryside in 'The Darkling Thrush'.

Examiner's Comment

This well-managed paragraph shows a very close reading of the poem. Suitable quotations are effectively used to highlight the contrast between human existence and the enduring world of nature. The short personal input and cross-reference to 'The Darkling Thrush' add to the engagement with Hardy's poetry. Grade A standard.

CLASS/HOMEWORK EXERCISES

1. 'Hardy's poetry is a mixture of a place and emotion.' Discuss this statement in relation to 'Drummer Hodge'.

2. Copy the table below into your own notes and fill in critical comments about the last two quotations.

Key Quotes

They throw in Drummer Hodge	The verb 'throw' exposes the army's callous treatment of casualties. Hodge's body is treated in an undignified way and disposed of without ceremony.
And foreign constellations west/Each night above his mound	The poet conveys the far-off land where the young soldier is buried by referring to the alien star groups which now watch over him.
The meaning of the broad Karoo	
Yet portion of that unknown plain/Will Hodge for ever be	

❷ THE DARKLING THRUSH

I leant upon a coppice gate
  When Frost was spectre-gray,
And Winter's dregs made desolate
  The weakening eye of day.
The tangled bine-stems scored the sky   5
  Like strings of broken lyres,
And all mankind that haunted nigh
  Had sought their household fires.

The land's sharp features seemed to be
  The Century's corpse outleant,   10
His crypt the cloudy canopy,
  The wind his death-lament.
The ancient pulse of germ and birth
  Was shrunken hard and dry,
And every spirit upon earth   15
  Seemed fervourless as I.

At once a voice arose among
  The bleak twigs overhead
In a full-hearted evensong
  Of joy illimited;   20
An aged thrush, frail, gaunt, and small,
  In blast-beruffled plume,
Had chosen thus to fling his soul
  Upon the growing gloom.

So little cause for carolings   25
  Of such ecstatic sound
Was written on terrestrial things
  Afar or nigh around,
That I could think there trembled through
  His happy good-night air   30
Some blessed Hope, whereof he knew
  And I was unaware.

31 December 1900

'When Frost was spectre-gray'

GLOSSARY

1	*coppice*: area of woodland or shrubs.	16	*fervourless*: without feeling or energy.
5	*bine-stems*: bindweed which winds itself around other plants.	19	*evensong*: Anglican church service held in the evening.
5	*scored*: scraped, marked; may also refer to sheet music.	20	*illimited*: infinite, endless.
6	*lyres*: stringed instruments similar to harps.	22	*blast-beruffled plume*: feathers ruffled in the breeze.
10	*Century's corpse*: the 19th century which has passed away.	25	*carolings*: joyful Christmas songs.
10	*outleant*: laid out.	27	*terrestrial*: earthly.
13	*pulse*: seed; throbbing beat.	28	*nigh around*: close by.
		31	*whereof*: of which.

EXPLORATIONS

1. What sort of atmosphere does Hardy establish in stanza one? Refer closely to the text in your response.

2. Choose two images of decay or desolation. Comment on the effectiveness of each.

3. What conclusions does Thomas Hardy reach concerning the thrush's inspiration? Refer to the poem in your answer.

STUDY NOTES

Thomas Hardy wrote 'The Darkling Thrush' as evening fell on the final hours of the 1900s. It originally had a sub-title, 'By the Century's Deathbed'. The bleak, wintry landscape is a metaphor for the close of the 19th century, which was anxiously emerging from the Victorian era. Although not actually written on the date, Hardy placed '31 December 1900' after the final line as a dramatic flourish to mark the end of a day, the end of a year, the end of a century. The song of the solitary thrush at the conclusion of the poem can be seen as a symbol of the dawning of modern times.

Stanza one invites readers into **Hardy's internal monologue**. In meditative mood, the poet leans on the gate of a small wood, observing and contemplating, 'I leant upon a coppice gate'. For him, it is a crucial moment of transition, as one century passes and another arrives. There is a compelling sense of nature in mourning. To illustrate the dramatic scene, Hardy makes effective use of personification ('Frost', 'Winter's'). The compound phrase, 'spectre-gray', emphasises this momentous occasion. Even the frost is seen as a ghost-like creature stalking the haunted countryside. Hardy's despair and pessimism is embodied in the bitter remnants of this dead season's 'dregs' which alter the sun's appearance to that of a blood-shot eye, 'The weakening eye of day'. The dismal landscape is shown as a mess of 'tangled bine-stems' whose silhouettes have 'scored' and slashed the sky. An insistent repetition of hard aural effects ('coppice', 'spectre', 'weakening') mimics the sounds of breaking ice. Everyone except the poet himself has fled from this inhospitable place to 'the household fires'. Is this symbolic of the deadening effect of the Industrial Revolution?

Stanza two sketches the end of the harsh day when 'The Century's corpse outleant'. This graphic picture of the 'land's sharp features' laid out with the sky as its 'crypt' and the wind howling a 'death-lament' intensifies the grimness of the scene. The poet makes readers experience chill nature as time conspires against mankind. An important metaphor for Hardy is the germination of the seed which then grows and develops into a plant. But **in this seemingly desolate place, the very essence of life is absent**: 'The ancient pulse of germ and birth/Was shrunken hard and dry'. The downward spiralling lines, 'And every spirit upon earth/Seemed fervourless as I' increase the despondent mood, suggesting that all energy and vigour has been sapped. Hardy is melodramatically portraying the landscape as populated by the living dead, 'spirit'. In this disconsolate world, the traditional comforts of religion seem to have been lost forever.

The phrase, 'All at once', heralds a sudden change of mood and a quickening of pace in **stanza three**. A bird is suddenly heard singing: 'a voice arose'. The 'joy illimited' **thrush's song contrasts sharply with Hardy's listless mood**. Unexpectedly, the bird is described in precise terms as 'frail, gaunt, and small'. It also suffers amid the harsh winter surroundings, 'In blast-beruffled plume'. However, unlike the weary poet, this plucky creature has chosen to 'fling' its song into the air. The spontaneous verb captures the thrush's energetic abandon. Despite the 'growing gloom' and encompassing darkness, the small, ragged bird defiantly perseveres.

Run-on lines gather momentum in the **fourth stanza** suggesting Hardy's bewilderment at the bird's action, 'So little cause'. The upbeat language – 'carolings' and 'ecstatic' – implies religious fervour, something that would appear to be denied to those who do not contemplate anything beyond the 'terrestrial'. So if the source of the thrush's joy is not found on earth, where else might it come from? Surprisingly, the thrush seems to be expressing what is within the human spirit, 'Some blessed Hope'. Its singing immediately lightens the gloom which is now transformed to 'happy good-night air'. In contrast to the poet who was 'unaware', the bird instinctively knew that spring returns after winter and that regeneration is possible. Perhaps Hardy's intellectual wisdom has misled him and he is incapable of understanding this. He had already abandoned belief in God and viewed life as being of little consequence when set against the vast expanse of time and the universe. Can the poet now leave behind his fatalistic attitude and gain access to the hope which sustains the little bird?

The **tone of this well-crafted transitional poem is solemn, almost hymn-like**. Hardy had a great love for Anglican church services. His spare, hard diction emphasises both the frozen landscape and his own melancholy. The constant conventional rhythm reflects the continuum of the pulse of life. There is a clear sense of the regular sequence of nature, the rollover of the seasons, life followed by death. The traditional lilting movement is paralleled by the conventional structure of the poem, four stanzas of eight lines and a standard rhyme scheme. This comforting sound clashes with the subject matter and mood. The poet is reliving his private encounter with the thrush throughout this downcast reflection. Despite himself, he is greatly impressed by the thrush's determination to sing, even though there are good reasons to stay quiet. Hope emerges out of the long bitter struggle with darkness. Is the thrush a celebration of new birth and new beginnings? Or is such happiness always beyond the reach of human comprehension?

ANALYSIS

'The dominant emotion in Hardy is sadness.' To what extent is this true of 'The Darkling Thrush'? Refer to the poem in your answer.

Sample Paragraph

At the start of 'The Darkling Thrush', the heavy-hearted poet stands in the gathering gloom of the turn of the century's last day in a land gripped by ice, 'When Frost was spectre-gray'. Hardy's typically melancholy mood is intensified with dramatic images of death, 'Century's corpse', 'crypt', 'death-lament'. The harsh 'c' and 'k' sounds in the first two stanzas ('weakening', 'cloudy canopy') impersonate the brittle land as it cracks under the weight of ice and frost. All is filled with sadness. Even the little bird who is a symbol of 'Some blessed Hope' is 'frail, 'gaunt, and small'. The short monosyllabic words emphasise the bird's bedraggled appearance. But hope is being swamped by the enveloping darkness, vividly captured in the alliterative phrase, 'growing gloom'. The conclusion of the poem is downcast as the poet admits he was 'unaware' of any hope. My initial impression was that Hardy could never understand the 'joy' of the thrush as he kept trying to work out why the little bird should sing, 'So little cause'. The dark conclusion of the poem reminds me of the ending of 'During Wind and Rain' where 'Down their carved names the raindrop ploughs'. Hardy's fatalistic attitude prevails!

Examiner's Comment

A very well-written paragraph which addresses the question directly. Suitable quotations are handled effectively throughout and the cross-reference to 'During Wind and Rain' is impressive. There is also some good personal interaction. Grade A.

CLASS/HOMEWORK EXERCISES

1. In your opinion, what is the central theme or message in 'The Darkling Thrush'? Refer closely to the poem in your response.

2. Copy the table below into your own notes and fill in critical comments about the last two quotations.

Key Quotes

When Frost was spectre-gray	Hardy's personification of the frost creates a vivid picture of a ghost-like figure. English poets traditionally used a capital letter for seasons and nature. Hardy liked the old ways and tradition.
And Winter's dregs made desolate/ The weakening eye of day	The emphatic alliteration of the letter 'd' reinforces the sharp wintry scene with its gloomy weather. Even the sun is depicted as a sick eye.
And every spirit upon the earth/ Seemed fervourless as I	
An aged thrush, frail, gaunt, and small,/In blast-beruffled plume	

3 THE SELF-UNSEEING

Here is the ancient floor,
Footworn and hollowed and thin,
Here was the former door
Where the dead feet walked in.

She sat here in her chair,   5
Smiling into the fire;
He who played stood there,
Bowing it higher and higher.

Childlike, I danced in a dream;
Blessings emblazoned that day;   10
Everything glowed with a gleam;
Yet we were looking away!

'Everything glowed with a gleam'

EXPLORATIONS

1. What does the poem's title, 'The Self-Unseeing', suggest to you? Refer closely to the text in your answer.

2. How would you describe the mood in each of the three stanzas? Comment on how Hardy achieves particular moods.

3. What do you understand by the final line, 'Yet we were looking away!'?

STUDY NOTES

'The Self-Unseeing' examines the idea that we can never appreciate the present, except in retrospect – when it's too late. This poem was written in 1898, after a visit by the poet to his childhood home. Thomas Hardy's father had died in 1892. This memory poem juxtaposes present and past, at the moment of remembering. Hardy once wrote: 'The business of the writer is to show the sorriness underlying the grandest of things'. He believed that the transient happiness of life gives way to sorrow.

In **stanza one**, the poet observes his childhood home which he describes in detail. Its 'ancient floor' is now 'Foot-worn and hollowed and thin'. The reader's viewpoint is brought to child-level, and the simple rhyme scheme echoes a child's lilting voice. Hardy manages to evoke both the past ('Here was') and the present ('Here is') simultaneously. Looking back down the years, he notes that the room has changed: 'the former door' is now gone. From the outset, the **tone is wistful and reflective**, as if Hardy is close to being overwhelmed with feelings of loss. Into this austere setting comes the recollection of the 'dead feet' of previous generations who once lived there.

The coldness of stanza one gives way to a dramatic flashback in **stanza two**. The tone is much more uplifting as Hardy recalls the warmth and high spirits (presumably of his parents or close friends) in happier times. In presenting his tableau of this cherished moment, **the poet emphasises commonplace details**. A woman stares 'into the fire' while a man plays the violin. The intensity of the memory is strengthened by the repetitious sound of the musician's 'bowing' as the sound rises 'higher and higher'.

In **stanza three**, Hardy has regressed into childhood. The alliteration 'danced in a dream' transports the reader into the energetic memory of the child poet. The overwhelming beauty of that time is caught by the line, 'Blessings emblazoned the day'. For Hardy, the experience was illuminated with a dreamlike serenity. The explosive letter 'b' and broad vowels slow the line so the reader can savour the moment with the poet. The past now seems to glow 'with a gleam'. The dynamic words, 'danced', 'emblazoned', 'glowed' mirror the dizzying motion of the dancing child. However, the last line, ('Yet we were looking away!') signals a regretful note which counteracts the nostalgic tone. **The poet's final comment has a universal relevance**: people do not appreciate life's simple joys until they have slipped away.

Thomas Hardy was a significant influence on many other poets, including Robert Frost and W. B. Yeats. Another admirer, Philip Larkin, felt that **he made the everyday details of his life the basis for tough unsparing poems**. At eighty-six Hardy wrote a poem entitled, 'He Never Expected Much'; 'Well world, you have kept faith with me,/Kept faith with me.../Never, I own, expected I/That life would all be fair'.

ANALYSIS

Hardy has been described as 'The author who loves the art of concealing art'. Discuss this statement in relation to 'The Self-Unseeing'. Refer closely to the poem in your exploration.

Sample Paragraph

In 'The Self-Unseeing', a complex theme, the duality of time, past and present, is caught in the one instant. Hardy is observing his younger self in a magic moment from his past family life, 'Childlike I danced in a dream'. He is mourning the reality that unawareness means the moment's importance is lost: 'Yet we were looking away'. The viewpoint is that of a child and the young voice is caught as he points out 'Here is', 'Here was', 'She sat here', 'He… stood there'. The poem's regular rhyme scheme has the rise and fall of a nursery rhyme. The beauty of that special day is marked by alliteration ('danced', 'dream'; 'glowed', 'gleam'). A typical youthful excitement is shown by the repetition of 'higher and higher' as Hardy recalls his father playing his violin in this happy family scene. The childish, simple diction sums up the sad truth that parts of Hardy's life have slipped by too quickly, 'we were looking away!' The exclamation mark at the poem's conclusion underpins his disappointment. In the simplest of reflective poems, Hardy has quietly demonstrated that people tend to take for granted the happiest moments of their lives. Here is a poet who understood the art of concealing art.

Examiner's Comment

This is a very competent response to a challenging question. The paragraph shows a good knowledge of the poem and a clear appreciation of Hardy's deceptively simple writing skill. References and quotations are carefully chosen and used effectively. Grade A.

CLASS/HOMEWORK EXERCISES

1. 'Hardy's poetry is often autobiographical, but it is never without universal significance.' Discuss this view with close reference to 'The Self-Unseeing'.

2. Copy the table below into your own notes and fill in critical comments about the last two quotations.

Key Quotes

Footworn and hollowed and thin	Hardy's detailed description of the floor clearly focuses the reader's attention on the ravages of time. The slender vowel in the adjective 'thin' emphasises a lack of substance.
Here was the former door	The use of the past tense and the adjective 'former' gently moves the reader from the present condition of the house to its previous state.
Childlike, I danced in a dream	
Blessings emblazoned that day	

4 CHANNEL FIRING

That night your great guns, unawares,
Shook all our coffins as we lay,
And broke the chancel window-squares,
We thought it was the Judgement-day

And sat upright. While drearisome   5
Arose the howl of wakened hounds:
The mouse let fall the altar-crumb,
The worms drew back into the mounds,

The glebe cow drooled. Till God called, 'No;
It's gunnery practice out at sea   10
Just as before you went below;
The world is as it used to be:

'All nations striving strong to make
Red war yet redder. Mad as hatters
They do no more for Christés sake   15
Than you who are helpless in such matters.

'That this is not the judgement-hour
For some of them's a blessed thing,
For if it were they'd have to scour
Hell's floor for so much threatening...   20

'Ha, ha. It will be warmer when
I blow the trumpet (if indeed
I ever do; for you are men,
And rest eternal sorely need).'

So down we lay again. 'I wonder,   25
Will the world ever saner be,'
Said one, 'than when He sent us under
In our indifferent century!'

And many a skeleton shook his head.
'Instead of preaching forty year,'   30
My neighbour Parson Thirdly said,
'I wish I had stuck to pipes and beer.'

Again the guns disturbed the hour,
Roaring their readiness to avenge,
As far inland as Stourton Tower,   35
And Camelot, and starlit Stonehenge.

April 1914

'Again the guns disturbed the hour,/Roaring their readiness to avenge'

GLOSSARY

'Channel Firing' refers to a military exercise in the English Channel, when British battleships engaged in gunnery practice shortly before the First World War.

3   *chancel*: space surrounding a church altar enclosed by railing or lattice.

4   *Judgement-day*: the dead are awakened and God judges who will go to heaven or hell for all eternity.

5   *drearisome*: monotonous, depressing.

7   *altar-crumb*: small piece of consecrated bread.

9   *glebe-cow*: cow grazing on parish land.

14 *Red war*: according to the Bible, one of the four horses of the Apocalypse (the destruction of the world) was red.

15 *Christés*: Christ's (Hardy uses the old-fashioned possessive form)

19 *scour*: cleanse, burnish.

21 *Ha, ha*: God's mocking tone, according to the Book of Job.

28 *indifferent*: unconcerned, apathetic.

35 *Stourton Tower*: a tower erected to the memory of Alfred the Great who repelled the Danes.

36 *Camelot*: mythical name of King Arthur's court.

36 *Stonehenge*: pre-historic monument which was thought to have been a place of worship for the Druids.

EXPLORATIONS

1. How does the poet use humour to make serious points about his fear of war? Refer closely to the poem in your response.

2. Sound is an important feature in this poem. Choose one sound, image (or aural effect) which you find particularly interesting. Briefly explain your choice.

3. Would you consider this a pessimistic poem? Is it showing us man's progress or his lack of progress? Refer to the text in your answer.

STUDY NOTES

'Channel Firing' was written shortly before the outbreak of World War One when gunnery practice in the English Channel was being undertaken by the navy. In his bitterly humorous poem, Hardy presents this event as a dramatic dialogue, an imagined conversation between two unidentified dead people, God, and a country parson. The poet believed strongly that warfare was both brutal and irrational. Here, an incensed God echoes this outlook, branding war-mongering humans 'Mad as hatters' (an oblique reference to the chaotic world of Alice in Wonderland). In an unusually derisive way, Hardy's poem mockingly uses death to symbolise the uselessness of war.

The poem opens with a sharp, accusatory tone as Hardy imagines a dead person complaining that the deceased are being awoken by the sound of these powerful naval guns. The speaker makes the mistake of thinking that it is an act of God, 'Judgement-day'. The **dark, irreverent humour of this haunting Gothic image** dominates **stanza one**. Alliteration emphasises the thunderous sound of gunfire. Hardy suggests the military's heedless approach to the consequences of their actions. Even the beautiful windowpanes of the church are smashed by the heavy reverberations of the 'great guns'. The growing confusion is mirrored in the form of the poem as the first stanza rushes into **stanza two**.

Amid the continuing upheaval, the animal world is also disturbed. The polysyllabic 'drearisome' and broad vowel effects of the line, 'Arose the howl of wakened hounds', convey the monotonous barking of the startled dogs. The mouse, usually a symbol of decay and destruction, lets fall an 'altar-crumb', while the worms retreat underground. Hardy's choice of the onomatopoeic verb 'drooled' (**stanza three**) vividly records the action of the unsettled glebe-cow dribbling and perplexed. An exasperated God suddenly appears and delivers his abrupt explanation, 'No;/It's gunnery practice out at sea'. He then scathingly observes that just as war has occurred before the dead passed on, so it continues: 'The world is as it used to be'. **God's voice then reflects on Europe's political divisions where countries try to outdo one another in more efficient methods of deadly destruction**, 'All nations striving strong to make/Red war yet redder'. The alliterative phrasing and dramatic colour imagery illustrate man's furious efforts to cause deadly destruction. Readers are left in no doubt about Hardy's gloominess regarding the future of the power-crazed human race, 'Mad as hatters'.

God's words continue to be heard throughout **stanzas five** and **six**. He observes that those responsible for warfare are fortunate that it is not 'judgement-hour' because they would all be punished severely. Indeed, they would have to 'scour/Hell's floor', a fitting place for violent men. This cynical God admits that his judgement day is 'warmer when/I blow the trumpet'. But he seems uncertain about how to deal with the masters of war, and wonders if they might be better left to rest in their graves for all eternity: 'for you are men,/And rest eternal sorely need'. **Hardy's portrayal of God is curious**. The Biblical image of the blowing of the trumpet that signals the end of time seems rather surreal. The poet is obviously condemning man's wickedness. But is he also criticising ineffective Christianity as something which does not deserve to be taken seriously? (Hardy had rejected his own childhood faith.)

Having listened to these bleak pronouncements, the unnamed dead return to their graves and resignedly 'lay again' (**stanza seven**) before voicing their own opinions about the gunnery exercise. One of them wonders if man will ever achieve sanity (by rejecting armed conflict). The speaker's reference to the 'indifferent' 20th century typifies **Hardy's underlying frustration with both God and humanity**. In **stanza eight**, the voice of an ineffectual clergyman is introduced as Parson Thirdly laments his 'preaching forty year' and wishes he had spent his life 'stuck to pipes and beer'. Again, the poet is suggesting that the Christian Church has failed in ridding man of his violent desires.

The poem's pessimistic tone continues into its **concluding stanza** which is focused on the endless human desire for conflict. All the surreal humour is now replaced by Hardy's emphasis on the resounding naval guns, 'Roaring their readiness to avenge'. Their alarming sound transcends time and place, reaching back to 'Stourton Tower', 'Camelot' and 'starlit Stonehenge'. Ironically, these three historic places represent people who were defeated by a succeeding conflict, reinforcing the poet's warnings about any future wars. **Hardy's historical perspective hammers home his message that nations do not learn from the past, and that all civilisations only last for a limited period**. In expressing the dark foreshadowing of the months leading up to the Great War, the poem's poignant conclusion is reflected in the place-names' broad assonance which dominate the final lines, suggesting that mankind will never make any moral advance. Instead, preoccupied with the senseless pursuit of conflict, man fails to notice the cool, calm beauty of 'starlit Stonehenge'.

ANALYSIS

'Hardy's war poetry is characterised by fatalistic pessimism and earthly realism.' Discuss this statement in relation to the poems of Thomas Hardy on your course. Quote carefully to illustrate your response.

Sample Paragraph

I agree that much of Hardy's poetry has a morose depressing quality, especially in the searing anti-war poem, 'Drummer Hodge', where innocence is sacrificed to the war-machine. But Hardy manages to incorporate a dry, mocking tone and a macabre sense of humour which shows the poet is well-rooted in reality, as even the bleakest scene can be borne better with a wry smile. The opening of 'Channel Firing', for example, is gruesomely comic as skeletons sit bolt upright, woken by guns firing in the English Channel in 1914. This ludicrous scene continues, almost like a cartoon, as dogs bay and cows dribble, 'The glebe-cow drooled'. All were disturbed from their normal routine by the preparations for war. God is portrayed as a scornful school principal thinking up even more extreme punishments for his unruly students. He wonders if he might skip Judgement Day altogether and let troublesome sinners sleep in their graves forever. Even the clergyman wishes he had not wasted his life 'preaching forty year', but had spent his life 'stuck to pipes and beer'. This tongue-in-cheek approach shows a poet who really understands people's true nature, life's cruel fortunes and the unknowable will of God. Hardy is truly aware that man has learnt nothing from history as the roll call of ancient monuments in the final stanza illustrates, 'Stourton Tower', 'Camelot', 'starlit Stonehenge'. So, in my opinion, Thomas Hardy is a poet who is characterised by his use of black humour when discussing humanity and life, rather than sunk beneath the weight of fatalistic pessimism.

Examiner's Comment

This A-grade personal response succeeds in addressing both aspects of the discussion effectively. There is a controlled, confident approach throughout, and the accurate references to two of Hardy's war poems work very well in examining the poet's attitudes to war.

CLASS/HOMEWORK EXERCISES

1. 'Hardy's poetry has a tragic vision, a sense that life has to be endured.' Do you agree or disagree with this statement? Support your opinions with careful quotation from the poems by Hardy on your course.

2. Copy the table below into your own notes and fill in critical comments about the last two quotations.

Key Quotes

Shook all our coffins as we lay	Hardy imagines the dead complaining that the great reverberations from the gunnery practice in the Channel have disturbed their rest. The hard 'k' sound mimics the movement.
Mad as hatters	The poet presents God's comment in a droll, comic way. But the humour has a serious purpose – to highlight the foolishness of people in choosing not to follow Christian teaching.
It will be warmer when/I blow the trumpet	
Roaring their readiness to avenge	

5

THE CONVERGENCE OF THE TWAIN

(LINES ON THE LOSS OF THE 'TITANIC')

1
In a solitude of the sea
Deep from human vanity,
And the Pride of Life that planned her, stilly couches she.

2
Steel chambers, late the pyres
Of her salamandrine fires,   5
Cold currents thrid, and turn to rhythmic tidal lyres.

3
Over the mirrors meant
To glass the opulent
The sea-worm crawls – grotesque, slimed, dumb, indifferent.

4
Jewels in joy designed   10
To ravish the sensuous mind
Lie lightless, all their sparkles bleared and black and blind.

5
Dim moon-eyed fishes near
Gaze at the gilded gear
And query: 'What does this vaingloriousness down here?'   15

6
Well: while was fashioning
This creature of cleaving wing,
The Immanent Will that stirs and urges everything

7
Prepared a sinister mate
For her – so gaily great –   20
A Shape of Ice, for the time far and dissociate.

8
And as the smart ship grew
In stature, grace, and hue,
In shadowy silent distance grew the Iceberg too.

9
Alien they seemed to be: 25
No mortal eye could see
The intimate welding of their later history,

10
Or sign that they were bent
By paths coincident
On being anon twin halves of one august event,   30

11
Till the Spinner of the Years
Said 'Now!' And each one hears,
And consummation comes, and jars two hemispheres.

'By paths coincident/On being anon twin halves of one august event'

GLOSSARY

Convergence: Meeting, coming together.
Twain: two
Titanic: gigantic, all-powerful. It was also the name of the famous passenger ship that struck an iceberg in the North Atlantic on her maiden voyage and sank on 15 April 1912.

3 *stilly*: calmly.

3 *couches*: lies.

4 *pyres*: material burning in heaps; ritual cremations.

5 *salamandrine*: referring to a mythical lizard-like creature said to live in fire; also to the furnaces which powered the ship.

6 *thrid*: pick a way through; a vibrating noise produced by engines.

6 *lyres*: musical instruments similar to small harps.

8 *glass the opulent*: show the reflections of wealthy passengers.

11 *ravish*: overwhelm.

12 *bleared*: blurred, indistinct.

15 *vaingloriousness*: excessive vanity, boastfulness.

17 *cleaving wing*: motion of the ship's prow (forward part) dividing the sea.

18 *Immanent Will*: most powerful force of nature, fate, God.

19 *sinister*: ominous, evil.

21 *dissociate*: disconnected, separate.

23 *hue*: type, appearance.

30 *anon*: soon.

30 *august*: impressive, admirable.

31 *Spinner of the Years*: God, fate, underlying force of the universe.

33 *consummation*: satisfactory completion; transaction.

33 *jars*: challenges, strikes against.

EXPLORATIONS

1. How does Hardy describe the present state of the decaying Titanic? Support your response with suitable reference to the poem.

2. Why, in your opinion, does the poet concentrate on the ship, rather than on the tragic loss of human life? Refer closely to the text in your answer.

3. How would you describe the concluding mood of the poem? Is it pessimistic, fatalistic, realistic, full of moral conviction, etc? Refer to the text in support of your view.

The Titanic was once the pride of marine craftsmanship, but on its maiden voyage, it struck an iceberg at 2.20 am on 15 April 1912 and sank three hours later. More than 1500 people lost their lives. This great ship was believed to be unsinkable, and consequently the management did not provide sufficient lifeboats. 'The Convergence of the Twain' focuses on the devastation brought about by human excess and hubris. Hardy's poem illustrates the sometimes cruel fate that awaits those who glorify material objects. Although he was personally acquainted with some of the victims, the poet does not mourn the dead, but concentrates on the passionate encounter between ship and iceberg.

The **opening stanzas** of this tightly rhymed poem **contrast the dazzling display of the Titanic as the most colossal moving object of its time with the corroded ship** on the ocean floor, 'stilly couches she'. The vessel is personified, following the naval tradition of referring to ships as female. She was once a symbol of human strength and capability, 'the Pride of Life that planned her'. This is a Biblical reference, 'For all that is in the world... the pride of life is not of the Father, but is of the world'. Although he usually reserved capital letters for nature's elemental forces, Hardy now uses capitals to refer to those who built this glorious liner. Is he suggesting that man is daring to regard himself as an equal to nature? His coldly moralistic tone criticises the stupidity of human presumption as he invites us to observe the motionless wreck's empty chambers.

Stanza two details these 'Steel chambers' of the ship throbbing with the power of the furnaces ('pyres'). Now that they are extinguished, it is the 'Cold currents' which sound ('thrid') as the sea plays its 'tidal lyres'. Ironically, the ocean has made the Titanic an ugly sight. Slimy invertebrates crawl over the mirrors which previously flattered those privileged passengers. Hardy's grotesque imagery emphasises the foolishness of human self-delusion in challenging fate and coincidence by believing that any ship was unsinkable. In the dark undersea world, jewels are worthless – 'Lie lightless'. Their sparkle is now extinguished, aptly described by the alliterative phrase, 'bleared and black and blind'. Instead, 'Dim moon-eyed fishes near/Gaze at the gilded gear', prompting the question: 'What does this vaingloriousness down here?' **Hardy is not mourning the lost passengers, but is mocking their self-satisfied arrogance** as their lavish possessions are without value on the sea floor.

The poem changes direction on the conversational expression, 'Well'. The focus moves from the present state of the wrecked liner to an exploration in **stanzas 6–11** of how the Titanic came to be lost. While man built his proud ship, nature was fashioning her nemesis, 'A Shape of Ice', in the distance, 'far and dissociate'. **Stanza 6** runs into **stanza 7** mirroring the unstoppable might of Fate 'that stirs and urges everything' as it fashions 'a sinister mate/For her'. The ponderous alliteration and assonance ('so gaily great') mimics the stately motion of the great ship as it moves through the sea with 'cleaving wing'. Hardy accentuates the point that hidden destinies frustrate man's intentions, 'the smart ship grew/In stature, grace, and hue'. Unfortunately, humans have no control over their destiny: 'No mortal eye could see' what was about to happen when the two forces (ship and iceberg) would meet – 'The Convergence of the Twain'. For the poet, this tragic encounter is a 'welding', a reference to the engineering work on the ship, and also the seamless bonding of two opposites.

In Hardy's view, this frightening union ('august event') is inevitable – 'they were bent/By paths coincident' (**stanza 10**). The beautiful Titanic is like a bedecked bride, a victim set on a course of blind vanity. Fate emphatically declares 'Now!' and each, ship and iceberg, 'hears' the command. They are the epitome of all-consuming love, but the unstoppable force meeting the immovable object results in devastation. Two 'hemispheres', the continents of America and Europe, are united in tragedy as the great ship collides with the wonderful natural phenomenon, ice. **Hardy's didactic poem shows man his true place in the universe**. Fate reigns supreme. Man ignores the 'Spinner of the Years' at his peril.

Throughout the poem, alliteration, ('gilded gear', 'gaily great', 'mirrors meant', 'Jewels in joy') suggests the decadent atmosphere aboard ship. Hardy also uses repetition of sound to show this world destroyed ('solitude of the sea', 'consummation comes'). Nature's power supersedes man's efforts. The eleven stanzas indicate an unfinished work, just as the Titanic's maiden voyage was cut short. The three-line shape of each stanza can be seen as mimicking the view of a vessel at sea (two short lines followed by an extended third line). Onomatopoeia allows readers to experience the cold, ugly world of the shipwreck where 'The sea-worm crawls'. The rhythm changes at the poem's conclusion as short punctuated phrases copy the abrupt halting of the ship, 'And consummation comes, and jars two hemispheres' (**stanza 11**). While Hardy's final lines present a salutary **picture of predestination and cosmic indifference**, we are left to decide about our own views about the Titanic disaster and similar catastrophes.

ANALYSIS

Hardy once said, 'Fear is the mother of foresight'. Discuss this statement in relation to 'The Convergence of the Twain'. Refer to the poem in your response.

Sample Paragraph

In my opinion, Thomas Hardy shows in his poem, 'The Convergence of the Twain', that if man does not fear, if he chooses to be over-confident and challenge Fate ('And the Pride of Life that planned her') then Fate ('The Immanent Will') comes into play. The engineers were not afraid as they built their huge ship. The Titanic was going to be a 'smart ship' great in 'stature, grace, and hue'. They lacked foresight, 'No mortal eye could see'. They did not take into account the chance encounters of life, 'paths coincident'. The management company was so confident that it did not provide adequate life-boats for the ship; it was unthinkable that it would ever sink. The rich passengers in jewels designed to 'ravish the sensuous mind' never thought for a moment that sea-worms would be crawling over the mirrors which had reflected them. All lacked the foresight that Fate, the 'Spinner of the Years', calls time, 'Now!' everything changes in an instant, 'jars two hemispheres'. Simon Armitage, the English poet, wrote a poem with the same title which was read at a memorial service for the September 11 victims. Man's hubris is also shown in how the twin towers were viewed as indestructible. Armitage, unlike Hardy, focuses on mourning the victims, 'shop windows are prepared/with faces of the disappeared'. Both poems show the recklessness of man's arrogance in assuming that he has control over his destiny... 'And consummation comes'. Man, be afraid!

Examiner's Comment

A very well focused response showing clear understanding of the poem. Suitable quotations support discussion points effectively. The brief cross-reference to the Simon Armitage poem adds further interest and enhances the personal engagement with Hardy's views. Grade A.

CLASS/HOMEWORK EXERCISES

1. 'Cruelty is the law pervading nature and society.' Would you agree or/and disagree that this is the view of Thomas Hardy in 'The Convergence of the Twain'? Refer closely to the poem in your answer.

2. Copy the table below into your own notes and fill in critical comments about the last two quotations.

Key Quotes

late the pyres/Of her salamandrine fires	Hardy describes the furnace fires of the ship as funeral pyres where a force of nature, such as the salamander lizard, could survive – unlike man. Sibilant 's' effects echo the fire's hissing sounds.
slimed, dumb, indifferent	The sea-worm is described as grotesque, stupid and uncaring of its appearance – in contrast to the Titanic's affluent passengers who were well dressed, smart and cared about out-doing one another.
Alien they seemed to be	
On being anon twin halves of one august event	

WHEN I SET OUT FOR LYONNESSE

When I set out for Lyonnesse,
A hundred miles away,
The rime was on the spray,
And starlight lit my lonesomeness
When I set out for Lyonnesse   5
A hundred miles away.

What would bechance at Lyonnesse
While I should sojourn there
No prophet durst declare,
Nor did the wisest wizard guess   10
What would bechance at Lyonnesse
While I should sojourn there.

When I came back from Lyonnesse
With magic in my eyes,
All marked with mute surmise   15
My radiance rare and fathomless,
When I came back from Lyonnesse
With magic in my eyes!

'What would bechance at Lyonnesse'

GLOSSARY

1   *Lyonnesse*: the legendary home of King Arthur and his wizard, Merlin. It was also the name of the house belonging to Hardy's first wife.
3   *rime*: white frost which forms on plants as dew freezes.
3   *spray*: branch or shoot of a plant.

7   *bechance*: happen.
8   *sojourn*: stay for a short while.
9   *durst*: dared.
15 *mute surmise*: silent wonder.
16 *radiance*: delight.
16 *fathomless*: deep.

EXPLORATIONS

1. Choose one image from the poem that you found particularly interesting and effective. Briefly explain your choice.

2. 'With magic in my eyes.' How does Hardy convey 'magic' and wonder to the reader? Refer closely to the text in your answer.

3. Write your own personal response to the poem.

STUDY NOTES

Thomas Hardy wrote to a friend, '"When I set out for Lyonnesse" was exactly what happened forty four years ago'. Shortly after Hardy's first wife, Emma Gifford, died, the poet found two manuscripts belonging to her. In one, she criticised his behaviour towards her. They had been married for thirty-eight years, unhappily. The other manuscript described her youth up until she met and became engaged to Hardy. Everything about the meeting had been magical. This poem, with its fairy-tale atmosphere, reveals their love as a beautiful fantasy.

In **stanza one**, the poet recalls a journey he made. There is a sense of reluctance to travel such a long distance, 'A hundred miles away'. He eventually went to St Juliot in Cornwall to advise on repairs to a local church. It was there that Hardy met the rector's sister-in-law, Emma Gifford, and very soon they had fallen in love. Lyonnesse was the name of Emma's home, and also the name of the mythical kingdom of King Arthur and his knights. Is Lyonnesse also a metaphor for the enchantment of first love? Remarkably, the poet was able to capture **the vivid feeling of magic from that journey** as if memory had enriched the emotion in his own mind. The bewitching setting (a still night of 'starlight') matches Hardy's traditional ballad style. As he sets out at dawn for the mythical land of Lyonnesse, the young poet is full of 'lonesomeness'. Is he seeking love and adventure? A mood of dreamy romanticism is reinforced by the repeated sibilant 's' and gentle 'l' sounds, 'And starlight lit my lonesomeness'. The first two lines of the stanza are repeated at its conclusion suggesting a mantra, the making of a spell. Overall, a sweet, lyrical tone captures the excitement and optimism of youthful love.

Stanza two is filled with wonder. Hardy uses archaic language ('bechance', 'sojourn', 'durst') to create another time and place. Is he now living in an enchanted world? The euphoric emotion of the early stages of his relationship with Emma is palpable, 'What would bechance at Lyonnesse/While I should sojourn there?' Simple childlike language suggests his anticipation and astonishment. Recurring alliterative phrases ('should sojourn', 'durst declare') add to the dreamlike quality of this extraordinary experience. Hardy effortlessly slips into the style of fantastic fairy-tales to emphasise that no-one could have foretold what was about to happen, not even the 'wisest wizard' (who was Merlin the magician at King Arthur's court). Is the poet implying that the couple's young love was merely infatuation (a heightened state of fascination) rather than true feeling? Readers are left guessing about the nature of their relationship. This, of course, makes their love all the more mysterious – and universally appealing.

The focus is on Hardy's return journey in **stanza three**. The evocative image, 'With magic in my eyes', **delightfully describes his dramatic transformation**. Personal pronouns ('I' and 'my') emphasise the self-satisfaction of someone in love. The glow of passion is noticed by all who 'surmise' the reason for this sudden change. His 'radiance' is special ('rare') and incapable of being measured ('fathomless'). This truly magical experience has completely changed Hardy. Repetition is used to capture his otherworldly state. The poem is framed within the opening line, 'When I set out for Lyonnesse' and the mirrored conclusion, 'When I came back from Lyonnesse', as though a mythical journey has taken place. The regular rhyme scheme and steady rhythm (four strong beats alternating with three) provide the musicality of a ballad. But regardless of all the breathless joy, there is an underlying poignancy which leaves several questions unanswered. Is youthful romance transient and capable of destruction? Or is love permanent, because the memory, especially of first love, lingers forever? Hardy once wrote: 'I have a faculty... for burying an emotion in heart or brain for forty years, and exhuming it at the end of that time as fresh as when interred.'

ANALYSIS

'As a poet, Hardy can articulate emotions of which everyone has experience or knowledge.' Discuss this statement in relation to 'When I Set Out for Lyonnesse', referring closely to the poem.

Sample Paragraph

I think Hardy has effectively expressed the overwhelming emotions of first love, a universal experience, in his poem, 'When I Set Out for Lyonnesse'. He suggests the mystery and romance which young lovers experience. But he also omits background details and only gives readers a glimpse the emotional drama of first love. The wonder of the event is caught in the phrase, 'What should bechance'. I can imagine the poet marvelling at the unexpected sensation of first love. The cold, loneliness of the person who has not experienced true love is caught in the atmospheric image, 'The rime was on the spray'. The last stanza expresses the dramatic change that young love brings. Everyone notices the transformation but no-one openly comments. I think this describes exactly how everyone celebrates romantic love. When the poet uses archaic words like 'sojourn', 'durst', this places the poem outside of time so that readers can relate to the spell cast by love. The fairy-tale quality is increased by the simple childlike references and alliteration, 'durst dare' and 'wisest wizard'. All of us can share in the poet's delight as he repeats 'Lyonnesse' six times over the course of the poem. It reminds me of a love-sick student frantically scribbling that one special name on every schoolbook! Hardy, through his omissions, his tone of delight, his use of archaic words and emphatic repetition, allows the reader to share his astonishment and pleasure at being in love for the very first time.

Examiner's Comment

This is a good, solid response which addresses the question directly by focusing on the poem's universal significance. Effective use is made of reference and quotation. A little more discussion of Hardy's positive tone might have been included. There is also some sense of personal engagement. Grade B.

CLASS/HOMEWORK EXERCISES

1. 'Hardy is a poet who is out-of-date and hard to understand.' Discuss this view in relation to the poem, 'When I Set Out for Lyonnesse', using quotation to support your response.

2. Copy the table below into your own notes and fill in critical comments about the last two quotations.

Key Quotes

The rime was on the spray	The poet is describing not only the frosty morning, but also suggesting the isolation of anyone who has not yet experienced true love.
Nor did the wisest wizard guess	This is a reference to Merlin the magician who lived at King Arthur's court. The alliteration and sibilant sounds add to the sense of an elusive fantasy tale.
While I should sojourn there	
All marked with mute surmise	

7   UNDER THE WATERFALL

'Whenever I plunge my arm, like this,
In a basin of water, I never miss
The sweet sharp sense of a fugitive day
Fetched back from its thickening shroud of gray.
      Hence the only prime   5
      And real love-rhyme
      That I know by heart,
      And that leaves no smart,
Is the purl of a little valley fall
About three spans wide and two spans tall   10
Over a table of solid rock,
And into a scoop of the self-same block;
The purl of a runlet that never ceases
In stir of kingdoms, in wars, in peaces;
With a hollow boiling voice it speaks   15
And has spoken since hills were turfless peaks.'

'And why gives this the only prime
Idea to you of a real love-rhyme?
And why does plunging your arm in a bowl
Full of spring water, bring throbs to your soul?'   20

'Well, under the fall, in a crease of stone,
Though where precisely none has ever known,
Jammed darkly, nothing to show how prized,
And by now with its smoothness opalized,
      Is a drinking glass: 25
      For, down that pass
      My lover and I
      Walked under a sky
Of blue with a leaf-wove awning of green,
In the burn of August, to paint the scene,   30
And we placed our basket of fruit and wine
 By the runlet's rim, where we sat to dine;
And when we had drunk from the glass together,
Arched by the oak-copse from the weather,
I held the vessel to rinse in the fall,   35
Where it slipped, and sank, and was past recall,

Though we stooped and plumbed the little abyss
With long bared arms. There the glass still is.
And, as said, if I thrust my arm below
Cold water in basin or bowl, a throe   40
From the past awakens a sense of that time,
And the glass we used, and the cascade's rhyme.
The basin seems the pool, and its edge
The hard smooth face of the brook-side ledge,
And the leafy pattern of china-ware   45
The hanging plants that were bathing there.

'By night, by day, when it shines or lours,
There lies intact that chalice of ours,
And its presence adds to the rhyme of love
Persistently sung by the fall above.   50
No lip has touched it since his and mine
In turns therefrom sipped lovers' wine.'

'By night, by day, when it shines or lours,/There lies intact that chalice of ours'

GLOSSARY

A–Z

3	*fugitive*: escaped, runaway.	29	*awning*: shelter, cover.
5	*prime*: important, best, top-quality.	37	*plumbed*: explored, searched.
6	*real*: genuine.	37	*abyss*: deep hole, chasm.
8	*smart*: sharp stinging pain.	40	*throe*: spasm, severe pain.
9	*purl*: swirling motion, murmuring sound.	42	*cascade*: small waterfall.
10	*spans*: measurement using outstretched hand.	47	*lours*: sky looks dark or threatening.
13	*runlet*: small fast-running stream.	48	*chalice*: drinking cup; usually associated with Holy Communion.
24	*opalized*: semi-transparent, cloudy colour.	52	*therefrom*: from there.

EXPLORATIONS

1. Thomas Hardy changed the title of this poem from 'The Lost Glass' to 'Under the Waterfall'. Why, in your opinion, did he do this? Which title would you prefer? Give reasons to support your choice.

2. In lines 17–20, another voice enters, questioning why the woman's memory has such a powerful effect on her. To whom do you think this voice belongs? Give reasons for your answer.

3. How does the woman regard the glass in the last stanza? Comment on the use of the words 'chalice' and 'wine' in your response.

STUDY NOTES

'Under the Waterfall' was published in 1914 following the death of Hardy's first wife, Emma. Their relationship had deteriorated and they had been living almost separate lives. The poet found two personal manuscripts among his wife's belongings, one of which referred to a picnic the couple had enjoyed during their early courtship, beside 'a sparkling little brook… in which we lost a tiny picnic-tumbler'. Hardy is best known for poems in which he remembers personal experiences. In this case, he fills the recollection of this little event with the wonderful promise of their early years together.

This **memory poem explores love, its promise and disappointment**. The poet imagines his wife, Emma, recalling a picnic they had enjoyed in 1870, shortly after they had first met. Many of Hardy's poems describe his relationship with Emma from his viewpoint, but here Emma's perspective is predominant. The **opening lines** focus on a mundane act, an arm being immersed in a basin of water. Hardy's use of the present tense ('like this') brings the moment alive. We can even sense a second presence, eagerly listening to the telling of the tale. 'Whenever' suggests a repeated action. Is this special memory continually evoked? The run-on lines and insistent rhyme intensify the overwhelming emotion of the memory for the woman, 'I never miss/The sweet sharp sense of a fugitive day/Fetched back from its thickening shroud of gray'. Although her excited tone is clearly evident, this elusive experience remains buried in the distant past and proves hard to recapture.

The mood changes quite abruptly in line 5. The rhyme becomes childishly playful as if the speaker has reverted to her youth. Line lengths are shorter as four beats give way to two. Carefully-chosen words, such as 'prime' and 'real', suggest that this first dream-like experience of romantic love was truly happy, without any trace of pain or disappointment ('leaves no smart'). But as always with Hardy, a more disturbing sub-text implies that his wife's subsequent experience of love was very different.

Lines 9-16 contain a lengthy descriptive passage conveying the sounds and movements of an idyllic country scene. The photographic detail of the 'little valley fall/About three spans wide and two spans tall' flowing over a 'table of solid rock', gives authenticity to the recollection. **Hardy's onomatopoeic effects in 'The purl of a runlet' echo the lively, murmuring brook**. It is clear that the water continues to flow, regardless of what happens in human affairs, 'never ceases/In stir of kingdoms, in war, in peaces'. The stream's resonant sounds are further conveyed by emphatic assonance: 'With a hollow boiling voice it speaks'.

The description of nature's timeless power is interrupted by a second unnamed voice – presumably the poet himself – in lines **17-20**, inquiring as to why the woman's memory is the only 'real love-rhyme'. The question is immediately followed by another: why does the action of submerging her arm in water 'bring throbs to your soul'?

The response, which begins with a conversational 'Well', makes up the remainder of the poem and recounts how one of the picnic glasses was accidentally dropped into the water whilst being washed 'under the fall'. Mystery surrounded its whereabouts, 'Though where precisely none has ever known' (**line 22**) and its worth remains unrecognised, 'nothing to show how prized'. However, there is a recognition that the glass will have changed, 'with its smoothness opalized', now turning opaque. **Does first love also change and become tainted?**

Again, in **lines 25-28**, the woman's youthful voice re-appears as the jaunty rhythm moves along as carefree as the lovers, 'My lover and I/Walked under a sky'. But it is obvious that the memory has seared her as she recalls, with descriptive richness, the green leaves 'In the burn of August' shading the picnicking lovers with their 'basket of fruit and wine'. She vividly recalls rinsing the glass the lovers had shared, alliteration suggesting the moment when 'it slipped, and sank, and was past recall'. The lovers try to find it – 'Though we stooped and plumbed the little abyss/ With long bared arms' – but are unsuccessful. Their efforts are similar to the poem's initial action, a likely trigger for the memory. Hardy sums up the significance of the lost drinking-glass succinctly: 'There the glass still is'. **Is he saying that the past can never be recovered?** A surreal sequence follows as the woman imagines the floral designs of the basin merging with the pool water, 'The basin seems the pool', an enduring image which emphasises the intensity of the small drama.

In the **concluding lines**, the speaker realises that regardless of the weather, 'when it shines or lours', she is certain that the wine glass 'lies intact'. Because of its association with the couple, it has now become a special – almost sacred – object, 'that chalice of ours', a powerful symbol of their long lost love. It remains untouched since the day of their picnic: 'since his and mine/In turns therefrom sipped lovers' wine'. With the ordinary gesture of plunging her arm into a basin of water, **the woman has preserved this memorable event in defiance of time and life's disappointments**.

'Under the Waterfall' presents readers with a dual perspective as past love is immortalised. While there are many possible interpretations of the poem, most critics assume that Hardy is adopting the voice of his dead wife Emma, having her relay a **beautiful memory of their relationship, in contrast to all their later marital difficulties**. Others see the glass as a metaphor for their love – beyond reach and lost irrevocably. It has also been said that the waterfall is a symbol of ongoing life, a sign that the two lovers will be united in death.

ANALYSIS

'Hardy's love poetry explores transience and loss with tragic scepticism.' To what extent is this true of 'Under the Waterfall'? Support the points you make with reference to the text.

Sample Paragraph

In my opinion, 'Under the Waterfall' is a description of a moment in the Garden of Eden for the two young lovers. The carefree rhythm, 'My lover and I/Walked under a sky' is the romance of which dreams are made. The vivid description of the hot day, 'In the burn of August', the details, 'our basket of fruit and wine' placed near the 'runlet's rim' conjure up an idyllic scene of young love. They 'had drunk from the glass together', a golden scene worthy of any romantic film. However, as with most of Hardy's poetry, the dark clouds soon gather, their 'chalice' becomes 'Jammed darkly' in the 'little abyss'. The drinking glass, their symbol of the promise of love is now lost, as was the poet's relationship with his first wife, Emma. This relationship had begun with such expectation, as we are told in the poem 'When I Set Out for Lyonnesse'. The poet then had had 'magic' in his eyes, he was filled with a 'radiance rare and fathomless'. But life takes its toll and as the woman's voice explains that even a beautiful memory can lie hidden 'in its thickening shroud of gray'. Here is Hardy's tragic scepticism, unflinching in its portrayal of the transience and loss humans endure in life, 'its smoothness opalized'. Hardy's sceptical view of lost love dominates the poem. His underlying mood is bittersweet: 'There the glass still is'. I could detect a deep sense of his personal tragedy at the end of the poem – suggested by the 'sweet sharp sense' of the woman's recollection which is re-awakened every time she plunges her arm, 'like this,/In a basin of water'. Only the memory like 'that chalice' remains 'intact'.

Examiner's Comment

This is a penetrating, personal response which addresses the question directly by examining both content and style. Interesting cross-reference and the effective use of relevant quotations show very good engagement with the poem. The expression is fluent and controlled throughout. Grade A.

CLASS/HOMEWORK EXERCISES

1. 'Thomas Hardy can compose a poem from the smallest events.' Discuss this statement in relation to his poems on your course. Use suitable quotations to support the points you make

2. Copy the table below into your own notes and fill in critical comments about the last two quotations.

Key Quotes

I never miss/The sweet sharp sense of a fugitive day	The past is glorified through the poet's use of sibilance and alliteration which emphasise the sense of loss. All the adjectives suggest a moment of stolen delight.
The purl of a runlet that never ceases	The spiralling pattern of the flowing water is conveyed by the assonance and repetition of the letter 'r'.
Jammed darkly, nothing to show how prized	
under a sky/Of blue with a leaf-wove awning of green	

8   THE OXEN

Christmas Eve, and twelve of the clock.
    'Now they are all on their knees,'
An elder said as we sat in a flock
    By the embers in hearthside ease.

We pictured the meek mild creatures where   5
    They dwelt in their strawy pen,
Nor did it occur to one of us there
    To doubt they were kneeling then.

So fair a fancy few would weave
    In these years! Yet, I feel,   10
If someone said on Christmas Eve,
    'Come; see the oxen kneel

'In the lonely barton by yonder coomb
    Our childhood used to know,'
I should go with him in the gloom,   15
    Hoping it might be so.

                1915

'We pictured the meek mild creatures where/They dwelt in their strawy pen'

GLOSSARY

The title refers to adult male cattle, ox
(or oxen).

2   *on their knees*: according to legend, it was
said that cattle – like those in the stable at
Bethlehem – would kneel at midnight on
Christmas Eve.

3   *elder*: an old person, possibly one of Hardy's
grandparents.

9   *fancy*: fantasy; made-up story.

13   *barton*: cowshed.

13   *coomb*: valley.

15   *gloom*: dreariness; or perhaps a
metaphor for the poet's own ageing spirit.

EXPLORATIONS

1. In your opinion, what is the mood in the first stanza of the poem? Refer
particularly to Hardy's use of such words as 'flock' and 'embers' in your
response.

2. Explain the relationship between hope and doubt in Hardy's poem. Refer closely
to the text in your answer.

3. Write your own personal response to the poem, using reference and quotations
to illustrate your views.

STUDY NOTES

*'The Oxen' was first published on Christmas Eve, 1915, just one year into the horrors of
the Great War. In the poem, Hardy looks back with an affectionate, nostalgic eye to lost
faith and simple innocence. He still wishes for the old comforts of his childish beliefs.
There is a sense of deep wistfulness and regret in the final lines which reflect the ageing
poet's disappointment with 'these years' – the unsettling 20th century.*

Although Hardy's poem is set in rural England among country people, it
immediately conjures up the miraculous scene of the Nativity when Jesus was born
to Mary and Joseph in a stable in Bethlehem, attended by shepherds and an ox and
ass. The first line of **stanza one** establishes the setting: 'Christmas Eve, and twelve
of the clock'. The archaic syntax is evocative of centuries of comforting tradition.

The poet recalls his childhood, listening to an 'elder' recounting the old belief that the oxen always kneel at the stroke of midnight to commemorate the birth of Jesus. Hardy's use of direct speech dramatises the narrative. The first person plural ('we') conveys a sense of togetherness and belonging. As members of this close-knit society ('flock'), the children unquestioningly accept the traditional story. However, the 'embers' around which they gather indicate that this sheltered world of 'hearthside ease' and certain belief is coming to a close. In wistful mood, **the poet reminisces nostalgically on simpler times and regrets the passing of a secure world** which was fortified by superstition, tradition, community, and belief in God.

Throughout **stanza two**, Hardy continues to marvel at the lost innocence of childhood. He remembers how all the children by the fireside would have had a vivid picture in their mind's eye of the cattle kneeling to pray. The soft alliterative phrase, 'meek mild creatures', and colloquial adjective, 'strawy', convey the simple religious faith of country folk. In retrospect, the poet seems to think that such unquestioning belief was remarkable: 'Nor did it occur to one of us there/To doubt they were kneeling then'. The poem's **third stanza**, with its abrupt break in the second line, reflects Hardy's attempt to bridge the gap between maturity and youth. The idyllic past ('pictured') gives way to the realistic present ('feel'). Significantly, he now regards the old Christmas story as a mere fantasy ('fancy') although he admits that it is a beautiful one ('fair'). The verb 'weave' conjures up the intricate homespun beauty of the old beliefs. Is there a suggestion that the old traditions are unravelling? The adult Hardy had broken free from this childhood faith. Yet, there is **an underlying regard for the certainties of past times, in contrast with sceptical modern-day attitudes**. This is caught in the exclamatory phrase, 'In these years!' Hardy's dismissive tone reveals a deeply-felt response to the horrendous realities of trench warfare which reinforced his rejection of Christianity.

The meditative expression, 'Yet, I feel', seems like an afterthought as **emotion struggles with reason**. The poet now imagines himself invited to 'Come; see the oxen kneel'. In **stanza four**, Hardy reverts to West Country dialect ('In the lonely barton by yonder coomb') as he reclaims his place in 'Our childhood'. He still has a sentimental desire to return to a state of innocence. For Hardy, memories of early experience are comforting. He can now regard the past as a safe place in which there are no doubts. Although he no longer has faith in Christianity, he longs to re-live his childhood – particularly at Christmas-time when the old certainties return and are still deeply appealing. For the time being, the poet allows myth to overpower reality as he desires to cling on to the deceptions of his youth, a desire that would make him 'go with him in the gloom/Hoping it might be so'. Strong concluding lines are a recurring feature of Hardy's poetry. In this case, the final flourish is truncated, adding a dramatic poignancy to the poet's sense of longing. His reluctance to accept that what the 'elder' had said about the oxen was a 'fancy' leaves him wishing for the Christmas story to be true, and yearning for lost innocence.

ANALYSIS

'Thomas Hardy's poetry shows a nostalgia for Christian belief, which it ultimately rejects.' Discuss this statement with reference to 'The Oxen'.

Sample Paragraph

The simple ballad, 'The Oxen', paints a warm scene of English country-folk re-telling old religious stories about the ox kneeling at the crib of Jesus; 'Now they are all on their knees'. The homely picture illustrates a scene of comfort and security as the young listeners sat 'in hearthside ease'. The broad vowel sounds stretch endlessly as the children imagine the 'meek mild creatures' kneeling to honour Christ on Christmas Eve at 'twelve of the clock'. Sentimentality still attracts Hardy to the old certainties of Christianity. But a more intricate sentence immediately dispels this golden scene, 'So fair a fancy few would weave'. The elaborate alliteration ('f' and 'w') suggest the deception of the Christmas story. The adult poet realises it is out of place 'In these years' of uncertainty and brutal warfare. Hardy had rejected his childhood faith and had become increasingly sceptical of a world dominated by conflict. He was also writing in his mid-seventies which gave him a reflective view of life. He admits that if he were he invited, he would love to test the truth of the old Christmas story, but the short concluding line captures his deeper doubts, 'Hoping it might be so'. Hardy aches with a sense of loss and exclusion as his hollow scepticism remains and he rejects the story.

Examiner's Comment

This is a thoughtful and focused response which shows a clear understanding of the poem. Relevant points refer to both content and style. Although there is no explicit personal input, quotations are integrated effectively and the expression throughout is varied and assured. Grade A.

CLASS/HOMEWORK EXERCISES

1. 'Maturity changes a person's perspective.' How true is this statement in relation to 'The Oxen'? Refer to the text of the poem in your answer.

2. Copy the table below into your own notes and fill in critical comments about the last two quotations.

Key Quotes

An elder said as we sat in a flock	Both the use of the past tense and the old word 'elder' contribute to establishing a nostalgic view of the past. The word 'flock' has Biblical overtones (Jesus is referred to as The Good Shepherd) as well as illustrating the unquestioning attitude of the young listeners.
By the embers in hearthside ease	The low glow of the dying fire is vividly captured by the word 'embers'. It could also refer to a disappearing way of life. The simple security of the credulous Christian community is shown in the sibilant phrase, 'hearthside ease'.
So fair a fancy few would weave/In these years!	
In the lonely barton by yonder coomb	

9 DURING WIND AND RAIN

They sing their dearest songs –
He, she, all of them – yea,
Treble and tenor and bass,
    And one to play;
With the candles mooning each face...   5
    Ah, no; the years O!
How the sick leaves reel down in throngs!

They clear the creeping moss –
Elders and juniors – aye,
Making the pathways neat   10
    And the garden gay;
And they build a shady seat...
    Ah, no; the years, the years;
See, the white storm-birds wing across!

They are blithely breakfasting all –   15
Men and maidens – yea,
Under the summer tree,
    With a glimpse of the bay,
While pet fowl come to the knee...
    Ah, no; the years O!   20
And the rotten rose is ript from the wall.

They change to a high new house,
He, she, all of them – aye,
Clocks and carpets and chairs
    On the lawn all day,   25
And brightest things that are theirs...
    Ah, no; the years, the years;
Down their carved names the rain-drop ploughs.

'They change to a high new house'

GLOSSARY

A-Z

3	*Treble and tenor and bass*: three part harmony, high, medium and low voices.	15	*blithely*: happily, without thought or care.
5	*mooning*: illuminating.	21	*ript*: torn.
7	*reel*: dance wildly.	28	*ploughs*: erodes, cuts through.

EXPLORATIONS

1. Briefly describe the four scenes of family life presented in this poem, and comment on any similarities which you notice between them.

2. Select one image (or symbol) from the poem that you find particularly interesting and effective. Briefly explain your choice.

3. After reading this poem, do you think Thomas Hardy was very pessimistic in his view of life? Explain your views using close reference to the text.

STUDY NOTES

Hardy's poems are those of a man looking back on his life, and his memories are often tinged with a deep sense of remorse. In his seventies, he read vivid accounts of the girlhood of his first wife, Emma Gifford, who had recently died. This poem offers a double perspective on that time, recounting its happiness, but also expressing the poet's heartbreak at the pitiless ravages of time. 'During Wind and Rain' deals with one of Hardy's favourite themes – life's transience – with characteristic elegance and economy.

This haunting poem consists of four seven-line stanzas. The first five lines recall moments in Emma's life while the final two lines include dark images of decay and death. Such a regular structure suggests an obvious sense of the four seasons and the seven days of the week. In **stanza one**, a family group is enjoying a musical evening, singing 'their dearest songs' in harmony. Hardy accentuates the nostalgic mood through his use of broad assonant vowels and the image of glowing candlelight, 'mooning each face'. The resulting soft-focus halo effect permeates this dreamy scene where everyone seems blessed. But Hardy's poem also addresses **the inevitable passing of time**. The opening image of joyful celebration fades away at the end of line five. In a dramatic change of tone, the harsh reality of age and waste is emphasised in an uncompromising way. The heart-rending refrain, with its poignant broad vowels ('Ah, no; the years O!') reveals Hardy's awareness of life's transitory nature. The stanza closes with a disquieting image of dead leaves whirling wildly: 'the sick leaves reel down in throngs'. This depiction of inexorable decay is both mournful and lyrical.

Stanza two presents another happy family scene, this time set out-of-doors in springtime. As before, there is an atmosphere of tranquillity as 'Elders and juniors' work purposefully to 'clear the creeping moss'. The alliterative hard 'c' allows the reader to hear the scrape of garden tools on stone as the moss is removed. The family continues working, 'Making the pathways neat/And the garden gay'. The emphatic repetition adds to the **serene portrayal of cosy domesticity**. But this relaxed mood is soon interrupted by a variation on the refrain, 'Ah, no; the years, the years'. Hardy reinforces his philosophy that people misguidedly live their lives as if they will be here forever. The plaintive tone and evocative image of ominous 'white storm-birds' reminds us that no matter what we do to protect ourselves, death is inevitable.

In **stanza three**, the poet offers another picture of perfect domesticity as the various family members go about their lives, 'blithely' unaware of their ultimate fate. Hardy hints at their false sense of security 'Under the summer tree'. Even the 'glimpse of the bay' in the distance is not enough to warn them of oncoming storms. However, as in previous stanzas, **what starts as a pleasant experience ends with time's annihilating power**. The sharp alliteration of the rolling letter 'r' in the final image ('the rotten rose is ript from the wall') shows the cruel force with which human existence can be torn apart. Nature provides yet another sign of the cycle of life and death.

The **fourth stanza** shows the completion of the life-cycle. Set in autumn, the family is moving house. All their belongings are strewn outside, 'On the lawn all day'. Everything is displaced, further evidence of impermanence. The poet's message is a simple one: people spend a lifetime gathering material possessions (the 'brightest things') without realising that, eventually, **everything has to be left behind**. The regular rhyme scheme and repeated invocation of 'the years' speed the poem towards its chilling conclusion. Hardy leaves the reader with the grim image of the family's gravestone where even their 'carved names' are being eroded. In time, the writing will be erased as the 'rain-drop ploughs' through the headstone. The monosyllabic verb with its broad vowels reduces the poem's theme to the frightening realisation that the merest trace of a human being's existence will be consigned to oblivion. The seemingly gentle and life-sustaining drop of rain has been transformed into a destructive instrument of nature. Hardy's tone is one of ironic dismay as man's insignificance is vividly exposed in this dismal conclusion.

ANALYSIS

Thomas Hardy has written poems which 'mortify the human sense of self-importance by suggesting that human beings are of no matter or appreciable value in this indifferent universe'. Discuss this statement, referring closely to 'During Wind and Rain'.

Sample Paragraph

I agree that Hardy shows us life's insignificance in 'During Wind and Rain'. He uses four examples of a group of people living life to the full. They sing together by the soft candlelight 'mooning each face'. But they are unaware of time. They busily garden, 'Making pathways neat'. They eat outside in a beautiful setting 'With a glimpse of the bay'. Yet they behave as if there is no tomorrow, 'blithely' unconscious and full of their own self-importance. They are living materialistic lives, concerned only with the 'brightest things that are theirs'. But the uncaring universe is destructive, vividly described by the violent verbs, 'reel', 'ript', 'ploughs'. Hardy emphasises that nothing remains forever, not even 'their carved names' on their gravestones. All will die, defeated by 'the years, the years'. The use of the colloquial 'aye' and 'yea' make the poem's tone more moving and pessimistic. Hardy had visited his first wife's family graves after her death and I can imagine him standing there, realising that all these people were now gone forever. This poem was inspired by the writings of his wife about her childhood and is very different in tone from another of his poems, 'When I Set Out for Lyonnesse', which these writings also inspired. Hardy has, indeed, humbled our self-importance in this pessimistic poem by showing that humans are of no more importance than 'sick leaves' or a 'rotten rose' in the grand design of an indifferent universe.

Examiner's Comment

This is an assured response to a challenging question and includes some well-focused points about Hardy's dark view of human existence. Expression is controlled throughout. References are directly relevant to the discussion and accurate quotations provide suitable support. Grade A.

CLASS/HOMEWORK EXERCISES

1. Hardy once commented: 'The world does not despise us; it only neglects us.' How does the poet show this in 'During Wind and Rain'? Refer both to the content and style of the poem in your response.

2. Copy the table below into your own notes and fill in critical comments about the last two quotations.

Key Quotes

And one to play	One person accompanies the singers on a musical instrument. This form of house entertainment was very popular in the late 19th century. The word 'play' suggests the group's carefree mood.
How the sick leaves reel down in throngs	Before a storm breaks, the strengthening wind blows loose leaves from the trees. Describing the leaves as 'sick' creates an ominous atmosphere.
They clear the creeping moss	
They are blithely breakfasting all	

10 AFTERWARDS

When the Present has latched its postern behind my tremulous stay,
And the May month flaps its glad green leaves like wings,
Delicate-filmed as new-spun silk, will the neighbours say,
'He was a man who used to notice such things'?

If it be in the dusk when, like an eyelid's soundless blink,   5
The dewfall-hawk comes crossing the shades to alight
Upon the wind-warped upland thorn, a gazer may think,
'To him this must have been a familiar sight'.

If I pass during some nocturnal blackness, mothy and warm,
When the hedgehog travels furtively over the lawn,   10
One may say, 'He strove that such innocent creatures should
come to no harm,
But he could do little for them; and now he is gone'.

If, when hearing that I have been stilled at last, they stand at the door,
Watching the full-starred heavens that winter sees,
Will this thought rise on those who will meet my face no more,   15
'He was one who had an eye for such mysteries'?

And will any say when my bell of quittance is heard in the gloom,
And a crossing breeze cuts a pause in its outrollings,
Till they rise again, as they were a new bell's boom,
'He hears it not now, but used to notice such things'?   20

'And the May month flaps its glad green leaves like wings'

GLOSSARY

1	*tremulous*: frightened, uncertain.	10	*furtively*: cautiously.
6	*dewfall*: late evening.	17	*bell of quittance*: funeral bell.
7	*gazer*: observer.	18	*outrollings*: echoes.
9	*nocturnal*: night-time.		

EXPLORATIONS

1. How does Hardy convey a sense of time passing in 'Afterwards'? Refer both to the content and style of the poem in your response.

2. There are many beautiful nature images in the poem. Choose one that you like and briefly explain its appeal.

3. In your view, how does Hardy wish people to remember him after his death? Refer to the text in your response.

STUDY NOTES

'Afterwards' was written by Thomas Hardy in 1917 when he was seventy-seven. This self-portrait contrasts the permanence of nature with the transience of human life as the poet reflects on how he would like to be remembered after his death. His wish is to be regarded as an ordinary countryman who was aware of the seasonal changes in nature and one who felt compassion for 'innocent creatures'. The poem was read at Hardy's memorial service.

The title of the poem, 'Afterwards', is deceptively simple. It describes the aftermath of a significant event while also suggesting the unceasing movement of time. Hardy plays an intriguing game with the ambiguity of time since the poem is set in the future (after he has died).

Stanza one opens with a dramatic image of the poet's death. Hardy imagines a type of Grim Reaper (a personification of death) leading him through the back gate ('postern') after his earthly 'stay' in this world. The adjective 'tremulous' stresses the transitory nature of existence, and even brings to mind the shaking movements of a very old man. Is there a suggestion that the poet might also fear that his passing will not even be noticed? This melancholy thought is followed by a much more vigorous, colourful picture of life in all its glory. The 'May month', nature's time of growth, is seen as a newly-emerged butterfly with its 'glad green leaves like wings'. This energetic image is complemented by the skipping rhythm and energetic alliteration, 'glad green', 'new-spun silk'. The stanza concludes with a question as the poet wonders what people will say about him after he has passed away. **His hope is that he will be remembered as one who closely observed nature's most minute changes**. Hardy chooses conversational dialogue to show how his neighbours were likely to assess his personality: 'He was a man who used to notice such things'.

The poet imagines another dark scene in **stanza two** as he considers what would happen if he were to die 'in the dusk'. He introduces the image of a hawk arriving with 'an eyelid's soundless blink' to portray a sense of silence and suddenness. Run-on lines emphasise the smooth swift noiseless flight of this bird of prey. Has the poet's life slipped by in the blink of an eye? The alliterative description of the local landscape ('wind-warped upland') vividly shows how the thorn bushes have been shaped over time. But unlike Hardy himself, nature endures. The stanza ends with a hypothetical statement, 'a gazer may think' about the poet's familiarity with his surroundings: 'To him this must have been a familiar sight'. The **direct speech again contrasts the ordinary man with Hardy and his heightened sensibilities**.

In **stanza three**, the poet imagines his death taking place on a warm summer's night. **The close feel of the late evening is made palpable by soft-sounding adjectives: 'mothy', 'warm'.** Readers are presented with another nocturnal animal, a hedgehog moving 'furtively'. The adverb expresses its vulnerability, travelling nervously under the cover of darkness. Hardy concludes by conjecturing that perhaps he himself might be remembered as someone who cared for 'such innocent creatures', although he could do little for them. Is the hedgehog a metaphor for all the things the poet has been unable to accomplish in his life? This image reflects his philosophy that little could ever be changed. It might also relate to his lifelong campaign against cruelty to animals. Will anyone else continue his work when he is dead?

Stanza four considers the possibility of the poet dying in wintertime under 'full-starred heavens'. As usual, there are no explicit references to death. Instead, it is suggested by the night-time setting and the personification of the season: 'winter sees'. Hardy uses the present tense to convey the never-ending natural cycle which is in obvious contrast with his own mortality. **The wistful tone is in keeping with the underlying sense of life's essential wonder.** He hopes that he will be remembered as one who 'had an eye for such mysteries' in thoughts which 'rise' at times in his neighbours' minds. This carefully-chosen verb reflects nature's power and the effortless, mysterious movement of the moon.

The **concluding stanza** opens with the conjunction 'And', suggesting the inevitable momentum of transience. Assonant vowels reinforce the solemn mood as Hardy acknowledges the reality that death is part of the natural life-cycle. At the poet's funeral, the 'bell of quittance' is sounded 'in the gloom'. For him, this funeral knell is merely a marker of time. He imagines a momentary interruption in the bell's sound which occurs as a 'crossing breeze cuts a pause in its outrollings'. But the renewed sound of the 'bell's boom' is a final flourish suggesting rebirth and continuity – a recurring theme in the poet's writing. Once again, he wonders if people will remark that 'He hears it not now, but used to notice such things'. **The poem ends as it began – in uncertainty.** Will Hardy be remembered? By whom? Will he be spoken of as he would wish? Against this preoccupation is the poet's deep awareness of nature's constant beauty and permanence.

Precise language reinforces the poem's central message that Hardy was acutely appreciative of his natural environment. The changing scene in each stanza (May, a winter night and dusk) shows his sharp powers of observation. Hardy's regular rhyme mirrors the steady rhythm of the changing seasons. The extended lines describing nature suggest a man who took his time, who stood and stared. Each stanza is structured as one sentence and the verbs 'say' and 'think' introduce the imagined comments of his neighbours. **This formal structure lends a solemn, funereal quality to the poem**. The tone is hesitant throughout, echoing the poet's modest view of his own importance. He is simply one who commented on what he observed without ever losing his sense of wonder.

ANALYSIS

'Thomas Hardy is hopeful that he will be remembered by a few people, not as a poet, but simply as a loving observer of nature.' Discuss this statement in relation to 'Afterwards'.

Sample Paragraph

Thomas Hardy in his poem, 'Afterwards', is unsure although he hopes to be remembered. Each of the five stanzas depicts an imagined scene of what may happen after his death. Stanzas two, three and four begin with 'If'. The possible remarks of his local neighbours are introduced by 'will say' or 'may think'. It's very clear to me that he hopes they will remember him in a specific way. As a man who closely observed nature and appreciated nature, not as a famous English poet. The ordinary conversational tone of direct speech conveys his neighbours' imagined reactions, such as 'He was a man who noticed such things', 'To him it must have been a familiar sight'. I felt that Hardy's use of poetic language emphasised his sensitivity to nature. Its beauty is vividly described by compound words – 'Delicately-filmed', – 'like an eyelid's silent blink' and 'wind-warped'. Even one new word, 'outrollings'. In my view, there is no doubt that Hardy was a humble man, a true nature lover who understood the beauty of the seasons and 'used to notice such things'.

Examiner's Comment

This is a succinct, note-like response to the question, supported effectively with suitable quotation and reference. Points are focused clearly on Hardy' close affinity with nature. While there is good personal engagement, some of the quotations are slightly inaccurate. Grade C.

CLASS/HOMEWORK EXERCISES

1. Thomas Hardy has been described as 'a solitary person who listened and watched'. Based on your reading of 'Afterwards', how true is this statement? Support the points you make by reference to the poem.

2. Copy the table overleaf into your own notes and fill in critical comments about the last two quotations.

Key Quotes

Delicate-filmed as new-spun silk	Gentle sibilant effects and use of the compound phrase emphasise the amazing beauty of nature.
like an eyelid's soundless blink	This simile vividly describes the flight and arrival of the hawk. Soft 's' effects suggest silence while the abrupt monosyllable 'blink' mirrors the unexpected appearance.
But he could do little for them	
He was one who had an eye for such mysteries	

LEAVING CERT SAMPLE ESSAY

'Hardy's realistic view of the world is effectively conveyed by his hauntingly vivid language.' To what extent do you agree with this statement? Support the points you make with the aid of suitable reference to the poems on your course.

Marking Scheme Guidelines

Candidates are free to agree and/or disagree with the statement. Expect discussion on how Hardy uses language to communicate his realistic views. Evidence of genuine engagement with the poems should be rewarded.

Material might be drawn from the following:

- Themes of transience, disillusionment and war's harsh reality.
- Explores man's futile struggle against cosmic forces.
- Celebrates nature, innocence and young love.
- Past experiences presented as bittersweet memories.
- Varying tones – nostalgic, cynical, realistic, ironic.
- Spare, unadorned, unromantic writing style.
- Use of revealing symbols and evocative imagery, etc.

Sample Essay

(Hardy's realistic view conveyed by hauntingly vivid language)

1. *For me, Thomas Hardy is by far the most thought-provoking poet I have studied. There is no denying the bleakness of some poems, but his attitude to life is never completely without hope. Hardy's voice is a mature one, often reflecting on the*

world in a more realistic way. He was writing during troubled times – including the Boer War of 1899–1902 and the Great War of 1914–1918. While some poems obviously reflect these terrible conflicts in a broad political sense, what I found interesting, however, is that in 'Drummer Hodge' and 'Channel Firing', the poet relates these great moments of history to the lives of ordinary people.

2. *'Channel Firing' presents an extremely pessimistic view of man's foolish involvement in war. Hardy's humour is irreverently surreal, especially when he dramatises God's voice, re-assuring the corpses that it is not yet Judgement Day but simply 'gunnery practice' by the British navy preparing for war. The image of a frustrated God is certainly memorable. His frustration with war-torn nations is evident in the reference to the routine bloodshed of national armies intent on making 'red war yet redder'. The living are seen as hopelessly insane – 'Mad as hatters'. It is easy to relate to the poet's feeling of disillusionment about the sheer waste of war at every level.*

3. *There is little doubt that Hardy's grisly humour is meant to highlight the stupidity of those who engage in wars. In the final lines, the tone changes dramatically as the ominous sound of the guns are imagined ready 'to avenge' other conflicts. Hardy ends by remembering 'Stourton Tower'/And Camelot, and starlit Stonehenge'. His disturbing message seems to be that conflict and power struggles have always been part of history.*

4. *'Drummer Hodge' is a much more restrained poem containing no explicit condemnation of war, but the implied criticism can not be missed. I thought Hardy's quiet tone was very effective in quietly noting the waste of young life. He evokes great sympathy for Hodge who is thrown, without any dignity into his grave. He is not even placed in a coffin, but buried 'just as found'. Nor does a headstone mark his burial. Like countless others, he is treated as just another disposable casualty of war. In contrast, Hardy's tone in describing the beautiful South African veldt is gentle – 'his landmark is a kopje-crest'.*

5. *Ironically, Hardy conveys the horrific truth of battle through a series of simple images which suggest a deep sense of loss. Hodge is 'Uncoffined' and his lonely unmarked grave – 'mound' – is in a foreign place, under 'Strange stars amid the gloom'. In an understated way, the poem pays tribute to the young soldier who is now part of the South African landscape forever. He will nourish the roots of 'some*

Southern tree' watched over by 'strange-eyed constellations'. For me, as a teenager, the pathos of Hodge's tragic life is made more striking by the reserved manner in which Hardy honours his youthful innocence.

6. 'During Wind and Rain' effectively contrasts the happiness of Hardy's first wife's childhood with the inevitability of time. The contrast is effective. Much of the poem describes carefree moments in his wife's life, especially family gatherings, when 'They sing their dearest songs' or 'are blithely breakfasting'. The balance of the world is evident. But it is in the last two lines of each stanza that Hardy introduces dark images of ageing and death.

7. 'How the sick leaves reel down in throngs' suggests an overpowering sense of decay. 'See the white storm birds wing across' is an even stronger visual image warning of wild weather and symbolising the trauma of old age. Another dramatic image – 'the rotten rose is ript from the wall' further illustrates the tragedy of passing time, the emphatic alliterative 'r' effect adding to our understanding of the merciless power of time. I found the poet's final image most disturbing of all – 'Down their carved names the rain-drop ploughs'. The fact that even the tombstones of the dead will eventually be worn away is a depressing reminder of mortality.

8. It would be wrong to generalise and say that all Hardy's poems are pessimistic. 'When I Set Out for Lyonnesse' vividly captures the mystery and wonder of first love – 'with magic in my eyes'. 'The Darkling Thrush' is also essentially upbeat, reflecting Hardy's passion for country living. The poem personifies the 19th century as if it were 'The Century's corpse outleant' or 'His crypt the cloudy canopy'. Hardy uses the winter landscape to express the cold tone. The imagery is gaunt and violent – 'The tangled bine-stems scored the sky'. But nature is also awe-inspiringly beautiful and the 'illimited' bird lifts the sad mood by creating an 'ecstatic sound'. Although the poet is unsure about the future, he takes 'blessed hope' from the 'carolings' of the 'aged thrush'.

GRADE: A1
P = 15/15
C = 15/15
L = 12/15
M = 5/5
Total = 47/50

9. I would wholeheartedly agree that Hardy's world view is a realistic one. His language is both varied and fresh, something which readers find particularly inviting. It is refreshing to find a mature, intelligent approach to subjects, such as war and lost love. It is this balance and honesty in his poems that makes them so interesting.

(approx. 860 words)

Examiner's Comment

This is a well sustained response using wide-ranging references to poems which reveal Hardy's attitudes to the world. Suitable references and accurate quotes are used to support detailed discussion points. There is also good personal interaction with the poems. Although there is some awkward expression (in paragraphs 4 and 6), the overall standard is very high.

SAMPLE LEAVING CERT QUESTIONS ON HARDY'S POETRY

(45/50 MINUTES)

1. 'Thomas Hardy is a pessimistic poet and yet there are moments of insightful optimism in his work.' Write a response to this statement, supporting the points you make with suitable reference to the poetry on your course.

2. 'Hardy's meditative approach is well suited to his recurring themes of loss and disappointment.' To what extent would you agree with this view? In your response, refer to the poems by Hardy that you have studied.

3. 'Thomas Hardy presents interesting questions about human experience in a unique poetic voice.' Using the above title, write the text of a talk you would give to your Leaving Certificate class. You should refer to both Hardy's style and subject matter. Support the points you make by reference to the poetry on your course.

Sample Essay Plan (Q2)

'Hardy's meditative approach is well suited to his recurring themes of loss and disappointment.' To what extent would you agree with this view? In your response, refer to the poems by Hardy that you have studied.

- Intro: Hardy takes a thoughtful, nostalgic approach to central themes, such as first love, nature, transience, war, etc. Poems reflect his personal experiences and philosophy.

- Point 1: 'During Wind and Rain' – contrasts his late wife's happy childhood with the destructive force of time. Varying tones and vivid imagery highlight the intense conflict within the human experience. Images of darkness and desolation also convey Hardy's mixed feelings in 'The Darkling Thrush'.

- Point 2: 'Drummer Hodge' and 'Channel Firing' express Hardy's critical views on the tragic waste of warfare. His technique varies from restrained elegy to surreal drama.

- Point 4: Poignant recollections of lost innocence ('The Oxen') and the magical delights of first love ('When I Set Out for Lyonnesse') demonstrate the poet's skill at re-creating places and conveying atmosphere.

- Conclusion: Personal reflections relating to loss are central to Hardy's poems, many of which are based on bittersweet experiences. Control of mood, diction and imagery is an important feature of the poet's distinctive style.

Sample Essay Plan (Q2)

Develop one of the above points into a paragraph.

Sample Paragraph: Point 4

One of Hardy's shortest poems, 'The Oxen' is particularly memorable for its simple nostalgic reflection on a Christmas superstition from the poet's childhood. In rural Dorset, country people believed that the oxen (cattle) knelt on Christmas Eve as the animals once did at Christ's birth in the Bethlehem stable. Like most people who have been taught the Nativity story, I could understand the poet's sentimental memory of imagining the 'meek mild creatures'. The sibilant phrase itself is gently musical, in keeping with the poet's wistful mood. In the final lines, Hardy almost relives his childhood wonder, wishing he could believe the old story – 'Hoping it might be so'. The sense of loss even extends to his colloquial description of the Dorset locality – 'In the lonely barton by yonder coomb'. The simplicity of the language heightens our awareness of childhood innocence itself and the sadness of its passing. This is a universal experience, and Hardy is skilful in recreating such feelings. In 'When I Set Out for Lyonnesse', he evokes the intense fairytale joy of first love between young people. The memory can still bring back 'magic in my eyes'.

Examiner's Comment

As part of a full essay, this is a well controlled discussion which makes relevant points on the poet's meditative treatment of youthful experiences. Although it ends a little abruptly, there are interesting references to the poet's use of language. Quotes are accurate and effectively worked into the critical commentary. Grade B.

LAST WORDS

'This is how I like to think of him, a boy dancing on the stone cottage floor, outside time, oblivious, ecstatic, with his future greatness as unimaginable as the sorrows that came with it.'

Claire Tomalin

'A powerful imagination, a profound and poetic genius, a gentle and humane soul.'

Virginia Wolff

'One can read him for years and years and still be surprised.'

Philip Larkin

JOHN MONTAGUE

1929 –

'Poetry is a weapon,
a prayer before an
unknown altar.'

The author of many books of poetry, stories and essays, John Montague has been called 'the greatest Irish poet of his generation' by Derek Mahon. Born to Catholic parents in New York, he returned to Garvaghey, County Tyrone, at the age of four to be raised by his father's sisters. As a schoolboy in St Patrick's College, Armagh, Montague developed an interest in Irish poetry. His first poems were published when he was a student at University College Dublin in the late 1940s. He has since travelled the world as poet, teacher and journalist, but all the while keeping a literary and emotional anchor in Ireland. Family and personal history – as well as Irish history – are central themes in his poetry. The love and legend of Ireland permeate his work; people and places from his own past continually capture his attention. Other recurring themes include nature, isolation, relationships, exile and personal loss. The purposeful use of vowel sounds, line breaks and natural speech rhythms are all notable features of his writing style. Montague has succeeded in recording memories and expressing feelings of a common humanity. It has made him one of the most influential figures in the international evolution of Irish poetry in modern times.

Prescribed Poems

❶ KILLING THE PIG

The noise.

He was pulled out, squealing,
an iron cleek sunk in the roof
of his mouth.

(Don't say they are not intelligent: 5
they know the hour has come
and they want none of it;
they dig in their little trotters,
will not go dumb or singing
to the slaughter.)   10

That high-pitched final effort,
no single sound could match it –

a big plane roaring off,
a diva soaring towards her last note,
the brain-chilling persistence of an electric saw,   15
scrap being crushed.

Piercing & absolute,
only high heaven ignores it.

Then a full stop.
Mickey Boyle plants   20
a solid thump of the mallet
flat between the ears.

Swiftly the knife seeks the throat;
swiftly the other cleavers work
till the carcass is hung up   25
shining and eviscerated as
a surgeon's coat.

A child is given
the bladder to play with.
But the walls of the farmyard   30
still hold that scream,
are built around it.

'shining and eviscerated'

GLOSSARY

3   *cleek*: metal hook.
8   *trotters*: the pig's feet.
14 *diva*: famous female opera singer.
15 *persistence*: perseverance.
21 *mallet*: wooden hammer.

24 *cleavers*: instruments used for cutting meat.
25 *carcass*: dead body.
26 *eviscerated*: gutted.
29 *bladder*: the pig's inflatable urinary organ.

EXPLORATIONS

1. How, in your opinion, does Montague feel about the killing of the pig? Refer to the poem in your answer.

2. Comment on the four images the poet uses to describe the noise of the pig's screeching (lines 10–16). Which image conveyed the pig's squeals most effectively? Briefly explain why.

3. Write your own personal response to the poem. Were you shocked, disgusted, unperturbed…? Explain your answer.

STUDY NOTES

'Killing the Pig' is a powerful dramatisation of an event which is familiar and even routine to some people, but which shocks and disturbs others. Throughout the poem, John Montague is a compassionate witness at a slaughtering and he leaves readers to reflect on profound questions of morality and humanity. In recalling another childhood experience, the poet presents the farmyard killing through typically conversational language.

The fragmented form of the poem's opening creates a suitable subtext for the cruel event that is about to take place. Two terse words ('The noise'), set the scene in motion. The title clarifies the deed: 'Killing the Pig'. Montague chooses to use the definite article ('the') in obvious recognition of the animal's distinctiveness. In **line 2**, the pig is described as 'He', a further acknowledgement of the animal's unique life-force. All the focus is on the violence and indignity being wreaked on the pig as it is 'pulled out'. **The desperate terror of shrill resistance can be heard** in the onomatopoeic verb 'squealing'. Montague's haunting verbal music is dissonant and harsh, with hard 'k' sounds suggesting the brute force with which the pig is being handled. The disturbing image of a sharp iron hook sunk into the pale 'roof/of his mouth' contrasts with the pig's vulnerable pink flesh.

The poet's tone becomes increasingly didactic. Lines **5–10** anticipate the customary claim that animals are unaware of being slaughtered, an argument which is often used to justify their treatment. In an angry comment placed inside parentheses (brackets), Montague states: 'Don't say they are not intelligent'. Insisting that they know what is to happen 'and they want none of it', he humanises the terrified pigs: 'they dig in their little trotters'. The adjective 'little' underpins the animals' defencelessness. Readers are not given the luxury of imagining the pigs 'singing to the slaughter', happily going unawares to meet their fate. Instead, **the poet does not allow us to ease our consciences** by denying the reality of what is happening. He emphasises the terrible noise – 'That high pitched final effort' as the pig protests in vain. In **line 12**, its unique wail is alliteratively caught, 'no single sound could match it'.

Montague employs four contemporary **metaphors to convey the animal's frantic voice**. Like the ear-splitting noise of a plane 'roaring off', it drowns out all other sound. The onomatopoeic 'roaring' echoes the 'soaring' song of the famous opera singer striving to reach the glass-shattering 'last note'. Will the pig's traumatised scream also be his final note? The animal's relentless squeals are compared to a rasping 'electric saw' in the aptly extended **line 15**. A final aural image ('scrap being crushed') is brusque, perhaps suggesting that the pig is easily disposable and of as little consequence as everyday rubbish. Again, the discordant hard 'c' records the ordeal of the killing indelibly on both poet and reader.

For Montague, **this sound is beyond compare**, 'Piercing & absolute' (**line 17**). The pig's dying high-pitched cry forces its way into our consciousness. But surprisingly, 'high heaven ignores it'. Is the poet suggesting God's indifference to the suffering of his creation? Inevitably, the awful drama ends ('Then a full stop') marking a clear change of mood as Montague's observant eye pans around the farmyard. There is a cinematic quality to his description of the actual slaughtering process. Montague recalls the concentration of 'Mickey Boyle' who carries out the various stages of his task with impassive efficiency. Initially, he 'plants' the wooden mallet with a 'solid thump' to stun the pig before killing it. Like a surgeon, he acts deftly using deliberate movements. The butcher's knife is personified – 'it seeks the throat'. Montague carefully avoids giving any graphic details of blood-letting, but uses antiseptic imagery to depict the hanging carcass, 'shining and eviscerated'.

In the aftermath of the killing, the mood is lifted momentarily in the **last stanza** as a child is given the pig's bladder 'to play with'. **For the farming community, this has been an everyday act.** But the poet chooses to end the poem by singling out the unforgettable horror of what has happened – etched in his memory by 'that scream'. The walls where the animal suffered such a cruel fate reverberate with the alarming sound and Montague himself will forever associate that place with the fearful cry.

'Killing the Pig' typifies John Montague, the compassionate image-maker. Most of his subject matter comes from personal experience. As always, the **poet's tone is open to various interpretations**. Is he criticising people for their cruelty to animals? Or does he accept that suffering is a routine part of traditional farm practice? What is beyond doubt is his own sympathy for the terrified animal. The pig's frightened resistance to its imminent doom continues to echo through the deserted yard. 'The noise' remains.

ANALYSIS

'The harshness of life looms large in Montague's poetry.' Discuss this view with particular reference to 'Killing the Pig'.

Sample Paragraph

John Montague certainly does not shirk from the harsh cruelties of life. He faces them squarely and helps the reader to confront unpleasant realities. In 'Killing the Pig', the distress of the unfortunate animal is seen in the dramatic two-word opening, 'The noise'. The savage treatment of the pig is illustrated by the grim contrast of the brutal 'iron cleek sunk in the roof' of the pig's mouth. This poet spared me none of the brutality. He even dismisses the usual excuses of a 'dumb' animal totally unaware of knowing what is happening to it. Instead I was forced, just as the pig 'was pulled out', to face the awfulness of its cruel fate and his hopeless protest. I found the poem was most powerful in conveying the pig's terror through Montague's focus on the squeals, 'Piercing and relentless', 'no single sound could match it'. Four very powerful images of totally mind-blowing noise push the message home – the ear-shattering sound of the plane as it takes off, the tragic 'last note' of the opera singer, the totally 'brain-chilling' drone of the non-stop 'electric saw', the brutal image of 'scrap being crushed'. The last three lines compel us to recognise the pitiless reality of farm-life. Even though the pig ends up just a 'carcass', 'hung up/shining and eviscerated', its 'scream' still totally dominates the farmyard in the memory of the poet. Similarly in 'The Trout', Montague faces up to the harshness of life. Long after the fish has been caught, Montague can still 'taste' the fish's 'terror' on his hands.

Examiner's Comment

This is a generally focused attempt at addressing the question personally. Suitable references and quotations show good engagement with the poem. The expression varies from fluent control to being awkward at times, and the word 'totally' is over-used. Overall, however, there is some interesting discussion. Grade B.

CLASS/HOMEWORK EXERCISES

1. 'Montague's poetry describes the reality of being human.' Discuss this statement in relation to the poems of Montague studied by you on your course. Refer closely to the texts in your response.

2. Copy the table below into your own notes and fill in critical comments about the last two quotations.

Key Quotes

will not go dumb or singing/ to the slaughter	Montague prevents the reader from making cosy assumptions. The sing-song alliterative phrase is a chill contrast to the terrified pig's 'Piercing' protest.
Then a full stop	The poem is abruptly brought to a halt by the terse sentence. A split-second pause is marked before the bloody deed of slaughter is carried out. The punctuation mark signals not only the end of the sentence but the end of the pig's life.
Swiftly the knife seeks the throat;/swiftly the other cleavers work	
A child is given/the bladder to play with	

❷ THE TROUT

for Barrie Cooke

Flat on the bank I parted
Rushes to ease my hands
In the water without a ripple
And tilt them slowly downstream
To where he lay, tendril-light,   5
In his fluid sensual dream.

Bodiless lord of creation,
I hung briefly above him
Savouring my own absence,
Senses expanding in the slow   10
Motion, the photographic calm
That grows before action.

As the curve of my hands
Swung under his body
He surged, with visible pleasure.   15
I was so preternaturally close
I could count every stipple
But still cast no shadow, until

The two palms crossed in a cage
Under the lightly pulsing gills.   20
Then (entering my own enlarged
Shape, which rode on the water)
I gripped. To this day I can
Taste his terror on my hands.

'In his fluid sensual dream'

GLOSSARY

(A–Z)

Dedication: Barrie Cooke, prominent abstract impressionist artist and keen fisherman. Montague shared his fascination with the world of nature.

5 *tendril-light*: delicate, thread-like.

6 *fluid*: flowing, graceful.

6 *sensual*: pleasurable.

15 *surged*: sudden powerful movement.

16 *preternaturally*: beyond what is normal or natural.

17 *stipple*: speckled mark or dot.

20 *gills*: respiratory organs of fish.

EXPLORATIONS

1. Trace the poet's feelings as he pursues the fish and catches it. Refer closely to the poem in your response.

2. Choose two images from the poem which you found effective. Briefly explain your choice in each case.

3. Did you find the final two lines of the poem convincing or not? Refer to the text in your response.

STUDY NOTES

John Montague is a poet of place and emotion who is fascinated by the natural world and has great respect for its beauty. This eloquent poem is based on a vivid childhood memory when he used his hands to fish in a small stream. Montague's voice is clear and coherent, expressing an intensity of thought and emotion. The precision of image is characteristic of his work.

This lyrical memory poem captures two contrasting perspectives, the beauty of nature and the thrill of the hunt. Montague freeze-frames a specific moment from his childhood in compelling detail. He recalls his experience lying 'Flat on the bank', catching fish with his bare hands. **Stanza one** traces the **increasing anticipation and tension** as the boy gently eases his hands into 'the water without a ripple' so that the trout remains undisturbed. The line break, 'I parted/Rushes', mimics the movement of quietly separating the undergrowth to allow the sliding of his hands into position. The boy's concentration is presented through a series of dramatic verbs ('parted', 'ease', 'tilt') which highlight his close knowledge of the natural environment. The tranquil beauty of the trout is beautifully depicted, 'he lay, tendril-light/In his fluid sensual dream'. The compound word emphasises the fragility of this marvellous creature. Montague's understated verbal music (particularly the assonant vowel 'i' and sibilant 's' sounds) showcases the glistening fish as it lies in a secure womb-like state of innocence.

The boy's sense of wonder at this serene creature in its natural idyll gives way to a feeling of control in **stanza two**. Suddenly conscious that he can be considered a 'Bodiless lord of creation' who possesses the power of life or death over the fish, he imagines himself as a kind of divine being ('I hung briefly above him') who can now determine the trout's destiny. This feeling becomes transcendental and the boy is aware of the strangest sense ('Savouring my own absence') in what seems like an out-of-body encounter. The intensity of the boy's focus on the task in hand means that nothing else matters. **Time itself appears to be suspended**, 'Senses expanding in the slow/Motion'. Broad vowels restrain the rhythm of the line as meaning and movement harmonise to catch the shock of the moment.

Three final run-on lines in **stanza three** re-establish the pace as the boy acts swiftly: 'the curve of my hands/Swung under his body'. Momentarily, the fish 'surged', responding to the initial touch. The boy is now so 'preternaturally close' that he sees every mark ('stipple') on the trout's skin. For an instant, he instinctively understands the common life-force they share. Because the fish remains oblivious of its vulnerability, the sense of impending danger continues to intensify in **stanza four** as it is effectively trapped within the boy's 'two palms crossed in a cage'. Montague dramatises the confrontation and the boy's exhilaration as his 'own enlarged/Shape... rode on the water'. In this swiftly executed act, the trout's fate is decided: 'I gripped'. Finally, we hear the adult poet's reflective voice: 'To this day I can/Taste his terror on my hands.' The alliteration of the hard 't' sound suggests the **enduring guilt felt by the poet** at the memory of his attack on the panic-stricken fish. For Montague, the encounter between nature and human nature seems to mark a personal turning point. But what has he learned? Has he violated God's natural world?

ANALYSIS

John Montague has said: 'I think the ultimate function of the poet is to praise.' Discuss this statement in relation to his poem, 'The Trout'. Support the points you make with suitable reference to the text.

Sample Paragraph

Montague has called 'The Trout' his first love poem. He describes the fish – which he personifies throughout – in its natural element with all the tenderness of a lover. A magical, almost idealised figure of the dreaming trout is presented through visual detail and verbal music. The fish 'lay, tendril-light,/In his fluid sensual dream'. The soft 'l' combined with the assonance of the vowels 'i' and 'u' convey the stillness of the innocent creature. The beautiful patterns on the trout are depicted by the graphic word 'stipple' suggesting its glistening dotted markings. I also think the poet is praising the natural childhood activities of the countryside. The skill of the young boy as he slipped his hands into the water without disturbing the trout is evoked in the smooth run-on lines, 'ease my hands/In the water without a ripple/And tilt them slowly downstream/To where he lay'. But Montague is primarily a poet of compassion, especially for nature's creatures. In the alliterative last lines, he admits his guilt, 'To this day I can/Taste his terror on my hands'. The abrupt phrase, 'I gripped', describes the savage attack. He is aware that he disturbed the harmony of nature and killed one of its creatures. So, I think this poem is typical of Montague, the nature-lover. However, it is not only praising the beauty of nature, but it is also a poem of atonement as the poet seeks to remove his guilt over his act of desecration.

Examiner's Comment

This is a well-illustrated response which uses apt references to explore Montague's relationship with nature. Effective use is made of detailed reference and there is some good personal engagement with the poem. Expression throughout the paragraph is impressive. Grade A.

CLASS/HOMEWORK EXERCISES

1. 'Among the welter of the world's voices... you find your own voice.' In what ways do you think Montague has succeeded in speaking in his own unique voice in poems such as 'The Trout'? Refer to both subject matter and the use of stylistic devices in your response.

2. Copy the table below into your own notes and fill in critical comments about the last two quotations.

Key Quotes

And tilt them slowly downstream	The young boy's skill is conveyed by the vivid verb, 'tilt', and the assonance, 'ow'. Sibilance enhances the musical effect of the line.
Bodiless lord of creation	A spiritual, transcendental experience is described as the boy relishes his power of life and death over the trout. Broad vowel sounds suggest a sense of power.
the photographic calm/That grows before action	
The two palms crossed in a cage	

3 THE LOCKET

[handwritten annotations around the title:]
Superlative
Reflecting upon his mother
Negativity

Sing a last song
for the lady who has gone,   *died?*
fertile source of guilt and pain.   *Struggle from the start => giving birth*
The worst birth in the annals of Brooklyn,   *records*
Superlative that was my cue to come on,   *Signal*   5
my first claim to fame.   *Unwanted   Mistake*

Naturally she longed for a girl,
and all my infant curls of brown
couldn't excuse my double blunder
coming out, both the wrong sex,   10
and the wrong way around.   *breech*
Not readily forgiven, *stay with him*   *He has feelings of guilt and insecurity about himself → Feels not good enough*

So you never nursed me   *lack of Love and Care*
and when my father's songs   *begging?*   *He sees himself as a cause of all the problems.*
couldn't sweeten the lack of money,   *poor*   15
'when poverty comes through the door
love flies up the chimney',   *Love becomes inconsequential when you don't have the basics.*
your favourite saying.   *Journey of understanding*

Creates a difficult household

Then you gave me away,
Doesn't think twice might never have known me, *Abandoned*   20
if I had not cycled down
to court you like a young man,
teasingly untying your apron,
father drinking by the fire, yarning

Positive Of your wild, young days   *she didn't have it easy either*   25
which didn't last long, for you,
lovely Molly, the belle of your small town,
landed up mournful and chill
as the constant rain that lashes it
wound into your cocoon of pain.   30

Standing in that same hallway,   *she wants the father to leave*
'Don't come again', you say, roughly,
'I start to get fond of you, John,
He is beginning to acknowledge

John

and then you are up and gone';
the harsh logic of a forlorn woman   35
resigned to being alone.

Poignant, powerful conclusion

And still, mysterious blessing,
I never knew, until you were gone,
that always around your neck,
you wore an oval locket   40
with an old picture in it, *shows that she loved him.*
of a child in Brooklyn.   *She is poor at showing it.*

Relief

'mysterious blessing'

GLOSSARY

4	*annals*: records, files.		24	*yarning*: telling stories.
4	*Brooklyn*: New York suburb where Montague was born in 1929.		27	*lovely Molly*: the poet's mother.
5	*cue*: signal.		30	*cocoon*: heart, protected core.
11	*the wrong way round*: difficult breech birth.		35	*logic*: consideration, reasoning.
19	*you gave me away*: when he was four, Montague was sent home to Northern Ireland to be raised by his aunts.		35	*forlorn*: lonely, forsaken.

EXPLORATIONS

1. In your view, what is the meaning or significance of the locket to the poet? Refer to the text of the poem in your answer.

2. How do your feelings towards Montague's mother change over the course of the poem?

3. Write a short personal response to the poem, highlighting its impact on you.

STUDY NOTES

John Montague has described 'The Locket' as 'a kind of ballad sung at my mother's funeral'. This lyrical lament for 'the lady' recounts the childhood experience of living without a mother's love. He did not fully address his hurt until he became an adult and wrote this autobiographical poem marking her passing. Although there is an underlying sense of loss throughout, the poignant narrative tone, half-rhyme and wry humour lighten the pervading gloom as the locket and its picture ultimately console the poet.

The opening lines of **stanza one** have the lively effect of a nursery rhyme, 'Sing a last song/for the lady who has gone'. Montague reflects on his lonely childhood when there was no mother's rhyme for this little boy. **He recognises the reality of their distant relationship**, the bleak mood highlighted by the repetition of 'a' and 'ai' sounds. Growing up, the poet was made to feel at fault, 'fertile source of guilt and pain'. He remains haunted by his mother's voice, rejecting him: 'The worst birth in the annals of Brooklyn'. This reference to his breech birth is wryly acknowledged as 'my first claim to fame'.

Throughout the **second stanza**, Montague's attitude towards his mother seems to be caught between sympathy and bitterness: 'Naturally she longed for a girl'. Does the poet now understand her desire? Or is he still filled with anger and self-pity over his 'double blunder'? There is little doubt, however, about his mother's initial resentment which left him 'Not readily forgiven'. This blunt statement leads into **stanza three** and points accusingly to the heart of the matter as Montague addresses his mother directly: 'So you never nursed me'. Although apparently

Resentment

unflattering, there is a growing **awareness of the pressures resulting from family poverty and his parents' failing marriage**. The mother's voice is heard again: 'when poverty comes through the door/love flies up the chimney'.

Stanza four opens with another frank accusation: 'Then you gave me away'. The plain language resounds with **the pain of the abandoned child**. Montague's mother returned to Ireland when he was seven, but was unwilling to make contact with him. Later, as a young man, he knew that their relationship would never be salvaged 'if I had not cycled down'. Looking back, he sees himself re-enacting his father's role courting her, 'teasingly untying your apron'. The verb, 'yarning', with its broad vowel sound, spills over into **stanza five** mimicking their long conversations about his mother's 'wild, young days'. Compassionately, Montague notes that her carefree youth was short-lived. But while the lively repetition of 'l' highlights the prettiness of 'lovely Molly, the belle of our small town', this is immediately contrasted with the harsh reality of the woman she had become, 'mournful and chill'. Her difficult adult life is further emphasised by 'the constant rain', an effective simile for this sad woman. The final twisting line describes how Molly became wreathed in a claustrophobic state, 'wound into your cocoon of pain'.

Stanza six recalls the traumatic occasion when Montague's mother asked him to stop visiting: 'Don't come again'. Yet even here, there is a suggestion that he could appreciate her deep fear of expressing emotion and the prospect of further disappointment. It is difficult not to be moved by the tentative nature of their feelings. The poet now accepts the 'harsh logic of a forlorn woman' who would prefer to be alone rather than risk being touched by a close relationship. For her own reasons, she appears to be unable to communicate fully with her son. Despite the poem's central bleakness, the mood changes in **stanza seven**. Soft 's' sounds ease the desolate atmosphere as a 'mysterious blessing' occurs. Now that his mother is dead, Montague finds that in 'an oval locket' which she wore 'always', there is 'an old picture in it,/of a child in Brooklyn'. **The poet is both amazed and relieved by this secret gesture of unspoken love.** Significantly, he can come to terms with the past, knowing that she had never forgotten him and she did care for him, in her own way. He has finally been given the opportunity to forgive.

While most of Montague's memories have focused on the damaging influence of an unsatisfactory relationship, this is **essentially an unselfish poem** which explores his mother's life and decisions from her point of view. Moving between past and present, the poet allows us to hear her voice as well as his own. He also gives us an insight into an earlier time in Irish society when emotions were often oppressed. Such an intensely sensitive and honest approach is characteristic of Montague's poetry.

He wants answers and reality rather than feeling sorry for himself.

ANALYSIS

'Montague is an autobiographical poet.' In your opinion, does Montague attempt to live in the past? Explore this idea with reference to 'The Locket', supporting the points you make with reference to the poem.

Sample Paragraph

John Montague has written, 'A door closed when I was four, the separation from my mother… is at the centre of my emotional life'. In his poem, 'The Locket', Montague affectionately and openly re-evaluates the difficult relationship he had with his mother. She had endured a miserable life joining his father in New York in 1928 on the eve of the Great Depression. However, the emphasis of this poem is not, I believe, an effort to live or recapture the past. It is a study of the damaging influence of his mother on his own life. Montague makes the skeletons in the family cupboard 'dance' as he roundly accuses her of abandoning him three times, 'So you never nursed me', 'Then you gave me away', 'Don't come again'. But this poet and this poem are not like his mother, 'wound into' a 'cocoon of pain'. He is willing to accept her unspoken gesture, the 'mysterious blessing' of the 'oval locket/with an old picture in it/of a child in Brooklyn'. He is willing to forgive. There is the astonishment, 'I never knew', of the poet as he realises that she had always secretly cared for him, although she had not articulated this love. In this revealing memoir, the mental anguish of being a displaced, unwanted child dissolves into the 'mysterious blessing' given by the locket his mother 'always' wore. The poem ends happily. We can clearly sense Montague's personal relief at not being rejected.

Examiner's Comment

This focused paragraph succeeds very well in addressing the central importance of Montague's relationship with his mother. The ideas are interesting throughout and firmly rooted in the accurate quotations from the text. Expression is also mature and well controlled. Grade A standard.

CLASS/HOMEWORK EXERCISES

1. 'John Montague is a chillingly realistic poet.' Discuss this statement referring closely to the poems on your prescribed course.

2. Copy the table below into your own notes and fill in critical comments about the last two quotations.

Key Quotes

fertile source of guilt	Montague highlights the intensity of childhood experience. In this case, his mother was a rich cause of blame and heartbreak both to herself, her husband and her son.
that was my cue to come on	The theatrical phrase is suggestive of the applause and praise heaped on a performer and also the expected adulation given to a newborn child. Ironically, he felt excluded and unloved as a child.
So you never nursed me	
wound into your cocoon of pain	

4　THE CAGE

America

My father, the least happy
man I have known. His face
retained the pallor *[Pale look]*
of those who work underground:
[wasted] the lost years in Brooklyn　　　　　　5
listening to a subway
[Onomatopoeia] shudder the earth.

But a traditional Irishman
who (released from his grille
in the Clark Street IRT)　　　　　　　　　　10
drank neat whiskey until
he reached the only element *[to forget his troubles]*
he felt at home in
any longer: brute oblivion. *[unaware]*

And yet picked himself　　　　　　　　　　15
up, most mornings,
to march down the street
extending his smile
to all sides of the good,
(all-white) neighbourhood　　　　　　　　　20
belled by St Teresa's church.

Ireland

When he came back
we walked together *[Contrast between Rural and Urban life]*
across fields of Garvaghey
to see hawthorn on the summer *[positive]*　25
hedges, as though
he had never left;
a bend on the road

which still sheltered
primroses. But we　　　　　　　　　　　　30
did not smile in
the shared complicity
of a dream, for when
weary Odysseus returns *[Not a fairy tale ending]*
Telemachus should leave.　　　　　　　　　35

Often as I descend
into subway or underground
I see his bald head behind
the bars of the small booth;
the mark of an old car   40
accident beating on his
ghostly forehead.

Father dead.

'listening to a subway'

GLOSSARY

3   *pallor*: pale look, unhealthy appearance.
5   *Brooklyn*: district in New York.
9   *grille*: screen of iron bars.
10 *I.R.T.*: New York subway, the Interborough Rapid Transport rail line.
14 *oblivion*: unawareness, unconsciousness.
24 *Garvaghey*: Co. Tyrone, birth place of the Montague family.

32 *complicity*: close involvement, connivance.
34 *Odysseus*: in Greek mythology, when Odysseus returned home from his epic voyage, his son Telemachus was eventually forced to leave.
39 *booth*: kiosk, enclosed cubicle.

EXPLORATIONS

1. In your opinion, what does the poem's title suggest about John Montague's father and his life? Refer closely to the text in your answer.

2. Identify and comment on the atmosphere or mood created by the poet in lines 21–34.

3. Write your own personal response to the poem, explaining its impact on you.

STUDY NOTES

'The poem on my father, "The Cage", sways between gloom and gaiety [cheerful]. It sways also between the Brooklyn of my birth – an urban background and the secret rural world of Garvaghey in Tyrone, where I grew up, and which in a way, had become my father's dreamscape'. (John Montague) The poet was born into a family of Irish exiles in Brooklyn in 1929, the year of the Great Depression. His parents (James and Molly) struggled to make ends meet as their marriage faltered and failed. Montague was sent home to Northern Ireland to be reared by relatives while his father remained in New York for the next nineteen years.

Stanza one opens with a shocking admission as if Montague is answering the question, 'What was your father like?' His response is both poignant [emotional] and startling: 'the least happy/man I have known'. This blunt statement suggests someone who was **a prisoner of emigration, work and drink**. James Montague's face held 'the pallor' of the underground worker cut off from fresh air and light in his ticket-kiosk. His time in Brooklyn seems wasted, 'lost years', as if he has been incarcerated or doomed to dwell in Hades (the mythical underworld). There is no other sound except the 'shudder' of reverberating trains. We wonder if the father is also shuddering, trapped in this bleak place, almost buried alive.

The **second stanza** focuses on James Montague's solitary life as an emigrant worker – 'a traditional Irishman'. The poet imagines his father's daily routine, 'released' from his underground ticket-booth to spend his time drinking alone. Far from his family, he relies on 'neat whiskey' to escape from loneliness into 'the only element/he felt at home in'. **The poet's tone – describing his father's** *totally ignorant*

Turned back on family

drunken state as 'brute oblivion' – seems to combine sympathy and disgust.
The repulsive adjective and explosive 'b' sound suggest a savage animal. However, *attack directly* Montague does not condemn his father directly, but describes his painful *clever* existence with an air of intellectual detachment.

In **stanza three**, we see the smiling public face of the functioning alcoholic. Well used to morning hangovers, James Montague 'picked himself/up, most mornings'. **The tone is one of admiration for his father's plucky perseverance.** The alliterative 'm' sounds (in 'most mornings') emphasise the strong-minded nature of the man. His confident stride is captured in the verb 'march' as he charmingly displays 'his smile/to all sides'. Is the poet suggesting that his father could be a house devil and street angel? The carefully-placed brackets aptly illustrate the racism '(all-white)' prevalent in New York's working-class suburbs. This predominantly Irish Catholic neighbourhood is 'belled by St Teresa's church'. The onomatopoeic verb vividly suggests the chapel bell ringing to summon a compliant congregation. Montague powerfully summons up the uneasy atmosphere in urban America during the 1940s. Is this also a prison of sorts? *Poet blames both father and society.*

Stanza four signals a significant change of mood. The poet recalls his father's return in the 1950s to his home-place in Tyrone where he had grown up. Fast-flowing run-on lines convey the ease of life as father and son 'walked together' through the beautiful Northern Ireland countryside, 'to see hawthorn on the summer/hedges'. The long years spent in Brooklyn are momentarily forgotten; it is 'as though/he had never left'. Instead, the focus remains firmly on Garvaghey's natural beauty as stanza four runs into **stanza five**, describing 'a bend on the road/which still sheltered/primroses'. Unfortunately, father and son were unable to maintain their close family bond; they 'did not smile in/the shared complicity/ of a dream'. **Montague's personal disappointment is obvious.** The gulf between himself and his estranged father was simply too wide. In retrospect, he compares it to the uneasy relationship between Odysseus and Telemachus from classical mythology.

The **final stanza** reverts to the present and the poet's continuing fascination with his father's memory. In his mind's eye, he keeps seeing the old man 'as I descend/into subway or underground'. There seems to be no escape from the sad, defining image of a wasted life 'behind/the bars of the small booth'. The alliterative 'b' emphasises his father's confinement. Montague is also haunted by the mark of an old injury on his father's 'ghostly forehead'. **The stark images**

and slow rhythm are in keeping with the overwhelmingly remorseful mood.
In presenting this vivid character sketch of his father's vulnerable existence, Montague is characteristically compassionate. Just as in 'The Locket', written about his mother, he uses the poem to re-evaluate perceptions about his father, clarifying in the process his own personal and historical identity.

On a Journey

ANALYSIS

'One explores an inheritance to free oneself and others.' (Montague) Discuss this statement with close reference to 'The Cage'.

Sample Paragraph

I felt the poem, 'The Cage' was a very honest exploration by John Montague of his personal inheritance. He must have felt a tremendous hurt at being separated from his parents, and this is clearly seen in his poems, 'The Locket' and 'The Cage'. Yet, Montague never shows anger, but explains the situation as it was. In 'The Cage' he does not shy away from his father's alcoholism. He recounts how he drank 'neat whiskey' until he reached 'brute oblivion'. The poet does not judge. He records. Indeed, he is generous enough to respect his father's spirit as he 'picks himself/up, most mornings' to 'march down the street/extending his smile'. Montague remembers their reunion many years later and openly admits that although they spent time together in the beautiful countryside 'to see hawthorn on the summer/hedges', they did not feel at ease as father and son. Too much had passed unshared between them and so that special secret shared connection will forever be denied them. Montague avoids gushing, dishonest sentimentality, preferring to speak plainly. His father remains with him to the present day, but as a shadowy, sad figure, still cut off by 'the bars of the small booth'. The precise description, 'his ghostly forehead' rings true. Although Montague does not have the usual memories of his father, he has freed himself from bitterness by facing the past with candour and honesty. This has enabled him survive it. We also can now look at painful hurts in our own past, and if we look at them with detachment and honesty, we can free ourselves from crippling resentment.

Examiner's Comment

Close reading of the poem is evident in this focused Grade A response to how Montague comes to terms with the past. Quotations are integrated effectively into the discussion and the expression is well managed throughout. The brief cross-reference to 'The Locket' adds interest, as does the final personal comment.

CLASS/HOMEWORK EXERCISES

1. 'Never sentimental, yet full of sentiment, his is a talent that can recreate a memory or an emotion with almost preternatural precision.' Discuss this statement with reference to the poems by Montague on your course.

2. Copy the table below into your own notes and fill in critical comments about the last two quotations.

Key Quotes

the lost years in Brooklyn/ listening to a subway/ shudder the earth	Montague's use of alliteration emphasises the huge amount of time that his father spent working at a menial job. The onomatopoeic verb 'shudder' suggests the disorientating subway noise.
drank neat whiskey until/he reached the only element/he felt at home in	His father's alcoholism is honestly recorded in long run-on lines as he spirals downwards into total unawareness.
as though/he had never left	
But we/did not smile in/ the shared complicity/of a dream	

⑤ WINDHARP

for Patrick Collins

The sounds of Ireland,
that restless whispering
you never get away
from, seeping out of
low bushes and grass,   5
heatherbells and fern,
wrinkling bog pools,
scraping tree branches,
light hunting cloud,
sound hounding sight,   10
a hand ceaselessly
combing and stroking
the landscape, till
the valley gleams
like the pile upon   15
a mountain pony's coat.

'wrinkling bog pools'

GLOSSARY

(A–Z)

Windharp: an allusion to Greek mythology. The windharp has existed for over 3,000 years. Aeolus was appointed keeper of the winds and this Aeolian harp is named after him. It is a stringed instrument played not by hand but by the movement of the wind over its strings which are of different thicknesses but all tuned to the one note.

Dedication: Patrick Collins is an 'atmospheric' landscape artist who 'worked like a poet condensing, abstracting and interpreting fragments from memory'.

4   *seeping*: leaking, discharging.

15 *pile*: soft projected surface.

EXPLORATIONS

1. Why, in your opinion, has the poet dedicated this poem to a painter of the Irish landscape?

2. Does Montague convey a disturbing or a pleasant picture of Ireland? Refer particularly to the poet's choice of verbs in your response.

3. In what ways do you think the last image (the final five lines) contrasts with what went before in the poem? Comment on the poet's choice of image to conclude the poem.

STUDY NOTES

'Windharp', written in 1975, presents a word picture of the Irish landscape. John Montague, in one intricate sentence, evokes the unique sights and sounds of Ireland. The Romantic poets regarded the windharp as a symbol of poetic inspiration and Montague uses the windharp as a metaphor for the Irish landscape as it changes tonally, both visually and aurally, with the breath of the passing wind.

The **opening line** suggests that what is to follow is special to one place, 'The sounds of Ireland'. The rushing movement of the single fifteen-line sentence mimics the wind sweeping through the landscape unhampered by barriers or borders. The opening sounds are very particular to Ireland as the wind sighs over the bushes and grasses which act as strings and so produce **Ireland's delicate**

rustling sound which is beautifully captured in the sibilant phrase, 'restless whispering'. It is evocative of the soft babble of many voices and it hints at the folklore of the 'little people' said to populate the countryside of Ireland. This sound is always present, as is illustrated by the run-on line 'you never get away/from'. It is like a breath which oozes from the landscape. The verb 'seeping' with its long 'ee' vowel sound effectively conveys the exuding moan which comes 'out of/low bushes and grass'. It then rises as it tinkles melodiously through the higher flora, 'heatherbells and fern'.

In **line 6**, the poet switches his focus from the sounds the wind produces from the Irish landscape. Now the **centre of interest becomes the visual effects which the wind produces** on the countryside as it rearranges features, 'wrinkling bog pools'. The rippling effect of wind on water is described, the smooth plane now furrowed, ridged and fluted. The cacophony of 'scraping tree branches' is heard as its unpleasant grating friction is noted. Although this is a poem where there is no human present, it is very much a personal poem as Montague records his own impressions and invites the reader to partake too. He does not shirk from recording perturbing details, he is not an idealist. The mood now darkens further. The marauding aspect of the wind is shown in a phrase of internal rhyme, 'sound hounding sight'. The quickly changing light effects as shadow is followed by blindingly bright sunlight, is conjured up. The huge clouds scud across the sky in a never-ending relentless pursuit. Is there a suggestion of the loud clap of thunder before the flash of lightning?

In the final **five lines**, the **tone changes to one of quiet intimacy** as if the calm has arrived after the storm. The wind is personified – 'a hand' stroking an animal. Just as a pony's coat is groomed by 'combing and stroking' until the hair shines, so nature takes care of the landscape with the energising force of the wind, 'the valley gleams'. Nature has made the countryside beautiful with a luminous surface of the wind-animated land and water.

A wind knows no impediment. It moves freely where it will in its mysterious enigmatic timeless dance. Is Montague suggesting that the deep division of the North's Troubles can be healed by the remedy of inclusivity, that different voices and views can blend just as the different facets of the countryside's sounds and sights do under the **harmonising force** of the prevailing wind?

> ## ANALYSIS

'John Montague's poetry creates a definite sense of place through a clear and precise use of language.' Discuss this statement in relation to the poems by Montague prescribed on your course. Refer to both style and content in your response.

Sample Paragraph

I found the poem 'Windharp' beautifully evocative of the unique qualities of the landscape of Ireland. Its sounds are unsettling as there is rarely a day without a light breeze. The soft sibilant 's' in the phrase, 'restless whispering' caught this ceaseless music of the wind's rustling. I thought the clear light ringing sound of the wind whistling over the great bogs sounds in the assonant line 'heatherbells and fern'. The adjective 'wrinkling' suggested to me the corrugated appearance of the water disturbed and agitated by the wind's passing. It is almost as if the pool frowned at the interruption. The great play of light which is so much a feature of the Irish landscape and beloved of so many artists is uniquely described as shadow and light chase each other in hot pursuit, 'light hunting cloud'. Montague's language is deceptively simple because it is so carefully chosen and seems able to convey effortlessly the exact impression to the reader of the reforming appearance and sounds of the land. This deeply personal poem affects the reader's sensibilities in a profound way, particularly the final tender image which personifies the wind as a caressing hand which leaves a valley gleaming like the burnished coat of a well-loved pony which has been brushed to perfection. The beautiful clear luminous quality of the landscape of Ireland with its whispering sounds has been seared indelibly into my mind.

Examiner's Comment

An assured response, focusing successfully on the poet's use of sound effects. There is a sustained emphasis on interesting details of Montague's language use. Accurate and apt quotations are effectively integrated into the discussion and the varied expression is well controlled throughout. Grade A.

> ## CLASS/HOMEWORK EXERCISES

1. 'John Montague is a realist not an idealist.' Discuss this view of the poet referring closely to the poems prescribed on your course.

2. Copy the table below into your own notes and fill in critical comments about the last two quotations.

Key Quotes

that restless whispering/you never get away/from	Montague uses the run-on line and the sibilant 's' to recreate the endless sound of the wind as it passes through the Irish landscape.
scraping tree branches	The hard 'c' sound evokes the harsh abrasive noise made when wood rubs on wood. Montague's music includes discord.
light hunting cloud	
sound hounding sight	

⑥ ALL LEGENDARY OBSTACLES

All legendary obstacles lay between   *Waiting for someone being carried on the train*
Us, the long imaginary plain,   *long 'o' sound*   *anxiety/uncertainty*
The monstrous ruck of mountains   *Longing for her*   *Worried about relationship?*
And, swinging across the night,   *Shows his unease?*
Flooding the Sacramento, San Joaquin,   *Assonance*   5
The hissing drift of winter rain.

All day I waited, shifting   *uses the geographical to highlight the distance / separation.*
Nervously from station to bar   *Sense that we wonder where is she?*
As I saw another train sail
By, the San Francisco Chief or   10
Golden Gate, water dripping
From great flanged wheels.

At midnight you came, pale   *Not a romantic fashion*
Above the negro porter's lamp.   *emotional uncertainty.*
I was too blind with rain   15
And doubt to speak, but   *Waited all day*
Reached from the platform   *dual purpose*
Until our chilled hands met.

You had been travelling for days   *Maybe he is worried that she has time to think and reflect on their relationship.*
With an old lady who marked
A neat circle on the glass   20
With her glove, to watch us
Move into the wet darkness
Kissing, still unable to speak.

'As I saw another train sail/By'

GLOSSARY

1 *legendary*: famous, fabled.
2 *imaginary*: imagined by the waiting poet.
2 *plain*: extensive expanse of open country.
3 *ruck*: stack, heap.
5 *Sacramento, San Joaquin*: Californian rivers.

10 *San Francisco Chief*: well-known North American train.
11 *Golden Gate*: another famous American train.
12 *flanged*: protected, rimmed.

EXPLORATIONS

1. How does the poet convey the nervousness of the waiting lover at the train station? Support your answer with suitable reference or quotation.

2. Montague makes effective use of sound in the poem. Select one aural image that you consider particularly effective. Briefly explain your choice.

3. Write your own short personal response to the poem.

STUDY NOTES

John Montague is a romantic poet whose material comes from lived experience and direct observations. 'All Legendary Obstacles' explores both the delights and difficulties of love. This short lyric resonates with the uncertainty of love's early stages. Set against the dramatic landscape of the western plains of America, the poem refers to an incident which occurred in 1956 when Montague's future wife, Madeleine de Brauer, was visiting him in California, 'but her train got delayed in the Mojave Desert when the rains came'. Shortly after she arrived, the poet proposed to her.

Stanza one opens with a sweeping introduction, 'All legendary obstacles lay between/Us', as the poet lists the impediments the trains carrying his loved one faces. The adjective, 'legendary' suggests that these obstructions are majestic. They also refer to the barriers the early pioneers had to overcome in their great trek west. The physical deterrents are the American flatlands, the mountains and the pouring rain. **Montague's precise eloquence is seen in his descriptions.**

highlights the gap between them.

Broad vowels stretch the line, 'long imaginary plain'. The grandeur of Mid-West America's prairies is laid before the reader. It is 'imaginary' because the poet is picturing this place in his mind as he constructs the journey his lover is making. *highlights the uncertainty* The harshly onomatopoeic 'ruck' is used to describe the jagged mountain ranges. Montague suggests the flux and movement of the enormous sheets of 'hissing' rain 'swinging across the night' when the swollen rivers, 'Sacramento, San Joaquin' burst their banks. The enormous physical space between the lovers is marked by placing the pronoun 'Us' at the beginning of line 2. It also references the emotional gap which has to be overcome by any couple in a long-distance relationship. Do the mountains and rainstorm symbolise doubts and fears? Just as the train has to overcome physical barriers to arrive safely at its destination, lovers must often negotiate emotional hurdles before they can find happiness.

The panoramic scene gives way to a more personal, intimate setting at the rail station in **stanza two**. The poet anxiously scans each train in anticipation. This place of countless arrivals and departures emphasises transience. Montague's restless mood is illustrated by his edgy movements, 'shifting/Nervously from station to bar'. He describes his growing disappointment, 'As I saw another train sail/By'. The line break stresses the powerful locomotive's flashing movement as it passed. **John Montague is a poet of place**, and he firmly locates his narrative using familiar names of the great trains which travel vast distances over the American plains, 'San Francisco Chief, or/Golden Gate'. The visual detail and technical terms ('water dripping/From great flanged wheels') brings us onto the platform to wait alongside the apprehensive poet and to marvel at the grace and majesty of these impressive machines. For a moment, we share the poet's apprehension. Will she really come? What will the reunion be like?

Stanza three describes the **delicate moment of that crucial meeting** through a series of short detailed descriptions. The anxious wait is over. Dark and light are contrasted as his loved one is 'pale/Above the negro porter's lamp'. She arrives, rather like Eurydice in the Orpheus legend, from a threatening place. This, however, is no clichéd lovers' meeting. Little awkwardnesses are described, 'I was too blind with rain/And doubt to speak'. Their hands meet, but are 'chilled', from the cold or the long separation.

In the **fourth stanza**, we see the lovers from the viewpoint of the old lady 'who marked/A neat circle on the glass/With her glove'. Had her young travelling companion been regaling her with the purpose of her journey? Is she blessing their reunion or is she a little envious? Meanwhile, the lovers on the platform 'Move into the wet darkness/Kissing'. Has Orpheus managed to rescue his Eurydice from the unknown? Two circles ring-fence the couple, the porter's lamp and the old lady's drawing, as love triumphs despite all the problems encountered. Montague concludes with a **haunting, cinematic image** worthy of any Hollywood romance. But is there an underlying tinge of darkness? They are 'still unable to speak'. A cool sense of unease lingers in the air.

The poet's use of verbal music, assonance, onomatopoeia, cacophony (harsh *Not* *Prominant* sounds) and sibilance conjure up an authentic picture of the waiting lover at the rain-swept station. The **controlled structure** of four six-line stanzas juxtaposes the various scenes clearly as each stanza concludes with a full stop. This tense little drama culminates in a heartening final scene of the lovers' departure from uncertainty, old age and transience.

ANALYSIS

'Montague does not offer an overly idealistic view of love and relationships.' Discuss this assessment of the poet's work with reference to 'All Legendary Obstacles'. Refer closely to the poem in your response.

Sample Paragraph

I agree that Montague does not offer a utopian view of romantic love and relationships. In 'All Legendary Obstacles', the poet explores the expectation, the intimacy and difficulties of early love. The list of 'legendary obstacles' with which the poem opens, 'the long imaginary plain', the 'monstrous ruck of mountains' and 'hissing drift of winter rain' not only refer to the physical barriers between the lovers, but also to the emotional barriers they will have to overcome. The lover on the platform is anxious, unsure of his loved one, 'shifting/Nervously' as he waits. The difficulty of easy, natural communication is revealed, the poet 'too blind with rain/And doubt to speak'. Their hands are 'chilled'. This image economically conveys their predicament. Even the conclusion of the poem has a slight hint of doubt. Yes, they kiss and seem to be given a blessing as the old lady on the train draws a 'neat circle' on the carriage window. But their inability to communicate remains – they are 'still unable to speak'. Perhaps there was no need for words. I was left wondering if the couple's relationship will survive after the initial passion has passed. Montague is a poet of romance, but he is also a poet who observes reality – including the various facets of bright and dark in a relationship exactly as it occurs in the real world, not as it does in a fairy-story.

Examiner's Comment

This is a well-focused response, with very good discussion of the development of thought in the poem. Apt and accurate quotations are effectively used to support points. There is some evidence of personal engagement, and the expression throughout is assured. Grade A.

CLASS/HOMEWORK EXERCISES

1. 'John Montague's poetic style can be strikingly cinematic.' To what extent is this true of 'All Legendary Obstacles'? Support the points you make with suitable reference to the poem.

2. Copy the table below into your own notes and fill in critical comments about the last two quotations.

Key Quotes

All legendary obstacles	This precise phrase encompasses the physical barriers as well as the emotional constraints between the lovers. It also refers to the legend of Orpheus who went to the Underworld to rescue his loved one, Eurydice. They left the darkness behind as they travelled to the light. But Orpheus looked back contravening his agreement with the god of the Underworld. He lost his beloved forever.
All day I waited	The repetition of 'All' and the long vowel 'a' sounds emphasise the tetchiness of the poet as the waiting seems interminable.
Until our chilled hands met	
who marked/A neat circle on the glass with her glove	

7   THE SAME GESTURE

There is a secret room
of golden light where
everything – love, violence,
hatred is possible;
and, again, love.   5

Such intimacy of hand
and mind is achieved
under its healing light
that the shifting of
hands is a rite   10

like court music.
We barely know our
selves there though
it is what we always were –
most nakedly are –   15

and must remember
when we leave, re-
suming our habits
with our clothes:
work, phone, drive   20

through late traffic
changing gears with
the same gesture as
eased your snowbound
heart and flesh.   25

'changing gears with/the same gesture'

GLOSSARY

10	*rite*: ritual, ceremony.	24	*snowbound*: encased by snow and ice.
11	*court music*: elegant, formal music.		

EXPLORATIONS

1. What does the image, 'a secret room/of golden light' convey to you? Briefly explain your answer.

2. How would you describe the mood of the poem in the last two stanzas? Refer to the text in support of your views.

3. Briefly comment on the significance of 'The Same Gesture' as a title for the poem.

STUDY NOTES

John Montague's love poetry explores a great range of emotions, including delight, desire, pleasure, devotion, betrayal and serenity. He has said: 'I'm fascinated by the whole idea of love... its intimacy, its harshness, its tenderness'. This moving celebration of romance is part of a longer sequence called 'Anchor' from Montague's collection 'The Great Cloak'. Here he explores the realisation that the same gesture can take on a different meaning depending on the setting and circumstances.

Stanza one begins on a confidential note: 'There is a secret room/of golden light'. This **private hideaway is depicted as being an almost heavenly place** to which the poet and his lover can escape. Montague evokes an extraordinarily dramatic atmosphere 'where/everything – love, violence,/hatred is possible'. Although the intricacies of a real relationship are acknowledged, the poet highlights the most powerful emotion of all: 'and, again, love'.

Run-on lines catch the overwhelming nature of the lovers' passionate feelings in **stanza two**. Their closeness is conveyed sensitively, 'Such intimacy of hand/and mind is achieved'. Montague's mystical reference suggests the **spiritual bond they share** within this special room, 'under its healing light'. Even the couple's physical caresses have religious overtones, with the affectionate motion of their hands described as a 'rite'. They move as if performing a graceful dance. Montague's apt simile considers how in tune they both are, 'like court music'. For them, romance is a refined, complex experience. It is almost timeless as they seem to exist in their own exclusive world.

Stanza three focuses on the **intensity of the lovers' relationship**: 'We barely know our/selves there'. The line break emphasises how their normal individual identity is shed as their true selves emerge, 'though/it is what we always were'. Their souls had been laid bare to each other while the real world – and its usual worries – disappears. For a short time, the room they are sharing becomes their whole existence. However, **stanza four** makes it clear that they must always return to their mundane lives, 're-/suming our habits/with our clothes'. Again, Montague uses another obvious line break to convey this recommencement of routine responsibilities. The couple's psychic bond dissolves and their magical, self-enclosed sanctuary is left behind. The outside world's demands are economically shown: 'work, 'phone, drive/through late traffic'.

Nevertheless, through all the humdrum routine of life, the memory of romance is never forgotten. Indeed, Montague even finds echoes of their precious time in such banal acts as 'changing gears'. This everyday gesture immediately loses its functionality when he recalls how a similar movement 'eased your snowbound/heart and flesh'. The gentle sibilant 's' sounds here reflect the poet's depth of emotion. In an earlier moment of intimacy, the same action had meant excitement and pleasure for the couple. **Montague's poem is cleverly structured** within a compact five-line stanza form. The Italian word for room is stanza and 'The Same Gesture' is organised like a suite of familiar rooms which suggest this fleeting love story. In keeping with the confident mood throughout, **stanza five** is carefully rounded off with a beautifully positive image celebrating the genuine warmth of the lovers' relationship.

> ANALYSIS

'John Montague's poetry, though rich in imagery and description, deals with ordinary events in economical, everyday language.' Discuss this statement in relation to 'The Same Gesture', supporting your opinions with accurate quotation.

Sample Paragraph

John Montague's poetry is filled with vibrant imagery, whether the 'mysterious blessing' of his mother's locket or the cage-like booth of his father's job. In 'The Same Gesture' the poet invites us to share a discreet love-nest, 'There is a secret room/of golden light'. This image of a private heavenly space is economically conveyed. Religious imagery is used to show the sacred bond between the couple. I particularly liked the idea of love's 'healing light' which transformed the couple into a harmonious unit. The simile, 'like court music', is equally striking as it suggested the elegance of the couple's movements. Real life's interruptions are also present, 'work, 'phone, drive/through late traffic' and soon bring Montague down to earth. The dual interpretation of the routine action of 'changing gear' was most impressive. Any action has different meanings depending on the context. In this case, the poet is more interested in remembering how he caressed his lover when they were alone together rather than concentrating on the functional action of changing gear. The adjective, 'snowbound', to describe the 'heart and flesh' of his loved one created for me a picture of how an individual is isolated on his own and how we all need the loving touch of another to bring us to life. For me, Montague's concise use of language and rich imagery were the basis of this powerful love poem.

Examiner's Comment

The paragraph succeeded in analysing the text of the poem very well to address the effectiveness of key images. There was clear evidence of personal engagement and the focused points were explored with clarity and confidence. Early cross-references to other poems by Montague added weight to the discussion. Grade A.

CLASS/HOMEWORK EXERCISES

1. 'John Montague explores his personal and historical identity through lively character sketches and clever stylistic devices.' Discuss this statement in relation to the poems on your course by John Montague. Quote in support of your opinions.

2. Copy the table below into your own notes and fill in critical comments about the last two quotations.

Key Quotes

There is a secret room/of golden light	The run-on line suggests the endless possibilities which love can bring. The 'golden light' image indicates a sacred dimension to the couple's relationship.
it is what we always were	Montague seems to be saying that a couple in love will bring out each other's true, essential being.
re-/suming our habits/with our clothes	
work, phone, drive/through late traffic	

Not a restorative [handwritten] place

8 LIKE DOLMENS ROUND MY CHILDHOOD

Permanence   influence on the landscape   old people shaped him in another way [handwritten]

Like dolmens round my childhood, the old people. *View of life is shaped by* [handwritten]

Jamie MacCrystal sang to himself,
A broken song without tune, without words;   *Negative image of rural* [handwritten]
He tipped me a penny every pension day,   *Positive description* [handwritten]
Fed kindly crusts to winter birds.   5
When he died, his cottage was robbed,   *People will take advantage even though he was a generous man.* [handwritten]
Mattress and money-box torn and searched.
Only the corpse they didn't disturb.

Maggie Owens was surrounded by animals,   *shared her house with animals* [handwritten]
A mongrel bitch and shivering pups,   10
Even in her bedroom a she-goat cried.
She was a well of gossip defiled,   *she spreads rumours* [handwritten]
danger Fanged chronicler of a whole countryside;   *Tells stories* [handwritten]
vicious Reputed a witch, all I could find
Was her lonely need to deride. *To give out, gave her contempt*   15 *e   Sound emphasised → lingers* [handwritten]

The Nialls lived along a mountain lane
Where heather bells bloomed, clumps of foxglove.
odd All were blind, with Blind Pension and Wireless,
Dead eyes serpent-flicked as one entered
To shelter from a downpour of mountain rain.   20
Crickets chirped under the rocking hearthstone
Until the muddy sun shone out again.

Mary Moore lived in a crumbling gatehouse,   *Symbol of poverty* [handwritten]
Famous as Pisa for its leaning gable.
Come from kitchen   Bag-apron and boots, she tramped the fields   25
Skinny Driving lean cattle from a miry stable.   *Hardship of Tyrone in 1940's* [handwritten]
A by-word for fierceness, she fell asleep
Over love stories, *Red Star* and *Red Circle*,   *She works indoor + outdoor* [handwritten]
Dreamed of gypsy love-rites, by firelight sealed.

Wild Billy Eagleson married a Catholic servant girl   30
When all his Loyal family passed on:
We danced round him shouting 'To Hell with King Billy',
And dodged from the arc of his flailing blackthorn.
Forsaken by both creeds, he showed little concern
Until the Orange drums banged past in the summer   35
And bowler and sash aggressively shone.

Curate and doctor trudged to attend them,
Through knee-deep snow, through summer heat,
From main road to lane to broken path,
Gulping the mountain air with painful breath.   40
Sometimes they were found by neighbours,
Silent keepers of a smokeless hearth,
Suddenly cast in the mould of death.

Ancient Ireland, indeed! I was reared by her bedside,
The rune and the chant, evil eye and averted head,
Fomorian fierceness of family and local feud.
Gaunt figures of fear and of friendliness,
For years they trespassed on my dreams,
Until once, in a standing circle of stones,
I felt their shadows pass   50

Into that dark permanence of ancient forms.

'their shadows pass'

GLOSSARY

dolmens: pre-historic tombs with a large flat stone laid on top of upright stones, like an altar.

12 *defiled*: contaminated, infected, polluted.

13 *Fanged*: sharp-toothed.

13 *chronicler*: recorder of events.

14 *Reputed*: gossiped about.

15 *deride*: ridicule, sneer at.

17 *foxglove*: tall plant with purple or white flowers.

24 *Pisa*: well-known Italian town with a famous leaning tower.

26 *miry*: muddy, boggy.

27 *by-word*: sign.

32 *King Billy*: King William of Orange who defeated the Irish Catholic forces at the Battle of the Boyne in 1690. He remains a popular hero for Ulster Loyalists.

33 *blackthorn*: walking stick.

37 *Curate*: assistant to parish priest.

45 *rune*: magical symbol.

46 *Fomorian*: war-like (Fomorians in Irish mythology were a fiendish race).

47 *Gaunt*: lean, bony.

48 *trespassed*: intruded.

EXPLORATIONS

1. Why, in your opinion, does John Montague compare the old people to dolmens? Refer closely to the poem in your answer.

2. Which one of the old people described in the poem made the greatest impact on you? Explain your choice.

3. Identify and comment on Montague's tone in the last stanza.

STUDY NOTES

According to John Montague himself, 'Like Dolmens Round My Childhood' is 'riddled with human pain'. A series of cinematic long-shots and close-ups vividly portray some of the eccentric individuals who inhabited the poet's childhood in his adopted County Tyrone. This eerie poem shows how the resonance of other people's distant voices forge his identity. Montague writes sensitively about communities which belong to an older lifestyle.

The poem begins with two contrasting pictures, one of inert matter (the dolmens) and another of pulsing life (the elderly neighbours he remembers from his youth). **Line 1** presents a dramatic simile of dolmens and people. The stones are from ancient pre-historic time, protecting and imprisoning old burial places. **These boulders loom large, forming a frightening circle around Montague's vulnerable childhood**. Similarly, the old people he knew also confine the boy. Lively character sketches list these memorable individuals and their distinctive households. For the poet, people and places merge as he recalls their scarred lives in this harsh environment.

In **line 2**, we are given the first vibrant pen picture – of Jamie MacCrystal who 'sang to himself'. Montague recalls the old man's 'broken song', with neither tune nor words. Readers are left wondering if Jamie sang to break the silence of his isolated existence. His generosity is noted, 'He tipped me a penny every pension day', the repetition of 'p' suggesting his natural kindness. The poet has fond memories of a simple man who fed 'crusts to winter birds'. However, **the pitiless reality of Montague's childhood world is soon revealed** when we learn that MacCrystal's home was ransacked shortly after his death: 'Mattress and money-box' are 'torn and searched'. Montague is not directly judgemental. But the facts themselves are enough to show us how undeserved this shameful incident is: 'Only the corpse they didn't disturb.'

Line 9 introduces the lonely figure of Maggie Owens 'surrounded by animals'. Widely perceived as a vicious, poisonous gossip ('Reputed a witch'), she even keeps a she-goat in her bedroom. The striking phrase, 'Fanged chronicler' reveals the old woman's corrupting reputation as if the bitter saliva of gossip flowed from her very teeth. Her spiteful stories are endless as 'a well'. But characteristically, Montague also makes us look at Maggie's hidden personality, the vulnerable underside. He remarks that all he could find 'Was her lonely need to deride'. Her gossip is merely a response to the cold isolation of her own unhappy life.

The poet turns his attention to an entire family in **line 16**. Ironically, the Nialls live in a beautiful setting that they themselves cannot see: 'All were blind'. Alliteration memorably captures the sight of the exuberant flowers, 'heather bells bloomed'. Again, Montague portrays the family sympathetically. They existed in a dark world, dependent on the 'Blind Pension and the Wireless'. The **effect on the boy is registered dramatically in grotesque imagery**: 'Dead eyes serpent-flicked'. The colourless darting eyes of a snake are contrasted with the traditional warm Irish hospitality of the open door ready to receive anyone who needed 'shelter from a downpour of mountain rain'. The 'muddy sun' image further emphasises the tragic irony of this unusual family.

The curious figure of Mary Moore ('A by-word for fierceness') appears in **line 23**. Her 'crumbling gatehouse' seems to be poised on the edge of a disappearing way of life associated with the fading Anglo-Irish influence. Montague's dry humour is evident in the comparison of the 'leaning gable' to the world famous Leaning Tower of Pisa. Poverty is Mary's true reality as she struggles to survive on subsistence farming, 'Driving lean cattle from a miry stable'. But there are other sides to her character. We are told 'she fell asleep/Over love stories' and devoured popular romance magazines, '*Red Star*', '*Red Circle*'. She even dreamt of romantic trysts, 'gypsy love-rites, by firelight sealed'. **From the poet's nostalgic perspective, all these individuals tried to survive by whatever means they could.** In Mary's case, she coped by dreaming of finding love.

Montague's final character, Wild Billy Eagleson, is named in **line 30**. This Protestant man marries a 'Catholic servant girl/When all his Loyal family passed on'. **The poet highlights the blatant sectarianism on both sides of the Northern Ireland divide.** Isolated as a suitable target for ridicule, Billy Eagleson is taunted by local children. The use of alliteration in 'danced' and 'dodged' stresses the persistent nature of this routine abuse: 'To Hell with King Billy'. Although Eagleson ineffectually retaliates with his 'flailing blackthorn', he is in a no-win situation, forsaken by both communities in a deeply divided society. In the bitter mid-summer marching season, however, he realised what an obvious outcast he had become. Montague's dramatic imagery suggests the tense atmosphere of such occasions through stirring onomatopoeia and ominous assonance: 'Orange drums banged past'. *Hinting at danger*

In **line 37**, the common humanity of all these marginalised individuals is underlined by the inescapable fact that they inevitably get sick and die. The difficult environment in which they attempted to exist is shown by the verb 'trudged' to describe the laborious visits of priest and doctor. The disconnection of these scattered people is evident in the description of the 'main road' turning into a 'lane' and finally to a 'broken path'. Sadly, they lived and died alone: 'Sometimes they were found by neighbours' who recognised them as 'Silent keepers of a smokeless hearth'. **For Montague, their corpses are like megalithic tombs, marking a place of death.** Their individuality has passed on as all are 'Suddenly cast in the mould of death'. The lively country characters of old are now mere shadows.

The poet considers the impact of these eccentric people on his own life. **Line 44** signals an abrupt change of tone as he pours scorn on the idea of 'Ancient Ireland, indeed!'. Montague is dismissive of any idealised version of Ireland's past. From bitter experience ('I was reared by her bedside'), he is well aware Irish poverty, loneliness, and pagan superstition, 'The rune and the chant'. The alliterative line, 'Fomorian fierceness of family and local feud' shows his deep-seated resentment of such disputes. The poet's **final lines** focus again on the unusual individuals who dominated his early years. These 'Gaunt figures' – uninvited and unwelcome – have haunted the young boy: 'For years they trespassed on my dreams'. But Montague also knows that he is liberated from the fearful grip of superstition and hate-fuelled feuds. He now stands as a young man in a circle of stones. **These 'shadows' have passed into memory and myth.** The poem's last line – like the first – stands apart. People merge into place, into 'that dark permanence of ancient forms'. The young man has acquired a clearer perspective. Montague has undergone a rite of passage as he asserts his own unique personal identity.

struggle , disconnected , unhappy people.

ANALYSIS

short message – to reach you a lesson.

'Montague's cinematic imagination and anecdotal skill conjure up a lost way of life.' Write your response to this statement, supporting the points you make with suitable reference to 'Like Dolmens Round My Childhood'.

Sample Paragraph

I fully agree that John Montague uses the techniques of cinema to establish the lost lonely figures scattered through the harsh rural terrain in his poem, 'Like Dolmens Round My Childhood'. The poem is book-ended with two dark long shots of shadowy shapes crowding in on the young boy's days. These people and places are resented in stand-alone lines, 'Like dolmens round my childhood, the old people' and 'Into that dark permanence of ancient forms' – and define the poem like the ancient monuments. In between there is a bright series of close-ups of unique characters doing their best to survive a harsh world. Jamie MacCrystal who 'Fed kindly crusts to winter birds' is followed by Maggie Owens 'surrounded by animals'. Then come the Nialls with their 'Dead eyes serpent-flicked' and Mary Moore at her 'crumbling gatehouse'. Wild Billy Eagleson and his 'flailing blackthorn' is another dramatic figure. Sad poignant images of all these solitary people create a tragic image of 'Ancient Ireland, indeed!' The country's dark side is glimpsed through Jamie's ransacked cottage, 'mattress and moneybox torn and searched', the image of Mary who 'tramped the fields' falling asleep dreaming of 'gypsy love-rites, by firelight sealed', followed by the bravado of the Orange March when 'bowler and sash aggressively shone' and from which Wild Billy is excluded forever. They are all forsaken. Montague's ability for story-telling is shown in vigorous images, 'Crickets chirped... until the muddy sun shone out again', 'Fanged chronicler of a whole countryside', 'the miry stable'. These dramatically realised characters come alive for me through visual images and the poet's capacity for reminiscence.

Examiner's Comment

This paragraph is filled with interesting and penetrating analysis. Quotations are used very effectively to support several perceptive points about Montague's visual and narrative techniques. Varied expression and some good personal engagement contribute to the high Grade A standard.

CLASS/HOMEWORK EXERCISES

1. It has been said that John Montague writes 'contemporary but formal poems about ancestors, lost rural ways, neighbours, place and language'. Discuss this statement with reference to 'Like Dolmens Round My Childhood'.

2. Copy the table below into your own notes and fill in critical comments about the last two quotations.

Key Quotes

Like dolmens round my childhood, the old people	The syntax has echoes of the phrasing found in native Gaelic language. Strong assonance of the letter 'o' ominously crowds in on the young Montague.
Crickets chirped under the rocking hearthstone	Onomatopoeia mimics the lively sound of the insects which appears to reverberate around the fireside.
Bag-apron and boots, she tramped the fields	
Silent keepers of a smokeless hearth	

9 THE WILD DOG ROSE

In memoriam of Minnie Kearney

1

I go to say goodbye to the *cailleach*,
that terrible figure who haunted my childhood
but no longer harsh, a human being
merely, hurt by event.
         The cottage,   5
circled by trees, weathered to admonitory
shapes of desolation by the mountain winds,
straggles into view. The rank thistles
and leathery bracken of untilled fields
stretch behind with – a final outcrop –   10
the hooped figure by the roadside,
its retinue of dogs
         which give tongue
as I approach, with savage, whingeing cries
so that she slowly turns, a moving nest   15
of shawls and rags, to view, to stare
the stranger down.
         And I feel again
that ancient awe, the terror of a child
before the great hooked nose, the cheeks   20
dewlapped with dirt, the staring blue
of the sunken eyes, the mottled claws
clutching a stick
         but now hold
and return her gaze, to greet her,   25
as she greets me, in friendliness.
Memories have wrought reconciliation
between us, we talk in ease at last,
like old friends, lovers almost,
sharing secrets   30
         of neighbours
she quarrelled with, who now lie
in Garvaghey graveyard, beyond all hatred;
of my family and hers, how she never married,

though a man came asking in her youth.   35
'You would be loath to leave your own,'
she sighs, 'and go among strangers' –
his parish ten miles off.
                    For sixty years
since, she has lived alone, in one place.   40
Obscurely honoured by such confidences,
I idle by the summer roadside, listening,
while the monologue falters, continues,
rehearsing the small events of her life.
The only true madness is loneliness,   45
the monotonous voice in the skull
that never stops
                    because never heard.

    2

And there
where the dog rose shines in the hedge   50
she tells me a story so terrible
that I try to push it away,
my bones melting.
                    Late at night
a drunk came beating at her door   55
to break it in, the bolt snapping
from the soft wood, the thin mongrels
rushing to cut, but yelping as
he whirls with his farm boots
to crush their skulls.   60
                    In the darkness
they wrestle, two creatures crazed
with loneliness, the smell of the
decaying cottage in his nostrils
like a drug, his body heavy on hers,   65
the tasteless trunk of a seventy-year-
old virgin, which he rummages while
she battles for life
                    bony fingers
reaching desperately to push   70
against his bull neck. 'I prayed

to the Blessed Virgin herself
for help and after a time
I broke his grip.'
                    He rolls   75
to the floor, snores asleep,
while she cowers until dawn
and the dogs' whimpering starts
him awake, to lurch back across
the wet bog.   80

            3

And still
the dog rose shines in the hedge.
Petals beaten wide by rain, it
sways slightly, at the tip of a
slender, tangled, arching branch   85
which, with her stick, she gathers
into us.
                'The wild rose
is the only rose without thorns,'
she says, holding a wet blossom   90
for a second, in a hand knotted
as the knob of her stick.
'Whenever I see it, I remember
the Holy Mother of God and
all she suffered.'   95
                    Briefly
the air is strong with the smell
of that weak flower, offering
its crumbling yellow cup
and pale bleeding lips   100
fading to white
                at the rim
of each bruised and heart-
shaped petal.

'the dog rose shines'

GLOSSARY

Wild Dog Rose: thornless rose with pink or white flowers, widespread in Ireland.
1 *cailleach*: a hag; offensive Gaelic term for elderly woman.
6 *admonitory*: hostile, uninviting.
7 *desolation*: barrenness, despair.
8 *straggles*: drifts, rambles.
8 *rank*: foul, rancid.
9 *untilled*: uncultivated.
10 *outcrop*: rock formation.
12 *retinue*: pack.

21 *dewlapped*: loose skin.
22 *mottled*: blotchy, freckled.
27 *wrought reconciliation*: found agreement.
36 *loath*: hate.
41 *Obscurely*: faintly.
43 *monologue*: long speech.
57 *mongrels*: dogs of unknown or mixed breeds.
71 *bull*: thick.
77 *cowers*: crouches, trembles.

EXPLORATIONS

1. Why does Montague no longer see the old woman as 'that terrible figure who haunted my childhood'? Refer closely to the poem in your response.

2. Select two interesting metaphors from the poem and comment on the effectiveness of each.

3. Write your own personal response to the poem, supporting the points you make with reference to the text.

STUDY NOTES

'The Wild Dog Rose' first appeared in John Montague's collection 'Tides' (1970) and vividly portrayed the brutal experience of a lonely seventy-year-old spinster ('the cailleach'). Set in the barren Irish landscape of his youth, the writing is haunting and uncomfortable throughout. The poem includes various contrasts, between past and present, ugliness and beauty, violence and prayer, and between the child and adult viewpoint. It is also a good example of Montague's skilful use of carefully-chosen language.

At the start of **section 1**, Montague describes how he visits an elderly neighbour 'to say goodbye to the cailleach'. The Gaelic word brings us into the darkness of Irish folklore, with its images of banshees and evil spirits. The poet recalls his earliest impression of the old woman: 'that terrible figure who haunted my childhood'. **His lingering sense of terror is graphically captured** in a subsequent description of her appearance as an archetypical witch – 'great hooked nose, the cheeks/dewlapped with dirt… the sunken eyes, the mottled claws/clutching a stick'. As always, there are notable aural effects. The deadening alliteration of the letter 'd' emphasises the dirty folds of the old woman's excess skin while the harsh 'c' sound suggests the sinister impact she had on the child.

From an adult perspective, however, Montague recognises the woman's vulnerability: 'a human being/merely, hurt by event'. No longer a great embodiment of dread, she now appears as just another ordinary person who has simply been wounded by circumstances. The poet's **sympathetic tone is evident from the outset**. He describes the woman's remote cottage and the surrounding land, 'weathered to admonitory/shapes of desolation' as an extension of herself. Like the unwelcoming landscape itself, she has also been exposed to trauma. In personifying her small dwelling (which 'straggles into view') Montague suggests the old woman's shambling walk: 'the hooped figure by the roadside' accompanied by her yelping dogs. She herself is unkempt and uncared for, 'a moving nest/of shawls and rags'. This vivid metaphor is typical of his detailed description and highlights the isolated cocoon into which the woman has retreated. Yet she is not completely reclusive and comes to 'view, to stare/the stranger down'. Under such intense scrutiny, the poet reverts to his youthful feelings of 'ancient awe' towards the woman. The line break at **line 24** – 'but now hold/and return her gaze' – shows the sudden change of attitude. Montague seems intrigued by her presence and they greet each other 'in friendliness'.

For a while, they share memories 'of my family and hers', now dead. There is an atmosphere of 'reconciliation' between the two. They even exchange secrets as the neighbour explains how she chose not to leave her family for marriage. We hear her voice in direct speech. Montague frequently uses **dialogue to reveal characters in their cultural and religious context**. The conversation recalls old times and forgotten disputes between local families who are now 'beyond all hatred'. The insular nature of this countrywoman is shown in her explanation that she did not want to 'go among strangers' even though her would-be husband only lived 'ten miles off'. Her decision has meant living alone for 'sixty years' in 'one place'. It is clear that the poet feels secretly 'honoured by such confidences'.

As the woman remembers some of the 'small events of her life', the poet's sympathetic understanding of her isolated existence is conveyed in his reflective comment: 'The only true madness is loneliness'. He realises that because she has no-one to converse with, her voice is 'never heard'. It exists only 'in the skull'.

Section 2 leads to the climax of the poem. Although it starts brightly ('And there/where the dog rose shines in the hedge'), the mood darkens unexpectedly as the woman recounts a 'story so terrible' that the poet can hardly listen: 'I try to push it away'. In fact, Montague's reaction is shown even before the story is told: 'my bones melting'. The disturbing account of a violent attack on the woman reveals the stark reality of Irish rural life at its worst. The frenzied assault is conveyed in the relentless pounding alliteration: 'a drunk came beating at her door/to break it in, the bolt snapping'. Forceful verbs illustrate the increasing aggression ('whirls', 'crush') as the drunken man attacks her dogs. **The horror is devastatingly relayed**, 'In the darkness/they wrestle'. Yet even in the midst of all this hideous activity, Montague can find it in himself to attempt to understand the motives, 'crazed/with loneliness'. Throughout the ordeal, the woman fiercely resists: 'bony fingers/reaching desperately to push/against his bull neck'. Again, the poet allows the reader to hear the victim's desperate voice praying to 'the Blessed Virgin herself' until she manages to break 'his grip'. The broad rolling 'o' assonance echoes the involuntary action of the drunken intruder, 'He rolls/to the floor' and sleeps. Verbs economically and dramatically convey the terrible scene as the woman 'cowers', the dogs are 'whimpering' and the man wakes to 'lurch back across/the wet bog'.

In **section 3**, Montague focuses on the beautiful **image of the shimmering wild rose**, 'And still/the dog rose shines in the hedge'. Is this nature's indifference to the sufferings of man? Or is it showing that life goes on despite the occurrence of terrible events? The rose has been battered by the rain, just as the woman has been hurt by life. Her voice is heard once more, explaining that the fragile flower is the 'only rose without thorns', without the ability to hurt. She admits that it is her enduring religious faith which sustains her: 'I remember/the Holy Mother of God and/all she suffered'. Montague also shows his regard for the natural world where the 'air is strong' because of the sweet-smelling aroma of 'that weak flower'. Momentarily, the old woman and wild rose become personified as one: 'offering/ its crumbling yellow cup/and pale bleeding lips'. The poet's compassionate description of human loneliness concludes with the evocative image of 'each bruised and heart-/shaped petal'. Significantly, both nature and human nature continue to endure. Readers are left to consider all that has been damaged by violence... the old woman, the rose, and perhaps Ireland itself.

ANALYSIS

'Montague can bring characters before our eyes through the precision of his language and his descriptive flair.' Discuss this statement with particular reference to 'The Wild Dog Rose'.

Sample Paragraph

In 'The Wild Dog Rose', John Montague presents an unforgettable image of an old woman and her unwavering religious belief and resilience in the midst of life's darkness. We see her through two pairs of eyes, a young boy's terrified stare and the compassionate, empathetic gaze of the adult poet. At first she seems like a stereotypical witch figure, 'cailleach', 'hooped figure', 'great hooked nose', 'mottled claws'. Each precise, descriptive detail conveys the 'ancient awe' in which the young boy held the woman. But then the poet allows us to hear her. We hear the lilt of the woman's voice in internal rhyme and alliteration as she explains why she never married, 'You would be loath to leave your own'. Her simple faith is conveyed in the colloquial, 'I prayed/to the Blessed Virgin herself for help'. Like generations of Irish Catholics, she holds onto her religion, 'I remember the Holy Mother of God and/all she suffered'. There is no trace of self-pity. The care with which Montague captures everyday speech rhythms vividly brings this woman to life. His detailed description of the dog rose battered by weather, 'each bruised and heart-/shaped petal', is both sweet and sad. It conveys the beauty and ugliness of life. Montague's portrayal of Minnie Kearney teaches us that we must look beyond the surface of a person before we judge, and we must see their unique beauty. This 'moving nest/of shawls and rags' stands revealed in all its beauty and it 'shines' thanks to the careful skill of Montague's language and his ability to describe what we don't always see.

Examiner's Comment

This response shows a sensitive reading of the poem and focuses clearly on the task. While personal engagement might have been more explicit, there is very good use made of supportive reference and quotation. Expression throughout is varied and generally well-controlled. Grade A.

CLASS/HOMEWORK EXERCISES

1. 'John Montague is a deeply compassionate poet who reserves judgement on people and issues.' Discuss this statement with reference to the poems prescribed on your course.

2. Copy the table below into your own notes and fill in critical comments about the last two quotations.

Key Quotes

The rank thistles/and leathery bracken of untilled fields	The poet's description of neglected land echoes the unkempt appearance of the old woman herself. The adjectives, 'rank' and 'leathery' portray a somewhat sinister image.
Memories have wrought reconciliation	The repetitive 'r' and assonant 'o' sounds reflect the torturous route to agreement between the pair.
the monotonous voice in the skull/that never stops	
it/sways slightly, at the tip of a/slender, tangled, arching branch	

Liberated ≠ Freed

© John Burns

10 A WELCOMING PARTY

Wie war das möglich?

Liberated Concentration Camps

That final newsreel of the war:
A welcoming party of almost shades
Met us at the cinema door
Clicking what remained of their heels. People are poor

From nests of bodies like hatching eggs   graphic   5
Flickered insectlike hands and legs   Limbs that contain life → want safety
And rose an ululation, terrible, shy;   unusual for a young lad to go
Children conjugating the verb 'to die'.   and see in the cinema.

One clamoured mutely of love
From a mouth like a burnt glove;   Abused   physically distressed   10
Others upheld hands bleak as begging bowls
Claiming the small change of our souls.

natural instinct
Some smiled at us as protectors.   opportunity to escape
Can these bones live?   Being filmed gives
                                          an opportunity to
Montague can   Our parochial brand of innocence   them to   15
only give   Was all we had to give.   fee away.
them pity,
→disconnected

To be always at the periphery of incident   Ireland is at the edge.
Gave my childhood its Irish dimension; drama of unevent:
Yet doves of mercy, as doves of air,
Can falter here as anywhere.   Lack of tolerance   20

highlights death in Europe
That long dead Sunday in Armagh
I learnt one meaning of total war   • run on lines
                Without rule
And went home to my Christian school   How can be
To belt a football through the air.   people systematically
        • He can live a normal life   kill people?

'almost shades'

GLOSSARY

(A–Z)

	German epigraph: How was it possible?	14	*Can these bones live?* (a biblical reference):
7	*ululation*: howling, wailing.		'Son of man, can these bones live?'
8	*conjugating*: listing.	15	*parochial*: localised, small-minded.
9	*clamoured*: cried out.	17	*periphery*: the edge; in the Second World
9	*mutely*: noiselessly.		War, Ireland was neutral.
		20	*falter*: fall away.

EXPLORATIONS

1. Comment on the significance of the poem's title, 'A Welcoming Party'.

2. Choose one image or phrase from the poem that you find particularly effective, and say why you found it so.

3. In your opinion, what lesson did Montague learn about 'total war'? Explain your response.

STUDY NOTES

As a sixteen-year-old student in St Patrick's College, Co. Armagh, Montague and his classmates were brought to the local cinema to see the 'final' newsreel films of the Second World War. This was the ultimate result of the conflict, the liberation of the concentration camps and the horrifying conditions found there. 'A Welcoming Party' is Adds to the unease *the adult poet's response to the deep impact these images made on him on that 'dead Sunday in Armagh'. The poem's title is an ironic one, suggesting a happy event with people lining up to greet important guests. Yet the German epigraph sounds a jarring note ('Wie war das möglich?'). Who is asking the question: 'How was it possible?'*

From the outset, Montague establishes an atmosphere of uncertainty, shock and disbelief. **Stanza one** opens with the poet's memory of the **crucial moment when he watched 'That final newsreel of the war' and understood the significance of the Nazi death camps**. The detainees who greeted the liberating armies are described as 'almost shades', excessively thin emaciated, skeletal figures who are so insubstantial that they seem to scarcely exist. These images are so shocking to the young Montague that the distinction between appearance and reality is blurred. The experience suddenly becomes surreal and he imagines that he is actually meeting these incarcerated [imprisoned] victims 'at the cinema door'.

The horrendous realism of the newsreel is continued into **stanza two** with graphic effect. Montague's description of the prisoners' wasted bodies conveys **a shocking sense of war's dehumanising consequences**: 'From nests of bodies like hatching eggs/Flickered insectlike heads and legs'. The 'hatching eggs' simile should suggest new life. Instead, it evokes a truly gruesome sight. Assonance captures the piercing wail ('ululation') of these degraded people. Children who ought to be in school conjugating verbs are making lists of different ways to die.

Stanza three begins with an oxymoron (apparent contradiction) which focuses on one helpless child who 'clamoured mutely' in a desperate search for 'love'. The grotesque simile, 'From a mouth like a burnt glove', [Harrowing ideas.] attempts to describe the indescribable. Is it a reference to the incineration which occurred routinely in these prison camps? The mood of despair is heightened by alliteration of the blunt 'b' and long vowel sounds: 'Others upheld hands bleak as begging bowls'. These distraught inmates beg not for coins ('small change') but for simple compassion, which is the basic currency of all human 'souls'.

Vividly recalling the haunting experience in **stanza four**, Montague felt that he and his schoolmates were being directly drawn into the horrific scene: 'Some smiled at us as protectors'. His response is incredulous: 'Can these bones live?' He can hardly understand how these starving figures are able to breathe. **Faced with such inhumanity, he becomes acutely conscious of his own powerlessness.** All he has to offer is 'Our parochial brand of innocence'. His youthful inexperience is no match for such terror. The poet develops this idea through **stanza five**, commenting on Ireland's remote geographical location, 'always at the periphery of incident'. For many Irish citizens, World War Two was a 'drama of unevent' as they were not actively involved. Montague recounts that 'doves of air' can tire and rest 'here as anywhere'. Is he suggesting that pacifists like himself ('doves of mercy') failed to respond adequately to the conflict?

The poet's critical tone becomes increasingly frustrated in the **final stanza** as he reflects on 'That long dead Sunday in Armagh'. However, this seemingly colloquial expression marks **a life-changing moment for Montague, a coming-of-age experience when he 'learnt one meaning of total war'**. The young man's enduring outrage at his helplessness is caught in the aggressive image of him returning to his comfortable boarding-school to 'belt a football through the air'. It is characteristic of Montague that his compelling imagery can seem impenetrable at times as he struggles to fully realise the incomprehensible events of war. Nonetheless, the harrowing lessons of the on-screen images remain etched indelibly on his young mind. 'A Welcoming Party' succeeds in combining the actual and metaphorical to explore the poet's reaction to the genocide of six million Jewish people. Typically, the poem reflects Montague's emotional honesty in addressing important themes which have a resonant universal significance.

Its about more than his experience he saw
⇒ He understands he is geographically disconnected. ⇒ Makes us aware of the world

ANALYSIS

'Montague's poetry is often concerned with victims.' Discuss this statement referring to both the content and style of the poems prescribed on your course. Support the points you make with suitable reference or quotation.

Sample Paragraph

In many of Montague's poems, childhood experiences are stored and distilled in the poet's memory until he is ready to confront them in adulthood. The event which inspired 'A Welcoming Party' occurred when the poet was brought from his school to the local cinema in Armagh to watch a newsreel film about the liberation of Nazi concentration camps. I wondered if Auschwitz was a suitable subject for poetry. But Montague has created a moving poem from the horrific sights, 'almost shades', 'nests of bodies'. Their terrible cries are heard in the assonance of 'ululation'. The gruesome reality of the incinerator is conveyed in the dramatic simile, 'mouth like a burnt glove'. I can now see that the language of poetry is exactly right for expressing the tragedy and the feelings of these nameless victims. All of us should be affected. We should ask, like Montague, 'Can those bones live?' We must ask, 'Wie war das möglich?' The heart-rending impact of these sights on the young poet is shown by the blurring of boundaries between fact and fiction as he imagines himself in the company of the victims, 'Some smiled at us as protectors'. The distasteful truth is confronted by Montague, the young student who is unable to help these desperate people. Is he himself also a victim of this war, feeling frustration as he goes home to 'belt a football through the air'? There are no winners in this poem, no comfortable solutions for anyone, even the reader. All are victims.

onomatopoeia
frustrated
⇒ what can he do.

Examiner's Comment

This is a successful personal response to the question and engages directly with the poem. Points are focused effectively on Montague's use of language and supported throughout by apt quotation. The final discussion about war's wider diminishing effects is particularly interesting. Grade A.

CLASS/HOMEWORK EXERCISES

1. 'John Montague's poetry is personal and anecdotal.' Discuss this statement, referring to the poems by Montague on your prescribed course. Refer closely to the texts in your answer.

2. Copy the table below into your own notes and fill in critical comments about the last two quotations.

Key Quotes

Clicking what remained of their heels	Onomatopoeia chillingly re-creates the sound of the confused prisoners as the hard 'c' and 'ck' sounds echo.
From nests of bodies like hatching eggs	The horrible sight of packed human bodies is vividly portrayed in this dramatic metaphor. Sibilant 's' sounds suggest a struggling life-force.
Can these bones live?	
To be always at the periphery of incident	

LEAVING CERT SAMPLE ESSAY

'John Montague addresses questions of personal identity and belonging in a compassionate manner.' Discuss this view, support the points you make with suitable reference to the poems on your course.

Marking Scheme Guidelines

Candidates are free to agree and/or disagree with the statement. Expect discussion on how Montague uses language to explore themes of identity. Evidence of genuine engagement with the poems should be rewarded.

Material might be drawn from the following:

- Insightful reflections on childhood settings.
- Contrasting attitudes to nature, family and community.
- Various views on relationships, romantic love.
- Poems explore pain, brutality, harshness of life.
- Questions relate to the past and Irish identity.
- Varying tones – sympathetic, nostalgic, critical.
- Revealing stylistic devices – imagery, mood and atmosphere, etc.

Sample Essay

(Montague's compassionate approach in addressing themes of personal identity)

1. In studying John Montague's poems, I was very aware of how so many were autobiographical. He seemed to be someone who is constantly searching to understand his own self in terms of his origins and early influences in N. Ireland. To a great extent, he explores his childhood experiences and early relationships, perhaps to explain the adult he has become. What I found interesting was the honesty of the self-analysis, his sensitive treatment of other people and the subtle use of language throughout his poems.

2. Montague's awareness of place is a recurring feature of his work. Rural Tyrone – and particularly Garvaghey – provides a familiar setting for interesting glimpses of his early life. From my reading of 'The Trout' and 'Killing the Pig', I get the impression that he has been deeply affected by the realities of life during the 1930s onwards. His earliest years have clearly been marked by the unusual characters and everyday poverty around him. His terror of the 'screeching' pig being slaughtered was an incident of farmyard violence that has never been forgotten. The excitement of handling a terrified fish has created in him a lifelong respect for nature. What Montague seems to be saying is that he has been shaped by places and people from his past. In addition to his parents, the eccentric local characters he remembers have taught him to empathise with individuals. It's evident that particular locations define his coming of age – whether as a young boy beside a river-bank, a small farmyard

or a 'bend of the road' in Co. Tyrone. He associates places with turning-points in his life. In 'A Welcoming Party', for example, he discovered the atrocities of Nazi death camps while watching a film one 'long dead summer in Armagh'.

3. Family life – especially the poet's awkward relationships with his parents – are taken up in 'The Locket' and 'The Cage'. He faces up to the truth of being rejected by his mother – 'you never nursed me', but uses the poem to accept his mother for what she was – a disappointed person afraid of showing emotion – 'a forlorn woman'. The poet's tone seems gentle throughout, even when he describes how he was abandoned, 'So you never nursed me', as though he can imagine her loss as well as his own. He is overjoyed at the 'mysterious blessing' of his late mother's 'oval locket/with an old picture in it/of a child in Brooklyn'. I found this to be a very sincere poem, revealing Montague's generosity. He is never bitter, seemingly more concerned for his mother than himself. Instead of feeling anger, he puts himself in her place, 'Naturally, she longed for a girl'. His account of 'lovely Molly' who ended up 'mournful and chill' is typical of his considerate attitude.

4. Similarly, the dramatic opening lines of 'The Cage' reflect Montague's heartfelt sympathy for his father – 'the least happy/man I have known'. Background details give a harrowing picture of this desperate Irish exile – working in the New York underground and relying on 'neat whiskey' to survive. As in 'The Locket', Montague never judges, but merely outlines his father's troubled ritual, drinking himself into 'brute oblivion'. The symbol of the small ticket kiosk with its window grille is a simple metaphor for a life of captivity. Once again, the poet's tone is sensitive, fully aware that he never really knew his father and had little opportunity to have a normal relationship with him. Despite this, the poet still honours the failed life of this unfortunate emigrant. For me, this tribute is characteristic of Montague. His own sense of self has been shaped by the obvious sympathy he has for both his parents.

5. It seems clear that John Montague has mellowed in later life and uses his poems to express a more tolerant understanding of people. 'Like Dolmens Round My Childhood' recalls some of the elderly rural people who once terrified him. But he now sees them as tragic individuals, a product of a distinctively superstitious Irish community. Jamie MacCrystal and his 'broken song' was peculiar but kind-hearted. Montague realises that the old man was a victim of local crime – 'his cottage was robbed'. Ironically, the adult poet can now see the darker side and

he has no sympathy for the local thugs who took advantage of the old bachelor. Other characters in the poem, such as Maggie Owens and Mary Moore are also remembered with fondness. The poet's dual perspective – as child and adult – helps him to understand his own divided life. Montague almost seems to be apologising for not understanding Mary Moore's frustrated existence in her 'crumbling gatehouse'. He still imagines her sad night-time routine, reading romantic stories and dreaming of 'gypsy love-rites'. Montague presents a series of images of such solitary people. For him, they are like the ancient dolmens, in that they maintain a mysterious hold over him. These 'Gaunt figures of fear' are ingrained in his own personality and clearly reflect his sense of being Irish.

6. *I believe that Montague's poems allow him to come to terms with his own identity. His compassion is based on a realistic vision of the past. His poems will have meaning for anyone who tries to understand the influence of childhood on forming adult character. In his case, he becomes resigned to seeing himself as the child of distant parents and the product of a sometimes harsh 1930s rural Ireland.*

(approx. 900 words)

Examiner's Comment

This is a well-prepared and focused response to a challenging question. It shows genuine personal engagement with Montague's poems. While there are useful references to the text, a little more on the poet's compassionate tone would be welcome. Overall, the expression is clear and controlled throughout.

GRADE: A2
P = 13/15
C = 13/15
L = 12/15
M = 5/5
Total = 43/50

SAMPLE LEAVING CERT QUESTIONS ON MONTAGUE'S POETRY

(45/50 MINUTES)

1. 'John Montague's distinctive poetic world is primarily concerned with trying to make sense of the past.' Write a response to this statement, supporting the points you make with suitable reference to the poetry on your course.

2. 'Personal memories and a unique writing style are the defining hallmarks of John Montague's poetry.' Discuss this view, supporting your points with reference to the poems by Montague on your course.

3. 'While Montague's poetic voice is essentially located within Ireland, his work has a universal significance.' To what extent would you agree with this statement? In your response, refer to the poems you have studied.

Sample Essay Plan (Q2)

'Personal memories and a unique writing style are the defining hallmarks of John Montague's poetry.' Discuss this view, supporting your points with reference to the poems by Montague on your course.

- Intro: Montague – the sympathetic image-maker. Poems of people and places – family, childhood, the natural world. A unique poetic voice – varying tones, moods, dramatic moments, vivid images and sound effects.

- Point 1: 'The Trout' – dramatic reconstruction – the boy's developing appreciation of nature. Montague's controlled onomatopoeic effects.

- Point 2: 'Windharp' – recalls the beauty of Ireland's remote landscape – sibilant sounds, visual and tactile imagery.

- Point 3: 'The Cage' and 'The Locket' – acute and revealing memories of the poet's parents. Underlying mood of sadness and sympathy.

- Point 4: The reality of 1930s rural Ireland seen in 'Like Dolmens Round My Childhood' and 'The Wild Dog Rose' – poverty, loneliness, sectarianism, brutality. Characteristic language use – memorable imagery, descriptive details, compassionate tone, etc.

- Conclusion: Poetry defined by two elements. Montague's intensely personal poems – significant moments based around specific characters and settings. Unique style dominated by a sense of empathy.

Sample Essay Plan (Q2)

Develop one of the above points into a paragraph.

Sample Paragraph: Point 2

Montague's regard for the Irish landscape is really typical of his sense of being Irish. I thought that his poem 'Windharp' sums up his memories of the remote countryside – and really symbolises his love for windswept rural places – especially the 'sounds of Ireland'. But the poem is much more than a description. The 'restless whispering' seems to represent the country's unsettled history which in turn makes Irish people distinct. It is really not unusual for Montague to use such a haunting metaphor to represent the subtle aspects of what it means to be Irish. The sound of the wind on the hillsides is suggested by the run-through line 'you never get away/from'. The poet uses effective personification to bring the countryside to life. The verb 'seeping' with its elongated vowel sounds conveys the poignant noise which comes 'out of low bushes and grass'. But as always, there is a realistic recognition of a darker Ireland, echoed in the tactile image of the sharp wind 'scraping tree branches'. Montague's vision of the country is never a sentimental or idyllic one. However, there is no denying his underlying love for its rugged beauty. The short poem ends on a note of really intense intimacy, with the low wind compared to 'a hand' stroking an animal. Ingrained in Montague's memory is an appreciation of the Irish landscape as somewhere mysterious and luminous.

Examiner's Comment

As part of a full essay, this is a reasonably engaging personal response which shows a confident understanding of the poem. Quotations are well integrated into the general discussion points. The adverb 'really' is over-used, but the overall expression is clear throughout. Grade B standard.

LAST WORDS

'John Montague is a poet of enormous lyrical gifts, but he has as well an acute and dramatic sense of history.'

C. K. Williams

'Ulster past, present and future is in the marrow of his bones.'

Hugh MacDiarmid

'He is a world-class poet, one of that extraordinary group – perhaps a dozen? – who illuminate our lives, not just for now, but for as long as words have meaning.'

Carolyn Kizer

EILÉAN NÍ CHUILLEANÁIN

1942 –

'I chose poetry because it was different.'

Eiléan Ní Chuilleanáin is regarded by many as one of the most important contemporary Irish women poets. Her subject matter ranges from social commentary and considerations of religious issues to quiet, introspective poems about human nature. She has also translated poetry from a number of languages. Ní Chuilleanáin is noted for being mysterious and complex; her poems usually have subtle messages that unfold only through multiple readings. She is well-read in history, and a strong sense of connection between past and present characterises her work, in which she often draws interesting parallels between historical events and modern situations. Many of her poems highlight the contrast between fluidity and stillness, life and death, and of the undeniable passing of time and humanity's attempts to stop change. They are usually intricately-layered, often subtle half-revelations, but always both carefully controlled and even startling. She herself has frequently referred to the importance of secrecy in her poetry. Most critics agree that Ní Chuilleanáin's poems resist easy explanations and variously show her interest in explorations of transition, the sacred, women's experience, and history.

Prescribed Poems   HIGHER LEVEL

6

❶ LUCINA SCHYNNING IN SILENCE OF THE NICHT

Moon shining in silence of the night
The heaven being all full of stars
I was reading my book in a ruin
By a sour candle, without roast meat or music
Strong drink or a shield from the air   5
Blowing in the crazed window, and I felt
Moonlight on my head, clear after three days' rain.

I washed in cold water; it was orange, channelled down bogs
Dipped between cresses.
The bats flew through my room where I slept safely.   10
Sheep stared at me when I woke.

Behind me the waves of darkness lay, the plague
Of mice, plague of beetles
Crawling out of the spines of books,
Plague shadowing pale faces with clay   15
The disease of the moon gone astray.

In the desert I relaxed, amazed
As the mosaic beasts on the chapel floor
When Cromwell had departed and they saw
The sky growing through the hole in the roof.   20

Sheepdogs embraced me; the grasshopper
Returned with a lark and bee.
I looked down between hedges of high thorn and saw
The hare, absorbed, sitting still
In the middle of the track; I heard   25
Again the chirp of the stream running.

'shining in silence of the night'

GLOSSARY

Title: Lucina is another name for Diana, the moon goddess. In Roman mythology, Lucina was the goddess of childbirth. Ní Chuilleanáin's title comes from the opening line of 'The Antichrist', a satirical poem by the Scottish poet, William Dunbar (c.1460–1517).

9   *cresses*: small strongly flavoured leaves.

12   *plague*: curse, diseased group.

14   *spines*: inner parts, backs.

16   *astray*: off course.

18   *mosaic*: mixed, assorted.

19   *Cromwell*: Oliver Cromwell (1599–1658), controversial English military and political leader who led an army of invasion in 1649–50, which conquered most of Ireland. Cromwell is still regarded largely as a figure of hatred in the Irish Republic, his name being associated with massacre, religious persecution, and mass dispossession of the Catholic community.

26   *chirp*: lively sound, twitter.

EXPLORATIONS

1. How would you describe the atmosphere in the poem's opening stanza? Refer to the text in your answer.

2. Choose one image taken from the natural world that you found particularly interesting. Comment briefly on its effectiveness.

3. Based on your reading of this poem, do you think Ní Chuilleanáin presents a realistic view of Irish history? Give reasons for your response.

STUDY NOTES

Eiléan Ní Chuilleanáin takes her title from a Middle Scots poem by William Dunbar. 'Lucina Schynning in Silence of the Nicht' is set in a ruin somewhere in Ireland, after Oliver Cromwell had devastated the country in 1649. However, Ní Chuilleanáin's beautiful and haunting poem is much more than a meditation on an historical event. The poet achieves immediacy by means of a dramatic monologue that recreates the whisperings of desolation in the aftermath of Cromwell's march through Ireland.

As in so many of her poems, Ní Chuilleanáin invites readers into a **strangely compelling setting**. The poet personifies the moon, creating an uneasy atmosphere. Silence enhances the dramatic effect: 'The heaven being all full of stars'. This eerie scene is described in a series of random details. The language – with its archaic Scottish dialect – is note-like and seemingly timeless. There is a notable absence of punctuation and a stilted rhythm as the unknown speaker's voice is introduced: 'I was reading my book in a ruin' (**line 3**). The series of fragmentary images – 'a sour candle', 'the crazed window' – are immediately unsettling, drawing us back to a darker age in Ireland's troubled history.

Characteristically, Ní Chuilleanáin leaves readers to unravel the poem's veiled meanings and the identity of the dispossessed narrator is never made known. Instead, this forlorn figure 'without roast meat or music' is associated with material and cultural deprivation – **a likely symbol of an oppressed Ireland**? Does the absence of 'Strong drink or a shield' add to the notion of a defeated people? Despite the obvious indications of almost incomprehensible suffering, some respite can still be found: 'I felt/Moonlight on my head, clear after three days' rain' (**line 7**). This simple image of nature – illuminating and refreshing – suggests comforting signs of recovery.

Ní Chuilleanáin's startling drama moves into the wild Irish landscape: 'I washed in cold water; it was orange'. The sense of native Irish resistance against foreign invasion is clearly evident in the reference to Dutch-born Protestant William of Orange, who defeated the army of Catholic James II at the Battle of the Boyne in 1690. But the poet focuses on the speaker's experience of displacement, illustrating the **alienation which existed within nationalist Ireland**. The narrator, surrounded by animal life and the open sky, becomes an extension of animate and inanimate nature: 'The bats flew through my room… Sheep stared at me' (**line 10**).

In an increasingly surreal atmosphere, the mood becomes much more disturbed. The poet's apocalyptic dream-vision highlights the 'waves of darkness' in an uninterrupted nightmarish sequence of repulsive images: 'plague/Of mice, plague of beetles/Crawling'. The **emphatic repetition of 'plague' resonates with images of widespread misery, disease and famine**. Nor does the poet ignore the distorted history of Ireland which has resulted from prejudice, propaganda and vested interest 'Crawling out of the spines of books' (**line 14**). What stands out, however, is Ní Chuilleanáin's ability to suggest distressing glimpses of our island's dark past, poignantly depicted in her heart-rending language describing innocent death: 'Plague shadowing pale faces with clay/The disease of the moon gone astray.'

There is a distinctive change of mood in lines **17–20** as the speaker reflects on the aching aftermath in the period after 'Cromwell had departed'. References to Christian retreat and renewal indicate the **consolation provided by religious faith**, 'In the desert I relaxed, amazed/As the mosaic beasts on the chapel floor'. This sense of wonder through the possibility of spiritual fulfilment is developed in the metaphorical image of 'The sky growing through the hole in the roof'. As always, landscape and nature are features of Ní Chuilleanáin's poem, allowing readers access to her subtle thinking.

In sharp contrast to the earlier trauma, the final tone is remarkably composed and harmonious. The language – which has been somewhat archaic throughout much of the poem – is noticeably biblical: 'Sheepdogs embraced me; the grasshopper/Returned with a lark and bee'. **There is an unmistakable sense of survival and new-found confidence** in **line 23**: 'I looked down between hedges of high thorn'. Ní Chuilleanáin's recognition of 'The hare, absorbed, sitting still' (a cross-reference to her poem, 'On Lacking the Killer Instinct') reinforces the feeling of quiet resignation. Is she alluding to the maturity and relative peace of the present Irish state? At any rate, the poem ends on a hopeful note of vigorous resilience, with one of nature's liveliest sounds, 'the chirp of the stream running'.

Throughout this elusive poem, Ní Chuilleanáin has explored fascinating aspects of Irish history – a story that has been often lost in the 'silence of the night'. So much of Ireland's past is marked by exploitation and resistance. The poem has deep undercurrents of countless conflicts springing from both without and within. The moon has long been associated with love, beauty, loneliness, lunacy and death. Some critics have suggested that Ní Chuilleanáin's poem uses the moon to symbolise the struggle of women through the centuries. As usual, readers are free to judge for themselves. However, there is little doubt that 'Lucina Schynning in Silence of the Nicht' presents us with **an intense, self-enclosed world** – but one where the tensions and aspirations of Ireland's complex story are imaginatively encapsulated.

ANALYSIS

'Eiléan Ní Chuilleanáin's poems offer rich rewards to the perceptive reader.'
Discuss this view, with particular reference to 'Lucina Schynning in Silence of the
Nicht'.

Sample Paragraph

While I first found Ní Chuilleanáin's poetry obscure and quite difficult, I really
enjoyed reading 'Lucina Schynning'. The strange title and eerie atmosphere
under the moonlight is typical of a poet who makes us, the reader, imagine the
'world' of the poem. I found it all very dramatic. The narrative voice seemed
very traumatised and was convincing as it represented Ireland's troubled
history – 'I washed myself in cold water', 'Behind me, waves of darkness'. What
I really liked about the poet was that she suggested, rather than explained. The
description of Irish people starving and dying was very moving – especially
because of the word 'plague'. Ní Chuilleanáin's images of suffering were
balanced by the positive ending. The character in the poem was at one with
nature – 'sheep embraced me'. The poem asked many questions about how
people today look at the past. I thought the final lines were really encouraging.
The poet used many simple nature images of the hare 'sitting still' and the
'chirp of the stream' to show a present-day Ireland where there is peace and
contentment – unlike the war-torn past of the history books. Overall, I did enjoy
'Lucina Schynning' as it reminded me that there is still meaning in the beauty of
nature.

Examiner's Comment

This is a reasonably good response to a general question on the poem. There
is evidence of personal engagement and some worthwhile discussion points
which show an appreciation of Ní Chuilleanáin's poetic voice. Some of the
quotations are slightly inaccurate and the adverb 'really' is overused. Grade C.

CLASS/HOMEWORK EXERCISES

1. 'Ní Chuilleanáin's distinctive poetry is filled with subtle messages.' Discuss this statement, with particular reference to 'Lucina Schynning in Silence of the Nicht'.

2. Copy the table below into your own notes and fill in critical comments about the last two quotations.

Key Quotes

Blowing in the crazed window	Ní Chuilleanáin's central character is depicted as being overwhelmed by forces which cannot be controlled. The adjective 'crazed' emphasises the feeling of an absurd and dangerous world.
Plague shadowing pale faces with clay	The poem has many powerful images of Ireland's past – in this case, there are harrowing traces of terrified victims facing death.
The sky growing through the hole in the roof	
the chirp of the stream running	

2 THE SECOND VOYAGE

Odysseus rested on his oar and saw
The ruffled foreheads of the waves
Crocodiling and mincing past: he rammed
The oar between their jaws and looked down
In the simmering sea where scribbles of weed defined   5
Uncertain depth, and the slim fishes progressed
In fatal formation, and thought
                    If there was a single
Streak of decency in these waves now, they'd be ridged
Pocked and dented with the battering they've had,   10
And we could name them as Adam named the beasts,
Saluting a new one with dismay, or a notorious one
With admiration; they'd notice us passing
And rejoice at our shipwreck, but these
Have less character than sheep and need more patience.   15

I know what I'll do he said;
I'll park my ship in the crook of a long pier
(And I'll take you with me he said to the oar)
I'll face the rising ground and walk away
From tidal waters, up riverbeds   20
Where herons parcel out the miles of stream,
Over gaps in the hills, through warm
Silent valleys, and when I meet a farmer
Bold enough to look me in the eye
With 'where are you off to with that long   25
Winnowing fan over your shoulder?'
There I will stand still
And I'll plant you for a gatepost or a hitching-post
And leave you as a tidemark. I can go back
And organise my house then.   30
                    But the profound
Unfenced valleys of the ocean still held him;
He had only the oar to make them keep their distance;
The sea was still frying under the ship's side.

He considered the water-lilies, and thought about fountains   35
Spraying as wide as willows in empty squares,

The sugarstick of water clattering into the kettle,
The flat lakes bisecting the rushes. He remembered spiders
    and frogs
Housekeeping at the roadside in brown trickles floored
    with mud,
Horsetroughs, the black canal, pale swans at dark;   40
His face grew damp with tears that tasted

Like his own sweat or the insults of the sea.

'the simmering sea'

GLOSSARY

1   *Odysseus*: Greek mythic king and warrior. He is also the literary hero of Homer's epic tale, *The Odyssey*, which tells of Odysseus's ten-year struggle to return home from the Trojan War.
2   *ruffled:* wrinkled, tangled.
3   *Crocodiling*: gliding.

3   *mincing*: moving daintily.
10   *Pocked*: disfigured.
12   *notorious*: infamous.
21   *herons*: long-necked wading birds.
21   *parcel*: mark, measure.
26   *Winnowing*: probing.
38   *bisecting*: cutting through.

EXPLORATIONS

1. From your reading of the first stanza (lines 1–15), describe Odysseus's relationship with the sea. Refer to the text in your response.

2. Select two interesting images from the poem and comment on the effectiveness of each.

3. Write your own personal response to 'The Second Voyage', supporting the points you make with reference to the text.

STUDY NOTES

The relationship between past and present is one of Eiléan Ní Chuilleanáin's recurring themes. In addressing the present within the context of history, she often explores contrasts, such as life and death, motion and stillness, and of the inevitable tension between time passing and people's desire to resist change. 'The Second Voyage' refers to the Greek hero Odysseus, whose first epic journey was a relentless battle with the treacherous ocean. But growing frustrated by the endless struggle against nature, he decides that his next voyage will be on land and therefore less demanding.

From the outset, Odysseus is presented as a slightly bemused and ridiculous figure. There is a cartoon-like quality to the exaggerated ocean setting as Ní Chuilleanáin immediately portrays this legendary hero resting on his oar and watching the 'ruffled foreheads of the waves/Crocodiling and mincing past' (**line 3**). The poet expands this metaphor, describing the waves as great beasts to be challenged: 'he rammed/The oar between their jaws'. **Ní Chuilleanáin's derisive humour mocks the great wanderer's inflated sense of his own masculinity.** But there is no denying that Odysseus is still excited by the 'Uncertain depth' beneath him. For him, anything is possible at sea where he is truly in his element. The personification is childlike, suggesting his peevish annoyance at being unable to conquer the ocean waves which don't possess 'a single/Streak of decency' (**line 9**).

Ní Chuilleanáin's tone is playfully critical. As always, the poet's skill lies in her vigorous images, such as the 'slim fishes' beneath 'scribbles of weeds'.

Odysseus's powerful physicality is contrasted with the seemingly pretty waves which somehow resist the 'battering they've had'. Lording over this surreal scene and filled with disappointment, the egotistical Greek warrior thinks about the Garden of Eden. He is soon envying Adam who was given God-given control over all living things and had 'named the beasts' of the earth. Completely unaware of the irony of his excessive pride, Odysseus is overwhelmed by self-pity and resorts to ridiculing these foolish waves which fail to 'rejoice at our shipwreck' (**line 14**).

Ní Chuilleanáin develops the whimsical drama by letting us hear Odysseus's petulant voice as he prepares to seek recognition onshore. Armed with renewed confidence and his trusty oar – ('I'll take you with me he said to the oar'), he sets out to 'face the rising ground' and seek affirmation far away 'From tidal waters'. But despite the purposeful rhythm and self-assured tone, there is a strong underlying sense that he is deluding himself. The landscape might be serenely beautiful, but it is confined. Unlike the boundless sea, birds define it: 'herons parcel out the miles of stream' (**line 21**). Yet the brave warrior is eager to boast of his exploits in the outside world and hopes to tell his story to the first farmer he meets, 'Bold enough to look me in the eye'. **Odysseus even tries to convince himself that it is time to put down roots**, to plant his oar as 'a gatepost or a hitching-post'. Then he will be ready to return home and 'organise my house'. However, the laboured rhythm and imposing multi-syllabic language conveys his half-heartedness about settling down.

Indeed, there are already signs that Odysseus will never surrender the freedom and adventure of dangerous ocean voyages. The powerful oar which once signified dynamism and exhilaration is now seen as a decorative symbol of stillness, a 'Winnowing fan'. Unable to deny his true destiny any longer, **he accepts that he cannot ignore his urge to control the sea**: the 'Unfenced valleys of the ocean still held him' (**line 32**). But his ironic situation remains; while the freedom he yearns for is unattainable on land, he is still unable to conquer the seemingly infinite sea.

The poem's final section is sympathetic to Odysseus's dilemma. Ní Chuilleanáin replaces the pompous first-person pronouns with her own measured narrative account: 'He considered the water-lilies, and thought about fountains' (**line 35**). The poet makes extensive use of **contrasting water images to highlight land and sea**. Unlike the water 'frying under the ship's side', settled life appears controlled, but unattractive ('Horsetroughs, the black canal'). His uneasy memories of home ('water clattering', 'pale swans at dark') are ominous. For Odysseus, his second excursion into landlocked civilisation offers so little fulfillment that 'His face grew damp with tears'. The hero is forever drawn to that first epic voyage and the wonderful experience of ocean living, with which he is inextricably bound: 'Like his own sweat or the insults of the sea'.

The fluctuating water images – another familiar feature of Eiléan Ní Chuilleanáin's writing – reflect the complex narrative threads throughout the poem. Transitions of various kinds are central to her work. The poet has also been very involved in translating texts, and believes that because of the limits imposed by the translator, the process can never be completely true to the original language. Some literary critics see 'The Second Voyage' as an **extended metaphor exploring how language and culture resist translation**, but like so many of Ní Chuilleanáin's enigmatic poems, the ultimate interpretation is left to individual readers themselves.

ANALYSIS

'Ní Chuilleanáin's poetry makes effective use of contrasts to illuminate her themes.' Discuss this view, with particular reference to 'The Second Voyage'.

Sample Paragraph

Contrasting themes, such as life and death, permanence and transience, and motion and stillness are all prominent within Eiléan Ní Chuilleanáin's 'The Second Voyage'. Such contrasts make it easier to understand her poetic world. The opening description of arrogant Odysseus who 'rammed' his oar against the waves shows a macho larger-than-life character whose extrovert behaviour could not be more unlike the silent sea with its 'Uncertain depth' which he will never tame. Momentarily, the irritated hero makes up his mind to undertake a new 'voyage' by seeking glory on land. But the reality of settled life disappoints him. Revealing images of fixed landmarks – 'a gatepost', 'hitching-post', 'tidemark' – all convey the sense of motionless disinterest. Odysseus is immediately aware of the contrasting dynamic qualities of the sea's 'Unfenced valleys'. Throughout the last stanza, Odysseus debates the relative attractions of land and sea. I found it interesting that the man-made images were all water-based – 'fountains', 'brown trickles', 'the black canal' – and all lacking the mystery and danger of the open sea which Odysseus longs for. The ending of the poem rounds off the choices facing Odysseus. Once again, Ní Chuilleanáin succeeds in juxtaposing his love-hate obsession with the mysterious ocean as his tears taste 'Like his own sweat or the insults of the sea'.

Examiner's Comment

The introductory overview established a very good basis for exploring interesting contrasts within the poem. There is some well-focused and worthwhile personal engagement with the text, and suitable quotations provide valuable support. Diction and expression are also excellent throughout. Grade A.

CLASS/HOMEWORK EXERCISES

1. 'Eiléan Ní Chuilleanáin presents readers with unsettling scenes, both real and other-worldly.' Discuss this statement, with particular reference to 'The Second Voyage'. Refer to the text in your answer.

2. Copy the table below into your own notes and fill in critical comments about the last two quotations.

Key Quotes

The ruffled foreheads of the waves/ Crocodiling and mincing past	Ní Chuilleanáin's sardonic humour personifies the sea to reflect Odysseus's irritation that it ignores him and is beyond his control.
In the simmering sea where scribbles of weed defined/Uncertain depth	Alliterative sibilant effects add to this vivid image of the inscrutable ocean which Odysseus finds so challenging and mysterious.
herons parcel out the miles of stream,/ Over gaps in the hills, through warm/ Silent valleys	
But the profound/Unfenced valleys of the ocean still held him	

❸   DEATHS AND ENGINES

We came down above the houses
In a stiff curve, and
At the edge of Paris airport
Saw an empty tunnel
– The back half of a plane, black   5
On the snow, nobody near it,
Tubular, burnt-out and frozen.

When we faced again
The snow-white runways in the dark
No sound came over   10
The loudspeakers, except the sighs
Of the lonely pilot.

The cold of metal wings is contagious:
Soon you will need wings of your own,
Cornered in the angle where   15
Time and life like a knife and fork
Cross, and the lifeline in your palm
Breaks, and the curve of an aeroplane's track
Meets the straight skyline.

The images of relief: 20
Hospital pyjamas, screens round a bed
A man with a bloody face
Sitting up in bed, conversing cheerfully
Through cut lips:
These will fail you some time.   25

You will find yourself alone
Accelerating down a blind
Alley, too late to stop
And know how light your death is;

You will be scattered like wreckage,   30
The pieces every one a different shape
Will spin and lodge in the hearts
Of all who love you.

'snow-white runways'

GLOSSARY

7   *Tubular*: cylindrical, tube-shaped.
13 *contagious*: catching.
23 *conversing*: chatting.

27 *Accelerating*: speeding.
32 *lodge*: settle.

EXPLORATIONS

1. Describe the atmosphere at the airport in the first two stanzas. Refer to the text in your response.

2. Based on your reading of lines 13–25, choose one image that you found particularly memorable and comment on its effectiveness.

3. Write your personal response to 'Deaths and Engines', referring closely to the poem in your answer.

STUDY NOTES

'Deaths and Engines' contextualises Eiléan Ní Chuilleanáin's experience of death – and particularly her father's death – within the setting of another 'burnt-out' ruin, the abandoned wreckage of an aircraft engine. Characteristically, the poet's metaphorical sense is so complete that at times it dominates the poem, constantly inviting readers to tease out meaningful connections within the language.

As with so many of her poems, Ní Chuilleanáin begins mid-narrative – as dreams often do – with an aeroplane coming in to land in Paris. The sense of danger as the plane descends in 'a stiff curve' is typical of the edgy imagery found in **stanza one**. **The memory immediately suggests a moment of insight – of coming down to earth**: 'We came down above the houses/In a stiff curve'. Details are stark – particularly the absorbing description of the 'empty tunnel' and the peculiar sight of the 'back half of a plane' which has been 'burnt-out and frozen' against the wintry landscape. The contrast of the deserted 'black' wreckage 'On the snow' accentuates the visual effect, adding drama to the memory.

Stanza two emphasises the surreal nature of the hushed 'snow-white runways in the dark'. The poet continues to construct a dreamlike sense of uneasy silence and chilling alienation. The only sounds coming over the loudspeakers are the unsettling 'sighs/Of the lonely pilot'. There is an underlying suggestion of a weary individual – perhaps facing death. This is given a wider relevance by the unnerving opening of **stanza three**: 'The cold of metal wings is contagious'. For the poet, this insightful moment marks a changing perspective; 'Soon you will need wings of your own'. The 'you' might refer Ní Chuilleanáin's dying father or the poet herself or possibly the reader. From this point onwards, the metaphor of the wrecked aircraft is central to the fragmentary memories of her father's illness and death. **The poet interweaves two narratives**; the trajectory of the plane as it 'Meets the straight skyline' and the mark of her father's natural life span ('the lifeline in your palm'). Ní Chuilleanáin uses the memorable image of the crossed knife and fork to suggest the inescapable destiny which confronts the dying.

The poet's familiar preoccupations of tension and mystery are even more obvious in **stanza four**. Disjointed scenes of 'Hospital pyjamas, screens round a bed' are introduced as 'images of relief'– at least temporarily. **But the prevailing mood is of inevitable death** – 'These will fail you some time'. The poet expresses the final reality of every human being in **stanza five**: 'You will find yourself alone'. Ní Chuilleanáin conveys the nightmarish realisation of irreversible death through recognisable images of losing control: 'Accelerating down a blind/Alley, too late to stop'. Run-on lines and a persistent rhythm add to the sense of powerlessness. Once again, there are echoes of the 'empty tunnel' and the 'burnt-out' plane. Nevertheless, in imagining her father's final moments, the poet can relate to his experience of dying as a release, so that they both understood 'how light your death is'.

The resigned tone of **stanza six** reflects Ní Chuilleanáin's deeper understanding of mortality. In celebrating her father's life within a context of enduring love, the poet is able to simultaneously dismantle and preserve the relationship she has had with her father. She returns to the image of the wrecked aeroplane, accepting that in death, 'You will be scattered like wreckage'. However, far from feeling sadness for her father's loss, **Ní Chuilleanáin takes comfort in knowing that he will live 'in the hearts/Of all who love you'**. The sentiment is subdued and poignant, and all the more powerful since it comes from a poet who rarely expresses her feelings directly.

To a great extent, the poem is about families and how they process their personal tragedies. As always, Ní Chuilleanáin's oblique approach is open to many interpretations. But she seems to be suggesting that it takes the sudden shock of death to acknowledge the closeness of relationships in our lives. Typically, in dealing with such emotional subjects as separation, grief and the death of a loved one, **the poet never lapses into sentimentality**. 'Deaths and Engines' was written during the escalation of violence in Northern Ireland, and some critics have understood the poem as a commentary on the human cost of conflict. In the end, readers are left to make up their own minds.

ANALYSIS

'Ní Chuilleanáin's poems of separation and estrangement transcend the limits of personal experience.' Discuss this view, with particular reference to 'Deaths and Engines'.

Sample Paragraph

One of the most interesting aspects of Eiléan Ní Chuilleanáin's poetry is her focus on the natural life cycle. Even though she deals with the distressing subject of her father's death in 'Deaths and Engines', I found the poem to be more uplifting than depressing. In closely comparing his death to the wrecked plane she saw in Paris, 'Tubular, burnt-out and frozen', she eventually realises that all the 'pieces' of the wreckage 'Will spin and lodge in the hearts/Of all who love you'. Just because death has separated her from her father physically does not mean the end of their love. The poem also shows Ní Chuilleanáin empathising with her father and stressing the individual experience of death for every human being: 'You will find yourself alone/Accelerating down a blind/Alley, too late to stop'. Her message is simple – every individual must face death unaccompanied. In her poems, Ní Chuilleanáin can really accept the natural cycle – and this has meaning for every reader. In 'Fireman's Lift', for example, she also came to terms with a close family death – that of her mother by comparing her passing to the glorious Assumption of the Virgin Mary. I believe that such poems transcend the individual and emphasise the naturalness of separation and loss.

Examiner's Comment

This is a well-focused response to the question and shows a close understanding of the poem. Accurate quotations are used effectively to support key points. Expression is clear and there is some good personal engagement. The cross-reference is also welcome. Grade A.

CLASS/HOMEWORK EXERCISES

1. 'What defines Eiléan Ní Chuilleanáin's poetry is its imaginative power and precision of language.' Discuss this statement, with particular reference to 'Deaths and Engines'.

2. Copy the table below into your own notes and fill in critical comments about the last two quotations.

Key Quotes

The back half of a plane, black/On the snow, nobody near it	Ní Chuilleanáin's graphic description of the abandoned aircraft – associating it with disaster and violent death – is surreal and unnerving. Like so much of her writing, it transports readers into states of refreshed perception.
The cold of metal wings is contagious:/Soon you will need wings of your own	The frozen wings of the wrecked plane makes an immediate impact on the poet who connects the image to her father. There is an underlying sense of realisation and the suggestion of angels leading the dying soul to heaven.
The images of relief:/ Hospital pyjamas, screens round a bed	
And know how light your death is	

4 STREET

He fell in love with the butcher's daughter
When he saw her passing by in her white trousers
Dangling a knife on a ring at her belt.
He stared at the dark shining drops on the paving-stones.

One day he followed her   5
Down the slanting lane at the back of the shambles.
A door stood half-open
And the stairs were brushed and clean,
Her shoes paired on the bottom step,
Each tread marked with the red crescent   10
Her bare heels left, fading to faintest at the top.

'And the stairs were brushed and clean'

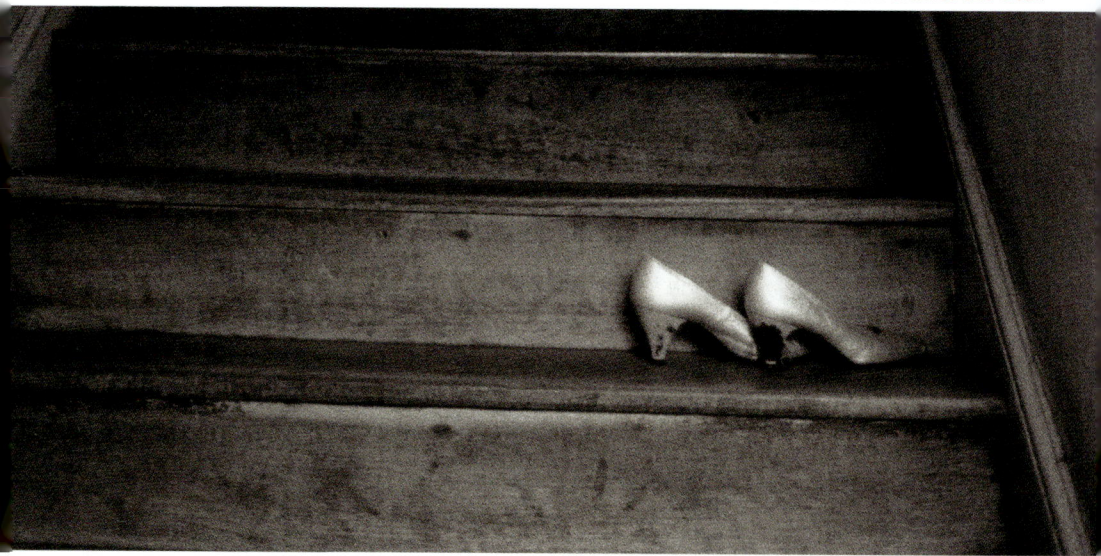

GLOSSARY

3	*Dangling*: hanging freely, displaying.	10	*crescent*: half-moon; sickle-shape.
6	*shambles*: untidy market scene; place of slaughter.	11	*fading*: dwindling, perishing.
		11	*faintest*: weakest, exhausted.
10	*tread*: undersole of a shoe; top surface of a step in a staircase.		

EXPLORATIONS

1. Why do you think Ní Chuilleanáin chose to name her poem 'Street' and yet gives the street no name? Give reasons for your response.

2. Which image did you find most intriguing in the poem? Refer closely to the text in your answer.

3. Were you satisfied by the poem's conclusion? Briefly explain your response.

STUDY NOTES

'Street' is a short lyric poem from Ní Chuilleanáin's collection, 'The Magdalene Sermon' (1989). Mary Magdalene was the first person to witness the Resurrection of Christ and these poems reflect on women's religious experiences. The poems also depict edges, borders and crossings between different kinds of worlds as though passing through thresholds and intersections from one realm of experience to another, just as Christ rose from the dead. Characteristically, the poet reveals and conceals women and their strange responsibilities in a graceful, luminous voice.

Ní Chuilleanáin believed in the importance of the ordinary and the domestic as new metaphors for human experience. In the **first section** of the poem, she quietly tells a somewhat unusual tale, giving readers a memorable glimpse into another reality. It is the story of a man falling in love with a woman, 'the butcher's daughter'. Flowing run-on lines depict the rising emotions of the man as he catches sight of her 'in her white trousers'. This colour is often associated with purity and innocence, but it is also the traditional colour butchers wear in their work. **A close-up shot captures a disturbing detail.** 'Dangling' describes the careless movement of the knife as it sways from the 'ring at her belt'. The verb is carefully positioned at the beginning of the line as it tantalises and entices like a piece of shining jewellery; yet this knife has a deadly purpose. The man is captivated: 'He stared at the dark shining drops on the paving-stones'. Has this knife recently been used? Has blood just been spilled? Is he, as if in a fairytale, suddenly enthralled, by the glittering yet lethal trade of the slaughterer?

In the **second section**, the narrative continues, becoming increasingly menacing:

'One day he followed her'. The assonant 'ow' sound disquietly enhances his journey. Ní Chuilleanáin specialises in the 'poetic of descriptive places'. The man's journey takes him 'Down the slanting lane at the back of the shambles'. **Varying line lengths add to the growing tension**. The adjective 'slanting' suggests a sinister backstreet where everything is oblique, tilted, half-concealed. The 'shambles' is a rough market where meat is carved and animals are slaughtered. To the outside world, it is a place of violence and mayhem. Is Ní Chuilleanáin making a hidden reference to the slaughter of Christ on the cross? 'A door stood half-open'. Does the door admit or shut out? Is this a symbol of the threshold between life and death which Christ breached? As always, the poet invites the reader to make sense of the clues. A secret is being half-revealed, a mystery is being highlighted. Where does the door lead?

Eiléan Ní Chuilleanáin often peoples her poems with women who studiously attend to their chores. (Mary Magdalene attended to Jesus washing his feet with her tears and drying them with her hair.) Here 'the stairs were brushed and clean'. Are they awaiting a visit or is this the attention to hygiene which is normal in the butchering trade? This poet's population of silent figures disclose little information. The 'butcher's daughter' had left 'shoes paired on the bottom step'. Yet even this tangible detail reveals only mystery. The full narrative is missing. Is there a suggestion that the man and woman will soon be a pair as well? An inviting flight of stairs leads to all sorts of possibilities. **Ní Chuilleanáin has created a typically ambivalent scenario** filled with underlying danger and excitement. This dreamlike encounter is imbued with an unforgettable atmosphere of edgy anticipation as profound silence echoes.

The poem concludes with a defined image. The girl's 'bare heels' have left traces which become more indistinct as they ascend the stairs. This is emphasised by the alliterative phrase, 'fading to faintest'. These are 'marked with the red crescent' like a secret sign beckoning through the enjambed lines. **The mystery resonates.** What really is marked with the bow-shapes? The stairs? Her shoes? The heels? Readers are kept wondering. What does the future hold for this couple? Detailed close-ups have been presented, yet there are tantalising gaps in the narrative as we are left like the man who was enticed by the 'Dangling' knife, lured into this ominous atmosphere. As in so many of her elusive dramas, disrupting patterns of communication allows the poet to draw attention to the problem of communication itself. Is this the rounded insight to be glimpsed in the poem?

'Poems of waiting, dramatic and incident rich, are told quietly by Ní Chuilleanáin.' Discuss this statement in relation the poem 'Street'.

Sample Paragraph

I felt that the poem 'Street' inveigled me into its dreamlike, surreal yet tangible world rather like the man is lured by the 'butcher's daughter'. I was caught as if in a dream, that state of consciousness which shimmers between sleep and wakefulness, where details are clearly recognisable, 'the dark shining drops', 'the red crescent/her bare heels left', yet their meaning is shrouded in mystery. Just as the 'half-open' door both invites and repels, this poem reveals and conceals as the reader wonders what is about to happen. Will the encounter take place between the man and the woman? Will he disappear at the top of the steps? Is she waiting for him there or has she disappeared? What has she been doing? What will she do? The reader has been brought like the man on a 'slanting' journey. The full view of the lane was obscured from him, the full story is hidden from the reader by the obliqueness of the poem. Yet just like a dream the atmosphere is unforgettable, the waiting is palpably ominous. The poem disappears at its conclusion as the 'red crescent' marks flow 'fading to faintest at the top'. Suspense and tension reverberate. As in life nobody knows what will happen next. This tale is told calmly as the poet carefully positions the instrument of allure at the edge of the line 'Dangling' to highlight its swaying inviting movement. The reader is led like the man, by well-realised signs, 'drops', a 'lane', a 'door', 'stairs' and footprints as if following a trail in a fairy tale. Yet the poet does not release the dramatic tensions at the poem's conclusion leaving it to resonate in the reader's consciousness.

Examiner's Comment

This response shows a remarkably close reading of the poem, using suitable reference and quotation to address the question throughout. Discussion points are clear and there is good engagement with the text. Expression is impressive – fluent, varied and well controlled. Grade A.

CLASS/HOMEWORK EXERCISES

1. 'Ní Chuilleanáin's poetry is oblique, yet concrete.' Discuss this statement in relation to 'Street'.

2. Copy the table below into your own notes and fill in critical comments about the last two quotations.

Key Quotes

He fell in love with the butcher's daughter	This poem opens in the manner of a fairy tale with clear, uncluttered narrative. Neither the people nor the street are named, giving the poem a universal significance and the mystery of myth.
dark shining drops on the paving-stones	The evidence of the butcher's trade lies on the ground, yet the attraction of the blood stains is pinpointed by the focus on their lurid, glistening appearance.
A door stood half-open	
Each tread marked with the red crescent	

5 FIREMAN'S LIFT

I was standing beside you looking up
Through the big tree of the cupola
Where the church splits wide open to admit
Celestial choirs, the fall-out of brightness.

The Virgin was spiralling to heaven,   5
Hauled up in stages. Past mist and shining,
Teams of angelic arms were heaving,
Supporting, crowding her, and we stepped

Back, as the painter longed to
While his arm swept in the large strokes.   10
We saw the work entire, and how light

Melted and faded bodies so that
Loose feet and elbows and staring eyes
Floated in the wide stone petticoat
Clear and free as weeds.   15

This is what love sees, that angle:
The crick in the branch loaded with fruit,
A jaw defining itself, a shoulder yoked,

The back making itself a roof
The legs a bridge, the hands   20
A crane and a cradle.

Their heads bowed over to reflect on her
Fair face and hair so like their own
As she passed through their hands. We saw them
Lifting her, the pillars of their arms   25

(Her face a capital leaning into an arch)
As the muscles clung and shifted
For a final purchase together
Under her weight as she came to the edge of the cloud.

Parma 1963 – Dublin 1994

'spiralling to heaven'

GLOSSARY

Fireman's Lift: The term refers to a technique commonly used by emergency service workers to carry someone to safety by placing the carried person across the shoulders of the carrier.

The Assumption of the Virgin: Roman Catholic Church teaching states that the Virgin Mary, having completed the course of her earthly life, was assumed (or elevated) body and soul into heavenly glory.

Antonio Allegri da Correggio (1489–1534), usually known as Correggio, was the foremost painter of the Parma school of the Italian Renaissance. One of his best-known works, *The Assumption of the Virgin*, is a fresco which decorates the dome of the Duomo (Cathedral) of Parma, in Northern Italy.

2   *cupola*: dome-shaped roof.
4   *Celestial*: heavenly, divine.
5   *spiralling*: whirling, twisting.
17   *crick*: arch, strain.
18   *yoked*: forced, strained.
26   *capital*: upper section of a column supporting a ceiling or arch.

EXPLORATIONS

1. Based on your reading of the poem, comment on the appropriateness of the title, 'Fireman's Lift'.

2. Choose one visual image from the poem which you consider particularly effective. Briefly explain your choice.

3. Write your own short personal response to the poem.

STUDY NOTES

This extraordinary poem describes the scene depicted in the painter Correggio's masterpiece, Assumption of the Virgin. *In 1963 Eiléan Ní Chuilleanáin and her mother had visited Parma Cathedral. Following her mother's death in 1994, the poet used the visit as the setting for 'Fireman's Lift', describing it as a 'cheering-up poem, when my mother was dying because I absolutely knew that she would want me to write a poem about her dying…'*

The poem begins with Ní Chuilleanáin's vivid memory of the moment when she and her mother were looking up at Corregio's celebrated ceiling mural. In the **opening stanza**, she invites readers into the Italian setting: 'I was standing beside you looking up/Through the big tree of the cupola'. There is an **immediate dreamlike sense of intimacy and closeness between mother and daughter**, as though they were both aware that something significant was happening. From the outset, the focus is on the majestic painting's mystery and symbolism, reaching heavenwards to imagined 'Celestial choirs'.

Stanza two emphasises the struggle of the angels to lift Mary into the heavens, and the awkwardness and wonder of being pushed in such a similar manner to birth. We are encouraged to become part of the dynamic scene within the reality of this great spectacle. The dynamic verbs 'spiralling' and 'heaving' suggest **the physical effort involved in raising the Virgin from her earthly life**. Line breaks and frequent commas are used to create a sluggish pace. Ní Chuilleanáin is drawn to the collective energy which becomes a fireman's lift of 'Teams of angelic arms', and the effort to raise Mary 'Past mist and shining' is relentless.

Ní Chuilleanáin then considers the overwhelming effect of Corregio's 'work entire', designed to give the illusion of real and simulated architecture within the painted fresco. This awe-inspiring achievement is reflected in the pulsating run-through rhythms and hushed tones of **stanzas three** and **four**. **Dramatic images of the angelic figures and saints assisting Mary's Assumption give expression to the artist's powerful vision**: 'Melted and faded bodies' are intermingled with 'elbows and staring eyes'. Within the dome/petticoat image, Ní Chuilleanáin describes Correggio's Virgin passing into another glorious life. All the time, this vortex of bodies and faces around her are fully engaged in assisting Mary to reach the waiting Christ.

Stanza five defines an important turning point for the poet who can now make sense of her mother's death through a fresh understanding of Corregio's perspective: 'This is what love sees, that angle'. **The assured tone marks a coming-to-terms with deep personal loss.** Ní Chuilleanáin's renewed appreciation of the painting enables her to accept the burden of letting the dead go. Her resignation is evident in the poignant image of a 'branch loaded with fruit', an obvious symbol of the natural cycle.

Stanzas six and **seven** return to **Corregio's mesmerising skill in his interaction of art and architecture** within the cathedral dome. This intricate collusion is seen in sharper focus, providing a context for Ní Chuilleanáin to re-assert her changing relationship with her mother. The restless limbs of the painted angels are in perfect harmony with the great Duomo ceiling: 'The back making itself a roof/The legs a bridge'. This intriguingly harmonious composition merging paint and plaster adds to the urgency of ensuring that the dying soul achieves its ultimate ascension to heaven.

The **final stanzas** observe the figures attending on Mary, 'heads bowed over to reflect on her/Fair face'. Their tenderness is evident in both sound and tone. The poet has said that, on one level, 'Fireman's Lift' is about the nurses who looked after her mother when she was dying. Typically, the poet broadens our understanding of suffering, showing people caring and concerned. The concluding lines, however, acknowledge **the strength of spirit which Ní Chuilleanáin singles out as the hallmark of her mother's life and death**. This is reflected in the purposeful expression on the Virgin's face: 'As the muscles clung and shifted/For a final purchase'. Tactile 'u' sounds ('usc', 'ung', 'urch', etc.) and the drawn-out rhythms emphasise that body goes with soul in the movement across this threshold: 'to the edge of the cloud.'

Death and rebirth are recurring themes in Ní Chuilleanáin's work. But in honouring her mother's life and associating her passing with the Assumption of the Virgin, the poet has brought together Italian art, religion and a deep sense of sorrow. Essentially, however, **'Fireman's Lift' is a moving expression of the poet's enduring love** for her mother. It is not unusual for readers of Ní Chuilleanáin's poetry to encounter beautiful images which leave them searching. Nevertheless, this poem has a universal significance. It is infused with an astounding sense of love, loss and triumph as the ascending figure disappears into the clouds. Poised on the edge of this unknowable boundary, the rest is mystery.

ANALYSIS

'For Eiléan Ní Chuilleanáin, boundaries and transitions are central concerns.' Discuss this view with particular reference to 'Fireman's Lift'.

Sample Paragraph

I found 'Fireman's Lift' both puzzling and interesting. Ní Chuilleanáin managed to link her mother's death with the famous painting by Antonio Correggio, *The Assumption of the Virgin*. In describing her memory of a holiday visit to Parma Cathedral, the poet seemed to enter the reality of the mural and see her own relationship with her mother in a new way – almost like one of the angels who desperately tries to raise Mary to heaven, 'Teams of angelic arms were heaving'. The transition is shown in terms of brute strength – the Virgin is 'Hauled up in stages'. But the poet also reflects the transition between this life and the next in the optical illusions painted on the dome's structure. Everything appears to be integrated – for example, the hands of angels act as a 'crane and a cradle' supporting Mary. She leans on the 'pillars of their arms'. This metaphor blurs the distinction between stonework and painted figures. The poet sees no difference between her own prayers for her mother's soul and the work of the saints who raise the Virgin. To me, Ní Chuilleanáin is absorbed in the art work. I found this typical of her poetry in that she wanders beyond borders and margins, just as Correggio did within his celebrated painting.

Examiner's Comment

This is a very well-written response which addresses the question directly and uses references effectively. There is good engagement with the poem throughout. Clear points explore the poet's emphasis on the blurred lines within the Correggio painting, and between it and Ní Chuilleanáin's own attitude. Grade A standard.

CLASS/HOMEWORK EXERCISES

1. 'Eiléan Ní Chuilleanáin's poems explore the persistence of memory in a highly distinctive style.' Discuss this statement with particular reference to 'Fireman's Lift'.

2. Copy the table below into your own notes and fill in critical comments about the last two quotations.

Key Quotes

I was standing beside you looking up	Ní Chuilleanáin's simple, opening image is not only applicable to a shared moment in Parma Cathedral, but suggests the tender memories of children and the lasting influence of parents.
Teams of angelic arms were heaving	The energetic language and forceful alliteration reflect the enormous collective effort to ensure the Virgin Mary's ascension to heaven.
As she passed through their hands	
the muscles clung and shifted	

6 ALL FOR YOU

Once beyond the gate of the strange stableyard, we dismount.
The donkey walks on, straight in at a wide door
And sticks his head in a manger.

The great staircase of the hall slouches back,
Sprawling between warm wings. It is for you.   5
As the steps wind and warp
Among the vaults, their thick ribs part; the doors
Of guardroom, chapel, storeroom
Swing wide and the breath of ovens
Flows out, the rage of brushwood,   10
The roots torn and butchered.

It is for you, the dry fragrance of tea-chests
The tins shining in ranks, the ten-pound jars
Rich with shrivelled fruit. Where better to lie down
And sleep, along the labelled shelves,   15
With the key still in your pocket?

'steps wind and warp/Among the vaults'

GLOSSARY

6   *wind*: curve, meander.
6   *warp*: bend, buckle.
7   *vaults*: large rooms often used for storage; chambers beneath a church.

7   *ribs*: curved structures which support a vault.
10 *brushwood*: undergrowth, small twigs and branches.

EXPLORATIONS

1. Based on your reading of the poem, comment on the appropriateness of the title, 'All for You'.

2. Choose one memorable image from the poem and briefly explain its effectiveness.

3. Write your own individual response to the poem, referring closely to the text in your answer.

STUDY NOTES

'All for You' comes from Eiléan Ní Chuilleanáin's 'The Brazen Serpent' (1994). The book's title refers to the Biblical story of Moses and the Israelites in the desert. God had become angry with his people as they had spoken against their leader Moses and He let fierce snakes crawl among them and bite them. Moses prayed for the people and God instructed Moses to make a bronze serpent and place it upon a pole in public view. Anyone who was bitten could then look on the brazen snake and they would be cured. This foreshadows the raising onto the Cross of Jesus Christ who died to save sinners. Therefore, God made this sacrifice 'All for You'. Ní Chuilleanáin's collection of poems brings the possibility of hope, of getting through bad times, of being redeemed.

Ní Chuilleanáin **collapses time and distinctions betweeen places** in 'All for You'. Line by line, the reader is drawn into deeper water until the bottom can no longer be touched, a recurring feature of this poet's complex work. The **first three lines** describe a scene which resonates with detail from the Bible story of the birth of Jesus, 'the strange stableyard', 'The donkey', the 'manger'. Why is the stableyard 'strange'? In the Biblical account, Joseph and Mary had to leave their home town and travel to Bethlehem to be listed for a tax census. As often is the case with Ní Chuilleanáin's dramatic presentations, the reader must piece together a bare minimum of narrative sense. However, there is a sense of inevitability about the journey being described.

In **lines 4–11**, a noticeably different time and space is realised. What follows is **a series of evocative images and metaphors relating to a transitional experience**. Personification brings a staircase vividly to life as it 'slouches back' lolling and slumping – 'Sprawling' almost like a reclining animal as it sits between the 'warm wings' of the hall. Is it ominous or welcoming? It is waiting, as the bronze serpent awaited the Israelites, like a gift 'for you'. Ní Chuilleanáin does not determine the identity of 'you', instead leaving it open to speculation, so that 'you' could have a universal application and refer to anyone. Is this gift for all? The poet's descriptive talent engages the reader as the grand staircase is depicted with great clarity, yet its full significance is never defined. Alliteration ('wind and warp') conveys the stairs' sinuous movement, curling like an uncoiling animal through the 'thick ribs' of the intimidating vaults.

The architectural metaphor is a strong element in Ní Chuilleanáin's poetry which is full of mysterious crannies and alcoves. Could this imposing building be a convent waiting to welcome a young woman as its doors open, revealing the imposing interior of 'guardroom, chapel' and 'storeroom'? The poet's three aunts were nuns and she has commented, 'One is constantly made aware of the fact that the past does not go away, that it is walking around the place causing trouble at every moment'. Is this reference therefore autobiographical or does it encompass a wider significance? Could the staircase lead to salvation and heaven?

A rush of heat from the nearby ovens is suddenly palpable – again conveyed through the poet's effective working of personification, 'the breath of ovens/Flows out'. Ní Chuilleanáin uses a violent image to describe the fierce temperature, 'the rage of brushwood'. This is continued in the savagery with which the kindling has been collected, 'roots torn out and butchered'. Is there an echo of the Biblical tale of the burning bush from the **Book of Exodus** where God directed Moses to the Promised Land? This story teaches that we should be able to obey God whenever he calls us. Is the poet also referencing the story of Christ, 'butchered' on the cross for the sins of the world? The forceful rhythm of these dramatic lines creates an intensity, a climax of dread, almost like an ecstatic spiritual experience.

There is a marked **change of tone** in the **last five lines**. All the tension eases within the ordered space of the building's provisions store. Readers are now immersed in the moment, smelling the 'dry fragrance of tea-chests', observing 'tins shining in ranks, the ten-pound jars'. Repetition of the rich 'r' sound suggests the store's abundance of goods. Yet there is also an unease secreted in this image of confined order. The fruit is 'shrivelled', the fragrance is 'dry'. Is there a life withering, unable to reproduce? Is this another central dimension of religious life? The poem concludes with a rhetorical question intimating that there is nowhere better to take rest, just as Joseph and Mary did long ago in that 'strange stable yard', than here 'along the labelled shelves'. The body's surrender and submission to God's will enables it to act.

Another Biblical reference is suggested in the final detail of the 'key still in your pocket'. In Isaiah 33:6, faith is the key of salvation: 'He will be the sure foundation of your times, a rich store of salvation and wisdom and knowledge; the fear of the Lord is the key to this treasure.' Ní Chuilleanáin's poem focuses on the experience of Christian faith as imagined through the imposing challenge and triumph of religious vocations. The 'key' image is typically contradictory – symbolising both confinement and freedom. Is the poet presenting the central paradox of Christian belief? Can the soul's redemption only be achieved through submission to God's will? Characteristically, Ní Chuilleanáin's multi-layered narrative has been subtly woven, offering a glimpse, perhaps of salvation and hope.

ANALYSIS

'Eiléan Ní Chuilleanáin's poetry is an unshaped fire demanding to be organised into a sequence of words and images.' Discuss this statement in relation to 'All for You'.

Sample Paragraph

'All for You' is an unsettling poem which seems to emerge from the subconscious like an unformed fire. This poet's work resists containment as she wanders beyond borders. The poem springs from the idea of a gift which is 'All for You'. This can be the reward of spiritual salvation as the continuous references to the Bible – the story of Christ's birth is interwoven with references to Old Testament scenes, such as 'the rage of brushwood'. Like an 'unshaped fire', the poem's religious theme 'Flows out' like the heat from the ovens. Yet it is carefully layered. Fragmentary narratives are overlaid and remain long after the poem is read. I thought the image of the writhing staircase which 'slouches back' was very effective as it suggested the brazen serpent which Moses erected to gain salvation for his own people. The image also symbolised the harsh ladder of life which Christians must climb to reach salvation. Ní Chuilleanáin's use of alliteration, 'wind and warp', emphasised the twisting turns life takes and also called to mind the uncoiling serpent – the devil, perhaps. The poet has often written about nuns and she includes several interesting images relating to the enclosed life of a convent. I got the sense of being in a strange building with old-fashioned rooms and vaults. The storeroom imagery reflected the enclosed religious world, with 'the dry fragrance of tea-chests' and 'shrivelled fruit'. The sense of routine and order was also present: 'The tins shining in ranks'. Ironically, this strict religious life of submission represented the 'key' to salvation. The repetition of 'It is for you' suggests a generous God wishing to give a precious gift and what gift could be more important than the gift of hope? All the poet's ideas are expressed in patterns of visionary and spiritual language which can be seen as a powerful 'unshaped fire'.

Examiner's Comment

A clear personal response to a challenging question. Key discussion points are effectively illustrated, showing a good understanding of this complex poem – and particularly the poet's use of dense symbols and overlapping images. Expression throughout is varied, fluent and well controlled. Grade A.

CLASS/HOMEWORK EXERCISES

1. 'Ní Chuilleanáin's language is supple and acute enough to undertake its most difficult subject, how we perceive and understand the world.' Discuss this statement in relation to the prescribed work of the poet on your course.

2. Copy the table below into your own notes and fill in critical comments about the last two quotations.

Key Quotes

The donkey walks on, straight in at a wide door/ And sticks his head in a manger	This scene is echoed in the following image of the hall where doors 'Swing wide'. The donkey does not hesitate to follow its instincts to take sustenance at its trough. Is it equally natural for someone entering a religious order to accept the gift being offered?
the steps wind and warp	Alliteration vividly conveys the twisting movement of the great staircase. The image could also be seen as a metaphor for the difficulties encountered in the Christian journey to salvation.
guardroom, chapel, storeroom	
the ten-pound jars/Rich with shrivelled fruit	

7 FOLLOWING

So she follows the trail of her father's coat through the fair
Shouldering past beasts packed solid as books,
And the dealing men nearly as slow to give way –
A block of a belly, a back like a mountain,
A shifting elbow like a plumber's bend –   5
When she catches a glimpse of a shirt-cuff, a handkerchief,
Then the hard brim of his hat, skimming along,

Until she is tracing light footsteps
Across the shivering bog by starlight,
The dead corpse risen from the wakehouse   10
Gliding before her in a white habit.
The ground is forested with gesturing trunks,
Hands of women dragging needles,
Half-choked heads in the water of cuttings,
Mouths that roar like the noise of the fair day.   15

She comes to where he is seated
With whiskey poured in two glasses
In a library where the light is clean,
His clothes all finely laundered,
Ironed facings and linings.   20
The smooth foxed leaf has been hidden
In a forest of fine shufflings,
The square of white linen
That held three drops
Of her heart's blood is shelved   25
Between the gatherings
That go to make a book –
The crushed flowers among the pages crack
The spine open, push the bindings apart.

'And the dealing men nearly as slow to give way'

GLOSSARY

(A–Z)

Title: Following: coming after in time or sequence, people about to be mentioned or listed; those who admire or support somebody.

2 **beasts**: animals at an Irish mart.

3 **dealing men**: dealers, men who bargain as they buy and sell animals at an Irish fair.

5 **plumber's bend**: length of 18 inches from the bend of the elbow to the tip of the middle finger.

7 **brim**: edge.

10 **wakehouse**: house, particularly in Ireland where a dead person is laid out; people come to console the grieving relatives and to pay their respects to the deceased.

14 **cuttings**: small pieces of plants.

20 **facings**: strengthening linings; collar, cuffs and trimmings on a uniform coat.

20 **linings**: layers of material used to cover and protect.

21 **foxed**: soiled; marked with fox-like reddish spots and stains, often found on old books and documents.

21 **leaf**: single sheet of paper.

22 **shufflings**: walking slowly and awkwardly.

29 **spine**: vertical back of book to which pages are attached.

29 **bindings**: material which holds pages together.

EXPLORATIONS

1. Based on your reading of the poem, show how Eiléan Ní Chuilleanáin conjures up the atmosphere of an Irish fair day? Refer closely to the text in your response.

2. In your opinion, how many settings are there in this poem? Which one did you prefer? Give reasons for your choice quoting to support your answer.

3. Choose one vivid image from the third stanza of the poem and briefly explain its effectiveness.

STUDY NOTES

Eiléan Ní Chuilleanáin often assumes a storytelling role in her poems as she relates memories from the past. She re-adjusts the perspective of readers by taking us into the lives of ordinary people who literally and physically made history. In her collection, 'The Brazen Serpent', Ní Chuilleanáin highlights family and women as makers of history.

She hints at the untold, through her use of characters, silences and secrets. These confidential witnesses, like the poet herself, reconstruct subtle revelations of family unease and discontentment. Female imagery expresses what is silenced. The poet frequently explores religious themes as well as death and rebirth. Quietly and precisely, she offers us the comfort that the past does not go away.

In the **opening section**, the poet begins her story in her usual oblique, non-confessional style, yet deeply engaging the reader despite her seeming detachment. A vividly realised journey by a girl through the hurly-burly of an Irish fair day catapults the reader into the story. She is trying to follow her father through the dense crowds, 'the trail of her father's coat through the fair'. Long run-on lines and broad vowels convey the difficulty of negotiating the route as she attempts to push past 'beasts packed as solid as books'. This unusual simile illustrates the tightly-packed rows of animals. Nor could she easily make her way through the dealers, men caught up in the very serious business of buying and selling, making a deal. Their thick-set bodies, bulky like their animals, are described through a tumbling list of similes and metaphors to highlight their immobile weight, 'A block of a belly, a back like a mountain'. A 'shifting elbow' is like the measure used in plumbing. All these images reinforce the **tough, masculine world of the fair**. Ní Chuilleanáin has pushed the reader, through her unwavering gaze, into the poem's self-enclosed world.

Suddenly, in **line 6**, the girl catches a glimpse of her father. This is shown by a list of his clothing: 'a shirt-cuff, a handkerchief,/Then the hard brim of his hat'. His progress is swift and effortless. He moves as swiftly as the punctuation (a series of fast-moving commas) accelerates the motion of the line. Sharp contrast in the verbs used to describe the progress of the girl and her father **highlight their different rates of success in moving through the fair**. The girl is struggling, 'Shouldering past', while the father moves with ease, 'skimming along'. Is Ní Chuilleanáin suggesting that a woman finds it difficult to negotiate a man's world? The poet has hypnotically caught the excitement as well as the danger of the fair day.

Distance and time blur in the **second section**. Ní Chuilleanáin shifts the scene and time frame from the noise and physical bulk of the fair to the **'shivering bog'**. Personification and slender vowels effectively convey the cold 'starlight' scene as she is revisiting, 'tracing light footsteps', mapping faint prints. **A surreal, nightmarish world is presented**, as 'The dead corpse risen from the wakehouse' appears 'before her in a white habit'. Whose corpse is this? The effortless sense of 'Gliding' suggests the agile movement of the father. Momentarily, the packed animals of the fair have given way to the ground 'forested with gesturing trunks'. Now the heavy trees are highlighting her way, as she will ultimately follow her father into death. Thin waving rushes are evocatively described as 'Hands of women dragging needles'. Their slow cumbersome movement is presented in visionary terms. Is this a reference to the story from the Bible when the Pharaoh of Egypt decreed that, because of the increasing numbers of Israelites all first-born boys were to be drowned on the river Nile? Are these the half-choked heads? Is this the wail of Israelite women and children as they cry and 'roar' like the beasts in the fair, aware of their fate? Or is it a reference to the subordination of women as they work?

In the poem's **concluding section**, the girl meets her father in a much more hospitable setting with 'whiskey poured in two glasses', 'His clothes all finely laundered'. Within these domestic interiors of the poet's imagination lies the remote **possibility of utopia**. The 'square of white linen', redolent of the survivor's suffering, shrunk and stained by the body's signifiers of hurt, becomes a relic of love and loss. Ní Chuilleanáin has commented, 'A relic is something you enclose, and then you enclose the reliquary in something else. In the The Book of Kells exhibition, the book satchel is in leather, which is meant to protect, and there is a shrine which in turn is meant to protect the book'. A relic is associated with people seeking comfort in difficult times. The past is beautifully evoked in the phrase, 'The smooth foxed leaf has been hidden' with its haunting image of time-stained pages. Inside the book are 'crushed flowers', reminders that love was violated, yet something of it remains. These memories have tremendous power; they 'crack' and push apart as if being reborn. Living and dead touch each other through such memories. The dust and noise of the cattle market, the cold starry bog have all evaporated to be replaced by this interior where the 'light is clean', making it easy to see. Comfort and hope are being offered as the poem suggests that the past is not dead.

ANALYSIS

'Ní Chuilleanáin's poems explore how the most basic legends – family stories – fragment and alter in each individual's memory.' Discuss the statement with particular reference to the poem, 'Following'.

Sample Paragraph

I think we tell ourselves stories about the past and I wonder do we need to revisit them in order to see the past differently, to assimilate it and move on in hope? Ní Chuilleanáin's poem, 'Following', dredges up fragments of uniquely Irish family stories (the fair day, a wake, women sewing) and rearranges them, as cards are moved in 'shufflings'. This reconstructs and transforms the past so that we can see and understand from a new perspective. We are brought as followers, just like the girl in the fair, on a journey to discover that the past is not dead, but resonates through the present by means of relics, 'The square of white linen', and so gives hope and comfort to those left behind. The title suggests to me that we are all following one another on the same journey through life, but at different paces, as the girl and the father in the fair. In the masculine world of the fair, 'beasts packed solid as books' the girl found it hard to negotiate her way. The poet has identified the difficult role women have in life, 'dragging needles', employed in repetitive domestic drudgery. These women are unable to express their opinions and concerns, 'Half-choked'. The legends become 'crushed flowers' yet the poet suggests that they are so potent that they can 'crack' open and push apart the book in which they are enclosed. I felt that she was communicating the message of hope that the past does not stay in the past but reverberates and pulses through the present. Our memories do not remain 'shelved' but live again in the present through the power of relics.

Examiner's Comment

This is an assured response, focused throughout and very well illustrated. Quotations are integrated effectively and the answer ranges widely. There is clear evidence of good engagement with the poet's central theme of memory. Expression is also varied and well controlled. Grade A.

> ## CLASS/HOMEWORK EXERCISES

1. 'The mysterious writing style of Ní Chuilleanáin allows the reader to explore the poems on many levels, each tracking a different aspect of the cycle of life.' Discuss this statement in relation to the prescribed poems of this poet on your course.

2. Copy the table below into your own notes and fill in critical comments about the last two quotations.

Key Quotes

Following	This title not only refers to the girl's efforts to follow her father, but also to her admiration of him and how he was about to be remembered. It also suggests that she is following her father as he moves through life to death.
Half-choked heads in the water of cuttings	Two stories merge, the Biblical account of the drowned children of the Jews and the contemporary story of women's subordination in the sharp world of dominant men. Their lack of opportunity and importance is graphically conveyed in the compound word, 'Half-choked'.
In a forest of fine shufflings	
The square of white linen	

8   KILCASH

From the Irish, c.1800

What will we do now for timber,
With the last of the woods laid low –
No word of Kilcash nor its household,
Their bell is silenced now,
Where the lady lived with such honour,   5
No woman so heaped with praise,
Earls came across oceans to see her
And heard the sweet words of Mass.

It's the cause of my long affliction
To see your neat gates knocked down,   10
The long walks affording no shade now
And the avenue overgrown,
The fine house that kept out the weather,
Its people depressed and tamed;
And their names with the faithful departed,   15
The Bishop and Lady Iveagh!

The geese and the ducks' commotion,
The eagle's shout, are no more,
The roar of the bees gone silent,
Their wax and their honey store   20
Deserted. Now at evening
The musical birds are stilled
And the cuckoo is dumb in the treetops
That sang lullaby to the world.

Even the deer and the hunters   25
That follow the mountain way
Look down upon us with pity,
The house that was famed in its day;
The smooth wide lawn is all broken,
No shelter from wind and rain;   30
The paddock has turned to a dairy
Where the fine creatures grazed.

Mist hangs low on the branches
No sunlight can sweep aside,
Darkness falls among daylight   35
And the streams are all run dry;
No hazel, no holly, no berry,
Bare naked rocks and cold;
The forest park is leafless
And all the game gone wild.   40

And now the worst of our troubles:
She has followed the prince of the Gaels –
He has borne off the gentle maiden,
Summoned to France and to Spain.
Her company laments her   45
That she fed with silver and gold:
One who never preyed on the people
But was the poor souls' friend.

My prayer to Mary and Jesus
She may come safe home to us here   50
To dancing and rejoicing
To fiddling and bonfire
That our ancestors' house will rise up,
Kilcash built up anew
And from now to the end of the story   55
May it never again be laid low.

'long walks affording no shade now'

GLOSSARY

(A–Z)

Title: Eiléan Ní Chuilleanáin's translation of the early 19th-century ballad, *Caoine Cill Chais* (The Lament for Kilcash), an anonymous lament that the castle of Cill Chais stood empty, its woods cut down and all its old grandeur disappeared. Kilcash was one of the great houses of a branch of the Butler family near Clonmel, Co. Tipperary, until well into the 18th century. Ní Chuilleanáin's poem encompasses several generations of the Butler family, but the presiding spirit is that of Margaret Butler, Viscountess Iveagh (who died in 1744).

2   **the last of the woods**: a reference to the mass clearance of native Irish forests by plantation settlers to create agricultural land and to fuel the colonial economy. The woodland belonging to the Butlers of Kilcash were sold in 1797 and 1801.

5   **the lady**: Margaret Butler, Viscountess Iveagh, a staunch Catholic (d.1744).

16   **The Bishop**: Catholic clergy – including Lady Iveagh's brother-in-law – were often given shelter in Kilcash.

17   **commotion**: noise, clamour.

24   **lullaby**: soothing song.

31   **paddock**: enclosure.

42   **prince of the Gaels**: probably a reference to the 18th Earl of Ormonde.

43   **the gentle maiden**: Countess wife of the 18th Earl.

47   **preyed**: harmed, took advantage of.

EXPLORATIONS

1. From your reading of the poem, what is your impression of Lady Iveagh? Refer to the text in your answer.

2. Choose one interesting image from 'Kilcash' which you consider particularly effective. Give reasons to explain why this image appealed to you.

3. Write your own individual response to the poem, referring closely to the text in your answer.

STUDY NOTES

'Kilcash' comes from Eiléan Ní Chuilleanáin's 'The Girl Who Married the Reindeer' (2001). Many of the poems in this collection deal with outsiders and the dispossessed. Kilcash was the great house of one of the branches of the Butler family near Clonmel, Co. Tipperary, until the 18th century. The Butlers were Catholic landed gentry who

had come to Ireland as part of an Anglo-Norman invasion during the 12th century and had taken over vast amounts of land. Over time, the family became absorbed into Irish ways. Ní Chuilleanáin's version of the traditional Irish elegy, Caoine Cill Chais, *mourns the death of Margaret Butler, Viscountess Iveagh.*

Stanza one opens with a plaintive voice lamenting 'What will we do now for timber'. The ballad was originally composed in the early 1800s following the demise of the Butlers of Kilcash and the eventual clearing of the family's extensive woodlands which had supplied timber for local people. **The early tone typifies the entire poem's sense of hopelessness, now that the woods are 'laid low'**. The systematic felling of trees is symbolic of the decline of this aristocratic Catholic family. Following colonisation, the Irish were consigned to Nature as a symbol of their barbarity. In some British circles, they were referred to as the 'natural wild Irish' because the country's remote boglands and forests offered shelter to Irish rebels. The poem emphasises the uneasy silence around Kilcash and the speaker pays extravagant tribute to 'the lady' of the house who is immediately associated with Ireland's Catholic resistance: 'Earls came across oceans to see her'.

As always, Ní Chuilleanáin's approach is layered, recognising the genuine feelings of loss while suggesting a misplaced dependence on all those who exploited the native population. For the most part, however, the poem's anonymous narrator appears to express the desolation ('long affliction') felt by the impoverished and leaderless Irish of the time. There is no shortage of evidence to illustrate what has happened to the 'fine house'. Throughout **stanzas two** and **three**, broad assonant sounds add to the maudlin sentiments. **The 'neat gates knocked down' and the 'avenue overgrown' reflect the dramatic turnaround in fortunes.** But is Ní Chuilleanáin's translation of the old song also unearthing an underlying sense of delight in the sudden fall of the mighty? There is 'no shade now' for the once powerful gentry as well as the impoverished community. Many of the references to the 'stilled' birds and animals can also be seen as both a loss and a possible release from an unhappy phase of oppression and dependence.

Images of hardship taken from nature dominate **stanzas four** and **five**. The abandoned peasants are depicted as pitiable. The atmosphere becomes increasingly disturbing as the natural world order is transformed: 'Darkness falls among daylight/And the streams are all run dry'. **As in so many other Irish legends, the landscape reflects the terms of the Butlers' exile**: 'The forest park is leafless'. Negative language patterns – 'No sunlight', 'No hazel, no holly' – highlight the sense of mordant despondency resulting from abandonment. Relentlessly, the regular lines and ponderous rhythm work together to create a monotonous trance-like effect. The extravagant praise for 'the gentle maiden' (a likely reference to the wife of the 18th Earl) dominates stanza six. As a representative of the Butler dynasty, her absence is seen as 'the worst of our troubles' and she is glorified as someone 'who never preyed on the people' despite her privileged lifestyle.

The prayer-like tone of the **final stanza** is in keeping with the deep yearning for a return to the old ways in Kilcash. The Catholic allusion also reinforces the central importance of religion in expressing political and cultural identity. In wishing to restore the former Gaelic order, the speaker imagines lively scenes of communal celebration: 'fiddling and bonfire'. **The aspiration that the castle will be 'built up anew' offers a clear symbol of recovery.** This rallying call is in keeping with traditional laments and is characteristic of the poet's sympathies for the oppressed. Ní Chuilleanáin has retained the rhetorical style of Gaelic poetry throughout, revealing the experience of isolated communities through numerous images of restless desolation and uncomfortable silences.

'Kilcash' marks a significant transition in Irish history. As the old native aristocracy suffered military and political defeat and, in many cases, exile, the world order that had supported the bardic poets disappeared. In these circumstances, it is hardly surprising that much Irish poetry of this period laments these changes and the poet's plight. However, **Ní Chuilleanáin's translation of the old ballad differs from other versions in being more ambivalent towards Viscountess Iveagh and what she represented**. Is the poem a poignant expression of loss and a genuine tribute to those landlords who were seen as humane? Does the poet satirise the subservient native Irish who had been conditioned to accept some convenient generosity from the Catholic gentry? To what extent did the original lament present a romantic distortion of Ireland's history? Readers are left to decide for themselves.

'Eiléan Ní Chuilleanáin's poems retain the power to connect past and present in ways that never cease to fascinate.' Discuss this statement, with particular reference to 'Kilcash'.

Sample Paragraph

On a first reading, I thought that 'Kilcash' was a simple adaptation of the old Gaelic ballad, 'Caoine Cill Chais'. After studying the poem, however, I feel that Eiléan Ní Chuilleanáin has raised many interesting questions about Irish history. For a start, the poem is a translation and the original bard's view of the 18th century Butler line is buried beneath Ní Chuilleanáin's. The opening lament of the deprived peasants seems self-pitying – 'What will we do now for timber'. The compliments paid to Lady Iveagh (Margaret Butler) are lavish and focus on her Catholic faith and support for the old Gaelic culture – 'Earls came across oceans to see her'. As a young person looking back on this period of upheaval, I could appreciate the way disposed Irish people had become dependent on the Catholic gentry as symbols of freedom. The poem repeatedly places 'the lady' as the epitome of hope – 'the poor souls' friend'. It was interesting to see how the flight of the Butlers reduced people to complete dependence, so that all they could do was pray for a miraculous reversal of history 'that our ancestors' house will rise up'. The main insight I gained from the poem was that colonisation – whether by Catholic or Protestant landlords – had broken the Irish spirit. Ní Chuilleanáin manages to link past and present very subtly, broadening our view of the complex relationships between powerful interests and a conquered population.

Examiner's Comment

An assured personal response, focused throughout and very well illustrated with suitable quotations. The paragraph carefully highlights Ní Chuilleanáin's exploration of the plight of the native Irish community in various ways. Points are clearly expressed throughout. Grade A.

CLASS/HOMEWORK EXERCISES

1. 'Ní Chuilleanáin's distinctive poetic world provides an accessible platform for voices from the margin.' Discuss this view, with particular reference to 'Kilcash'.

2. Copy the table below into your own notes and fill in critical comments about the last two quotations.

Key Quotes

What will we do now for timber,/With the last of the woods laid low	The opening admission of loss and dependence sets the nostalgic tone for the rest of this traditional ballad.
the sweet words of Mass	Ní Chuilleanáin emphasises the 'sweet words' of Catholicism as being of crucial importance to native Irish communities in expressing their cultural identity.
Darkness falls among daylight	
Her company laments her/ That she fed with silver and gold	

9   TRANSLATION

for the reburial of the Magdalenes

The soil frayed and sifted evens the score —
There are women here from every county,
Just as there were in the laundry.

White light blinded and bleached out
The high relief of a glance, where steam danced   5
Around stone drains and giggled and slipped across water.

Assist them now, ridges under the veil, shifting,
Searching for their parents, their names,
The edges of words grinding against nature,

As if, when water sank between the rotten teeth   10
Of soap, and every grasp seemed melted, one voice
Had begun, rising above the shuffle and hum

Until every pocket in her skull blared with the note —
Allow us now to hear it, sharp as an infant's cry
While the grass takes root, while the steam rises: 15

  Washed clean of idiom · the baked crust
  Of words that made my temporary name ·
  A parasite that grew in me · that spell
  Lifted · I lie in earth sifted to dust ·
  Let the bunched keys I bore slacken and fall ·   20
  I rise and forget · a cloud over my time.

'Washed clean of idiom'

GLOSSARY

Sub-title: The Magdalenes refers to Irish women, particularly unmarried mothers, who were separated from their children and forced to work in convent laundries. Inmates were required to undertake hard physical labour, including washing and needle-work. They also endured a daily regime that included long periods of prayer and enforced silence. In Ireland, such institutions were known as Magdalene laundries. It has been estimated that up to 30,000 women passed through such laundries in Ireland, the last one of which (in Waterford) closed on 25 September 1996.

1 *frayed*: ragged.
1 *sifted*: sorted, examined.
3 *the laundry*: clothes washing area.
13 *blared*: rang out, resounded.
16 *idiom*: language, misinterpretation.
18 *parasite*: bloodsucker.

EXPLORATIONS

1. Comment on the effectiveness of the poem's title, 'Translation', in relation to the themes which Ní Chuilleanáin addresses in the poem.

2. Choose one image from the poem that you found particularly interesting. Briefly explain your choice.

3. How does the poem make you feel? Give reasons for your response, supporting the points you make with reference to the text.

STUDY NOTES

During the early 1990s, the remains of more than 150 women were discovered at several Dublin religious institutions as the properties were being excavated. The bones, from women buried over a very long period were cremated and reburied in Glasnevin Cemetery. Eiléan Ní Chuilleanáin's poem was read at the reburial ceremony to commemorate Magdalene laundry women from all over Ireland. 'Translation' links the writer's work with the belated acknowledgement, in the late 20th century, of the stolen lives and hidden deaths of generations of Irishwomen incarcerated in Magdalene convents.

The poem begins with a macabre description of the Glasnevin grave where the reburial is taking place: 'The soil frayed and sifted evens the score'. Ní Chuilleanáin expresses the feelings of the mourners ('here from every county') who are **united by a shared sense of injustice**. This dramatic ceremony represents a formal acknowledgement of a dark period in Ireland's social history. **Line 4** takes readers back in time behind convent walls and imagines the grim laundry rooms in which the Magdelene women worked: 'White light blinded and bleached out/The high relief of a glance'.

The poet's delicate and precise language contrasts the grinding oppression of routine manual labour with the young women's natural playfulness. **Their stolen youth and lost gaiety is poignantly conveyed through familiar images of the laundry** 'where steam danced/Around stone drains and giggled and slipped across water' (**line 6**). Vigorous verbs and a jaunty rhythm add emphasis to the sad irony of their broken lives. The relentless scrubbing was intended to wash away the women's sins. However, no matter how much the women washed, they were considered dirty and sinful throughout their lives.

All through the poem, Ní Chuilleanáin focuses on the importance of words and naming as though she herself is aiming to make sense of the shocking Magdalene story. But how is she to respond to the women who have come to the graveyard, 'Searching for their parents, their names'? Typically, the language is dense and multi-layered. In death, these former laundry workers are mere 'ridges under the veil' of the anonymous earth. The metaphor in **line 7** also evokes images of the stern Magdalene nuns. **Ní Chuilleanáin sees all these women as victims of less enlightened times**, ironically recalled in the prayer-like note of invocation: 'Assist them now'.

The poem's title becomes clear as we recognise **Ní Chuilleanáin's intention to communicate ('translate') decades of silence into meaningful expression on behalf of the Magdalene laundry inmates**. Their relentless efforts to eventually become a 'voice' is compared to the almost impossible challenge of 'rising above the shuffle and hum' within the noisy laundry itself. In **line 9**, Ní Chuilleanáin visualises the women setting 'The edges of words grinding against nature' until their misrepresentation is overcome as it is turned to dust along with their bodies.

From **line 13**, much of the **focus is placed on exploring the experience of one of the nuns who managed the laundries**. As the true history emerges, she is also being cleansed of 'the baked crust/Of words that made my temporary name'. The 'temporary name' is her name in religion, that is, the saint's name she chose on entering strict convent life, which, as Ní Chuilleanáin notes, involved relinquishing her previous identity as an individual. She too has been exploited and the poet's generous tone reflects an understanding of this woman who is caught between conflicting influences of duty, care, indoctrination and doubt, 'Until every pocket in her skull blared'. The evocative reference to the 'infant's cry' echoes the enduring sense of loss felt by young mothers who were forced to give up their babies shortly after birth.

In the poem's **final lines**, we hear the voice of a convent reverend mother, whose role is defined by 'the bunched keys I bore'. The reburial ceremony has also cleansed her from 'that spell' which maintained the cruel system she once served. Almost overwhelmed, she now recognises the 'parasite' power 'that grew in me'; and only now can the keys she carries, an obvious symbol of her role as gaoler, 'slacken and fall'. **Bleak, disturbing images and broken rhythms have an unnerving timeless effect.** This woman's punitive authority over others has haunted her beyond the grave.

In the end, Ní Chuilleanáin's measured and balanced approach shows genuine compassion for all institutionalised victims, drawing together the countless young women and those in charge, in their common confinement. In addition to their time spent in convents, they are now reunited, sifting the earth that they have all become. **The tragic legacy of these institutions involves women at many levels.** Nevertheless, the poem itself is a faithful translation, as these victims have been raised from their graves by the poet's response to their collective dead voice. Ní Chuilleanáin relates their compelling story to: 'Allow us now to hear it'. She also tenderly acknowledges the complete silencing of the Irish Magdalenes as they did their enforced and, in some cases, lifelong penance.

Although Eiléan Ní Chuilleanáin's mournful 'translation' reveals glimpses of their true history, **none of these Magdalene women can ever be given back the lives they had before they entered the laundries.** The poem stops short of pretending to even the score in terms of power between those in authority and the totally subservient and permanently disgraced women under their control. At best, their small voices rise up together like 'steam' and form a 'cloud over my time' (**line 21**). This metaphor of the cloud can be construed as a shadow of shame over Irish society, but it can also be seen as a warning that the cycle of abuse is likely to be repeated.

ANALYSIS

'Ní Chuilleanáin's poems often address important aspects of women's experiences in an insightful fashion.' Discuss this view, with particular reference to 'Translations'.

Sample Paragraph

I would completely agree that 'Translations' deals with an issue which is important to Irish women. The scandal of what happened to the unfortunate girls who were locked up in Magdalene convents deserves to be publicised. Eiléan Ní Chuilleanáin's poem certainly gave me a deeper understanding of their disturbing story. The dramatic opening description of the reburial service was attended by relatives 'from every county', suggesting the scale of the mistreatment. The details of the cold laundries – where 'White light blinded' seemed a subtle way of symbolising the misguided actions of those religious orders who punished young girls. I admired the poet's fair treatment of those nuns who are also presented as being imprisoned, even replacing their own natural identities with 'temporary' saints' names. The poem's last stanza was revealing as it envisaged one of the severe nuns who was still confused by her part in the cruelty. She only recognises the 'parasite' of heartless authority within her when it is too late. The poet makes it clear that she was a product of an oppressive Catholic Ireland and under the 'spell' of misguided power. In my opinion, 'Translation' succeeds in explaining the true story of the Magdalene women. It is all the more powerful because Ní Chuilleanáin avoids being over-emotional. Her quiet tone conveys sensitivity and sadness for this dreadful period in Irish history which still lingers like 'a cloud over my time'.

Examiner's Comment

This succinct and focused response shows a clear understanding of the poem and of Ní Chuilleanáin's considered approach to her theme. Short quotations are well integrated and the discussion points range over much of the poem. There is also some very good personal interaction. Grade A.

CLASS/HOMEWORK EXERCISES

1. 'Eiléan Ní Chuilleanáin's poetry offers a variety of interesting perspectives which vividly convey themes of universal relevance.' Discuss this statement with particular reference to 'Translation'.

2. Copy the table below into your own notes and fill in critical comments about the last two quotations.

Key Quotes

The soil frayed and sifted evens the score	Ní Chuilleanáin's opening line sets the reburial scene in Glasnevin Cemetery. The description of the soil being spread evenly on the graves conveys a sense of finality, of coming to terms with the past.
White light blinded and bleached out/The high relief of a glance	Revealing details of conditions within the laundry are unsettlingly poignant. The sharply alliterative verbs are suggestive of how the Magdalene story was covered up for such a long time.
Assist them now, ridges under the veil	
Allow us now to hear it, sharp as an infant's cry	

10 THE BEND IN THE ROAD

This is the place where the child
Felt sick in the car and they pulled over
And waited in the shadow of a house.
A tall tree like a cat's tail waited too.
They opened the windows and breathed   5
Easily, while nothing moved. Then he was better.

Over twelve years it has become the place
Where you were sick one day on the way to the lake.
You are taller now than us.
The tree is taller, the house is quite covered in   10
With green creeper, and the bend
In the road is as silent as ever it was on that day.

Piled high, wrapped lightly, like the one cumulus cloud
In a perfect sky, softly packed like the air,
Is all that went on in those years, the absences,   15
The faces never long absent from thought,
The bodies alive then and the airy space they took up
When we saw them wrapped and sealed by sickness
Guessing the piled weight of sleep
We knew they could not carry for long;   20
This is the place of their presence: in the tree, in the air.

'This is the place'

GLOSSARY

A–Z

11 *creeper*: climbing plant.   13 *cumulus*: rounded, fluffy.

EXPLORATIONS

1. Based on your reading of the poem, comment on the appropriateness of the title, 'The Bend in the Road'.

2. Choose one image from 'The Bend in the Road' which you consider effective. Give reasons why this image appealed to you.

3. How would you describe the poem's conclusion? Is it mysterious? Hopeful? Comforting? Bitter? Briefly explain your response.

STUDY NOTES

'The Bend in the Road' is part of Eiléan Ní Chuilleanáin's poetry collection, 'The Girl who Married the Reindeer'. In many of these poems, the autobiographical becomes transformed as Ní Chuilleanáin takes a moment in time and fills it with arresting images, exact description, stillness and secrecy, linking together selected memories from various times and places. This poem's title suggests that the road will go on even though it is not visible at the moment.

Stanza one opens with Ní Chuilleanáin pointing to the exact place where 'the child/Felt sick in the car and they pulled over'. The memory of such a familiar occurrence is given significance by the use of the demonstrative pronoun, 'This'. Run-on lines catch the flurry of activity as concerned adults attend to the sick child. Everything is still as they 'waited' for the sickness to pass. This suspended moment resonates as they linger 'in the shadow of a house'. **For a split second, an ominous – almost surreal – atmosphere begins to develop.** The poet introduces a slightly sinister simile, 'A tall tree like a cat's tail', peeking in from the world of fairy tale. Then the tree is personified: it 'waited too' as people and landscape merge in the moment of hush. Suddenly, a simple action, ('They opened the windows') relieves the tension and everyone 'breathed/Easily'. The position of the adverb at the beginning of the line captures the relief at the recovery of the child. Yet, the stationary atmosphere remained, 'while nothing moved'. However, the routine narrative of everyday life quickly resumes, 'Then he was better'.

In the **second stanza**, this roadside location takes on the shared resonance of memory, 'Over twelve years'. Readers are left imagining how the adults and child, when passing 'the place' would point it out as 'Where you were sick one day on the way to the lake'. The length of the line mirrors the long car journey. There is a sense of time being concentrated. Ní Chuilleanáin marvels at how the child has grown to adulthood, 'You are taller now than us'. The place has also changed – and even the tree is 'taller'. Assonance pinpoints how the nearby house is becoming yet more mysterious, 'quite covered in/With green creeper'. The insidious 'ee' sound mimics the silent takeover of the house by nature, as it recedes more and more into the shadows. Nature is alive. Creepings and rustlings stir, dispersing solidity and sureness. The poet cleverly places the line as if on a bend at the turn of a line, 'the bend/In the road is as silent as ever it was on that day'. Everything seems focused on the serenity of the place. **A bend in a road prevents seeing what is coming next. Is this an obvious symbol of the human experience?** No-one knows what lies ahead. The tone of this reflective stanza is introspective as Ní Chuilleanáin considers the undeniable passing of time and the human condition.

In the **final stanza**, memory and place interplay with other recollections. The poet's attention turns towards the sky which she imagines 'Piled high' with past experiences. A lifetime's memories now tower 'like the one cumulus cloud/In a perfect sky'. The alliteration of the hard 'c' successfully captures the billowing cloud as it sails through the sky. **Similarly, the recollections of 'all that went on in those years' heave and surge as they drift through the poet's consciousness.** Naturally, they flow from the exact description of 'the bend/In the road'. They are now visible as feelings of loss expand into the present, 'The faces never long absent from thought'. Ní Chuilleanáin had lost not only her father and mother, but also her sister. But she remembers them **similarly** as they were, 'bodies alive then and the airy space they took up' just as the cloud in the sky. Poignantly, the poet also recalls them in their final sickness, 'wrapped and sealed by sickness', as if they had been parcelled for dispatch away from the ordinary routine of life by the ordeal of suffering.

However, the harsh reality of sickness and old age is also recognised: 'We knew they could not carry for long'. Just as the cloud grows bigger as it absorbs moisture, finally dissolving into rain, so did the poet's loved ones buckle beneath the weight of their illness, under the 'piled weight of sleep'. Ní Chuilleanáin finds constant reminders of her family's past in the natural world. She uses a simple image of cloud-like shapes of pillows and bed-covers as they surrender to sickness. Characteristically, the thinking within the poem has progressed considerably. The poet has widened its scope, its spatial dimension, to include those external experiences to which she so eloquently pays witness. Indeed, the poem now stands as a monument to silence and time, absence and presence, past and present. The moment of stillness is invoked. This roadside location takes on a special importance. It marks the place where lost family members now reside. Ní Chuilleanáin's alliterative language is emphatic: 'This is the place of their presence'. They belong 'in the tree, in the air'. As in so many of her poems, Ní Chuilleanáin honours the invisible, unseen presence of other thoughts and feelings that – just like the bend in the road – lie waiting in silence to be discovered and brought to life again.

ANALYSIS

'Eiléan Ní Chuilleanáin's poetry illuminates ephemeral moments of perception in exact description.' Discuss this view in relation to 'The Bend in the Road'. Use suitable reference and quotation to support the points you make.

[handwritten annotations: "Short" above "ephemeral", "understanding" above "perception"]

Sample Paragraph

I agree that Ní Chuilleanáin's poem, 'The Bend in the Road' is filled with meticulously accurate description. *[handwritten: "Precise" above "meticulously"]* The opening lines pinpoint the exact place where 'the child/Felt sick in the car' and they 'pulled over'. The ordinary conversational language, 'They opened the windows', 'Then he was better', brings me into this precise moment in time and place. I can see the dark, cool shadow of the house. I experience the tree as if a child through the almost cartoon-like simile, 'A tall tree like a cat's tail'. Yet, an otherworldly experience hovers as personification transforms the tree into a living being; it 'waited too'. The poet reveals that 'nothing moved' as if all was in suspense awaiting some dramatic revelation. And it is displayed. The place has become a metaphor for the reality of being human. Everything in life changes. The poet suddenly realises that the child has now grown into a man, 'You are taller than us now'. Nothing has remained the same, 'The tree is taller'. Assonance subtly illustrates the changed house now overgrown with 'green creeper'. Another layer is added with the perception that the place has become suffused with the 'presence' of those 'faces never long absent from thought'. This still, silent moment has allowed boundaries to be crossed as memories float 'Piled high, wrapped lightly, like the one cumulus cloud/In a perfect sky'. I now began to understand that in a static moment, the conventional distinctions between life and death, being and memory, all recede and become blurred. The past now lives again, 'in the tree, in the air'. Through carefully observed, precise description of material things, this poet transports readers into a different place to an understanding that many experiences, 'all that went on in those years', can be savoured in various forms, 'softly packed like the air'.

Examiner's Comment

This is a very successful personal response to the question. Accurate and apt quotes provide good support for discussion points which range through the poem effectively. There is evidence of genuine engagement with the poem and expression is also impressive throughout. Grade A.

CLASS/HOMEWORK EXERCISES

1. 'Space in Ní Chuilleanáin's poetry is used as an expression of one's experience of the world and is a metaphor for the linking together of self and the world, within and without.' Discuss this statement, with particular reference to 'The Bend in the Road'.

2. Copy the table below into your own notes and fill in critical comments about the last two quotations.

Key Quotes

A tall tree like a cat's tail waited too	The repetition of the hard 't' sound and the somewhat surreal comparison are reminiscent of a young child's story.
the bend/In the road is as silent as ever it was on that day	The mystery and suspense of what might be lurking around the corner is caught by a careful positioning of the line break and the emphasis on the silence of the day.
like the one cumulus cloud/ In a perfect sky	
wrapped and sealed by sickness	

11 ## ON LACKING THE KILLER INSTINCT

One hare, absorbed, sitting still,
Right in the grassy middle of the track,
I met when I fled up into the hills, that time
My father was dying in a hospital –
I see her suddenly again, borne back   5
By the morning paper's prize photograph:
Two greyhounds tumbling over, absurdly gross,
While the hare shoots off to the left, her bright eye
Full not only of speed and fear
But surely in the moment a glad power,   10

Like my father's, running from a lorry-load of soldiers
In nineteen twenty-one, nineteen years old, never
Such gladness, he said, cornering in the narrow road
Between high hedges, in summer dusk.
                          The hare   15
Like him should never have been coursed,
But, clever, she gets off; another day
She'll fool the stupid dogs, double back
On her own scent, downhill, and choose her time
To spring away out of the frame, all while   20
The pack is labouring up.
                The lorry was growling
And he was clever, he saw a house
And risked an open kitchen door. The soldiers
Found six people in a country kitchen, one   25
Drying his face, dazed-looking, the towel
Half covering his face. The lorry left,
The people let him sleep there, he came out
Into a blissful dawn. Should he have chanced that door?
If the sheltering house had been burned down, what good   30
Could all his bright running have done
For those that harboured him?
                And I should not
Have run away, but I went back to the city
Next morning, washed in brown bog water,   35
And I thought about the hare, in her hour of ease.

'While the hare shoots off to the left'

GLOSSARY

(A-Z)

1 *hare*: mammal resembling a large rabbit.
1 *absorbed*: engrossed, immersed, preoccupied.
7 *absurdly*: ridiculously, nonsensically.

7 *gross*: disgusting, outrageous.
16 *coursed*: hunted with greyhounds.
20 *frame*: picture, enclosure.
21 *labouring*: moving with difficulty.

EXPLORATIONS

1. Who, in your opinion, lacked the killer instinct in this poem? Was it the hare, the soldiers, the greyhounds, the father, the poet? Refer closely to the text in your response.

2. The poet alters time and place frequently in this poem. With the aid of quotations, trace these changes as the poem develops.

3. Did you find the poem's conclusion satisfying or mystifying? Give reasons for your response referring closely to the text.

STUDY NOTES

'On Lacking the Killer Instinct' is part of Eiléan Ní Chuilleanáin's 'The Sun-fish' collection. A sunfish is so-called due to its habit of basking on the water's surface. Ní Chuilleanáin often presents daily life with a sense of mystery and otherworldliness as the poems move between various realms of experience. Each scene lies open to another version of the narrative. She blurs the distance between past and present in this three-part poem. History, which is something of an Irish obsession, always informs the present. This poet discovers and remembers. As she herself has said: 'In order for the poem to get written, something has to happen.'

The title of the poem immediately intrigues and unsettles. The **opening lines** focus on a stationary hare, silent, engrossed, 'absorbed', at rest. It is a vivid picture. Why is this hare preoccupied? The sibilant alliterative phrase, 'sitting still', captures the motionless animal in 'the middle of the track'. This **naturalistic setting** and image is brought into high resolution as the poet recounts that her own journey 'up into the hills' caused her to meet this creature. Ní Chuilleanáin juxtaposes the stillness of the wild hare with her own headlong flight from the awful reality, 'that time/My father was dying in a hospital'. In describing this terrible experience, her tone is remarkably controlled – detached, yet compassionate.

Another narrative thread is introduced in **line 6** when the poet recalls the 'morning paper's prize photograph'. Here the predators are presented as ungainly, almost comical characters incapable of purposeful action: 'Two greyhounds tumbling over, absurdly gross'. The broad vowels and repetition of 'r' highlight the hounds' unattractively large appearance. Irish coursing is a competitive sport where dogs are tested on their ability to run and overtake the hare, turning it without capturing it. It is often regarded as a cruel activity which causes pain and suffering to the pursued creature. From the start of the poem, **readers are left wondering who exactly lacks the killer instinct**. Do the dogs not have the urge to pounce and kill? Has the hare got the killer instinct, running for its life, showing the strong will to survive against all odds? The rapid run-on lines mimic the speed and agility of the hare exulting in 'glad power'.

In **line 11**, the **reader is taken into another realm** – a common feature of Ní Chuilleanáin's interconnected narratives. In this case, she recalls another pursuit. Her father was a combatant in the Irish Civil War in 1922 and was on the run. Like the hare, he fled, 'cornering in the narrow road/Between high hedges, in summer dusk'. Both are linked through 'gladness' as they exult in their capacity to outrun their pursuers. For her father, this was a 'lorry-load of soldiers' – the compound word emphasising the unequal odds against which the poet's father struggled. This is similar to the hare's predicament against the 'Two greyhounds'. The precise placing of 'The hare' tucked away at the end of **line 15** suggests the animal's escape. Ní Chuilleanáin comments that neither the hare nor her father should ever have 'been coursed'. She is happy to think that on some other occasion, the hare is likely to outwit the 'stupid dogs' and will 'spring away out of the frame', nimbly escaping her pursuers. In Irish coursing, the hare is not run on open land but in a secure enclosure over a set distance. The heavy panting exertions of the pursuing dogs is illustrated in the run-through line, 'all while/The pack is labouring up'.

Ní Chuilleanáin returns to her father's story in **line 22**, imagining a moment of danger from his time as a fugitive. The scene is dominated by the threatening sound of a lorry, 'growling' like a pursuing hound. The repetition of the adjective 'clever' links her father and the hare as he too made his escape. Intent on surviving, 'he saw a house/And risked an open kitchen door'. The **enemy soldiers go through the motion of pursuit cursorily, seemingly lacking the killer instinct** when they 'Found six people in a country kitchen'. Ní Chuilleanáin is characteristically ambivalent about why the rebels were not challenged, reminding us of the contradictory attitudes among the various combatants of the Civil War. For whatever reason, the fugitives ('one/Drying his face, dazed-looking') were not arrested and their deception worked. The poet's father is allowed refuge: 'The people let him sleep there'. Throughout Ireland's troubled history, 'safe houses' existed which sheltered those on the run. In her mind's eye, the poet pictures her father emerging in triumph next day 'Into a blissful dawn' (**line 29**). In a series of questions, she considers his crucial decision to stand his ground and feign innocence. In retrospect, anything might have happened to affect the outcome at 'the sheltering house'. Ní Chuilleanáin emphasises how chance has played such a significant role – not just in her father's life – but in Ireland's history.

The poet concludes by returning to the opening scene. Having observed the hare and remembered her father's encounter during the Civil War, she now realises that she should never have run away from her dying father. Her decision to return is seen as a mature one – almost like a religious ritual in which the poet cleanses herself, 'washed in brown bog water'. Is this a form of absolution to remove her guilt for running away? Typically, she uses this unifying symbol to gently draw the poem's three narratives together. After the common experience of the turbulence of the run, all three (the hare, the father and the poet herself) have entered a new state of being – calm composure. Ní Chuilleanáin reflects on 'the hare, in her hour of ease', the soft monosyllabic final word gently conveying a sense of peace and reconciliation. The poem closes as it began with the **beautiful silent image of the hare**, self-possessed and serene after all the turmoil of the chase.

ANALYSIS

'Eiléan Ní Chuilleanáin is a quiet, introspective, enigmatic poet.' Discuss this statement with particular reference to 'On Lacking the Killer Instinct'.

own experience *mysterious*

Sample Paragraph

I thought the poem, 'On Lacking the Killer Instinct', moved effortlessly, mysteriously weaving three different narratives; the intently observed story of the hare and greyhounds, the quietly detached family history of her father's escape in 1921 and her own headlong flight from the city. Ní Chuilleanáin creates small clear windows into the narratives and the reader can then glimpse multi-views of human experience and discord, 'One hare... I met... that time/My father was dying in a hospital'. *disagreement* *dont give up* She celebrates resilience, the hare's 'bright eye' is full of 'a glad power'. Similarly, her father exulted in his cleverness, 'never/ Such gladness' as he out-manoeuvred the 'lorry-load of soldiers'. The poet also faced up to the *unbearable* unpalatable fact of death and 'went back to the city/Next morning'. Her impressionistic style is similar to watching a photograph as it slowly develops before our eyes. At first there are vague unconnected shapes, but as the order establishes itself, the meaning becomes clear. Ní Chuilleanáin gazes intently on a familiar sight, the still hare, which becomes more strange *broodens to wider meaning* under her spellbound observation and she links it to the flight and survival contest which underpins all of life. The reader is effortlessly guided through different times and places as the focus of the poet's gaze shifts from the hunt of the hare in coursing to the hunt of her father in his role in the Civil War, 'In nineteen twenty-one, nineteen years old'. She then quietly reflects on her own flight and concludes that running does not solve problems, 'what good/Could all his bright running have done/For those that harboured him?' In the end, this poet poses questions that resonate. *Lingers* Does she too lack the killer instinct, the capacity to seize and capture rather than suggest? The long monosyllabic word 'ease' suggests that staying calm and still is more effective than running. Yet who lacked the killer instinct, the hare, the greyhounds, the father, the soldiers, the poet? Is the killer instinct worth having? This enigmatic, introspective poet leaves us with an image of quiet stillness to ponder.

Examiner's Comment

This is a very clear and focused response to a testing question. Interesting critical points – aptly illustrated by accurate quotations – range widely, tracing the subtle development of the poem's various narrative threads. The questions posed at the end round off the discussion effectively. Grade A.

CLASS/HOMEWORK EXERCISES

1. 'Eiléan Ní Chuilleanáin's poems elude categories and invite and challenge the reader in equal measure.' Discuss this statement with particular reference to 'On Lacking the Killer Instinct'.

2. Copy the table below into your own notes and fill in critical comments about the last two quotations.

Key Quotes

I see her suddenly again, borne back	Ní Chuilleanáin's effortless movement between settings and time is clearly conveyed by the alliterative explosive phrase.
While the hare shoots off to the left	The dramatic verb captures the sudden darting movement of the elusive fleeing hare as she seeks to escape the pursuing hounds. The detailed direction conveys the poet's close observation.
cornering in the narrow road/Between high hedges	
Should he have chanced that door?	

12 ## TO NIALL WOODS AND XENYA OSTROVSKIA, MARRIED IN DUBLIN ON 9 SEPTEMBER 2009

When you look out across the fields
And you both see the same star
Pitching its tent on the point of the steeple –
That is the time to set out on your journey,
With half a loaf and your mother's blessing.   5

→ Relationship shall be equal

Leave behind the places that you knew:
Move foreward
All that you leave behind you will find once more,
You will find it in the stories;
The sleeping beauty in her high tower
With her talking cat asleep   10
Nobody can tell you what to do
Solid beside her feet – you will see her again.

When the cat wakes up he will speak in Irish and Russian
And every night he will tell you a different tale
About the firebird that stole the golden apples,
Gone every morning out of the emperor's garden,   15
And about the King of Ireland's Son and the Enchanter's Daughter.

The story the cat does not know is the Book of Ruth
And I have no time to tell you how she fared
When she went out at night and she was afraid,
In the beginning of the barley harvest,   20
Or how she trusted to strangers, and stood by her word:

You will have to trust me, she lived happily ever after.

'the firebird that stole the golden apples'

GLOSSARY (A–Z)

Title: An epithalamium is a poem (or song) in celebration of a wedding. Eiléan Ní Chuilleanáin has included this poem (to her son Niall and his bride, Xenia) as the introductory dedication in her poetry collection, *The Sun-fish*.

9   *sleeping beauty*: European fairytale from 'La Belle au bois dormant' (Beauty of the sleeping wood) by Charles Perrault and 'Dornroschen' (Little Briar Rose) by the Brothers Grimm.

14   *the firebird*: Russian fairytale; 'Tsarevitch Ivan, the Fire Bird and the Gray Wolf' by Alexander Afanasyev.

16   *the King of Ireland's Son*: Irish fairytale; 'The King of Ireland's Son' by Padraic Colum.

17   *Book of Ruth*: religious story from the Old Testament.

21   *Or how she trusted to strangers*: In the Bible story, Boaz owned the field Ruth harvested. He was a relative of the family and by law could 'redeem' her if he married her now that she was a widow. He wished to do so because he admired how she had stood by her mother-in-law, 'For wherever you go, I will go'.

EXPLORATIONS

1. Do you think the references to fairytales are appropriate on the occasion of Eiléan Ní Chuilleanáin's son's marriage? Give one reason for your answer.

2. In your opinion, what is the dominant tone of voice in the poem? Is it one of warning, reassurance, hope, consolation…? Briefly explain your response with reference to the poem.

3. Why do you think the poet placed the last line apart from the rest of the poem? Give one reason for your opinion.

STUDY NOTES

'I write poems that mean a lot to me.' (Eiléan Ní Chuilleanáin) This particular poem is dedicated to her son, Niall, and his new bride, Xenya, on the happy occasion of their marriage. Folklore is central to this poet's work. Her mother, Eilis Dillon, was a famous writer of children's stories. Fairytales allow Ní Chuilleanáin the opportunity to approach a subject from an oblique, non-confessional perspective. It gives distance. Story-tellers

rarely comment or explain what happens. They simply tell the tale. In this poem, Ní Chuilleanáin refers to folklore and a well-known Bible story as she addresses the young couple.

The **first stanza** opens with **warm advice** from a loving mother as she gives the young man leave to set out on his own journey through life with his new partner. Run-on lines contain a beautiful, romantic image of a harmonious vision, 'you both see the same star'. Personification and alliteration bring this natural image to radiant life, 'Pitching its tent on the point of the steeple', suggesting the new home which the young couple are about to set up for themselves. **Ní Chuilleanáin's gaze is one of relentless clarity and attentiveness. She illuminates details**. She also counsels that it is the right time to go, 'to set out on your journey' when you are prepared ('With half a loaf') and with good wishes ('and your mother's blessing'). She combines colloquial and fairytale language. The tone is warm, but also pragmatic – offering practical advice to the newlyweds to make the most of whatever they have to start with: 'half a loaf is better than none'.

Stanza two begins with the imperative warning: 'Leave behind'. The mother is recommending the couple to forget 'the places that you knew'. Is 'places' a metaphor for their actual homes, or their cultural environments? Or does it refer to values the young people hold sacred? She consoles them that past experiences can still be found 'in the stories'. Ní Chuilleanáin now weaves an intricate web of such stories from many different sources. The first tale is that of 'sleeping beauty in her high tower'. This classic folk story involves a beautiful princess, enchantment and a handsome prince who has to brave the obstacles of tall trees which surround the castle and its sleeping princess. **Is Ní Chuilleanáin illustrating that the path to true love is filled with difficulties and that only the brave will be successful?** The extended run-on lines suggest the hundred years sleep of the spellbound princess who can only be awakened by a kiss. The poet also makes use of another familiar element of fairytales – talking animals. In this case, the 'talking cat' probably refers to Irish folklore, and the King of Cats, a renowned teller of tales. Ní Chuilleanáin is able to link the basic characteristics of the animal with human behaviour. The cat slumbers with the princess 'Solid', stable and dependable, beside her feet. Despite the poet's realism, however, this fairytale allusion is primarily optimistic.

In **stanza three**, Ní Chuilleanáin imagines the cat awakening and telling stories in both 'Irish and Russian', a likely reference to the young couple's **two cultural backgrounds**. The poet has said that in her work she is trying 'to suggest, to phrase, to find a way to make it possible for somebody to pick up certain suggestions... They might not be seeing what I am seeing'. The poet continues to set her personal wishes for Niall and Xenya within the context of folktales, turning to the Russian tradition: 'Tsarevitch, the Fire Bird and the Gray Wolf'. Again, the hero of this story is on a challenging mission, as he attempts to catch the 'firebird that stole the golden apples... out of the emperor's garden'. The assonance of the broad vowel 'o' emphasises the exasperation of the repeated theft. As always in folklore, courage and determination are required before the hero can overcome many ordeals and find true happiness.

Ní Chuilleanáin introduces the Irish tradition, with the story of the King of Ireland's son who must pluck three hairs from the Enchanter's beard in order to save his own life. On his quest, he gains the hand of Fedelma, the Enchanter's youngest daughter. But he falls asleep and loses her to The King of the Land of Mist. **Is the poet simply advising her son and daughter-in-law that love must be cherished and never taken for granted?** Throughout the poem, she draws heavily on stories where heroes have to fight for what they believe in. All of these tales convey the same central meaning – that lasting love has to be won through daring, determination and sacrifice.

In the playful link into **stanza four**, Ní Chuilleanáin remarks that 'the story the cat does not know is the Book of Ruth'. This final story is not from the world of folklore, but from the Bible, (although the poet has commented that 'a lot of religious narrative is very folkloric'). The Book of Ruth teaches that **genuine love can require uncompromising sacrifice**, and that such unselfish love will be well rewarded. This particular tale of inclusivity shows two different cultures coming together. The Israelites (sons of Naomi) marry women from the Moab tribe, one of whom is Ruth. She embraces Naomi's people, land, culture and God. This is very pertinent to the newly-married couple as they are also from different lands and cultures. Not surprisingly, the Biblical tale is one of loving-kindness – but it also includes a realistic message. After her husband's death, Ruth chooses to stay with her mother-in-law and undertakes the backbreaking farm-work of gleaning to support the family. This involves lifting the grain and stalks left behind after the harvesting of barley. The metaphor of the harvest is another reminder that married couples will reap what they sow, depending on the effort and commitment made to their relationship.

The poem's last line is placed apart to emphasise its significance. Ní Chuilleanáin tells the newly-weds that they 'will have to trust me' – presumably just as Ruth did her mother-in-law, Naomi. For doing this, she was rewarded with living 'happily ever after' as in the best tales. The poet's quietly light-hearted approach, however, does not lessen her own deeply-felt hopes for Niall and Xenya. **All the stories she has used are concerned with the essential qualities of a loving relationship** – and share a common thread of courage, faithfulness and honesty as the couple journey to a happy future. Tales and dreams are the shadow-truths that will endure. Ní Chuilleanáin's final tone is clearly sincere, upbeat and forward-looking.

ANALYSIS

'The imagination is not the refuge but the true site of authority.' Comment on this statement in relation to the poem, 'To Niall Woods and Xenya Ostrovskia, Married in Dublin on 9 September 2009'.

Sample Paragraph

I feel that Ní Chuilleanáin's poem has subtle messages which only become clear after several readings. I think the poet is counselling her son and his new bride, Xenya, that stories, 'the imagination' are where truth, 'the true site of authority' lies. Stories are not escapism, although we may scoff in this modern age at 'Once upon a time'. The stories she chooses, 'sleeping beauty in her high tower', 'the firebird that stole the golden apples' and the 'King of Ireland's Son and the Enchanter's Daughter' all suggest that perseverance and sincerity win the day. I believe that this is a good message to give to the couple as they 'set out' on their journey. Nothing worthwhile is won easily. This is not escapism, but reality. While the language, 'half a loaf and your mother's blessing', and imagery (even the beautiful lines which describe the 'star/Pitching its tent on the point of the steeple') seem to be from the land of children's fiction, they resound with good sense. I thought the inclusion of the story of Ruth was very apt as it involved two cultures which is relevant to the couple's Irish and Russian origins, but also to many other situations in this time of immigration. People in this new era will have to 'trust to strangers'. But if integrity and loving kindness is shown, as Ruth's story demonstrated long ago, the prize of a happy future can be won. 'You will have to trust me, she lived happily ever after.' I understood that Ní Chuilleanáin is showing that no matter where these imaginative tales come from, Europe, Russia, Ireland or the Bible, obstacles have to be overcome in life through resolution and perseverance. This is a tough message, there is no hiding here. I thought the poet was clever because by putting this insight into the realm of a fairy story, it does not sound like preaching which the young couple might resent, yet the message rings true throughout time from this 'site of authority' the kingdom of story-telling.

Examiner's Comment

A well-supported and sustained personal response showing genuine engagement with the poem. The focused opening tackles the discussion question directly. This is followed by several clear points tracing the development of thought throughout the poem. Accurate quotations and clear expression are also commendable features of the paragraph. Grade A.

CLASS/HOMEWORK EXERCISES

1. What impression of Ní Chuilleanáin do you get from reading 'To Niall Woods and Xenya Ostrovskia, Married in Dublin on 9 September 2009'? Write at least one paragraph in response, illustrating your views with reference to the text of the poem.

2. Use the blank spaces to fill in critical comments about the last two quotations.

Key Quotes

When you look out across the fields/And you both see the same star	The poet is acknowledging that the time has come for the young couple to strike out on their own as they look at what the world has to offer. The simple, romantic image of the star conveys vividly that they share the same vision of the future.
You will find it in the stories	Ní Chuilleanáin offers strong support and advice to the newlyweds. The truths that the young couple have known will not be lost because they are moving on. The spirit and value of these old tales will always be available in folklore.
About the firebird that stole the golden apples	
the King of Ireland's Son and the Enchanter's Daughter	

LEAVING CERT SAMPLE ESSAY

'Eiléan Ní Chuilleanáin's extraordinary poetic world reveals compelling narratives which never cease to captivate readers.' Discuss this view, supporting your answer with suitable reference to the poems on your course.

Marking Scheme Guidelines

Candidates are free to agree and/or disagree with the given statement. The poet's treatment of themes and subject matter should be addressed, as well as her individual approach, distinctive writing style, etc. Reward responses that show clear evidence of genuine engagement with the poems. Expect discussion on how Ní Chuilleanáin's poetry appeals/does not appeal to readers.

Material might be drawn from the following:

- Poet's views on life/relationships.
- Recurring optimistic themes on life and rebirth; the continuous past.
- Fragmented narrative; innovative narrative blending.
- Collapse of time and place.
- Atmospheric detail; artistic and architectural references.
- Dispassionate, detached tone of storyteller.
- Focus on uniquely Irish phenomena.
- Biblical, historical and mythical references.
- Mystical/spiritual experience.
- Layered and interwoven nuances challenge the reader, etc.

Sample Essay

(Ní Chuilleanáin's extraordinary poetic world reveals compelling narratives which captivate readers)

1. *To me, Eiléan Ní Chuilleanáin's lyrical world thrives on the creeping rustlings and barely noticed stirrings of life. Enthralling stories are quietly let slip to bewitch and enchant her readers in a wide range of variety, from hopeful poems such as 'All for You' to the family stories of 'Fireman's Lift' and 'To Niall Woods and Xenya...'*

2. *'The Bend in the Road' takes a normal event, a child becoming car-sick, and transforms it with arresting images from the surreal, ominous world of the fairytale,*

'A tall tree like a cat's tail'. The poet links together selected memories from various times and places and so mesmerises the reader with the resonance from this 'bend/ In the road'. The family all point, on subsequent journeys to 'Where you were sick on the way to the lake'. Ní Chuilleanáin's intent gaze reminds us that a bend in the road, which is cleverly emphasised by its line placement, prevents seeing what is around the corner. Now the poet interjects another memory into the story, the death of loved ones 'Piled high, wrapped lightly, like the one cumulus cloud/In a perfect sky'. This place now becomes 'the place of their presence'. They live now 'in the tree, in the air' because this is where they are remembered. Ní Chuilleanáin fuses parallel narratives, the ill child, the revisited bend in the road, the sick and dying relatives to uncover the mystical truth, the past shines through the present.

3. The driving narrative of the young girl in 'Following' as she attempts to keep up with her father on a hectic fair day holds the readers who are pulled into this world by the unusual description of 'beasts packed solid as books'. The explosive 'b' links 'beasts' and 'books' and I can really picture the crammed animals standing in lines as they await sale. Other stories are woven into the poem, as the image of the dead father appears, not 'skimming' as before but 'Gliding' as the girl crosses the 'shivering bog'. He is now sitting in 'the library where the light is clear'. The poet is tantalising readers, challenging us to engage and 'push... open' the poem, just as the 'crushed flowers', an evocative image for past shared memories, force the book open. Once more the reader is comforted by the message that the past is not dead. The girl's suffering is represented by 'The square of white linen'. It is not 'shelved', never to be thought of or experienced again. It will emerge, 'crack/The spine open'.

4. Ní Chuilleanáin has remarked that she has been 'captivated by history'. She recounts a story in the poem, 'On Lacking the Killer Instinct', which her father had told her about running away from the Black and Tans when he was a young man. The reader is submerged into the Ireland of 1922 as the soldiers hunt her father. He seeks refuge in a 'safe house'. The blessed relief of the escape is graphically conveyed in the detail, 'he came out/Into a blissful dawn'. In my opinion, the reader is delighted at the father's breath-taking escape. It is similar to the escape of the hare, recounted in the earlier part of the poem, 'her bright eye/Full not only of speed and fear/But surely in the moment a glad power'. Narratives are blended together seamlessly as the poet relates her own flight from the awful reality of her father's final illness, 'I

fled up into the hills, that time/My father was dying a in hospital'.

5. *'Fireman's Lift' also deals with the harsh truth of her mother's death. They had both visited Parma Cathedral once and their close relationship is clearly caught. 'I was standing beside you looking up/Through the big tree of the cupola'. The strong verbs, 'spiralling' and 'heaving' capture the huge effort of the angels as they lifted Mary in to the heavens from her earthly life. The hands of the angels act as a 'crane and support' for Mary. 'Their heads bowed to reflect on her/Fair face' reminded the poet of the nurses who tended her mother in her final illness. Readers become immersed in the poem's storyline when the poet comments, 'This is what love sees, that angle'. The poet is coming to terms with the harsh reality that life has a natural cycle, 'The crick in the branch loaded with fruit'. The reader stands with mother and daughter marvelling as 'The Virgin was spiralling to heaven'. Now it is time for the poet's mother to go too.*

6. *Although Ní Chuilleanáin tells a story from an oblique, non-confessional perspective, this detachment does not prevent her engaging her reader. In the epithalamium, 'To Niall Woods and Xenya...' she intricately weaves Russian ('the firebird') and Irish ('the Enchanter's Daughter') stories as she celebrates the two diverse cultures of the young couple. She also uses the story to gently pass on her thoughts and advice on their new life together. I thought the phrase, 'you both see the same star', showed how she understood that the young couple had a shared vision of life. But Ruth's story from the Bible was most fascinating. She had to show courage to succeed as she trusted to strangers. The young people will also need these qualities if they are to succeed in the best tradition of the fairytale to 'live happily ever after'. This, of course, is what every reader dreams of.*

7. *For me, Ní Chuilleanáin has opened a poetic world in which she intertwines stories from the fabric of her own family life, 'poems that mean a lot to me', with those from many other varied sources. The reader stands fascinated and delighted by a bend in the road, a hare 'sitting still', 'The sleeping beauty in her high tower', the Virgin Mary as 'she came to the edge of the cloud', a 'key still in your pocket', all thanks to the gaze and skill of a remarkable poet.*

(approx. 990 words)

Examiner's Comment

This is a well sustained personal response that shows clear engagement with several of Ní Chuilleanáin's poems. Effective use is made of accurate quotations and reference to support the critical discussion. While some points could benefit from further development, the essay is organised effectively and is written confidently.

GRADE: A1
P = 15/15
C = 13/15
L = 13/15
M = 5/5
Total = 46/50

SAMPLE LEAVING CERT QUESTIONS ON NÍ CHUILLEANÁIN'S POETRY

(45/50 MINUTES)

1. 'Ní Chuilleanáin's beguiling poems emerge from an intense but insightful imagination.' Do you agree with this assessment of her poetry? Write a response, supporting your points with reference to the poems on your course.

2. 'Eiléan Ní Chuilleanáin is a truly original poet who leads us into altered landscapes and enhances our understanding of the world around us.' To what extent would you agree with this statement? In your response, refer to the poems on your course.

50 mins

3 'Ní Chuilleanáin's subject matter can be challenging at times, but her writing style is always highly impressive.' Write a response to this view, supporting the points you make with suitable reference to the poetry on your course.

Sample Essay Plan (Q1)

'Ní Chuilleanáin's beguiling poems emerge from an intense but insightful imagination.' *deep understanding* *Do you agree with this assessment of her poetry? Write a response, supporting your points with reference to the poems on your course.*

- Intro: Ní Chuilleanáin's innovative treatment of a broad thematic range – *different aspects* Irish history, *remains over time* myth, transience, memory, relationships, loss, religious life, the dispossessed, etc.

- Point 1: 'Fireman's Lift' – compelling treatment of her mother's death. Importance of dramatic setting as a context for personal experiences/memories. Poet's sympathetic tone, atmospheric detail, artistic references.

- Point 2: 'Translation' – perceptive account of the Magdalene laundry workers. Sensitive approach to women victims. Use of effective symbols. Collapse of time. Silence and understated meanings. Imaginative and interwoven nuances affect readers.

- Point 3: Dispassionate, detached tone of storyteller – 'Deaths and Engines', 'Kilcash'. Underlying sense of the poet's compassion. Interlinked layered narrative threads entice the reader.

- Conclusion: Poetry can challenge/excite responses – Ní Chuilleanáin's mesmeric exploration of universal themes invites readers to unravel the secrets of her work.

Sample Essay Plan (Q1)

Develop one of the above points into a paragraph.

Sample Paragraph: Point 2

'Translation' offers an intriguing account of a dark period in recent Irish history. Ní Chuilleanáin's quiet dramatisation of the Magdalene laundry victims begins in Glasnevin Cemetery, with an unnerving description: 'soil frayed and sifted evens the score'. This image is typical of the poet, suggesting both the surface of the communal grave and the horrifying injustice that has happened over the years. In death, these women have become 'ridges under the veil' of the earth. The reference also conveys a sense of the strict Magdalene nuns who are also viewed as victims of an unchristian era. Time and places blend throughout the poem. The poet's concentrated vision of the laundries is associated with their exploitation – 'where steam danced/Around stone drains and giggled and slipped across water'. She contrasts the girls' youthful spirit with the cold conditions around them. I could make sense of the poem's title as Ní Chuilleanáin's aim was to reveal (or 'translate') the true Magdalene story. Without a trace of sentimentality, 'Translation' movingly recalls a whole generation of women whose lives were ruined. Generously, the ending focuses on the authoritarian figure of an unnamed nun who is envisioned in death and who finally understands the tragedy – 'Allow us now to hear it, sharp as an infant's cry'. This line suggested the communal suffering shared by the nuns and the unmarried mothers who were separated from their babies. The poet's intense depiction of the Magdalene experience is highly compelling, allowing me to relate to this truly regrettable 'cloud over my time'.

Examiner's Comment

As part of a full essay, this is a focused and competent A-grade paragraph which offers clear personal engagement with the poem. The discussion relating to Ní Chuilleanáin's dense imagery is impressive. Apt – and accurate – quotes are used effectively throughout and expression is fluent.

LAST WORDS

'There is something second-sighted about Eiléan Ní Chuilleanáin's work. Her poems see things anew, in a rinsed and dreamstruck light.'

Seamus Heaney

'Ní Chuilleanáin's eccentric poems uncover hidden dramas in many guises, and she continually holds us captive by her luminous voice.'

Molly Bendall

'Her voice and technique are so solid, so secure, and contain deep echoes of older poetry, as Irish verse tends to do.'

Robert Hudson

SYLVIA PLATH

1932–63

'Out of the ash
I rise with my red hair
And I eat men like air.'

Born in Boston, Massachusetts, in 1932, Sylvia Plath is a writer whose best-known poems are noted for their intense focus and vibrant, personal imagery. Her writing talent – and ambition to succeed – was evident from an early age. She kept a journal during childhood and published her early poems in literary magazines and newspapers. After studying Art and English at college, Plath moved to Cambridge, England, in the mid-1950s. Here she met and later married the poet Ted Hughes. The couple had two children, Frieda and Nicholas, but the marriage was not to last. Plath continued to write through the late 1950s and early 1960s. During the final years of her life, she produced numerous confessional poems of stark revelation, channelling her long-standing anxiety and doubt into poetic verses of great power and pathos. At her creative peak, Sylvia Plath took her own life on 11 February 1963.

Prescribed Poems

❶ BLACK ROOK IN RAINY WEATHER

On the stiff twig up there
Hunches a wet black rook
Arranging and rearranging its feathers in the rain.
I do not expect a miracle
Or an accident   5

To set the sight on fire
In my eye, nor seek
Any more in the desultory weather some design,
But let spotted leaves fall as they fall,
Without ceremony, or portent.   10

Although, I admit, I desire,
Occasionally, some backtalk
From the mute sky, I can't honestly complain:
A certain minor light may still
Lean incandescent   15

Out of kitchen table or chair
As if a celestial burning took
Possession of the most obtuse objects now and then –
Thus hallowing an interval
Otherwise inconsequent   20

By bestowing largesse, honour,
One might say love. At any rate, I now walk
Wary (for it could happen
Even in this dull ruinous landscape); skeptical,
Yet politic; ignorant   25

Of whatever angel may choose to flare
Suddenly at my elbow. I only know that a rook
Ordering its black feathers can so shine
As to seize my senses, haul
My eyelids up, and grant   30

A brief respite from fear
Of total neutrality. With luck,
Trekking stubborn through this season
Of fatigue, I shall
Patch together a content   35

Of sorts. Miracles occur,
If you care to call those spasmodic
Tricks of radiance miracles. The wait's begun again,
The long wait for the angel,
For that rare, random descent.   40

'Hunches a wet black rook'

GLOSSARY

(A-Z)

8	*desultory*: unexceptional, oppressive.	21	*largesse*: generous, giving.
10	*portent*: omen.	24	*skeptical*: wary, suspicious
15	*incandescent*: glowing.	25	*politic*: wise and likely to prove
19	*hallowing*: making holy.		advantageous.
20	*inconsequent*: of no importance.	37	*spasmodic*: occurring in bursts.

EXPLORATIONS

1. What is the mood of the poet? How does the weather described in the poem reflect this mood?

2. In your opinion, why do you think Plath sees light coming from ordinary household objects such as kitchen tables and chairs?

3. What do you think the final stanza means? Consider the phrase 'The wait's begun again'. What is the poet waiting for?

STUDY NOTES

'Black Rook in Rainy Weather' was written while Plath was studying in Cambridge in 1956. It contains many of her trademarks, including the exploration of emotions, the use of weather, colour and natural objects as symbols, and the dreamlike world. She explores a number of themes: fear of the future, lack of identity and poetic inspiration.

Stanza one begins with the straightforward description of a bird grooming itself, which the poet observes on a rainy day. But on closer inspection, the mood of the poem is set with the words 'stiff' and 'Hunches'. The bird is at the mercy of the elements ('wet') and there is no easy movement ('stiff'). **This atmospheric opening is dull and low key.** The black rook is a bird of ill omen. But the bird is presenting its best image to the world as it sits 'Arranging and rearranging its feathers'. Plath longed to excel in both life and art. If she were inspired, the rook would take on a new light as if on fire. But she doesn't see this happening. Even the weather is 'desultory' in the fading season of autumn. Poetic inspiration is miraculous; it is not ordinary. The world is experienced in a heightened way. Notice the long line which seems out of proportion with the rest as she declares that she doesn't expect any order or 'design' in the haphazard weather. The decaying leaves will fall with no ritual, without any organisation, just as they will. **This is a chaotic world**, a random place with no design, just as poetic inspiration happens by chance. It is also accidental, like the falling leaves. We cannot seek it, we receive it. It is active, we are passive.

After this low-key opening, the poem starts to take flight in **stanzas three** and **four** when the poet states: 'I desire'. Plath employs a witty metaphor as she looks for 'some backtalk' from the 'mute sky'. **She would like to connect with it**. It could happen on her walk, or even at home if she were to experience a 'certain minor light' shining from an ordinary, everyday object like a chair. The association of fire and light makes an ordinary moment special. It is 'hallowing'; it is giving generously ('largesse'). She is hoping against hope. Plath may be sceptical, but she is going forward carefully in case she misses the magic moment. **She must stay alert and watchful.** She must be 'politic', wise.

Stanzas six, **seven** and **eight** discuss poetic inspiration. Plath doesn't know if it will happen to her or how it will happen. Two contrasting attitudes are at loggerheads: hope and despair. The rook might inspire her: '**Miracles occur**'. If she were motivated, it would relieve 'total neutrality', this nothingness she feels when living uninspired. Although she is tired, she is insistent, 'stubborn'. The poet will have to 'Patch' something together. She shows human vulnerability, but she is trying. This determination is a different tone from the negative one at the beginning.

Literature was as important to Plath as friends and family. What she can't live without, therefore, is inspiration – a dark, passionless existence. **Depression** is an empty state with no feeling or direction, yet her view of creativity is romantic. It is miraculous, available only to a chosen few. 'The long wait for the angel' has begun. Notice the constant use of the personal pronoun 'I'. This is a poet who is very aware of self and her own personal responses to events and feelings. The outside world becomes a metaphor for her own interior world.

Plath uses both archaic language and slang as if reinforcing the randomness of the world. This is also mirrored in the run-on lines. All is haphazard, but carefully arranged, so even the extended **third-to-last line** stretches out as it waits for the 'random descent' of inspiration. In this **carefully arranged disorder**, two worlds are seen. One is negative: 'desultory', 'spotted', 'mute', 'dull', 'ruinous', stubborn', 'fatigue'. This is indicative of her own bleak mood. The other world is positive: 'fire', 'light', 'incandescent', 'celestial', 'hallowing', 'largesse', 'honour', 'love', 'shine'. Here is the possibility of radiance.

ANALYSIS

'Plath's poems are carefully composed and beautifully phrased.' Write a paragraph in response to this statement, illustrating your answer with close reference to the poem 'Black Rook in Rainy Weather'.

Sample Paragraph

Just like the rook, Plath 'arranges and rearranges' her words with infinite care to communicate the contrast between the dull life of 'total neutrality' which occurs when she is not inspired, when nothing sets 'the sight on fire'. I particularly admire how she artfully arranges disorder in the poem. This mirrors the chance of poetic inspiration. Long lines poke untidily out of the first three stanzas, seeking the 'minor light' to 'Lean incandescent' upon them. I also like how the lines run in a seemingly untidy way into each other, as do some stanzas. Stanza three goes into four, as it describes the chance of a light coming from an ordinary object, such as a kitchen chair, which is seen only if the poet is inspired. The alliteration of 'rare, random' in the last line mirrors the gift of poetic technique which will be given to the poet if she can receive the blessed benediction of poetic inspiration. 'Miracles occur'.

Examiner's Comment

Close reading of the poem is evident in this brief original response to Plath's poetic technique. Quotations are very well used here to highlight Plath's ability to create disordered order. Grade-A standard.

CLASS/HOMEWORK EXERCISES

1. In your opinion, has the poet given up hope of being inspired? Use reference to the poem in your answer.

2. Copy the table below into your own notes and fill in critical comments about the last two quotations.

Key Quotes

But let spotted leaves fall as they fall	Decaying leaves drop as they will without ceremony without any ritual to mark the event.
As if a celestial burning took/Possession of the most obtuse objects now and then	Poetic inspiration allows Plath to see the most ordinary things in a state of heightened awareness. They appear transformed into objects of beauty.
If you care to call those spasmodic/Tricks of radiance miracles	
that rare, random descent	

2 THE TIMES ARE TIDY

Unlucky the hero born
In this province of the stuck record
Where the most watchful cooks go jobless
And the mayor's rôtisserie turns
Round of its own accord.   5

There's no career in the venture
Of riding against the lizard,
Himself withered these latter-days
To leaf-size from lack of action:
History's beaten the hazard.   10

The last crone got burnt up
More than eight decades back
With the love-hot herb, the talking cat,
But the children are better for it,
The cow milk's cream an inch thick.   15

'riding against the lizard'

GLOSSARY

(A–Z)

2   *province*: a remote place.
2   *stuck record*: the needle would sometimes get jammed on a vinyl music album.

4   *rôtisserie*: meat on rotating skewer.
7   *lizard*: dragon.
11 *crone*: old witch.

EXPLORATIONS

1. What is suggested by the poem's title? Is Plath being cynical about modern life? Develop your response in a short paragraph.

2. Select one image from the poem that suggests that the past was much more dangerous and exciting than the present. Comment on its effectiveness.

3. Do you agree or disagree with the speaker's view of modern life? Give reasons for your answer.

STUDY NOTES

'The Times Are Tidy' was written in 1958. In this short poem, Plath casts a cold eye on contemporary life and culture, which she sees as bland and unadventurous. The poem's ironic title clearly suggests Plath's dissatisfaction with the over-regulated society of her day. Do you think you are living in an heroic age or do you believe that most people have lost their sense of wonder? Is there anyone in public life whom you really admire? Perhaps you despair of politicians, particularly when their promises sound like a 'stuck record'.

Stanza one is dominated by hard-hitting images reflecting how the world of fairytale excitement has disappeared. From the outset, **the tone is scornful and dismissive**. Plath believes that any hero would be totally out of place amid the mediocrity of our times. True talent ('the most watchful cooks') is largely unrewarded. The unexpected imagery of the 'stuck record' and the mayor's rotating spit symbolise complacent monotony and lack of progress, particularly during the late 1950s, when Plath wrote the poem. Both images convey a sense of purposeless circling, of people going nowhere. It seems as though the poet is seething with frustration at the inertia and conformity of her own life and times.

Plath's **darkly embittered sense of humour** becomes evident in **stanza two**. She laments the current lack of honour and courage – something which once existed in the world of fairytales. Unlike the past, contemporary society is compromised. There are no idealistic dragon-slayers any more. The worker who dares to stand up and criticise ('riding against the lizard') is risking demotion. The modern dragon – a metaphor for the challenges we face – has even been reduced to a mere lizard. Despite this, we are afraid of confrontation and prefer to retreat. The verb 'withered' suggests the weakness and decay of our safe, modern world. The poet openly complains that 'History's beaten the hazard'. Over time, we have somehow defeated all sense of adventure and daring. These qualities belong in the distant past.

In **stanza three**, Plath continues to contrast past and present. Witches are no longer burned at the stake. This might well suggest that superstition has disappeared, and with it, all imagination. The last two lines are ironic in tone, reflecting the poet's deep **disenchantment with the excesses of our consumer society**. The final image – 'the cow milk's cream an inch thick' – signifies overindulgence. At one time, it was thought that supernatural forces could reduce the milk yield from cows.

The poet clearly accepts that **society has changed for the worse**. Children may have everything they want nowadays, but they have lost their sense of wonder and excitement. She laments the loss of legendary heroism. Medieval dragons and wicked witches (complete with magic potions and talking cats) no longer exist. Her conclusion is that life today is decidedly less interesting than it used to be. Unlike so much of Plath's work, the personal pronoun 'I' is not used in this poem. However, the views expressed are highly contemptuous and the weary, frustrated tone clearly suggests that Plath herself feels unfulfilled.

ANALYSIS

Write a paragraph on Plath's critical tone in 'The Times Are Tidy'.

Sample Paragraph

The tone of voice in 'The Times Are Tidy' is almost irrationally critical of modern life. Plath has nothing good to say about today's world as she sees it. The poem's title is glib and self-satisfied, just like the neatly organised society that Plath seems to despise. The opening comment – 'Unlucky the hero born/ In this province' – emphasises this negative tone. The poet's mocking attitude becomes increasingly disparaging as she rails against the unproductive images of easy living – 'the stuck record' and 'the mayor's rôtisserie'. Plath goes on to contrast today's apathetic society with the more spirited medieval era, when knights in armour existed. The poet deliberately omits all the positive aspects of modern life and chooses to give a very one-sided view of the world. Plath ends on a sarcastic note, sneering at the advances of our world of plenty – 'cream an inch thick'. The voice here – and indeed, throughout the entire poem – is both sardonic and superior.

Examiner's Comment

This A-grade paragraph demonstrates strong analytical skills and is firmly focused on Plath's judgmental tone. The supporting references range widely and effectively illustrate the poet's critical attitude. Quotations are particularly well integrated and the management of language is assured throughout.

CLASS/HOMEWORK EXERCISES

1. Outline the main theme in 'The Times Are Tidy'. In your answer, trace the way the poet develops her ideas during the course of the poem.

2. Copy the table below into your own notes and fill in critical comments about the last two quotations.

Key Quotes

Unlucky the hero born/In this province	Plath is clearly disillusioned with the unheroic world in which she lives.
the mayor's rôtisserie turns/ Round of its own accord	The image of automation suggests how complacent and predictable life has become. Nothing seems to change.
But the children are better for it	
The cow milk's cream an inch thick	

❸ MORNING SONG

Love set you going like a fat gold watch.
The midwife slapped your footsoles, and your bald cry
Took its place among the elements.

Our voices echo, magnifying your arrival. New statue.
In a drafty museum, your nakedness   5
Shadows our safety. We stand round blankly as walls.

I'm no more your mother
Than the cloud that distils a mirror to reflect its own slow
Effacement at the wind's hand.

All night your moth-breath   10
Flickers among the flat pink roses. I wake to listen:
A far sea moves in my ear.

One cry, and I stumble from bed, cow-heavy and floral
In my Victorian nightgown.
Your mouth opens clean as a cat's. The window square   15

Whitens and swallows its dull stars. And now you try
Your handful of notes;
The clear vowels rise like balloons.

'The clear vowels rise like balloons'

GLOSSARY

2　*midwife*: a person trained to assist at childbirth.
3　*elements*: primitive, natural, atmospheric forces.
9　*Effacement*: gradual disappearance

11　*pink roses*: images on the wallpaper.
18　*vowels*: speech sounds made without stopping the flow of the breath.

EXPLORATIONS

1. Comment on the suitability and effectiveness of the simile in line 1.

2. What is the attitude of the mother to the new arrival? Does her attitude change in the course of the poem? Refer to the text in your answer.

3. A metaphor links two things so that one idea explains or gives a new viewpoint about the other. Choose one metaphor from the poem and comment on its effectiveness.

STUDY NOTES

'Morning Song' was written in 1961. Plath explores the complex issues of the relationship between a mother and a child, celebrating the birth of the infant but also touching on deep feelings of loss and separation.

Do all mothers immediately welcome and fall in love with a new baby? Are some of them overwhelmed or even depressed after giving birth? Are parents often anxious about the new responsibilities a baby brings? Plath wrote this poem after two intensely personal experiences, celebrating the birth of her daughter, Frieda, who was 10 months old when she wrote the poem, and shortly after a miscarriage. The poem is realistic and never strays into sentimentality or cliché. The title 'Morning' suggests a new beginning and 'Song' a celebration.

Stanza one describes the arrival of the child into the world in a strong, confident, rhythmic sentence announcing the act of creation: 'Love set you going'.

The simile comparing the child to a 'fat gold watch' suggests a plump baby, a rich and precious object. The broad vowel effects emphasise the physical presence of the baby. The 'ticking' sound conveys action and dynamism, but also the passage of time. The child is now part of the mortal world where change and death are inevitable. At this moment of birth, the baby is the centre of attention as the midwife and parents surround her. But this is a cruel world, as we see from the words 'slapped' and 'bald'. The child is now part of the universe as she takes her place among the 'elements'. The verbs in this stanza are in the past tense – **the mother is looking back at the event**. The rest of the poem is written in the present tense, which adds to the immediacy of the experience.

Stanza two has a feeling of disorientation, as if the mother feels separated from the child now that she has left the womb. There is a nightmarish, surreal quality to the lines 'Our voices echo, magnifying your arrival'. Plath sees the child as a new exhibit ('New statue') in a museum. Commas and full stops break up the flow of the lines and **the tone becomes more stilted and detached**. The child as a work of art is special and unique, but the museum is 'drafty', again a reference to the harshness of the world. The baby's vulnerability is stressed by its 'nakedness'. The midwife's and parents' frozen response is caught in the phrase 'blankly as walls'. They anxiously observe, unsure about their ability to protect. This baby also represents a threat to their relationship as she 'Shadows' their safety. The child is perceived as having a negative impact on the parents, perhaps driving them apart rather than uniting them.

Stanza three catches the **complex relationship between child and mother**. Plath feels she can't be maternal ('no more your mother'). This is vividly shown in the image of the cloud that rains, creating a puddle. **But in the act of creation, it destroys itself and its destruction is reflected in the pool of water.** Throughout her life, the poet was haunted by a fear of her own personal disintegration and annihilation. Does she see a conflict between becoming a mother and remaining a writer? She also realises as the child grows and matures that she will age, moving closer to death, and this will be reflected in the child's gaze. The mood of this stanza is one of dislocation, estrangement and powerlessness. Notice how the three lines of the stanza run into each other as the cloud disappears.

In **stanza four**, the tone changes to one of intimate, maternal love as the caring mother becomes alert to her child's needs. The situation described is warm and homely – the 'flat pink roses' are very different to the chill 'museum' of a previous stanza. The fragile breathing of the little child is beautifully described as 'your moth-breath/Flickers'. **Onomatopoeia in 'Flickers' mimics the tiny breathing noises of the child**. The mother is anticipating her baby's needs as she wakes ('listen'). The breathing child evokes happy memories of Plath's seaside childhood ('A far sea moves in my ear'). The infant cries and the attentive mother springs into action. She laughs at herself as she describes the comical figure she makes, 'cow-heavy and floral'. She feels awkward as she 'stumble[s]' to tend her child, whose eager mouth is shown by a startling image ('clean as a cat's') as it opens wide to receive the night feed of milk. The stanza flows smoothly over into **stanza five**, just as nature flows to its own rhythm and does not obey clocks or any other man-made rules. Night becomes morning as the child swallows the milk and the window swallows the stars.

Children demand a parent's time and energy. **The child now defines herself** with her unique collection of sounds ('Your handful of notes'). This poem opened with the instinctive, elemental 'bald' cry of a newborn, but closes on a lovely, happy image of music and colour, as the baby's song's notes 'rise like balloons'.

ANALYSIS

The poem opens with the word 'Love'. Is this poem about parental love or parental anxiety?

Sample Paragraph

'Morning Song' contains both as the tone varies from the confident assertion that 'Love' was the source of the child to the curiously disengaged tone of the second stanza, where the parents 'stand round blankly as walls'. The enormity of the event of the birth of their child into a harsh world, 'drafty museum', seems to overwhelm them, particularly the mother. In the third stanza, she declares that she is not the child's mother, and explores her feelings of annihilation through the complex image of the disintegrating cloud, which creates only to be destroyed in the act of creation. However, the poem ends on a positive, loving note as the attentive mother feeds her child on demand, listening to her baby's song 'rise like balloons'. This poem realistically deals with the conflicting emotions new parents experience at a birth.

Examiner's Comment

The short paragraph deals confidently with both attitudes in a well sustained argument effectively using pertinent quotes. These references range widely over much of the poem and the expression is very well controlled. Grade B.

CLASS/HOMEWORK EXERCISES

1. Look at the different sounds described in the poem, such as 'slapped', 'bald cry', 'A far sea moves', 'The clear vowels rise', and comment on their effectiveness.

2. Copy the table below into your own notes and fill in critical comments about the last two quotations.

Key Quotes

The midwife slapped your footsoles	After a birth, the nurse slaps the child to make it cry and clear the mucus from its mouth and nose.
your nakedness/Shadows our safety	The baby's vulnerability is a threat to the parents' relationship.
Our voices echo, magnifying your arrival	
And now you try/Your handful of notes	

❹   FINISTERRE

This was the land's end: the last fingers, knuckled and rheumatic,
Cramped on nothing. Black
Admonitory cliffs, and the sea exploding
With no bottom, or anything on the other side of it,
Whitened by the faces of the drowned.   5
Now it is only gloomy, a dump of rocks –
Leftover soldiers from old, messy wars.
The sea cannons into their ear, but they don't budge.
Other rocks hide their grudges under the water.

The cliffs are edged with trefoils, stars and bells   10
Such as fingers might embroider, close to death,
Almost too small for the mists to bother with.
The mists are part of the ancient paraphernalia –
Souls, rolled in the doom-noise of the sea.
They bruise the rocks out of existence, then resurrect them.   15
They go up without hope, like sighs.
I walk among them, and they stuff my mouth with cotton.
When they free me, I am beaded with tears.

Our Lady of the Shipwrecked is striding toward the horizon,
Her marble skirts blown back in two pink wings.   20
A marble sailor kneels at her foot distractedly, and at his foot
A peasant woman in black
Is praying to the monument of the sailor praying.
Our Lady of the Shipwrecked is three times life size,
Her lips sweet with divinity.   25
She does not hear what the sailor or the peasant is saying –
She is in love with the beautiful formlessness of the sea.

Gull-colored laces flap in the sea drafts
Beside the postcard stalls.
The peasants anchor them with conches. One is told: 30
'These are the pretty trinkets the sea hides,
Little shells made up into necklaces and toy ladies.
They do not come from the Bay of the Dead down there,
But from another place, tropical and blue,
We have never been to.   35
These are our crêpes. Eat them before they blow cold.'

'and the sea exploding'

GLOSSARY

1	*land's end*: literally 'Finisterre'; the western tip of Brittany.	19	*Our Lady of the Shipwrecked*: the mother of Christ prayed for sailors.
3	*Admonitory*: warning.	30	*conches*: shells.
10	*trefoils*: three-leaved plants.	31	*trinkets*: cheap jewellery.
13	*paraphernalia*: discarded items.	36	*crêpes*: light pancakes.
14	*doom-noise*: hopeless sounds.		

EXPLORATIONS

1. Would you agree that this is a disquieting poem that is likely to disturb readers? Refer to the text in your answer.

2. There are several changes of tone in this poem. Describe two contrasting tones, using close reference to the text.

3. What does the poem reveal to you about Sylvia Plath's own state of mind? Use reference to the text in your response.

STUDY NOTES

'Finisterre' was written in 1960 following a visit by Plath to Brittany, France. As with many of her poems, the description of the place can be interpreted both literally and metaphorically.

The sea has always inspired poets and artists. It is at times welcoming, menacing, beautiful, peaceful and mysterious. Throughout her short life, Sylvia Plath loved the ocean. She spent her childhood years on the Atlantic coast just north of Boston. This setting provides a source for many of her poetic ideas. Terror and death loom large in her descriptive poem 'Finisterre', in which the pounding rhythm of storm waves off the Breton coast represents **Plath's inner turmoil**.

Stanza one opens dramatically and immediately creates a disturbing atmosphere. Plath describes the rocky headland as being 'knuckled and rheumatic'. In a series of powerful images ('the last fingers', 'Black/Admonitory cliffs', 'and the sea exploding'), the poet recreates the uproar and commotion of the scene. The **grisly personification** is startling, linking the shoreline with suffering and decay. There is a real sense of conflict between sea and land. Both are closely associated with death ('the faces of the drowned'). The jagged rocks are compared to 'Leftover soldiers' who 'hide their grudges under the water'. There is a noticeable tone of regret and protest against the futility of conflict, which is denounced as 'old, messy wars'.

Plath's **negative imagery** is relentless, with harsh consonant sounds ('knuckled', 'Cramped', 'exploding') emphasising the force of raging storm waves. The use of contrasting colours intensifies the imagery. As the 'sea cannons' against the headland, the atmosphere is 'only gloomy'. It is hard not to see the bleak seascape as a reflection of Plath's own unhappy state.

In **stanza two**, the poet turns away from the cruel sea and focuses momentarily on the small plants clinging to the cliff edge. However, these 'trefoils, stars and bells' are also 'close to death'. If anything, they reinforce the **unsettling mood** and draw the poet back to the ocean mists, which she thinks of as symbolising the souls of the dead, lost in 'the doom-noise of the sea'. Plath imagines the heavy mists transforming the rocks, destroying them 'out of existence' before managing to 'resurrect them' again. In a **surreal sequence**, the poet enters the water ('I walk among them') and joins the wretched souls who lie there. Her growing sense of panic is suggested by the stark admission: 'they stuff my mouth with cotton'. The experience is agonising and leaves her 'beaded with tears'.

Plath's thoughts turn to a marble statue of 'Our Lady of the Shipwrecked' in **stanza three**. Once again, in her imagination, she creates a **dramatic narrative** around the religious figure. This monument to the patron saint of the ocean should offer some consolation to the kneeling sailor and a grieving peasant woman who pray to the mother of God. Ironically, their pleas are completely ignored – 'She does not hear' their prayers because 'She is in love with the beautiful formlessness of the sea'. The feeling of hopelessness is all-pervading. Is the poet expressing her own **feelings of failure and despondency** here? Or is she also attacking the ineffectiveness of religion? The description of the statue is certainly unflattering. The figure is flighty and self-centred: 'Her marble skirts blown back in two pink wings'. In contrast, the powerful ocean remains fascinating.

In the **fourth stanza**, Plath describes the local Bretons who sell souvenirs to tourists. Unlike the previous three stanzas, **the mood appears to be much lighter** as the poet describes the friendly stall-keepers going about their business. It is another irony that their livelihood (selling 'pretty trinkets') is dependent on the sea and its beauty. Like the statue, the locals seem unconcerned by the tragic history of the ocean. Indeed, they are keen to play down 'the Bay of the Dead' and explain that what they sell is imported 'from another place, tropical and blue'. In the final line, a stall-holder advises the poet to enjoy the pancakes she has bought: 'Eat them before they blow cold'. Although the immediate mood is untroubled, **the final phrase brings us** back to the earlier – and more disturbing – parts of the poem where Plath described the raging storms and the nameless lost souls who have perished at sea.

ANALYSIS

Write a paragraph on Sylvia Plath's use of detailed description in 'Finisterre'.

Sample Paragraph

The opening images of the rocks – 'the last fingers, knuckled and rheumatic' – are of decrepit old age. The strong visual impact is a regular feature of Sylvia Plath's writing. The first half of the poem is filled with memorable details of the windswept coastline. In her careful choice of descriptive terms, Plath uses broad vowels to evoke a pervading feeling of dejection. Words such as 'drowned', 'gloomy', 'rolled' and 'doom' help to create this dismal effect. The dramatic aural image, 'The sea cannons', echoes the roar of turbulent waves crashing onto the rocks. Plath's eye for close observation is also seen in her portrait of the holy statue – 'Her lips sweet with divinity'. The poem ends with a painstaking sketch of the Breton traders selling postcards and 'Little shells made up into necklaces and toy ladies'. The local people seem to have come to terms with 'the Bay of the Dead' and are getting on with life. Overall, the use of details throughout the poem leaves readers with a strong sense of place and community.

Examiner's Comment

Quotations are very well used here to highlight Plath's ability to create specific scenes and moods through precise description. The examples range over much of the poem and the writing is both varied and controlled throughout. Grade A standard.

CLASS/HOMEWORK EXERCISES

1. It has been said that vivid, startling imagery gives a surreal quality to 'Finisterre'. Using reference to the poem, write a paragraph responding to this statement.

2. Copy the table below into your own notes and fill in critical comments about the last two quotations.

Key Quotes

Admonitory cliffs, and the sea exploding/ With no bottom	Striking and dramatic images are a recurring feature throughout the poem.
Souls, rolled in the doom-noise of the sea	The poem is dominated by the underlying themes of fear, hopelessness and death.
Now it is only gloomy, a dump of rocks	
These are our crêpes. Eat them before they blow cold	

5   MIRROR

I am silver and exact. I have no preconceptions.
Whatever I see I swallow immediately
Just as it is, unmisted by love or dislike.
I am not cruel, only truthful –
The eye of a little god, four-cornered.   5
Most of the time I meditate on the opposite wall.
It is pink, with speckles. I have looked at it so long
I think it is part of my heart. But it flickers.
Faces and darkness separate us over and over.

Now I am a lake. A woman bends over me,   10
Searching my reaches for what she really is.
Then she turns to those liars, the candles or the moon.
I see her back, and reflect it faithfully.
She rewards me with tears and an agitation of hands.
I am important to her. She comes and goes.   15
Each morning it is her face that replaces the darkness.
In me she has drowned a young girl, and in me an old woman
Rises toward her day after day, like a terrible fish.

'The eye of a little god, four-cornered'

1   *exact*: accurate, giving all details; to insist on payment.

1   *preconceptions*: thoughts already formed.

11   *reaches*: range of distance or depth.

14   *agitation*: shaking, anxious.

EXPLORATIONS

1. Select two images that suggest the dark, sinister side of the mirror. Would you consider that these images show an unforgiving way of viewing oneself?

2. What are the parallels and contrasts between a mirror and a lake? Develop your response in a written paragraph.

3. Write your own personal response to this poem, referring closely to the text in your answer.

STUDY NOTES

'Mirror' was written in 1961 as Sylvia Plath approached her twenty-ninth birthday. In this dark poem, Plath views the inevitability of old age and death, our preoccupation with image and our search for an identity.

Do you think everyone looks at themselves in a mirror? Would you consider that people are fascinated, disappointed or even obsessed by what they see? Does a mirror accurately reflect the truth? Do people actually see what is reflected or is it distorted by notions and ideals they or society have? Consider the use of mirrors in fairytales: 'Mirror, mirror on the wall, who's the fairest of them all?' Mirrors are also used in myths, such as the story of Narcissus, who drowned having fallen in love with his reflection, and *Through the Looking Glass* is a famous children's book. Mirrors are also used in horror films as the dividing line between fantasy and reality.

In this poem, Plath often gives us a startling new angle on an everyday object. The function of a mirror is to reflect whatever is put in front of it. **Stanza one** opens with a ringing declaration by the mirror: 'I am silver and exact'. This **personification has a sinister effect** in the poem as the mirror describes an almost claustrophobic relationship with a particular woman. The voice of the mirror is clear, direct and precise. It announces that it reports exactly what there is without any alteration. We have to decide if the mirror is telling the truth, as it says it has no bias ('no preconceptions'). It does not judge, it reflects the image received. The mirror adopts the position of an impartial observer, but it is active, almost ruthless ('I swallow'). It is not cruel, but truthful.

Yet how truthful is a mirror image, as it flattens a three-dimensional object into two dimensions? The image sent out has no depth. The voice of the mirror becomes smug as it sees itself as the ruler of those reflected ('The eye of a little god'). Our obsession with ourselves causes us to worship at the mirror that reflects our image. In the modern world, people are often disappointed with their reflections, wishing they were thinner, younger, better looking. But **the mirror insists it tells the truth**, it doesn't flatter or hurt. The mirror explains how it spends its day gazing at the opposite wall, which is carefully described as 'pink, with speckles'. It feels as if the wall is part of itself. This reflection is disturbed by the faces of people and the dying light. The passage of time is evoked in the phrase 'over and over'.

In **stanza two**, the mirror now announces that it is 'a lake'. Both are flat surfaces that reflect. However, a lake is another dimension, it has depth. **There is danger.** The image is now drawn into its murky depths. The woman is looking in and down, not just at. It is as if she is struggling to find who she really is, what her true path in life is. Plath frequently questioned who she was. Expectations for young women in the 1950s were limiting. Appearance was important, as were the roles of wife, mother and homemaker. But Plath also wanted to write: 'Will I submerge my embarrassing desires and aspirations, refuse to face myself?' The mirror becomes irritated and jealous of the woman as she turns to the deceptive soft light of 'those liars, the candles or the moon'. The mirror remains faithful, reflecting her back. **The woman is dissatisfied with her image.** In her insecurity, she weeps and wrings her hands. Plath always tried to do her best, to be a model student, almost desperate to excel and be affirmed. Is there a danger in seeking perfection? Do we need to be kind to ourselves? Do we need to love ourselves? Again, the mirror pompously announces 'I am important to her'.

The march of time passing is emphasised by 'comes and goes', 'Each morning' and 'day after day'. The woman keeps coming back. The mirror's sense of its importance is shown by the frequent use of 'I' and the repetition of 'in me'. As time passes, the woman is facing the truth of her human condition as her reflection changes and ages in the mirror. Her youth is 'drowned', to be replaced by a monstrous vision of an old woman 'like a terrible fish'. **The lonely drama of living and dying is recorded with a dreamlike, nightmarish quality.** There is no comforting rhyme in the poem, only the controlled rhythm of time. The mirror does not give what a human being desires: comfort and warmth. Instead, it impersonally reminds us of our mortality.

ANALYSIS

What is your personal response to the relationship between the mirror and the woman? Support your views with reference to the poem.

Sample Paragraph

I feel the mirror is like an alter ego, which is coolly appraising the woman in an unforgiving way. The mirror is 'silver'. This cold metal object is heartless. Although the mirror repeatedly states that it does not judge, 'I have no preconceptions', the woman feels judged and wanting: 'She rewards me with tears and an agitation of hands.' I think the relationship between the woman and the mirror is dangerous and poisonous. She does indeed 'drown' in the mirror, as she never feels good enough. Is this the payment the mirror exacts? The complacent mirror rules her like a tyrannical 'little god, four-cornered'. It reminds me of how today we are never satisfied with our image, always wanting something else, more perfect. Plath also strove to be perfect. This obsessive relationship shows a troubled self, a lack of self-love. Who is saying that the older woman is 'like a terrible fish'? I think the mirror has become the voice of a society which values women only for their looks and youth, rather than what they are capable of achieving.

Examiner's Comment

In this fluent and personal response, the candidate has given a distinctive and well-supported account of the uneasy relationship between the mirror and the woman. Grade A answer.

CLASS/HOMEWORK EXERCISES

1. How are the qualities of terror and despair shown in the imagery of the poem?

2. Copy the table below into your own notes and fill in critical comments about the last two quotations.

Key Quotes

I have no preconceptions	The mirror states that it objectively reflects reality.
The eye of a little god, four-cornered	Plath's metaphor emphasises how this rectangular mirror considers itself very important.
I am silver and exact	
in me an old woman/Rises toward her day after day, like a terrible fish	

⑥   PHEASANT

You said you would kill it this morning.
Do not kill it. It startles me still,
The jut of that odd, dark head, pacing

Through the uncut grass on the elm's hill.
It is something to own a pheasant,   5
Or just to be visited at all.

I am not mystical: it isn't
As if I thought it had a spirit.
It is simply in its element.

That gives it a kingliness, a right.   10
The print of its big foot last winter,
The tail-track, on the snow in our court –

The wonder of it, in that pallor,
Through crosshatch of sparrow and starling.
Is it its rareness, then? It is rare.   15

But a dozen would be worth having,
A hundred, on that hill – green and red,
Crossing and recrossing: a fine thing!

It is such a good shape, so vivid.
It's a little cornucopia.   20
It unclaps, brown as a leaf, and loud,

Settles in the elm, and is easy.
It was sunning in the narcissi.
I trespass stupidly. Let be, let be.

'in its element'

GLOSSARY

1   *You*: probably addressed to Plath's husband.
3   *jut*: extending outwards.
7   *mystical*: spiritual, supernatural.
13 *pallor*: pale colour.

14 *crosshatch*: criss-cross trail.
20 *cornucopia*: unexpected treasure.
23 *narcissi*: bright spring flowers.

EXPLORATIONS

1. Explain Sylvia Plath's attitude to nature based on your reading of 'Pheasant'.

2. Compile a list of the poet's arguments for not killing the pheasant.

3. Write a paragraph on the effectiveness of Plath's imagery in the poem.

STUDY NOTES

'Pheasant' was written in 1962 and reflects Plath's deep appreciation of the natural world. Its enthusiastic mood contrasts with much of her more disturbing work. The poem is structured in eight tercets (three-line stanzas) with a subtle, interlocking rhyming pattern (known as terza rima).

The poem opens with an urgent plea by Plath to spare the pheasant's life: 'Do not kill it'. In the **first two stanzas**, the tone is tense as the poet offers a variety of reasons for sparing this impressive game bird. She is both shocked and excited by the pheasant: 'It startles me still'. Plath admits to feeling honoured in the presence of the bird: 'It is something to own a pheasant'. The broken rhythm of the early lines adds an abruptness that heightens the sense of urgency. **Plath seems spellbound by the bird's beauty** ('The jut of that odd, dark head') now that it is under threat. But the poet is also keen to play down any sentimentality in her attitude to the pheasant. **Stanza three** opens with a straightforward explanation of her attitude: 'it isn't/As if I thought it had a spirit'. Instead, **she values the bird for its graceful beauty and naturalness**: 'It is simply in its element.' Plath is keen to show her recognition of the pheasant's right to exist because it possesses a certain majestic quality, 'a kingliness'. In **stanza four**, the poet recalls an earlier winter scene when she marvelled at the pheasant's distinctive footprint in the snow. The bird has made an even greater impression on Plath, summed up in the key phrase 'The wonder of it', at the start of **stanza five**. She remembers **the colourful pheasant's distinguishing marks against the pale snow**, so unlike the 'crosshatch' pattern of smaller birds, such as the sparrow and starling. This makes the pheasant particularly 'rare' and valuable in Plath's eyes.

The poet can hardly contain her regard for the pheasant and her tone becomes increasingly enthusiastic in **stanza six** as she dreams of having first a 'dozen' and then a 'hundred' of the birds. In a few **well-chosen details**, she highlights their colour and energy ('green and red,/Crossing and recrossing') and adds an emphatic compliment: 'a fine thing!' Her delight continues into **stanza seven**, where Plath proclaims her ceaseless admiration for the pheasant: 'It's a little cornucopia', an inspirational source of joy and surprise.

Throughout the poem, Plath has emphasised that the pheasant rightly belongs in its natural surroundings, and this is also true of the final lines. **Stanza eight** is considered and assured. From the poet's point of view, **the pheasant's right to live is beyond dispute**. While the bird is 'sunning in the narcissi', she herself has become the unwelcome intruder: 'I trespass stupidly'. Plath ends by echoing the opening appeal to spare the pheasant's life: 'Let be, let be.' The quietly insistent repetition and the underlying tone of unease are a final reminder of the need to respect nature.

It has been suggested that the pheasant symbolises Plath's insecure relationship with Ted Hughes. For various reasons, their marriage was under severe strain in 1962 and Plath feared that Hughes was intent on ending it. This interpretation adds a greater poignancy to the poem.

ANALYSIS

There are several mood changes in 'Pheasant'. What do you consider to be the dominant mood in the poem? Refer to the text in your answer.

Sample Paragraph

The mood at the beginning of 'Pheasant' is nervous and really uptight. Plath seems to have given up hope about the pheasant. It is facing death. She repeats the word 'kill' and admits to being shocked at the very thought of what the bird is facing. She herself seems desperate and fearful. This is shown by the short sentence, 'Do not kill it'. But the outlook soon changes. Plath describes the pheasant 'pacing' and 'in its element'. But she seems less stressed as she describes the 'kingliness' of the pheasant. But the mood soon settles down as Plath celebrates the life of this really beautiful bird. The mood becomes calmer and ends in almost a whisper, 'Let be, let be'. The dominant mood is calm and considered in the poem.

Examiner's Comment

This is a reasonably well-focused response to the question. The candidate points out the change of mood following the first stanza. Some worthwhile references are used to show the poem's principal mood. The expression, however, is flawed in places (e.g. using 'but' to start sentences). The standard is C-grade overall.

CLASS/HOMEWORK EXERCISES

1. Plath sets out to convince the reader of the pheasant's right to life. Does she succeed in her aim? Give reasons for your answer.

2. Copy the table below into your own notes and fill in critical comments about the last two quotations.

Key Quotes

pacing/Through the uncut grass on the elm's hill	Plath is a keen observer of the pheasant and uses details to capture its steady movement.
That gives it a kingliness, a right	Man's relationship with the world of nature is central to 'Pheasant'.
I am not mystical	
It unclaps, brown as a leaf	

7 ## ELM

For Ruth Fainlight

I know the bottom, she says. I know it with my great tap root;
It is what you fear.
I do not fear it: I have been there.

Is it the sea you hear in me,
Its dissatisfactions?   5
Or the voice of nothing, that was your madness?

Love is a shadow.
How you lie and cry after it
Listen: these are its hooves: it has gone off, like a horse.

All night I shall gallop thus, impetuously,   10
Till your head is a stone, your pillow a little turf,
Echoing, echoing.

Or shall I bring you the sound of poisons?
This is rain now, this big hush.
And this is the fruit of it: tin-white, like arsenic.   15

I have suffered the atrocity of sunsets.
Scorched to the root
My red filaments burn and stand, a hand of wires.

Now I break up in pieces that fly about like clubs.
A wind of such violence   20
Will tolerate no bystanding: I must shriek.

The moon, also, is merciless: she would drag me
Cruelly, being barren.
Her radiance scathes me. Or perhaps I have caught her.

I let her go. I let her go   25
Diminished and flat, as after radical surgery.
How your bad dreams possess and endow me.

I am inhabited by a cry.
Nightly it flaps out
Looking, with its hooks, for something to love.   30

I am terrified by this dark thing
That sleeps in me;
All day I feel its soft, feathery turnings, its malignity.

Clouds pass and disperse.
Are those the faces of love, those pale irretrievables?   35
Is it for such I agitate my heart?

I am incapable of more knowledge.
What is this, this face
So murderous in its strangle of branches? –

Its snaky acids hiss.   40
It petrifies the will. These are the isolate, slow faults
That kill, that kill, that kill.

'I am terrified by this dark thing'

GLOSSARY

The wych elm is a large deciduous tree, with a massive straight trunk and tangled branches. It was once a favourite timber of coffin makers. Plath dedicated the poem to a close friend, Ruth Fainlight, another American poet.

1   *the bottom*: lowest depths.
1   *tap root*: the main root.

15   *arsenic*: poison.
18   *filaments*: fibres, nerves.
24   *scathes*: injures, scalds.
33   *malignity*: evil.
34   *disperse*: scatter widely.
35   *irretrievables*: things lost forever.
40   *snaky acids*: deceptive poisons.
41   *petrifies*: terrifies.

EXPLORATIONS

1. There are many sinister nature images in this poem. Select two that you find particularly unsettling and comment on their effectiveness.

2. Trace and examine how love is presented and viewed by the poet. Support the points you make with reference to the text.

3. Write your own individual response to this poem, referring closely to the text in your answer.

STUDY NOTES

Written in April 1962, 'Elm' is one of Sylvia Plath's most challenging and intensely dramatic poems. Plath personifies the elm tree to create a surreal scene. It 'speaks' in a traumatic voice to someone else, the 'you' of line 2, the poet herself – or the reader, perhaps. Both voices interact throughout the poem, almost always expressing pain and anguish. Critics often associate these powerful emotions with the poet's own personal problems – Plath had experienced electric shock treatment for depression. However, this may well limit our understanding of what is a complex exploration of many emotions.

The **opening stanza** is unnerving. The poet appears to be dramatising an exchange between herself and the elm by imagining what the tree might say to her. The immediate effect is eerily surreal. From the start, **the narrative voice is obsessed with instability and despair**: 'I know the bottom'. The tree is described in both physical terms ('my great tap root' penetrating far into the ground) and also as a state of mind ('I do not fear it'). The depth of depression imagined is reinforced by the repetition of 'I know' and the stark simplicity of the chilling comment 'It is what you fear'.

The bizarre exchange between the two 'speakers' continues in **stanza two**. The elm questions the poet about the nature of her **mental state**. Does the wind blowing through its branches remind her of the haunting sound of the sea? Or even 'the voice of nothing' – the numbing experience of madness?

Stanzas three and **four** focus on the dangers and disappointments of love – 'a shadow'. The tone is wary, emphasised by the comparison of a wild horse that has 'gone off'. The relentless sounds of the wind in the elm will be a bitter reminder, 'echoing' this loss of love 'Till your head is a stone'. **Assonance** is effectively used here to heighten the sense of hurt and abandonment. For much of the middle section of the poem (**stanzas five** to **nine**), the elm's intimidating voice continues to dramatise a series of horrifying experiences associated with madness. The tree has endured extreme elements – rain ('the sound of poisons'), sunshine ('Scorched to the root'), wind ('of such violence') and also the moon ('Her radiance scathes me'). **The harsh imagery and frenzied language** ('burn', 'shriek', 'merciless') combine to create a sense of shocking destructiveness.

Stanzas 10 and **11** mark a turning point where the voices of the tree and the poet become indistinguishable. This is achieved by the seemingly harmless image of an owl inhabiting the branches, searching for 'something to love'. The speaker is haunted by 'this dark thing'. The **poet's vulnerability** is particularly evident in her stark admission: 'I feel its soft, feathery turnings, its malignity'. Plath has come to relate her unknown demons to a deadly tumour.

In the **last three stanzas**, the poet's voice seems more distant and calm before the final storm. The image of the passing clouds ('the faces of love') highlight the notion of rejection as the root cause of Plath's depression. The poem ends on a visionary note when she imagines being confronted by a 'murderous' snake that appears in the branches: 'It petrifies the will'. The scene of **growing terror builds to a hideous climax** until her own mental and emotional states (her 'slow faults') end up destroying her. The intensity of the final line, 'That kill, that kill, that kill', leaves readers with a harrowing understanding of Plath's paralysis of despair.

ANALYSIS

Do you think that 'Elm' has a surreal, nightmarish quality? In your response, refer to the text to support your views.

Sample Paragraph

I would agree that Sylvia Plath has created a very disturbing mood in the poem, 'Elm'. Giving the tree a speaking voice of its own is like something from a child's fairy story. Plath compares love to a galloping horse. The poem is mainly about depression and madness. So it's bound to be out of the ordinary. The speaker in the poem is confused and asks weird questions, such as 'Is it the sea you hear inside me?' She is obsessive and totally paranoid. Everything is against her, as far as she imagines it. The weather is seen as an enemy even, 'the rain is like arsenic' and 'sounds like poisons'. The end is as if she is having a bad dream with imagining a fierce hissing snake in the tree coming after her. This represents Plath's deepest nightmare, the fear of loneliness. The whole poem is surreal and confusing – especially the images.

Examiner's Comment

This short paragraph includes some worthwhile references to the poem's disturbing aspects. The points are note-like, however, and the writing style lacks control. Some of the quotations are also inaccurate. C-grade standard.

CLASS/HOMEWORK EXERCISES

1. What evidence of Plath's deep depression and hypersensitivity is revealed in the poem 'Elm'? Refer closely to the text in your answer.

2. Copy the table below into your own notes and fill in critical comments about the last two quotations.

Key Quotes

I know it with my great tap root	Through the 'voice' of the elm, Plath uses the tree metaphor to suggest her own depths of despair.
My red filaments burn and stand, a hand of wires	This image of suffering may relate to the poet's own experience of electric shock treatment for depression.
the atrocity of sunsets	
Its snaky acids hiss	

8 POPPIES IN JULY

Little poppies, little hell flames,
Do you do no harm?

You flicker. I cannot touch you.
I put my hands among the flames. Nothing burns.

And it exhausts me to watch you   5
Flickering like that, wrinkly and clear red, like the skin of a mouth.

A mouth just bloodied.
Little bloody skirts!

There are fumes that I cannot touch.
Where are your opiates, your nauseous capsules?   10

If I could bleed, or sleep! –
If my mouth could marry a hurt like that!

Or your liquors seep to me, in this glass capsule,
Dulling and stilling.

But colorless. Colorless.   15

'You flicker. I cannot touch you'

GLOSSARY

1	*hell flames*: most poppies are red, flame-like.	10	*nauseous*: causing sickness.	
9	*fumes*: the effects of drugs.	13	*liquors*: drug vapours.	
10	*opiates*: sleep-inducing narcotics.	13	*capsule*: small container.	
		15	*colorless*: drained, lifeless.	

EXPLORATIONS

1. Examine the title, 'Poppies in July', in light of the main subject matter in the poem. Is the title misleading? Explain your answer.

2. What evidence can you find in 'Poppies in July' that the speaker is yearning to escape?

3. Colour imagery plays a significant role in the poem. Comment on how effectively colour is used.

STUDY NOTES

Like most confessional writers, Sylvia Plath's work reflects her own personal experiences, without filtering any of the painful emotions. She wrote 'Poppies in July' in the summer of 1962, during the break-up of her marriage.

The **first stanza** is marked by an uneasy sense of foreboding. The speaker (almost certainly Plath herself) compares the blazing red poppies to 'little hell flames' before directly confronting them: 'Do you do no harm?' **Her distress is obvious** from the start. The poem's title may well have led readers to expect a more conventional nature poem. Instead, the flowers are presented as being highly treacherous, and all the more deceptive because they are 'little'.

Plath develops the fire image in **lines 3–6**. However, even though she places her hands 'among the flames', she finds that 'Nothing burns' and she is forced to watch them 'Flickering'. It almost seems as though she is so tired and numb that **she has transcended pain** and can experience nothing: 'it exhausts me to watch you'. Ironically, the more vivid the poppies are, the more lethargic she feels.

The uncomfortable and disturbed mood increases in the **fourth stanza** with two **startling images**, both personifying the flowers. Comparing the poppy to 'A mouth just bloodied' suggests recent violence and physical suffering. The 'bloody skirts' metaphor is equally harrowing. There is further evidence of the poet's overpowering weariness in the prominent use of broad vowel sounds, for example in 'exhausts', 'mouth' and 'bloodied'.

In the **fifth stanza**, Plath's disorientated state turns to a distracted longing for escape. Having failed to use the vibrancy of the poppies to distract her from her pain, she now craves the feeling of oblivion or unconsciousness. But although she desires the dulling effects of drugs derived from the poppies, her **tone is hopelessly cynical** as she describes the 'fumes that I cannot touch'.

The mood becomes even more distraught in **lines 11–12**, with the poet begging for any alternative to her anguished state. 'If I could bleed, or sleep!' is an emphatic plea for release. It is her final attempt to retain some control of her life in the face of an overwhelming sense of powerlessness. Plath's **growing alienation** seems so unbearably intense at this point that it directly draws the reader's sympathy.

The **last three lines** record the poet's surrender, perhaps a kind of death wish. Worn down by her inner demons and the bright colours of the poppies, Plath lets herself become resigned to a 'colorless' world of nothingness. Her **complete passivity** and helplessness are emphasised by the dreamlike quality of the phrase 'Dulling and stilling'. As she drifts into a death-like 'colorless' private hell, there remains a terrible sense of betrayal, as if she is still being haunted by the bright red flowers. The ending of 'Poppies in July' is so dark and joyless that it is easy to see why the poem is often seen as a desperate cry for help.

ANALYSIS

'Poppies in July' is one of Plath's most disturbing poems. What aspects of the poem affected you most?

Sample Paragraph

'Poppies in July' was written at a time when Plath was struggling with the fact that her husband had deserted her. This affected her deeply and it is clear that the poppies are a symbol of this excruciating time. Everything about the poem is negative. The images of the poppies are nearly all associated with fire and blood. Plath's language is alarming when she compares the poppies to 'little hell flames' and also 'the skin of a mouth'. The most disturbing aspect is Plath's own unstable mind. She seems to be in a kind of trance, obsessed by the red colours of the poppies, which remind her of blood. I got the impression that she was nearly going insane in the end. She seems suicidal – 'If I could bleed'. For me, this is the most disturbing moment in the poem. I can get some idea of her troubled mind. Plath cannot stand reality and seeks a way out through drugs or death. The last image is of Plath sinking into a dull state of drowsiness, unable to cope with the world around her.

Examiner's Comment

Overall, a solid B-grade response which responds personally to the question. While the candidate dealt well with the disturbing thought in the poem, there could have been a more thorough exploration of Plath's style and how it enhances her theme of depression.

CLASS/HOMEWORK EXERCISES

1. Would you agree that loneliness and pain are the central themes of 'Poppies in July'? Refer to the text of the poem when writing your response.

2. Copy the table below into your own notes and fill in critical comments about the last two quotations.

Key Quotes

You flicker. I cannot touch you	The contrast between the poppies' energy and Plath's own passive state is a memorable feature of the poem.
And it exhausts me to watch you	Plath's overwhelming sense of despair is central to the poem.
Where are your opiates, your nauseous capsules?	
If my mouth could marry a hurt like that!	

9 THE ARRIVAL OF THE BEE BOX

I ordered this, this clean wood box
Square as a chair and almost too heavy to lift.
I would say it was the coffin of a midget
Or a square baby
Were there not such a din in it.   5

The box is locked, it is dangerous.
I have to live with it overnight
And I can't keep away from it.
There are no windows, so I can't see what is in there.
There is only a little grid, no exit.   10

I put my eye to the grid.
It is dark, dark,
With the swarmy feeling of African hands
Minute and shrunk for export,
Black on black, angrily clambering.   15

How can I let them out?
It is the noise that appalls me most of all,
The unintelligible syllables.
It is like a Roman mob,
Small, taken one by one, but my god, together!   20

I lay my ear to furious Latin.
I am not a Caesar.
I have simply ordered a box of maniacs.
They can be sent back.
They can die, I need feed them nothing, I am the owner.   25

I wonder how hungry they are.
I wonder if they would forget me
If I just undid the locks and stood back and turned into a tree.
There is the laburnum, its blond colonnades,
And the petticoats of the cherry.   30

They might ignore me immediately
In my moon suit and funeral veil.
I am no source of honey
So why should they turn on me?
Tomorrow I will be sweet God, I will set them free.   35

The box is only temporary.

'It is the noise that appalls me'

GLOSSARY (A-Z)

10   *grid*: wire network.
13   *swarmy*: like a large group of bees.
22   *Caesar*: famous Roman ruler.
29   *laburnum*: tree with yellow hanging flowers.

29   *colonnades*: long groups of flowers arranged in a row of columns.
32   *moon suit*: protective clothing worn by beekeepers; all-in-one suit.

EXPLORATIONS

1. How would you describe the poet's reaction to the bee box – fear or fascination, or a mixture of both? Write a paragraph for your response, referring to the poem.

2. Select two surreal images from the poem and comment on the effectiveness of each.

3. Would you describe this poem as exploring and overcoming one's fears and anxieties? Is the ending optimistic or pessimistic, in your opinion?

STUDY NOTES

'The Arrival of the Bee Box' was written in 1962, shortly after Plath's separation from her husband. Her father, who died when she was a child, had been a bee expert and Plath and her husband had recently taken up beekeeping. She explores order, power, control, confinement and freedom in this deeply personal poem.

The poem opens with a simple statement: 'I ordered this'. Straightaway, the emphasis is on order and control. The poet's tone in stanza one seems both matter-of-fact and surprised, as if thinking: 'Yes, I was the one who ordered this' and also 'Did I really order this?' **This drama has only one character, Plath herself.** We observe her responses and reactions to the arrival of the bee box. Notice the extensive use of the personal pronoun 'I'. We both see and hear the event.

The box is described as being made of 'clean wood' and given a homely quality with the simile 'Square as a chair'. But then a surreal, dreamlike metaphor, 'the coffin of a midget/Or a square baby', brings us into a **nightmare world**. The abnormal is suggested by the use of 'midget' and deformity by 'square baby'. The coffin conveys not only death, but also entrapment and confinement, preoccupations of the poet. The box has now become a sinister object. A witty sound effect closes the first stanza, as 'din in it' mimics the sound of the bees. They are like badly behaved children.

Stanza two explores the **poet's ambivalent attitude to the box**. She is fascinated by it, as she is curious to see inside ('I can't keep away from it'). Yet she is also frightened by it, as she describes the box as 'dangerous'. She peers in. The **third stanza** becomes claustrophobic and oppressive with the repetition of 'dark' and the grotesque image of 'the swarmy feeling of African hands/ Minute and shrunk for export'. The milling of the bees/slaves is vividly captured as they heave around in the heat in an atmosphere of menace and oppression, hopelessly desperate. We hear the bees in **stanza four**. The metaphor of a Roman mob is used to show how if they are let loose they will create **chaos and danger**. The assonance of 'appalls' and 'all' underlines the poet's terror. The phrase 'unintelligible syllables', with its onomatopoeia and its difficult pronunciation, lets us hear the angry buzzing. Plath is awestruck at their collective force and energy: 'but my god, together!' Notice the use of the exclamation mark.

The poet tries to listen, but only hears 'furious Latin' she does not understand. She doubts her capacity to control them, stating that she is 'not a Caesar', the powerful ruler of the Romans, in **stanza five**. She regards them as 'maniacs'. Then she realises that if she has ordered them, she can return them: 'They can be sent back'. **She has some control of this situation.** Plath can even decide their fate, whether they live or die: 'I need feed them nothing'. She has now redefined the situation as she realises that she is 'the owner'. They belong to her.

The feminine, nurturing side of her now emerges as she wonders 'how hungry they are'. The stereotype of the pretty woman surfaces in the description of the bees' natural habitat of trees in **stanza six**. Plath thinks if she releases them, they would go back to the trees, 'laburnum' and 'cherry'. She herself would then merge into the landscape and become a tree. This is a reference to a Greek myth where Daphne was being pursued by Apollo. After begging the gods to be saved, they turned her into a tree.

Now she refers to herself in her beekeeping outfit of veil and boiler suit in **stanza seven**. She rhetorically asks why they would attack her, as she is not a source of sustenance ('I am no source of honey'). **She decides to be compassionate**: 'Tomorrow I will be sweet God, I will set them free'. She realises that they are imprisoned only for now: 'The box is only temporary'.

This poem can also be read on another level. The box could represent the poet's attempt to be what others expect, the typical 1950s woman – pretty, compliant, nurturing. The bees could represent the dark side of her personality, which both fascinated and terrified Plath. She has to accept this: 'I have to live with it overnight'. **The box is like Pandora's box**: safe when locked, but full of danger when opened. Although she finds this disturbing, she also feels she must explore it in the interests of developing as a poet. The references to the doomed character of Daphne and the 'funeral veil' echo chillingly. Would these dark thoughts, if given their freedom, drive her to suicide? The form of this poem is seven stanzas of five lines. One line stands alone, free like the bees or her dark thoughts. If the box represents Plath's outside appearance or body, it is mortal, it is temporary. Will the thoughts, if freed from the body, stop?

ANALYSIS

How does this poem address the themes of order and power? Write a paragraph in response. Support your views with reference to the text.

Sample Paragraph

The poem opens with a reference to order, 'I ordered this'. It is an assertion of power, a deliberate act by 'I'. Throughout the poem the repetition of 'I' suggests a person who consciously chooses to act in a certain way. 'I put my eye to the grid', 'I lay my ear to furious Latin'. It is as if the poet wishes to confront and control her fears over the contents of the box. This box contains live, buzzing bees, whose wellbeing lies in the hands of the poet. 'I need feed them nothing, I am the owner'. Although she realises that she is not 'Caesar', the mighty Roman ruler, she can choose to be 'sweet God'. She alone has the power to release the bees, 'The box is only temporary'. This poem can also be read as referring to the control a person exercises when confronting their innermost fears and desires. These thoughts can be ignored or faced. The person owns these thoughts and can choose to contain them or confront them. Plath feared her own dark side, but felt it should be explored to enable her to progress as a poet. For her 'The box is only temporary'.

Examiner's Comment

This note-like response summarises parts of the poem that allude to order and power. However, it fails to address the question about the poet's approach to the central themes. There is little discussion about Plath's attitude to power. Grade C.

CLASS/HOMEWORK EXERCISES

1. How does Plath create a dramatic atmosphere in 'The Arrival of the Bee Box'?

2. Copy the table below into your own notes and fill in critical comments about the last two quotations.

Key Quotes

I have to live with it overnight/And I can't keep away from it	The poet refers to the intense relationship she has with the box, from which she cannot escape.
With the swarmy feeling of African hands/Minute and shrunk for export	The bees are described as miniature African slaves who are imprisoned as they are sent off to another country.
Tomorrow I will be sweet God	
The box is only temporary	

10 CHILD

Your clear eye is the one absolutely beautiful thing.
I want to fill it with color and ducks,
The zoo of the new

Whose name you meditate –
April snowdrop, Indian pipe,   5
Little

Stalk without wrinkle,
Pool in which images
Should be grand and classical

Not this troublous   10
Wringing of hands, this dark
Ceiling without a star.

'The zoo of the new'

GLOSSARY

4   *meditate*: reflect.
5   *Indian pipe*: American woodland flower.
7   *Stalk*: plant stem.

9   *classical*: impressive, enduring.
10   *troublous*: disturbed.

EXPLORATIONS

1. What was your own immediate reaction after reading 'Child'? Refer to the text in your answer.

2. Which images in the poem are most effective in contrasting the world of the child and the world of the adult?

3. Plath uses various sound effects to enhance her themes in 'Child'. Comment briefly on two interesting examples.

STUDY NOTES

Sylvia Plath's son was born in January 1962. A year later, not long before the poet's own death, she wrote 'Child', a short poem that reflects her intense feelings about motherhood.

The first line of **stanza one** shows the **poet's emphatic appreciation of childhood** innocence: 'Your clear eye is the one absolutely beautiful thing'. The tone at first is hopeful. Her love for the new child is generous and unconditional: 'I want to fill it with color'. The childlike language is lively and playful. Plath plans to give her child the happiest of times, filled with 'color and ducks'. The vigorous rhythm and animated internal rhyme in the phrase 'The zoo of the new' are imaginative, capturing the sense of **youthful wonder**.

In **stanza two**, the poet continues to associate her child with all that is best about the natural world. The baby is like the most fragile of flowers, the 'April snowdrop'. The assonance in this phrase has a musical effect, like a soft lullaby. Yet her own fascination appears to mask a deeper concern. Plath feels that such a perfect childhood experience is unlikely to last very long. Despite all her positive sentiments, what she wants for **the vulnerable child** seems directly at odds with what is possible in a **flawed world**.

Run-on lines are a recurring feature of the poem and these add to the feeling of freedom and innocent intensity. **Stanza three** includes two **effective comparisons**, again taken from nature. Plath sees the child as an unblemished 'Stalk' that should grow perfectly. A second quality of childhood's pure innocence is found in the 'Pool' metaphor. We are reminded of the opening image – the child's 'clear eye', always trusting and sincere.

The poet would love to provide a magical future for her young child, so that the pool would reflect 'grand and classical' images. However, as a loving mother, she is trapped between her **idealism** – the joy she wants for her child – and a **distressing reality** – an awareness that the child's life will not be perfectly happy. This shocking realisation becomes clear in **stanza four** and overshadows her hopes completely. The final images are stark and powerful – the pathetic 'Wringing of hands' giving emphasis to her helplessness. The last line poignantly portrays the paradox of the tension between Plath's dreams for the child in the face of the despair she feels about the oppressive world: this 'Ceiling without a star'. This dark mood is in sharp contrast with the rest of the poem. The early celebration has been replaced by anguish and an overwhelming sense of failure.

ANALYSIS

Do you think 'Child' is a positive or negative poem? Refer to the text in explaining your response.

Sample Paragraph

I think Plath's poem, 'Child', is essentially about a mother's inadequacy. The poet wants the best for her innocent son. Although the first half of the poem focuses on her wishes to protect him, this changes at the end. Plath starts off by wanting to fill the boy's life with happy experiences (bright colours and toys) and keep him close to nature. There are numerous references to nature right through the poem and Plath compares her son to an 'April snowdrop'. This tender image gave me a very positive feeling. Everything about the child is wonderful at first. He is 'absolutely beautiful'. This all changes at the end of the poem. The mood turns negative. Plath talks of being confined in a darkened room which has a 'Ceiling without a star'. This is in total contrast with the images early on which were of the bright outdoors. The poet was positive at the start. This has been replaced with negative feelings. The ending is dark and 'troublous' because Plath knows that her child will grow up and experience pain just as she has.

Examiner's Comment

This paragraph addresses the question well and offers a clear response. The candidate effectively illustrates the changing mood from optimism to pessimism and uses apt quotations in support. The style of writing is a little note-like and pedestrian. A basic B-grade standard.

CLASS/HOMEWORK EXERCISES

1. Write a paragraph comparing 'Child' with 'Morning Song'. Refer to theme and style in both poems.

2. Copy the table below into your own notes and fill in critical comments about the last two quotations.

Key Quotes

Your clear eye	The newborn child is innocent and is still unaffected by the corrupt world.
I want to fill it with color and ducks	The childlike language reflects the mother's desire to be part of her child's innocent world.
Not this troublous/Wringing of hands	
this dark/Ceiling without a star	

LEAVING CERT SAMPLE ESSAY

'Reading Sylvia Plath's poetry can be an uncomfortable experience.' Write a personal response to the above statement. Your answer should focus clearly on her themes and the manner in which she explores them. Support your points by reference to the poetry of Sylvia Plath on your course.

Marking Scheme Guidelines
Reward responses that show clear evidence of personal engagement with the poems. The key term ('uncomfortable experience') may be addressed implicitly or explicitly. Candidates may choose to focus on the positive aspects of Plath's poetry. Allow for a wide range of approaches in the answering.

Material might be drawn from the following:
• Recurring themes of nature, disillusionment, transience, etc.
• Complexity of mother–child relationships.
• Contrasting images and tones.
• Startling and unusual language.
• The poet's life and how it links with her poetry.

Sample Essay
(Reading Sylvia Plath's poetry)

1. *The poetry of Sylvia Plath awakes a multitude of emotions in the reader, many of them disturbing. Plath's engulfing depression led her to take a view of the world that is alarming and often perverse. However, Plath's great understanding of life and love for her children led her to write poems that bring both joy and contentment to the reader. It is this diversity of approach that makes Plath one of the finest poets of the modern age.*

2. *Motherhood had a highly potent effect on Plath as a person. This is presented to the reader in the poem 'Morning Song', which is addressed to her daughter. She refers to her child with three words: 'fat gold watch'. This image suggests that the baby is valuable, to be treasured and praised. However, the image of a watch may symbolise the dark undercurrent that time is passing, it is slipping away for both mother and daughter. This ambiguity exists in much of Plath's work and, when examined, may*

be a cause for distress and discomfort for the reader. The poet chooses to present the notion that her daughter is a work of art with the words 'New statue./In a drafty museum'. It is into this harsh world that her child will venture, a disturbing thought for both the poet and the reader.

3. The final image of the poem is of the baby herself trying a 'handful of notes'. The poet refers to the 'vowels' as they 'rise like balloons'. While the image seems to be a warm, content one, the image of a balloon seems to suggest something fragile, flimsy and transient. Even in her upbeat poems, Plath subtly presents disconcerting thoughts to the reader. The poem 'Black Rook in Rainy Weather' arises from the poet's feelings of contentment with life. She expresses this with the words 'I do not expect a miracle/Or an accident'. This inner peace leads the poet to rejoice in the mundane and urge us 'to let spotted leaves fall as they fall,/Without ceremony'. The poet becomes aware that 'Miracles occur' even if they are only 'spasmodic/Tricks of radiance'.

4. 'Poppies in July' is undoubtedly one of the most disturbing poems by Plath. It deals with the horrors of her depression. The title seems to suggest a joyful image, but this could not be further from the truth. Plath refers to the poppies as 'little hell flames', seeing them as instruments which add to her suffering. Plath, it seems, would rather feel pain than feel nothing at all. She is horrified when she puts her hand 'among the flames' and 'Nothing burns'. Plath longs to find the poppies 'Dulling and stilling' and for everything to be 'colorless'. This poem gives a vivid description of how Plath feels choked by her destructive feelings. The depth of the poet's despair is evident in the troubling effect 'Poppies in July' has on the reader.

5. Plath explores a similar experience in 'Elm', which starts with the words, 'I know the bottom... I know it with my great tap root'. The reference to a root suggests that the poet not only knew the lowest point, but draws her entire existence from that dark, hopeless place. We are told that Plath has 'suffered the atrocity of sunsets'. This hatred of something generally considered to be beautiful and joyous is a startling indication of the depth of her depression. Plath sees her sorrow as something that exists within herself – it is interior – and reveals that all day she feels 'its dark, feathery turnings, its malignity'. This horrifying image portrays the utter helplessness of the poet. It fills the reader with dread and fear, as Plath herself must have felt about her helplessness when she wrote the poem.

6. 'Child' was written to Plath's son shortly before she died. She expresses the wish that life should not be 'this troublous/Wringing of hands, this dark/Ceiling without a star'. The absence of the star symbolises the absence of any hope. We get the sense that Plath will never manage to break free of this depression and it is this thought that horrifies the reader.

7. Even in poems that seem peaceful and loving, the echoes of Plath's depression exist as undercurrents. The explicit nature of her darker poems affects the reader deeply, revealing to them the horrors and terrible reality of utter despair. Few, if any, could read Plath's poetry and remain unchanged by it.

(approx. 740 words)

Examiner's Comment

A solid answer showing an excellent knowledge of Plath's poetry. The emphasis on the effect that the poems have on the reader is sustained throughout. Some points are well developed, often in detail (e.g. in paragraph 2) and apt quotations are well used. Apart from occasional repetition (paragraph 5), the overall expression is fluent and varied.

GRADE: A2
P = 13/15
C = 13/15
L = 12/15
M = 5/5
Total = 43/50

SAMPLE LEAVING CERT QUESTIONS ON PLATH'S POETRY

(45/50 MINUTES)

1. 'Introducing Sylvia Plath'
   Using the above title, write an article for your school magazine. Support your points by close reference to the prescribed poems by Plath that you have studied.

2. 'Although Sylvia Plath's poetry deals with intense experiences, her skill with language ensures that she is always in control of her subject matter.' Discuss this view, supporting your points with the aid of suitable reference to the poems by Plath on your course.

3. 'Sylvia Plath's poems emerge from an unsettled world of anguish and personal torment.' Do you agree with this assessment of her poetry? Write a response, supporting your points with reference to the poems by Plath that you have studied.

Sample Essay Plan (Q2)

'Although Sylvia Plath's poetry deals with intense experiences, her skill with language ensures that she is always in control of her subject matter.' Discuss this view, supporting your points with the aid of suitable reference to the poems by Plath on your course.

- Intro: Identify the elements to be addressed – Plath's intensely disturbing themes and her innovative use of language.

- Point 1: Inner torment of 'Elm' presented through complex imagery and unsettling symbolism, allowing the reader to appreciate a nightmare world.

- Point 2: Contrast is effectively used in 'Poppies in July'. The speaker's deep yearning to escape is highlighted by the startling imagery of the flowers.

- Point 3: The depression in 'Black Rook in Rainy Weather' is also emphasised by conflicting images from nature and religion.

- Point 4: 'Child' and 'Morning Song' express strong themes about intense relationships through her mastery of language.

- Conclusion: Many poems deal with extreme emotional states, but Plath's poetic technique never lapses.

Sample Essay Plan (Q2)

Develop one of the above points into a paragraph.

Sample Paragraph: Point 2

'Poppies in July' is an intense poem about Plath's desperation to escape from her unhappy world. It begins on a disturbing note. The speaker is troubled by the sight of poppies, which she calls 'little hell flames'. The references to Hell and fire are developed through the rest of the poem, suggesting an extremely disturbed mind. The image of the red flames is both dramatic and terrifying – and typical of Plath's intense poetry. Readers can sense a standoff between the poppies and Plath herself. The flowers almost seem to mock the poet: 'You flicker. I cannot touch you'. Other images in the poem add to our understanding of the poet's deep pain – 'A mouth just bloodied' and 'fumes that I cannot touch'. Plath describes the poppies in a way that reveals her own troubled mental state. She is exhausted, almost beyond despair. We see her control of language when she contrasts the colour of the poppies with her own lifeless mood. We are left with a genuine sense of Plath's anguish. Unlike the blazing red flowers, the poet herself is 'colorless'.

Examiner's Comment

This is a well-focused paragraph that concentrates on Plath's ability to use language in an inventive and controlled fashion. The contrast between the vivid appearance of the poppies and the poet's own bleak mood is well illustrated. There is also a sense of engagement with the feelings expressed in the poem. A very good A-grade standard.

LAST WORDS ""

'Her poems have that heart-breaking quality about them.'

Joyce Carol Oates

'Artists are a special breed. They are passionate and temperamental. Their feelings flow into the work they create.'

J. Timothy King

'I am a genius of a writer; I have it in me. I am writing the best poems of my life.'

Sylvia Plath

W. B. YEATS

1865-1939

'I have spread my dreams under your feet.'

William Butler Yeats was born in Dublin in 1865. The son of a well-known Irish painter, John Butler Yeats, he spent much of his childhood in Co. Sligo. As a young writer, Yeats became involved with the Celtic Revival, a movement against the cultural influences of English rule in Ireland that sought to promote the spirit of our native heritage. His writing drew extensively from Irish mythology and folklore. Another great influence was the Irish revolutionary Maud Gonne, a woman as famous for her passionate nationalist politics as for her beauty. She rejected Yeats, who eventually married another woman, Georgie Hyde Lees. However, Maud Gonne remained a powerful figure in Yeats's writing. Over the years, Yeats became deeply involved in Irish politics and despite independence from England, his work reflected a pessimism about the political situation here. He also had a lifelong interest in mysticism and the occult. Appointed a senator of the Irish Free State in 1922, he is remembered as an important cultural leader, as a major playwright (he was one of the founders of Dublin's Abbey Theatre) and as one of the greatest 20th-century poets. Yeats was awarded the Nobel Prize in 1923 and died in 1939 at the age of 73.

Prescribed Poems

❶ THE LAKE ISLE OF INNISFREE

I will arise and go now, and go to Innisfree,
And a small cabin build there, of clay and wattles made:
Nine bean-rows will I have there, <u>a hive for the honey-bee,</u>
<u>And live alone in the bee-loud glade.</u> *alliteration*

Quiet place where time moves slowly
<u>And I shall have some peace there, for peace comes dropping slow,</u>   5
<u>Dropping from the veils of the morning to where the cricket sings;</u>
There midnight's all a glimmer, and noon a purple glow,
And evening full of the linnet's wings.

no end to cycle of peace

I will arise and go now, for always night and day   *can hear Innisfree calling him*
<u>I hear lake water lapping with low sounds by the shore;</u>   10
While I stand on the roadway, <u>or on the pavements grey,</u>   *alliteration + onomatopoeia*
I hear it in the deep heart's core.

idylic vision of rural seclusion

to Yeats, city is boring and grey

'I hear lake water lapping with low sounds by the shore'

GLOSSARY

Ⓐ-Z

Innisfree: island of heather.
2   *clay and wattles*: rods and mud were used to build small houses.
7   *midnight's all a glimmer*: stars are shining very brightly in the countryside.

8   *linnet*: songbird.
10   *lapping*: gentle sounds made by water at the edge of a shore.
12   *heart's core*: essential part; the centre of the poet's being.

EXPLORATIONS

1. This poem was voted number one in a recent *Irish Times* poll of the top 100 poems. Why do you think it appeals to so many readers?

2. What does the poem reveal to you about Yeats's own state of mind? Use reference to the text in your response.

3. How does the second stanza describe the rhythm of the passing day? Use quotations to illustrate your response.

STUDY NOTES

'The Lake Isle of Innisfree' was written in 1890. Yeats was in London, looking in a shop window at a little toy fountain. He was feeling very homesick. He said the sound of the 'tinkle of water' reminded him of 'lake water'. He was longing to escape from the grind of everyday life and he wrote an 'old daydream of mine'.

This timeless poem has long been a favourite with exiles everywhere, as it **expresses a longing for a place of deep peace**. The tone in **stanza one** is deliberate, not casual, as the poet announces his decision to go. There are Biblical overtones here: 'I will arise and go to my father,' the prodigal son announces. This lends the occasion solemnity. Then the poet describes the idyllic life of self-sufficiency: 'Nine bean-rows' and 'a hive for the honey-bee'. These details give the poem a timeless quality as the poet lives 'alone in the beeloud glade'.

Stanza two describes Innisfree so vividly that the future tense of 'I will arise' gives way to the present: 'There midnight's all a glimmer'. The **repetition** of 'peace' and 'dropping' suits the subject, as it lulls us into this tranquil place to which we all aspire to go at some point in our lives. Beautiful imagery brings us through the day, from the gentle white mists of the morning which lie like carelessly thrown veils over the lake to the blazing purple of the heather under the midday sun. The starry night, which can only be seen in the clear skies of the countryside, is vividly described as 'midnight's all a glimmer', with slender vowel sounds suggesting the sharp light of the stars. The soft 'l', 'm' and 'p' sounds in this stanza create a gentle and magical mood.

[handwritten margin note: clearly contrasting life in city to country side.]

The **third stanza** repeats the opening, giving the air of a solemn ritual taking place. The **verbal music** in this stanza is striking, as the broad vowel sounds slow down the line, 'I hear lake water lapping with low sounds by the shore', emphasising peace and tranquility. Notice the alliteration of 'l' and the assonance of 'o' all adding to the serene calm of the scene. The only **contemporary detail** in the poem is 'pavements grey', suggesting the relentless concrete of the city. The exile's awareness of what he loves is eloquently expressed as he declares he hears the sound 'in the deep heart's core'. Notice the monosyllabic ending, which drums home how much he longs for this place. Regular end rhyme (abab) and the regular four beats in each fourth line reinforce the harmony of this peaceful place.

ANALYSIS

What musical sounds did you find effective in this poem? Write a paragraph, illustrating your answer with references to the text.

Sample Paragraph

Yeats said that this poem was his 'first lyric with anything in its rhythm of my own music'. 'The Lake Isle of Innisfree' has a solemn, deliberate tone. It even has Biblical overtones. The steady end rhyme ('Innisfree', 'honeybee') adds to this stately music. The poet uses broad vowels to slow down the pace of the poem. This is an idyllic place where time almost stands still, 'alone in the bee-loud glade'. The repetition of 'peace' and 'dropping' creates a dreamy, soporific effect in this 'old daydream' of Yeats's. The brightly shining stars and the rapid movement of the bird's wings provide contrast as busy slender vowels in 'midnight's all a glimmer' and 'linnet's wings' tremble on the page. The soft 'l' sounds and alliteration in the line 'I hear lake water lapping with low sounds by the shore' bring us back to the calm, magical scene. I thought the consonance of 'la' and 'lo' also added to this effect. The final line beats out its message with five strong monosyllabic words: 'In the deep heart's core'. The phrase underlines the longing of the emigrant. This contrasts wonderfully with the slipping away of reality in 'pavements grey' as the exile relives his heart's desire.

Examiner's Comment

A good understanding of the techniques used by a poet to create music and the effect this has on the poem is displayed in the answer. Quotations are very well used here to back up this personal response. Grade-A standard.

CLASS/HOMEWORK EXERCISES

1. Pick out two images from the poem that appeal to you and discuss the reasons for their appeal.

2. Copy the table below into your own notes and fill in critical comments about the last two quotations.

Key Quotes

Nine bean-rows will I have there	Throughout the poem, Yeats is nostalgic for his homeland. He is yearning to return to the simple life he once enjoyed.
Dropping from the veils of the morning	The use of assonance emphasises the serene atmosphere of this magical place as the white mist lies over the lake.
peace comes dropping slow	
I hear it in the deep heart's core	

❷   SEPTEMBER 1913

Yeats is not happy with materialistic way of life

John Brennan Dances with Sluts in Rockies

What need you, being come to sense,
But fumble in a greasy till
And add the halfpence to the pence
And prayer to shivering prayer, until
You have dried the marrow from the bone?   5
For men were born to pray and save:
Romantic Ireland's dead and gone,
It's with O'Leary in the grave.

Yet they were of a different kind,
The names that stilled your childish play,   10
They have gone about the world like wind,
But little time had they to pray
For whom the hangman's rope was spun,
And what, God help us, could they save?
Romantic Ireland's dead and gone,   15
It's with O'Leary in the grave.

Was it for this the wild geese spread
The grey wing upon every tide;
For this that all that blood was shed,
For this Edward Fitzgerald died,   20
And Robert Emmet and Wolfe Tone,
All that delirium of the brave?
Romantic Ireland's dead and gone,
It's with O'Leary in the grave.

Yet could we turn the years again,   25
And call those exiles as they were
In all their loneliness and pain,
You'd cry, 'Some woman's yellow hair
Has maddened every mother's son':
They weighed so lightly what they gave.   30
But let them be, they're dead and gone,
They're with O'Leary in the grave.

'Romantic Ireland's dead and gone'

GLOSSARY

1   *you*: merchants and business people.
8   *O'Leary*: John O'Leary Fenian leader, one of Yeats's heroes.
9   *they*: the selfless Irish patriots.
17 *the wild geese*: Irish Independence soldiers forced into exile in Europe after 1690.

20 *Edward Fitzgerald*: 18th-century Irish aristocrat and revolutionary.
21 *Robert Emmet and Wolfe Tone*: Irish rebel leaders. Emmet was hanged in 1803. Tone committed suicide in prison after being sentenced to death in 1798.

EXPLORATIONS

1. Comment on the effectiveness of the images used in the first five lines of the poem.

2. How would you describe the tone of this poem? Is it bitter, sad, ironic, angry, etc.? Refer closely to the text in your answer.

3. Were the patriots named in the poem heroes or fools? Write a paragraph in response to Yeats's views.

STUDY NOTES

'September 1913' is typical of Yeats's hard-hitting political poems. Both the content and tone are harsh as the poet airs his views on public issues, contrasting the idealism of Ireland's heroic past with the uncultured present.

Yeats had been a great supporter of Sir Hugh Lane, who had offered his extensive art collection to the city of Dublin, provided the paintings would be on show in a suitable gallery. When the authorities failed to arrange this, Lane withdrew his offer. The controversy infuriated Yeats, who criticised Dublin Corporation for being miserly and anti-cultural. For him, it represented a **new low in the country's drift into vulgarity and crass commercialism**. The year 1913 was also a year of great hardship, partly because of a general strike and lock-out of workers. Poverty and deprivation were widespread at the time, particularly in Dublin's tenements.

The **first stanza** begins with a derisive **attack on a materialistic society** that Yeats sees as being both greedy and hypocritical. Ireland's middle classes are preoccupied with making money and slavish religious devotion. The rhetorical opening is sharply sarcastic, as the poet depicts the petty penny-pinching shopkeepers who 'fumble in a greasy till'. Yeats's tone is as angry as it is ironic: 'For men were born to pray and save'. Images of the dried bone and 'shivering prayer' are equally forceful – the poor are exploited by ruthless employers and a domineering Church. This disturbing picture leads the poet to regret the loss of 'Romantic Ireland' in the concluding refrain.

Stanza two develops the contrast between past and present as Yeats considers the **heroism and generosity of an earlier era**. Ireland's patriots – 'names that stilled' earlier generations of children – could hardly have been more unlike the present middle class. Yeats clearly relates to the self-sacrifice of idealistic Irish freedom fighters: 'And what, God help us, could they save?' These disdainful words echo the fearful prayers referred to at the start of the poem. The heroes of the past were so selfless that they did not even concern themselves with saving their own lives.

The wistful and nostalgic tone of **stanza three** is obvious in the rhetorical question about all those Irish soldiers who had been exiled in the late 17th century. Yeats's high regard for these men is evoked by comparing them to 'wild geese', a plaintive metaphor reflecting their nobility. Yet the poet's admiration for past idealism is diminished by the fact that **such heroic dedication was all for nothing**. The repetition of 'for this' hammers home Yeats's contempt for the pious materialists of his own imperfect age. In listing a roll of honour, he singles out the most impressive patriots of his own class, the Anglo-Irish Ascendancy. For the poet, Fitzgerald, Emmet and Tone are among the most admirable Irishmen.

In using the phrase 'All that delirium of the brave', Yeats suggests that their passionate dedication to Irish freedom bordered on a frenzied or misplaced sense of daring.

This romanticised appreciation continues into the **final stanza**, where the poet imagines the 'loneliness and pain' of the heroic dead. His empathy towards them is underpinned by an **even more vicious portrayal of the new middle class**. He argues that the establishment figures of his own time would be unable to comprehend anything about the values and dreams of 'Romantic Ireland'. At best, they would be confused by the ludicrous self-sacrifice of the past. At worst, the present generation would accuse the patriots of being insane or of trying to impress friends or lovers. Perhaps Yeats is illustrating the cynical thinking of his time, when many politicians courted national popularity. 'Some woman's yellow hair' might well refer to the traditional symbol of Ireland as a beautiful woman.

The poet's disgust on behalf of the patriots is rounded off in the last two lines: 'But let them be, they're dead and gone'. The refrain has been changed slightly, adding further emphasis and a **sense of finality**. After reading this savage satire, we are left with a deep sense of Yeats's bitter disillusionment towards his contemporaries. The extreme feelings expressed in the poem offer a dispirited vision of an unworthy country. It isn't surprising that some critics have accused Yeats of over-romanticising the heroism of Ireland's past, of being narrow minded and even elitist. At any rate, the poem challenges us to examine the values of the state we are in, our understanding of Irish history and the meaning of heroism.

ANALYSIS

'September 1913' is based on contrasting images of meanness and generosity. Which set of images makes the greater impact? Write your response in a paragraph, referring closely to the text in your answer.

Sample Paragraph

Although W. B. Yeats ridicules the greedy shopkeepers and landlords of Dublin, he makes a much greater impression in describing the patriots of old Ireland – 'names that stilled your childish play'. The image stops us in our tracks. We can imagine how children used to hold men like Wolfe Tone and Robert Emmet in such great respect. Yeats uses the beautiful image of the wild geese spreading 'The grey wing upon every tide' to describe the dignified flight of Irish soldiers who refused to accept colonial rule. The poet's simple imagery is taken from the world of nature and has a vivid quality that makes us aware of the poet's high opinion of those heroes who were prepared to die for their beliefs.

Examiner's Comment

Clearly written and well supported, this C-grade response addresses the question directly. There is evidence of close engagement with the poem. In addition, the expression is varied, fluent and controlled throughout. However, further development of key contrast points would be expected for a top grade.

CLASS/HOMEWORK EXERCISES

1. How relevant is 'September 1913' to present-day Ireland? Refer to the text of the poem when writing your response.

2. Copy the table below into your own notes and fill in critical comments about the last two quotations.

Key Quotes

What need you, being come to sense	Rhetorical questions satirise those smug people who knew how to exploit situations to their advantage.
Romantic Ireland's dead and gone	In his refrain, Yeats is caught between deep disillusionment towards his contemporaries and admiration for a more idealistic age.
You have dried the marrow from the bone	
For this that all that blood was shed	

❸ THE WILD SWANS AT COOLE

The trees are in their autumn beauty,
The woodland paths are dry,
Under the October twilight the water
Mirrors a still sky;
Upon the brimming water among the stones   5
Are nine-and-fifty swans.

The nineteenth autumn has come upon me
Since I first made my count;
I saw, before I had well finished,
All suddenly mount   10
And scatter wheeling in great broken rings
Upon their clamorous wings.

I have looked upon those brilliant creatures,
And now my heart is sore.
All's changed since I, hearing at twilight,   15
The first time on this shore,
The bell-beat of their wings above my head,
Trod with a lighter tread.

Unwearied still, lover by lover,
They paddle in the cold   20
Companionable streams or climb the air;
Their hearts have not grown old;
Passion or conquest, wander where they will,
Attend upon them still.

But now they drift on the still water,   25
Mysterious, beautiful;
Among what rushes will they build,
By what lake's edge or pool
Delight men's eyes when I awake some day
To find they have flown away?   30

'The bell-beat of their wings above my head'

GLOSSARY

5	*brimming*: filled to the very top or edge.	19	*lover by lover*: swans mate for life; this highlights Yeats's loneliness.
12	*clamorous*: loud, confused noise.	21	*Companionable*: friendly.
18	*Trod... tread*: walked lightly; carefree.	24	*Attend upon them still*: waits on them yet.

EXPLORATIONS

1. Why do you think the poet chose the season of autumn as his setting? What changes occur at this time of year? Where are these referred to in the poem?

2. In your opinion, what are the main contrasts between the swans and the poet? Describe two, using close reference to the text.

3. What do you think the final stanza means? Consider the phrase 'I awake'. From what does the poet awake?

STUDY NOTES

'The Wild Swans at Coole' was written in 1916. Yeats loved spending time in the West, especially at Coole, the home of Lady Gregory, his friend and patron. He was 51 when he wrote this poem, which contrasts the swans' beauty and apparent seeming immortality with Yeats's ageing, mortal self.

The poem opens with a tranquil, serene scene of **autumnal beauty** in the park of Lady Gregory's home in Galway. This romantic image is described in great detail: the 'woodland paths are dry'. It is evening, 'October twilight'. The water is 'brimming'. The swans are carefully counted, 'nine-and-fifty'. The use of the soft letters 'l', 'm' and 's' emphasise the calm of the scene in **stanza one**.

In **stanza two**, the poem moves to the personal as he recalls that it is 19 years since he first counted the swans. The word 'count' links the two stanzas. The poet's counting is interrupted as these mysterious creatures all suddenly rise into the sky. Run-through lines suggest the flowing movement of the rising swans.

Strong verbs ('mount', 'scatter') reinforce this elemental action. The great beating wings of the swans are captured in the onomatopoeic 'clamorous wings'. They are independent and refuse to be restrained. The ring is a symbol of eternity. The swans are making the same patterns as they have always made; they are unchanging. **Stanza two** is linked to **stanza three** by the phrases 'I saw' and 'I have looked'. Now the poet tells us his 'heart is sore'. He has taken stock and is **dissatisfied with his emotional situation**. He is 51, alone and unmarried and concerned that his poetic powers are lessening: '**All's changed**'. All humans want things to remain as they are, but life is full of change. He has lost the great love of his life, the beautiful Irish activist, Maud Gonne. He also laments the loss of his youth, when he 'Trod with a lighter tread'. Nineteen years earlier, he was much more carefree. The noise of the beating wings of the swans is effectively captured in the compound word 'bell-beat'. The alliterative 'b' reinforces the steady, flapping sound. The poet is using his intense personal experiences to express universal truths.

The swans in **stanza four** are **symbols of eternity**, ageless, 'Unwearied still'. They are united, 'lover by lover'. They experience life together ('Companionable streams'), not on their own, like the poet. He envies them their defiance of time: 'Their hearts have not grown old'. They do what they want, when they want. They are full of 'Passion or conquest'. By contrast, he is indirectly telling us, he feels old and worn out. The **spiral imagery** of the 'great broken rings' is reminiscent of the spirals seen in ancient carvings representing eternity. Yeats believed there was a cyclical pattern behind all things. The swans can live in two elements, water and air, thus linking these elements together. They are living, vital, immortal, unlike their surroundings. The trees are yellowing ('autumn beauty') and the dry 'woodland paths' suggest the lack of creative force which the poet is experiencing. Yeats is heartbroken and weary. Only the swans transcend time.

Stanza five explores a **philosophy of life**, linked to the previous stanza by the repetition of 'still'. The swans have returned to the water, 'Mysterious, beautiful'. The poem ends on a speculative note as the poet asks where they will 'Delight men's eyes'. Is he referring to the fact that **they will continue to be a source of pleasure to someone else** long after he is dead? The swans appear immortal, a continuing source of happiness as they practise their patterns, whereas the poet is not able to continue improving his own writing, as he is mortal. The poet is slipping into the cruel season of winter while the swans infinitely 'drift on the still water'.

ANALYSIS

Poets use patterns to communicate their message. With reference to 'The Wild Swans at Coole', write a paragraph on Yeats's use of pattern, referring to imagery, sound effects, rhyme, etc.

Sample Paragraph

The rhyme scheme in 'The Wild Swans at Coole' is abcbdd. When I look at the words which these rhymes stress, I see another layer in this poem. The marked contrast between the dry woodland paths, which are so suggestive of the drying up of creativity, and the water which 'Mirrors a still sky' is very effective. The water is teeming with life. In the second stanza the poet is anchored to the land as he makes his 'count', while the swans are free to fly at a moment's notice, 'All suddenly mount'. When Yeats first went to Coole, he was suffering from a broken heart and this is echoed in the rhyming lines 'And now my heart is sore', 'The first time on this shore'. Although the swans are in the 'cold', they have not 'grown old'. Finally, he wonders where these 'Mysterious and beautiful' creatures will be: 'By what lake's edge or pool'. Similarly, another layer of meaning is created by the rhyme of the last two lines of each stanza. I particularly liked the rhyme in the last stanza: 'when I awake some day/To find they have flown away'. This sums up for me the sadness of the poet as he realises he is mortal, whereas they are immortal. It may even suggest his dread that his poetic inspiration, which is as mysterious and beautiful as the swans, may suddenly desert him too. I think examining the carefully worked patterns of the poem increases both our enjoyment of the poem as well as our understanding of the poet's message.

Examiner's Comment

The student has engaged in a personal way to answer this question. Detailed attention has been given to the poet's use of rhyme. An effective, well-developed discussion that makes good use of quotations to sustain the argument. Confident expression adds to the A-grade standard.

CLASS/HOMEWORK EXERCISES

1. Is the poem more concerned with the poet than the swans? Write a paragraph responding to this statement, referring to the text.

2. Copy the table below into your own notes and fill in critical comments about the last two quotations.

Key Quotes

The woodland paths are dry	Using symbolism, Yeats expresses his fears of ageing and the loss of his poetic imagination.
And now my heart is sore	Yeats admits to being dissatisfied with his life. The assonance adds to the poignancy.
Unwearied still, lover by lover	
Mysterious, beautiful	

❹ AN IRISH AIRMAN FORESEES HIS DEATH

I know that I shall meet my fate
Somewhere among the clouds above;
Those that I fight I do not hate,
Those that I guard I do not love;
My country is Kiltartan Cross,   5
My countrymen Kiltartan's poor,
No likely end could bring them loss
Or leave them happier than before.
Nor law, nor duty bade me fight,
Nor public men, nor cheering crowds,   10
A lonely impulse of delight
Drove to this tumult in the clouds;
I balanced all, brought all to mind,
The years to come seemed waste of breath,
A waste of breath the years behind   15
In balance with this life, this death.

'I balanced all'

GLOSSARY

The Irish airman in this poem is Major Robert Gregory (1881–1918), son of Yeats's close friend, Lady Gregory. He was shot down and killed while on service in northern Italy.

3 *Those that I fight*: the Germans.

4 *Those that I guard*: Allied countries, such as England and France.

5 *Kiltartan*: townland near the Gregory estate in Co. Galway.

7 *likely end*: outcome.

12 *tumult*: turmoil; confusion.

EXPLORATIONS

1. 'This poem is not just an elegy or lament in memory of the dead airman. It is also an insight into the excitement and exhilaration of warfare.' Write your response to this statement, using close reference to the text.

2. Write a paragraph on Yeats's use of repetition throughout the poem. Refer to the text in your answer.

3. Imagine you are Robert Gregory. Write a short diary entry reflecting your thoughts and feelings about becoming a fighter pilot. Base your comments on the text of the poem.

STUDY NOTES

Thousands of Irishmen fought and died in the British armed forces during the First World War. Robert Gregory was killed in Italy at the age of 37. The airman's death had a lasting effect on Yeats, who wrote several poems about him.

Is it right to assume anything about young men who fight for their countries? Why do they enlist? Do they always know what they are fighting for? In this poem, Yeats expresses what he believes is the airman's viewpoint as he comes face to face with death. This **fatalistic attitude** is prevalent in the emphatic **opening line**. The poem's title also leads us to believe that the speaker has an intuitive sense that his death is about to happen. But despite this premonition, he seems strangely resigned to risking his life.

In **lines 3-4**, he makes it clear that he neither hates his German enemies nor loves the British and their allies. His thoughts are with the people he knows best back in Kiltartan, Co. Galway. Major Gregory recognises the irony of their detachment from the war. The ordinary people of his homeland are unlikely to be affected at all by whatever happens on the killing fields of mainland Europe. Does he feel that he is abandoning his fellow countrymen? What is the dominant tone of **lines 7–8**? Is there an underlying bitterness?

In **line 9**, the speaker takes time to reflect on why he joined the air force and immediately dismisses the obvious reasons of conscription ('law') or patriotism ('duty'). As a volunteer, Gregory is more openly cynical of the 'public men' and 'cheering crowds' he mentions in **line 10**. Like many in the military who have experienced the realities of warfare, **he is suspicious of hollow patriotism** and has no time for political leaders and popular adulation. So why did Robert Gregory choose to endanger his life by going to war? The answer lies in the key comments 'A lonely impulse of delight' (**line 11**) and 'I balanced all' (**line 13**). The first phrase is paradoxical. The airman experiences not just the excitement, but also the isolation of flying. At the same time, his 'impulse' to enlist as a fighter pilot reflects both his **desire for adventure** as well as his regret.

The **last four lines** explain the real reason behind his decision. It was neither rash nor emotional, but simply a question of balance. Having examined his life closely, Gregory has chosen the heroism of a self-sacrificing death. It is as though he only feels truly alive during the 'tumult' of battle. Yeats's language is particularly evocative at this point. Awesome air battles are effectively echoed in such dynamic phrasing as 'impulse of delight' and 'tumult in the clouds'. This **sense of freedom and power** is repeatedly contrasted with the dreary and predictable security of life away from the war – dismissed out of hand as a 'waste of breath'. From the airman's perspective, as a man of action, dying in battle is in keeping with 'this life' that he has chosen. Such a death would be his final adventurous exploit.

Some commentators have criticised Yeats's poem for glorifying war and pointless risk-taking. Others have suggested that the poet successfully highlights Anglo-Irish attitudes, neither exclusively Irish nor English. The poet certainly raises interesting questions about national identity and ways of thinking about war. However, in elegising Robert Gregory, he emphasises the **airman's daring solitude**. Perhaps this same thrill lies at the heart of other important choices in life, including the creative activity of artists. Is there a sense that the poet and the pilot are alike, both of them taking calculated risks in what they do?

ANALYSIS

What do you think is the poem's dominant or central mood? Write your response in a paragraph, referring closely to the text in your answer.

Sample Paragraph

The title itself suggests fear. However, the airman accepts his impending death as if it is a natural result. 'Fate' suggests destiny, the unavoidable. The rest of the poem is dominated by a strong mood of resignation. The slow rhythm is like a chant or a prayer. This airman has a fatalistic temperament. He seems completely relaxed when he says 'Those that I fight I do not hate'. In a way, he seems to have distanced himself from everything and everyone. He appears to have something of a death wish and his mood becomes very disillusioned towards the final section. For him, the past and future are a 'waste'. In general, his mood is quite resigned to death.

Examiner's Comment

This candidate focuses well on the negative moods within the poem. Apt quotes are also effectively used in reference. The paragraph might have included some mention of the contrasting euphoria of war. The language towards the end is also slightly stilted. Overall, a C-grade standard.

CLASS/HOMEWORK EXERCISES

1. Do you consider 'An Irish Airman Foresees his Death' to be an anti-war poem? Give reasons for your answer.

2. Copy the table below into your own notes and fill in critical comments about the last two quotations.

Key Quotes

I know that I shall meet my fate	The narrator, Robert Gregory, accepts that he will be killed in battle, yet his desire to take risks is more powerful.
waste of breath	The speaker's disenchantment with ordinary life is emphasised.
Nor law, nor duty bade me fight	
In balance with this life, this death	

❺   EASTER, 1916

I have met them at close of day
Coming with vivid faces
From counter or desk among grey
Eighteenth-century houses.
I have passed with a nod of the head   5
Or polite meaningless words,
Or have lingered awhile and said
Polite meaningless words,
And thought before I had done
Of a mocking tale or a gibe   10
To please a companion
Around the fire at the club,
Being certain that they and I
But lived where motley is worn:
All changed, changed utterly: 15
A terrible beauty is born.

That woman's days were spent
In ignorant good-will,
Her nights in argument
Until her voice grew shrill.   20
What voice more sweet than hers
When, young and beautiful,
She rode to harriers?
This man had kept a school
And rode our wingèd horse;   25
This other his helper and friend
Was coming into his force;
He might have won fame in the end,
So sensitive his nature seemed,
So daring and sweet his thought.   30
This other man I had dreamed
A drunken, vainglorious lout.
He had done most bitter wrong
To some who are near my heart,
Yet I number him in the song;   35
He, too, has resigned his part
In the casual comedy;

He, too, has been changed in his turn,
Transformed utterly:
A terrible beauty is born.   40

Hearts with one purpose alone
Through summer and winter seem
Enchanted to a stone
To trouble the living stream.
The horse that comes from the road,   45
The rider, the birds that range
From cloud to tumbling cloud,
Minute by minute they change;
A shadow of cloud on the stream
Changes minute by minute;   50
A horse-hoof slides on the brim,
And a horse plashes within it;
The long-legged moor-hens dive,
And hens to moor-cocks call;
Minute by minute they live: 55
The stone's in the midst of all.

Too long a sacrifice
Can make a stone of the heart.
O when may it suffice?
That is Heaven's part, our part   60
To murmur name upon name,
As a mother names her child
When sleep at last has come
On limbs that had run wild.
What is it but nightfall?   65
No, no, not night but death;
Was it needless death after all?
For England may keep faith
For all that is done and said.
We know their dream; enough   70
To know they dreamed and are dead;
And what if excess of love
Bewildered them till they died?
I write it out in a verse –
MacDonagh and MacBride   75

And Connolly and Pearse
Now and in time to be,
Wherever green is worn,
Are changed, changed utterly:
A terrible beauty is born.   80

'All changed, changed utterly'

GLOSSARY

On 24 April 1916, Easter Monday, about 700 Irish Republicans took over several key buildings in Dublin. These included the Four Courts, Bolands Mills, the Royal College of Surgeons and the General Post Office. The rebellion lasted six days and was followed by the execution of its leaders. The Rising was a pivotal event in modern Irish history.

1   *them*: the rebels involved in the Rising.
14 *motley*: ridiculous clothing.
17 *That woman*: Countess Markiewicz, friend of Yeats and a committed nationalist.
24 *This man*: Padraig Pearse, poet and teacher, was shot as a leader of the Rising.
25 *wingèd horse*: Pegasus, the mythical white horse that flies across the sky, was a symbol of poetic inspiration.
26 *This other*: Thomas MacDonagh, writer and teacher, executed in 1916.
31 *This other man*: Major John MacBride was also executed for his part in the rebellion. He was the husband of Maud Gonne.
33 *most bitter wrong*: there were recurring rumours that MacBride had mistreated Maud Gonne.
67 *needless death*: Yeats asks if the Rising was a waste of life, since the British were already considering independence for Ireland.
76 *Connolly*: Trade union leader and revolutionary, executed in 1916.

EXPLORATIONS

1. Describe the atmosphere in the opening stanza of the poem. Refer closely to the text in your answer.

2. 'Easter, 1916' has many striking images. Choose two that you find particularly interesting and briefly explain their effectiveness.

3. On balance, does Yeats approve or disapprove of the Easter Rising? Refer to the text in your answer.

STUDY NOTES

Yeats, who was in London at the time of the Rising, had mixed feelings about what had happened. He was clearly fascinated but also troubled by this heroic and yet in some ways pointless sacrifice. He did not publish the poem until 1920.

In the **opening stanza**, Yeats recalls how he used to meet some of the people who were later involved in the Easter Rising. He was unimpressed by their 'vivid faces' and he remembers routinely dismissing them with 'Polite meaningless words'. His admission that he **misjudged these insignificant Republicans** as subjects for 'a mocking tale or a gibe' among his clever friends is a reminder of his derisive attitude in 'September 1913'. Before 1916, Yeats had considered Ireland a ridiculous place, a circus 'where motley is worn'. But the poet confesses that the Rising transformed everything – including his own condescending apathy. In the stanza's final lines, Yeats introduces what becomes an ambivalent refrain ending in 'A terrible beauty is born'.

This sense of shock and the need to completely re-evaluate his views is developed in **stanza two**. The poet singles out individual martyrs killed or imprisoned for their activities, among them his close friend Countess Markiewicz. He also mentions Major John MacBride, husband of Maud Gonne, who had refused Yeats's proposal of marriage. Although he had always considered MacBride as little more than a 'drunken, vainglorious lout', Yeats now acknowledges that he too has been distinguished by his bravery and heroism. The poet wonders about

[handwritten margin note: They were all cork.]

the usefulness of all the passion that sparked the rebels to make such a bold move, but his emphasis is on the fact that **the people as well as the whole atmosphere have changed**. Even MacBride, whom he held in utter contempt, has grown in stature.

In **stanza three**, Yeats takes powerful images from nature and uses them to explore the meaning of Irish heroism. The metaphor of the stubborn stone in the stream might represent the defiance of the revolutionaries towards all the forces around them. **The poet evokes the constant energy and dynamism of the natural world**, focusing on the changes that happen 'minute by minute'. Image after dazzling image conjures up a vivid picture of unpredictable movement and seasonal regeneration (as 'hens to moor-cocks call') and skies change 'From cloud to tumbling cloud'.

For the poet, the Rising presented many contradictions, as he weighs the success of the revolt against the shocking costs. In contrasting the inflexibility of the revolutionaries with the 'living stream', he **indicates a reluctant admiration for the rebels' dedication**. Does Yeats suggest that the rebels risked the loss of their own humanity, allowing their hearts to harden to stone? Or is he also thinking of Maud Gonne and blaming her cold-hearted rejection of him on her fanatical political views?

In the **final stanza**, the poet returns to the metaphor of the unmoving stone in a flowing stream to warn of the dangers of fanaticism. The rhetorical questions about the significance of the rebellion reveal his **continuing struggle to understand** what happened. Then he asks the single most important question about the Rising: 'Was it needless death after all', particularly as 'England may keep faith' and allow Ireland its independence, all of which would prompt a more disturbing conclusion, i.e. that the insurgents died in vain.

Yeats quickly abandons essentially unanswerable questions about the value of the Irish struggle for freedom. Instead, he simply pays tribute to the fallen patriots by naming them tenderly, 'As a mother names her child'. The final assertive lines commemorate the 1916 leaders in dramatic style. Setting aside his earlier ambivalence, Yeats acknowledges that these patriots died for their dreams. The hushed tone is reverential, almost sacred. The rebels have been transformed into martyrs who will be remembered for their selfless heroism 'Wherever green is worn'. The insistent final refrain has a stirring and increasingly disquieting quality. The poem's central paradox, 'A terrible beauty is born', concludes that **all the heroic achievements of the 1916 Rising were at the tragic expense of human life**.

ANALYSIS

Write a paragraph outlining Yeats's feelings about the Irish patriots as expressed in the final stanza of 'Easter, 1916'. Support the points you make with suitable reference or quotation.

Sample Paragraph

The final verse reveals many of Yeats's unanswered questions and confused thinking about the 1916 patriots. However, he sees that his own role is to record what he knows to be true and to 'write it out in a verse'. This allows him to pay his own tribute to the 1916 leaders whom he lists formally, almost like a graveside oration. The slow, deliberate rhythm is deeply respectful. The mood is serious, almost sombre, in keeping with the poet's newfound respect for the dead heroes. Yeats ends with the keynote comment, 'A terrible beauty is born'. This oxymoron *Contradiction* derives its power from the obvious contrast between the terms. He believed that the Easter Rising was terrible because of all the unnecessary suffering that had occurred. Nevertheless, Yeats accepts that there was a transforming beauty that took the rebels, and perhaps many others, out of their lives of 'casual comedy' into the tragic drama of real life.

Examiner's Comment

This short paragraph is well focused and supported. The candidate touches on several interesting aspects of the poet's mixed feelings about 1916. The references to features of style contribute much to this well-written A-grade response.

CLASS/HOMEWORK EXERCISES

1. Yeats emphasises change of one kind or another throughout 'Easter, 1916'. List the main changes and comment briefly on them.

2. Copy the table below into your own notes and fill in critical comments about the last two quotations.

Key Quotes

All changed, changed utterly:/A terrible beauty is born	The 1916 Rising, in all its idealism and brutality, had transformed not just Ireland, but Yeats's own attitudes.
Enchanted to a stone	The poet uses the metaphor to show both the determination of the rebels and their unswerving fanaticism.
polite meaningless words	
Being certain that they and I/But lived where motley is worn	

6   THE SECOND COMING

Turning and turning in the widening gyre
The falcon cannot hear the falconer;
Things fall apart; the centre cannot hold;
Mere anarchy is loosed upon the world,
The blood-dimmed tide is loosed, and everywhere   5
The ceremony of innocence is drowned;
The best lack all conviction, while the worst
Are full of passionate intensity.

Surely some revelation is at hand;
Surely the Second Coming is at hand.   10
The Second Coming! Hardly are those words out
When a vast image out of *Spiritus Mundi*
Troubles my sight: somewhere in sands of the desert
A shape with lion body and the head of a man,
A gaze blank and pitiless as the sun,   15
Is moving its slow thighs, while all about it
Reel shadows of the indignant desert birds.
The darkness drops again; but now I know
That twenty centuries of stony sleep
Were vexed to nightmare by a rocking cradle,   20
And what rough beast, its hour come round at last,
Slouches towards Bethlehem to be born?

'somewhere in sands of the desert/A shape with lion body and the head of a man'

GLOSSARY

The Second Coming: This is a reference to the Bible. It is from Matthew and speaks of Christ's return to reward the good.

1   *in the widening gyre*: Yeats regarded a cycle of history as a gyre. He visualised these cycles as interconnecting cones that moved in a circular motion widening outwards until they could not widen any further, then a new gyre or cone formed from the centre of the circle created. This spun in the opposite direction to the original cone. The Christian era was coming to a close and a new disturbed time was coming into view. In summary, the gyre is a symbol of constant change.

2   *falcon*: a bird of prey, trained to hunt by the aristocracy.

2   *falconer*: the trainer of the falcon. If the bird flies too far away, it cannot be directed.

4   *Mere*: nothing more than; just; only.

4   *anarchy*: lack of government or order. Yeats believed that bloodshed and a worship of bloodshed were the end of an historical era.

5   *blood-dimmed*: made dark with blood.

12   *Spiritus Mundi*: Spirit of the World, the collective soul of the world.

14   *lion body and the head of a man*: famous statue in Egypt; an enigmatic person.

17   *desert birds*: birds of prey.

19   *twenty centuries*: Yeats believed that two thousand years was the length of a period in history.

20   *vexed*: annoyed; distressed.

20   *rocking cradle*: coming of the infant Jesus.

21   *rough beast*: the Anti-Christ.

22   *Bethlehem*: birthplace of Christ. It is usually associated with peace and innocence, and it is terrifying that the beast is going to be born there. The spiral has reversed its spinning. A savage god is coming.

EXPLORATIONS

1. This poem suggests that politics are not important. Does the poet convince you? Write a paragraph in response, with reference to the text.

2. Yeats uses symbols to express some of his most profound ideas. What symbols in this poem appeal to you? Use reference to the text in your response.

3. 'Yeats is yearning for order, and fearing anarchy.' Discuss two ways in which the poem illustrates this statement. Support your answer with reference to the text.

STUDY NOTES

'The Second Coming' is a terrifying, apocalyptic poem written in January 1919 against a background of the disintegration of three great European empires at the end of the First World War and against the catastrophic War of Independence in Ireland. These were bloody times. Yeats yearned for order and feared anarchy.

Sparked off by both disgust at what was happening in Europe as well as his interest in the occult, Yeats explores, in **stanza one**, what he perceives to be the failure at the heart of society: 'Things fall apart'. In his opinion, **the whole world was disintegrating** into a bloody, chaotic mess. This break-up of civilisation is described in metaphorical language. For Yeats, the 'gyre' is a symbol representing an era. He believed contrary expanding and contracting forces influence people and cultures and that the Christian era was nearing its end. Images of hunting show how the old world represented its failing – 'The falcon cannot hear the falconer'. We have lost touch with Christ, just as the falcon loses touch with the falconer as he swings into ever-increasing circles. This bird was trained to fly in circles to catch its prey. The circular imagery, with the repetitive '-ing', describes the continuous, swirling movement. Civilisation is also 'Turning and turning in the widening gyre' as it buckles and fragments.

The **tension** is reflected in a list of contrasts: 'centre' and 'fall apart', 'falcon' and 'falconer', 'lack all conviction' and 'intensity', 'innocence' and 'anarchy'. The strain is too much: 'the centre cannot hold'. The verbs also graphically describe this chaotic world: 'Turning and turning', 'loosed', 'drowned', 'fall apart'. Humans are changing amidst the chaos: 'innocence is drowned'. **Anarchy** is described in terms of a great tidal wave, 'the blood-dimmed tide', which sweeps everything before it. The compound word reinforces the overwhelming nature of the water. Yeats feels that the 'best', the leaders and thinkers, have no energy; they are indifferent and 'lack all conviction'. On the other hand, the 'worst', the cynics and fanatics, are consumed with hatred and violence, 'full of passionate intensity'.

Disillusioned, Yeats thinks **a new order has to be emerging**. He imagines a Second Coming. He repeats the word 'Surely' in a tone of both belief and fear in **stanza two**. The Second Coming is usually thought of as a time when Christ will return to reward the good, but the image Yeats presents us with is terrifying. **A blank, pitiless creature emerges**. It is straight from the Book of Revelations: 'And

I saw a beast rising out of the sea'. This was regarded as a sign that the end of the world was near. Such an unnatural hybrid of human and animal is the Anti-Christ, the opposite force of the gentle infant Jesus who signalled the end of the Greek and Roman Empires. The 'gaze blank' suggests its lack of intelligence. The phrase 'pitiless as the sun' tells us the creature has no empathy or compassion. It 'Slouches'. It is a brutish, graceless monstrosity.

The **hostile environment** is a nightmare scenario of blazing desert sun, shifting sands and circling predatory birds. The verbs suggest everything is out of focus: 'Reel', 'rocking', 'Slouches'. 'The darkness drops again' shows how disorder, disconnectedness and the 'widening gyre' have brought us to nihilism. This seems to be a prophetic statement, as fascism was to sweep the world in the mid-20th century. Then Yeats has a moment of epiphany: 'but now I know'. Other eras have been destroyed before. The baby in the 'rocking cradle' created an upheaval that resulted in the end of 'twenty centuries of stony sleep'.

Yeats believed that a **cycle of history** lasted two thousand years in a single evolution of birth, growth, decline and death. All change causes upheaval. The Christian era, with its qualities of innocence, order, maternal love and goodness, is at an end. The new era of the 'rough beast' is about to start. It is pitiless, destructive, violent and murderous. This new era has already begun: 'its hour come round at last'. It is a savage god who is coming, uninvited. The spiral has reversed its motion and is now spinning in the opposite direction. The lack of end rhyme mirrors a world of chaos. Yeats looks back over thousands of years. We are given a thrilling and terrifying prospect from a vast perspective of millennia.

ANALYSIS

Yeats declared that a poet should think like a wise man, but express himself as one of the common people. Write a paragraph in response to this view, using close reference to 'The Second Coming'.

Sample Paragraph

I feel that the themes of stability and anarchy are wisely considered by Yeats. When I look at the events of the mid to late 20th century from the perspective of the 21st century, I see a very prophetic voice warning of the dangers of the cynic, 'lack all conviction', and the fundamentalist fanatic, 'while the worst/Are full of passionate intensity'. The rise of fascism, the Second World War, the Vietnam War, the atom bomb – none of these were known when Yeats wrote this poem in 1919. Things did 'fall apart' and 'darkness' did drop again. However, the human spirit, 'Spiritus Mundi', rose again, and I would suggest that he was wrong to be so gloomy. Out of the turmoil and chaos of the Second World War came a cry. 'Surely some revelation is at hand'. But it was not the 'rough beast' with a 'gaze blank and pitiless as the sun'. Instead we had the foundation of the European Union, which has led to a long peace and stability. So, unlike Yeats's doom-laden prophecy, I think the 'centre' did 'hold'. In my opinion, the references to the Bible, Matthew, 'The Second Coming', and the Book of Revelations, 'I saw a beast', the phrases 'widening gyre', 'Spiritus Mundi' and the image of the Sphinx are not the language of the common man. It is very interesting to discover the meaning behind these phrases, but this is not the language of everyday speech. So although I do agree that Yeats did think like a wise man, I feel he was too pessimistic about the human race. I also think that although his expressions are powerful and thought provoking, they are not the language of the common man. This is in keeping with Yeats's view that the nobles and aristocrats should rule, not the masses.

Examiner's Comment

This impressive response focused clearly on the task, which was to consider Yeats's wisdom and his ability to express himself as one of the common people. A real sense of individual engagement with the poem came across in this well-argued answer. A grade.

> ## CLASS/HOMEWORK EXERCISES

1. This is a political poem. What kind of political vision does it convey? Illustrate your answer with reference to the text.

2. Copy the table below into your own notes and fill in critical comments about the last two quotations.

Key Quotes

Things fall apart	Yeats believed that civilisation was breaking up and a new, brutish order would be established.
The ceremony of innocence is drowned	This metaphor highlights that the rituals and celebration of goodness represented by the Christian era are swept away by anarchy.
Turning and turning in the widening gyre	
Surely the Second Coming is at hand	

Time passes

7 SAILING TO BYZANTIUM

I

That is no country for old men. The young

Ireland is a young Country

In one another's arms, birds in the trees

– Those dying generations – at their song,

The salmon-falls, the mackerel-crowded seas,

Fish, flesh, or fowl, commend all summer long   5

Whatever is begotten, born, and dies.

Caught in that sensual music all neglect

Everything has its place.

Monuments of unageing intellect.

Everything has a life space.

II

                                        worthless

An aged man is but a paltry thing,

People do not appreciate the old people.

         Scarecrow

A tattered coat upon a stick, unless   10

Soul must overcome this failing body.

Soul clap its hands and sing, and louder sing

For every tatter in its mortal dress, —

Nor is there singing school but studying

Monuments of its own magnificence;

Soul has to study the past

And therefore I have sailed the seas and come   15

To the holy city of Byzantium.

→ Istanbul in Turkey.
→ Tells us a lot about air port.

III

O sages standing in God's holy fire

As in the gold mosaic of a wall,

Come from the holy fire, perne in a gyre,

•He is almost calling the works of art to get his soul.

And be the singing-masters of my soul.   20

Consume my heart away; sick with desire

•Asking wise men to transform him from being an old man.

And fastened to a dying animal

         himself?

He wishes that body and soul could be separated

It knows not what it is; and gather me

Into the artifice of eternity.

• He wants to be consumed into the world of Art where he would be remembered.

He believes his soul would be eternalised in the work of Art.

Ambiguous

IV

Once out of nature I shall never take   25

once his soul is detached, he will never take the living form.

My bodily form from any natural thing,

But such a form as Grecian goldsmiths make

Of hammered gold and gold enamelling

To keep a drowsy Emperor awake;

People may become bored of the art.

Or set upon a golden bough to sing   30

To lords and ladies of Byzantium
Of what is past, or passing, or to come.

'the holy city of Byzantium'

GLOSSARY

A-Z

Sailing to Byzantium: for Yeats, this voyage would be one taken to find perfection. This country only exists in the mind. It is an ideal. The original old city of Byzantium was famous as a centre of religion, art and architecture.

1   *That*: Ireland – all who live there are subject to ageing, decay and death.

3   *dying generations*: opposites are linked to show that in the midst of life is death.

7   *sensual music*: the young are living life to the full through their senses and are neglecting the inner spiritual life of the soul.

9   *paltry thing*: worthless, of no importance. Old age is not valued in Ireland.

10   *tattered coat*: an old man is as worthless as a scarecrow.

10-11 *unless/Soul clap its hands and sing*: man can only break free if he allows his spirit

the freedom to express itself.

13-14 *Nor is there... own magnificence*: all schools of art should study the discipline they teach, while the soul should study the immortal art of previous generations.

17   *O sages*: wise men, cleansed by the holy fire of God.

19-24 *Come... artifice of eternity*: Yeats asks the sages to teach him the wonders of Byzantium and gather his soul into the perfection of art.

19   *perne in a gyre*: spinning; turning very fast.

22   *fastened to a dying animal*: the soul trapped in a decaying body.

32   *past, or passing, or to come*: in eternity, the golden bird sings of transience (passing time).

EXPLORATIONS

1. This poem tries to offer a form of escape from old age. Does it succeed? Write a paragraph in response, with support from the text.

2. Why are the 'Monuments of unageing intellect' of such importance to Yeats? What does this imply about contemporary Ireland?

3. The poem is defiant in its exploration of eternity. Discuss, using reference or quotation.

STUDY NOTES

'Sailing to Byzantium' confronts the universal issue of old age. There is no easy solution to this problem. Yeats found the idea of advancing age repulsive and longed to escape. Here he imagines an ideal place, Byzantium, which allowed all to enjoy eternal works of art. He celebrates what man can create and he bitterly condemns the mortality to which man is subject.

Yeats wrote, 'When Irishmen were illuminating the Book of Kells... Byzantium was the centre of European civilization... so I symbolise the search for the spiritual life by a journey to that city.'

The poet declares the theme in the **first stanza** as he confidently declaims that the world of the senses is not for the old – they must seek another way which is timeless, **a life of the spirit and intellect**. The word 'That' tells us he is looking back, as he has already started his journey. But he is looking back wistfully at the world of the lovers ('The young/In one another's arms') and the world of teeming nature ('The salmon-falls, the mackerel-crowded seas'). The compound words emphasise the dynamism and fertility of the life of the senses, even though he admits the flaw in this wonderful life of plenty is mortality ('Those dying generations'). The life of the senses and nature is governed by the harsh cycle of procreation, life and death.

The poet asserts in the **second stanza** that what gives meaning to a person is the soul, 'unless/Soul clap its hands and sing'. Otherwise an elderly man is worthless, 'a paltry thing'. We are given a chilling image of the thin, wasting frame of an old man as a scarecrow in tattered clothes. In contrast, we are shown the

(handwritten annotations:)
older people
senses
does not x
Everything gets its limit
vital
*There has to be more to life than the senses.
→ Soul has a role.

wonders of the intellect as the poet tells us that all schools of art study what they compose, what they produce – 'Monuments of unageing intellect'. These works of art are timeless; unlike the body, they are not subject to decay. Thus, music schools study great music and art schools study great paintings. The life of the intellect and spirit must take precedence over the life of the senses. Yeats will no longer listen to the 'sensual music' that is appropriate only for the young, but will study the carefully composed 'music' of classic art.

In Byzantium, the buildings had beautiful mosaics, pictures made with little tiles and inlaid with gold. One of these had a picture of martyrs being burned. Yeats addresses these wise men ('sages') in **stanza three**. He wants them to whirl through time ('perne in a gyre') and come to **teach his soul how to 'sing'**, how to live the life of the spirit. His soul craves this ('sick with desire'), **but it is trapped in the decaying, mortal body** ('fastened to a dying animal'). This is a horrendous image of old age. The soul has lost its identity: 'It knows not what it is'.

He pleads to be saved from this using two interesting verbs, 'Consume' and 'gather'. Both suggest a desire to be taken away. A fire consumes what is put into it and changes the form of the substance. Yeats wants a new body. He pleads to be embraced like a child coming home: 'gather me'. But where will he go? He will journey into the cold world of art, 'the artifice of eternity'. 'Artifice' refers to the skill of those who have created the greatest works of art, but it also means artificial, not real. Is the poet suggesting that eternity also has a flaw?

The **fourth stanza** starts confidently as Yeats declares that 'Once out of nature', he will be transformed into the ageless perfect work of art, the **golden bird**. This is the new body for his soul. Now he will sing to the court. But is the court listening? The word 'drowsy' suggests not. Isn't he singing about transience, the passing of time: 'what is past, or passing, or to come'? Has this any relevance in eternity? Is there a perfect solution to the dilemma of old age?

Yeats raises these questions for our consideration. He has explored this problem by contrasting the abundant life of the young with the 'tattered coat' of old age. He has shown us the golden bird of immortality in opposition to the 'dying animal' of the decaying body. The poet has lulled us with end-rhymes and half-rhymes. He has used groups of threes – 'Fish, flesh, or fowl', 'begotten, born, and dies', 'past, or passing, or to come' – to argue his case. At the end of the poem, do we feel that Yeats genuinely longs for the warm, teeming life of the senses with all its imperfections rather than the cold, disinterested world of the 'artifice of eternity'?

ANALYSIS

'Yeats is often concerned with finding ways of escape from the sorrows and oppressions which are so much a part of life.' What evidence do you find for this statement in 'Sailing to Byzantium'?

Sample Paragraph

I believe that Yeats was preoccupied with the inescapable fact of ageing and death. This poem, 'Sailing to Byzantium', concerns a voyage to perfection. In ordinary life there is no perfection, a fact that Yeats recognises in the phrase 'dying generations'. All must die so that more can be born into the abundant, mortal world of nature. He rages against the weaknesses of old age: an old man is a 'tattered coat upon a stick', 'a paltry thing'. The body is a 'dying animal'. Terrible, grotesque imagery vividly describes the ravages of the ageing process. Yeats intends to turn his back on this and seek immortality, hence his journey to Byzantium. This city, in his opinion, is the perfect city, as it was the cradle of European civilisation and religious philosophy. He wants the figures that are in the golden mosaics to come and instruct him how to live this life of the intellect: 'gather me'. He wants to escape the sorrows and oppressions of ordinary life. Then he paints an idyllic picture of himself, now in the shape of a golden bird, singing his songs. But this world seems cold, 'artifice of eternity', lifeless and a poor contrast to the warm, heaving, teeming 'salmon-falls, mackerel-crowded seas' world of stanza one. I don't believe Yeats has found the perfect solution to the problem of ageing. Is there one?

Examiner's Comment

A close reading of the poem is evident in this response to Yeats's search for escape. Engagement is evident in the response and was well supported by quotations. The student showed confidence in the concluding remarks. A-grade standard.

CLASS/HOMEWORK EXERCISES

1. Yeats often places himself at the centre of his work. Do you find this to be true in 'Sailing to Byzantium'? Give reasons for your answer.

2. Copy the table below into your own notes and fill in critical comments about the last two quotations.

Key Quotes

That is no country for old men	Yeats feels that Ireland is not a suitable place to live when old.
all neglect/Monuments of unageing intellect	Young people, because they are in the vigour of their youth, are only concerned with living life through their senses and have no time for matters of the mind or soul.
Into the artifice of eternity	
I shall never take/My bodily form from any natural thing	

8 *from* MEDITATIONS IN TIME OF CIVIL WAR:
THE STARE'S NEST BY MY WINDOW

The bees build in the crevices
Of loosening masonry, and there
The mother birds bring grubs and flies.
My wall is loosening; honey-bees,
Come build in the empty house of the stare.   5

We are closed in, and the key is turned
On our uncertainty; somewhere
A man is killed, or a house burned,
Yet no clear fact to be discerned:
Come build in the empty house of the stare.   10

A barricade of stone or of wood;
Some fourteen days of civil war;
Last night they trundled down the road
That dead young soldier in his blood:
Come build in the empty house of the stare.   15

We had fed the heart on fantasies,
The heart's grown brutal from the fare;
More substance in our enmities
Than in our love; O honey-bees,
Come build in the empty house of the stare.   20

'days of civil war'

GLOSSARY

Stare is another name for the starling, a bird with distinctive dark brown or greenish-black feathers.

3   *grubs*: larvae of insects.

12   *civil war*: the Irish Civil War (1922–23) between Republicans who fought for full independence and supporters of the Anglo-Irish Treaty.

13   *trundled*: rolled.

17   *fare*: diet (of dreams).

18   *enmities*: disputes; hatred.

EXPLORATIONS

1. Comment on how Yeats creates an atmosphere of concern and insecurity in stanzas two and three.

2. In your opinion, how effective is the symbol of the bees as a civilising force amid all the destruction of war? Support your answer with close reference to the poem.

3. How would you describe the dominant mood of the poem? Is it positive or negative? Refer closely to the text in your answer.

STUDY NOTES

The Irish Civil War prompted Yeats to consider the brutality and insecurity caused by conflict. It also made him reflect on his own identity as part of the Anglo-Irish Ascendancy. The poet wrote elsewhere that he had been shocked and depressed by the fighting during the first months of hostilities, yet he was determined not to grow bitter or to lose sight of the beauty of nature. He wrote this poem after seeing a stare building its nest in a hole beside his window.

Much of the poem is dominated by the images of building and collapse. **Stanza one** introduces this tension between creativity ('bees build') and disintegration ('loosening'). In responding to the bitter civil war, Yeats finds suitable **symbols in the nurturing natural world** to express his own hopes. Addressing the bees, he asks that they 'build in the empty house of the stare'. He is desperately conscious of the political vacuum being presently filled by bloodshed. His desperate cry for help seems heartfelt in tone. There is also a possibility that the poet is addressing himself – he will have to revise his own attitudes to the changing political realities caused by the war.

In **stanza two**, Yeats expresses a sense of being **threatened by the conflict** around him: 'We are closed in'. The use of the plural pronoun suggests a community under siege. He is fearful of the future: 'our uncertainty'. Is the poet reflecting on the threat to his own immediate household or to the once powerful Anglo-Irish ruling class? The constant rumours of everyday violence are highlighted in the stark descriptions: 'A man is killed, or a house burned'. Such occurrences almost seem routine in the grim reality of war.

Stanza three opens with a **haunting image**, the 'barricade of stone', an enduring symbol of division and hostility. The vehemence and inhumanity of the times is driven home by the stark report of soldiers who 'trundled down the road' and left one 'dead young soldier in his blood'. Such atrocities add greater depth to the plaintive refrain for regeneration: 'Come build in the empty house of the stare'.

In the **final stanza**, Yeats faces up to the root causes of war: 'We had fed the heart on fantasies'. Dreams of achieving independence have led to even greater hatred ('enmities') and intransigence than could have been imagined. It is a tragic irony that the Irish nation has become more divided than ever before. The poet seems despairing as he accepts the failure represented by civil conflict: 'The heart's grown brutal'. It is as though he is reprimanding himself for daring to imagine a brave new world. His **final plea for healing** and reconstruction is strengthened by an emphatic 'O' to show Yeats's depth of feeling: 'O honeybees,/ Come build in the empty house of the stare'.

ANALYSIS

'Images of ruin and renewal are in constant opposition in this poem.' Write a paragraph in response to this statement, supporting your points with reference from the text.

Sample Paragraph

'The Stare's Nest by my Window' is mainly about conflict, and particularly the Irish Civil War. It is not surprising that the poem contains many symbols and images of ruin and destruction. Yeats watches the bees building a nest in 'loosening masonry' outside his window. It's ironic. Something new is happening among the ruins. The bees are constructing. Building for the future. It is symbolic that something positive is taking place. This is a key theme in the poem. Yeats is hopeful in spite of the war. The poet's use of symbolism contrasts the two forces of ruin and renewal when he says 'build in the empty house'. There are other images of ruin e.g. the 'house burned' and the ruined life of the 'young soldier in his blood'. These images remind us of what happens in wartime. But Yeats seems to argue that we can learn from nature. He hopes that just as the birds take care of their young, Ireland will recover from war. In the future there will be renewal after all the ruin.

Examiner's Comment

There are a number of focused points made in this paragraph and the candidate makes a reasonable attempt to use supporting references. The expression is disjointed at times and the point about symbolism is repeated unnecessarily. A solid C-grade standard.

CLASS/HOMEWORK EXERCISES

1. Repetition is an important feature in this poem. Comment on its effectiveness in enhancing our understanding of the poet's themes.

2. Copy the table below into your own notes and fill in critical comments about the last two quotations.

Key Quotes

The mother birds bring grubs and flies	Details of nurturing in nature are used as a contrast to the background violence and devastation of warfare.
Yet no clear fact to be discerned	Many Irish people were confused by the Civil War and families were sometimes bitterly divided.
My wall is loosening	
The heart's grown brutal	

9 IN MEMORY OF EVA GORE-BOOTH AND CON MARKIEWICZ

The light of evening, Lissadell,
Great windows open to the south,
Two girls in silk kimonos, both
Beautiful, one a gazelle.
But a raving autumn shears   5
Blossom from the summer's wreath;
The older is condemned to death,
Pardoned, drags out lonely years
Conspiring among the ignorant.
I know not what the younger dreams –   10
Some vague Utopia – and she seems
When withered old and skeleton-gaunt,
An image of such politics.
Many a time I think to seek
One or the other out and speak   15
Of that old Georgian mansion, mix
Pictures of the mind, recall
That table and the talk of youth,
Two girls in silk kimonos, both
Beautiful, one a gazelle.   20

Dear shadows, now you know it all,
All the folly of a fight
With a common wrong or right.
The innocent and the beautiful
Have no enemy but time;   25
Arise and bid me strike a match
And strike another till time catch;
Should the conflagration climb,
Run till all the sages know.
We the great gazebo built,   30
They convicted us of guilt;
Bid me strike a match and blow.

'that old Georgian mansion'

GLOSSARY

1	*Lissadell*: the Gore-Booth family home in Co. Sligo.	11	*Utopia*: a perfect world.
3	*kimonos*: traditional Japanese robes.	22	*folly*: foolishness.
4	*gazelle*: graceful antelope.	28	*conflagration*: blazing inferno.
5	*shears*: cuts.	29	*sages*: philosophers.
9	*Conspiring*: plotting; scheming.	30	*gazebo*: ornamental summer house, sometimes seen as a sign of extravagance.

EXPLORATIONS

1. What mood does Yeats create in the first four lines of the poem? Explain how he achieves this mood.

2. Would you agree that this is a poem of contrasts? How does Yeats use contrasts to express his thoughts and feelings? Support your points with relevant reference.

3. What picture of Yeats himself emerges from this poem? Use close reference to the text to support the points you make.

STUDY NOTES

Yeats wrote this poem about the two Gore-Booth sisters shortly after their deaths. He was 62 at the time. Eva was a noted campaigner for women's rights and Constance was a revolutionary who took part in the 1916 Rising. She later became the first woman elected to the British House of Commons at Westminster. The poet had once been fascinated by their youthful grace and beauty, but he became increasingly opposed to their political activism. Although the poem is a memorial to the two women, it also reveals Yeats's own views about the changes that had occurred in Ireland over his lifetime.

Stanza one begins on a nostalgic note, with Yeats recalling a magical summer's evening in the company of the Gore-Booth sisters. The details he remembers suggest a **world of elegance and privilege** in the girls' family home, Lissadell House, overlooking Sligo Bay. 'Great windows' are a reminder of the grandeur to be found in the Anglo-Irish 'Big House'. Eva and Constance are portrayed as being delicately beautiful, their elusive femininity indicated by the exotic 'silk kimonos' they wear. The poet compares one of the girls to 'a gazelle', stylishly poised and graceful.

The abrupt contrast of mood in **line 5** disrupts the tranquil scene. Yeats considers the harsh effects of time and how it changes everything. He describes autumn (personified as an overenthusiastic gardener) as 'raving' and uncontrollable. The metaphor illustrates the way **time destroys** ('shears') the simple perfection of youth ('Blossom'). Typically, Yeats chooses images from the natural world to express his own retrospective outlook.

In **lines 7–13**, the poet shows his **deep contempt** for the involvement of both the Gore-Booth sisters in revolutionary politics. As far as Yeats is concerned, their activism 'among the ignorant' was a great mistake. These beautiful young women wasted their lives for a 'vague Utopia'. The graphic image of one of the girls growing 'withered old and skeleton-gaunt' is also used to symbolise the unattractive political developments of the era. Repulsed by the idea, Yeats retreats into the more sophisticated world of Lissadell's 'old Georgian mansion'.

The **second stanza** is in marked contrast to the first. Yeats addresses the spirits ('shadows') of Eva and Constance. The tone of voice is unclear. It appears to be compassionate, but there is an undertone of weariness as well. He goes on to scold the two women for wasting their lives on 'folly'. Yeats seems angry that their innocence and beauty have been sacrificed for nothing. It is as though he feels **they have betrayed both their own femininity and their social class**. If they had only known it, their one and only enemy was time.

In the **final lines** of the poem, Yeats dramatises his feelings by turning all his **resentment against time** itself. He associates the failed lives of the women with the decay of the Anglo-Irish Ascendancy. The energetic rhythm and repetition reflect his fury as he imagines striking match after match ('And strike another till time catch') and is consumed in a great 'conflagration'. The poet imagines that the significance of this inferno will eventually be understood by those who are wise, the 'sages'. In the last sentence, Yeats considers how 'They' (the enemies of the Anglo-Irish Ascendancy) hastened the end of a grand cultural era in Ireland. The 'great gazebo' is a symbol of the fine houses and gracious living that were slowly disappearing. The poem ends on a defiant note ('Bid me strike a match and blow'), with Yeats inviting the ghosts of Eva and Constance to help him resist the devastating effects of time.

ANALYSIS

To what extent is the poem a lament for the loss of youth and beauty? Refer closely to the text in your answer.

Sample Paragraph

'In Memory of Eva Gore-Booth and Con Markiewicz' is largely focused on the effects of time as an agent of destruction. Yeats begins by describing the two sisters as 'two girls'. I think his nostalgic portrayal of the time he shared with them at Lissadell is filled with regret. He remembers the summer evenings relaxing together 'and the talk of youth'. Yeats contrasts the beautiful girls in their silk kimonos with the way they were in their later years – 'withered old and skeleton-gaunt'. The image is startling, evidence of how he views the ravages of time. It is all the more shocking when compared with the exquisite kimonos – symbols of lost beauty. I think Yeats is also regretful of his own lost youth. At the end of the poem, he shows his anger at ageing and argues that youth has 'no enemy but time'.

Examiner's Comment

Although short, this is a well-focused paragraph which directly addresses the question. The references and quotes are carefully chosen and show a clear engagement with the poem. The use of the unnecessary 'I think' weakens the expression slightly. Otherwise, a good B-grade response.

CLASS/HOMEWORK EXERCISES

1. From your reading of the poem, how would you describe Yeats's true feelings towards the two women? Support the points you make with reference and/or quotation.

2. Copy the table below into your own notes and fill in critical comments about the last two quotations.

Key Quotes

The light of evening, Lissadell,/Great windows open to the south	These beautiful opening lines recreate the leisurely lifestyle associated with the Anglo-Irish gentry, the class to which Yeats belonged.
That table and the talk of youth	This is another reminder of the potential the sophisticated Gore-Booth sisters once had.
Two girls in silk kimonos	
Arise and bid me strike a match	

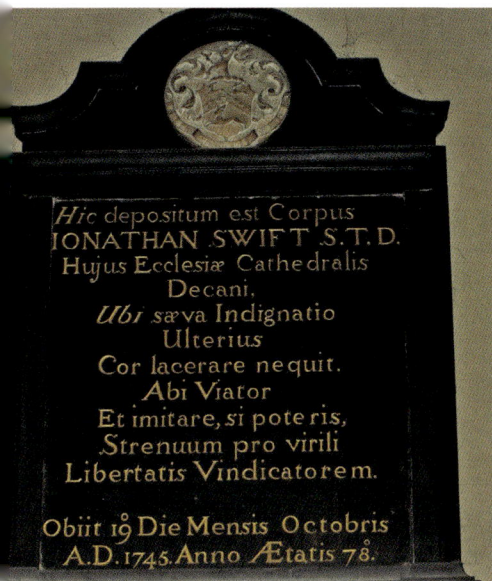

10 SWIFT'S EPITAPH

Swift has sailed into his rest;
Savage indignation there
Cannot lacerate his breast.
Imitate him if you dare,
World-besotted traveller; he   5
Served human liberty.

'Swift's Epitaph'

GLOSSARY

Swift: Jonathan Swift, satirist and clergyman, author of Gulliver's Travels and dean of St Patrick's Cathedral. The original inscription in Latin is on his memorial in the cathedral. Yeats liked to spend time there.

Epitaph: inscription for a tomb or memorial.

1 **his rest**: suggestion of afterlife; death is not an end.

2 **Savage indignation**: the driving force of Swift's satirical work. He believed in a society where wrong was punished and good rewarded.

3 **lacerate**: cut; tear.

5 **World-besotted**: obsessed with travelling or with material concerns rather than spiritual matters.

5-6 **he /Served human liberty**: Yeats believed Swift served the liberty of the intellect, not liberty for the common people. Yeats associated democracy with organised mobs of ignorant people.

> ## EXPLORATIONS

1. How would you describe the tone of this poem?

2. Comment on the poet's use of the verb 'lacerate'. What do you think Yeats is trying to convey?

> ## STUDY NOTES

'Swift's Epitaph' is a translation from the original Latin epitaph composed by Swift for himself. Yeats adds a new first line to the original. He regarded this epitaph as the 'greatest... in history'.

W. B. Yeats admired Swift, who was proud and solitary and belonged to the Anglo-Irish tradition, as did Yeats himself. He regarded the Anglo-Irish as superior. He once said, 'We have created most of the modern literature of this country. We have created the best of its political intelligence.' **Yeats's additional first line** to the epitaph conveys a dignified sailing into the spiritual afterlife by the deceased Swift. The rest of the poem is a **translation** from the Latin original. Swift is now free from all the negative reactions he was subjected to when alive: 'Savage indignation there/Cannot lacerate his breast.' Swift's self-portrait conveys the impression of a man of fierce **independence and pride**. 'Imitate him if you dare' is the challenge thrown down like a gauntlet to the reader to try to be like him. 'World-besotted traveller' can be read as a man who has travelled extensively in his imagination as well as in reality. His contribution to humanity is summed up in the final sentence: 'he/Served human liberty'. **He freed the artist** from the masses so that the artist could 'make liberty visible'. The tone of this short, compressed poem is proud and defiant, like Swift.

ANALYSIS

What impression of Swift do you get from this poem by Yeats? Write a paragraph in response, supporting your views with reference to the text.

Sample Paragraph

I thought that Swift was a confident, fearless man who dared to voice his own truth. The tone of the poem, from its opening, 'Swift has sailed into his rest', suggests a man who knew what he was doing and did it with style. It suggests a spiritual man, 'into his rest'. He is embarking on an afterlife of some sort. He was a man who braved the censure of the world, 'Savage indignation there/Cannot lacerate his breast'. He dared to say what he felt he had to say. A challenge is thrown down to the reader, 'Imitate him if you dare'. Obviously, both Swift and Yeats considered that Swift would be a hard act to follow. The phrase 'world-besotted traveller' could mean that the poet considered that modern man was too obsessed with material possessions, while Swift was concerned with loftier matters such as the moral good. The final sentence, 'he/Served human liberty', states that he improved the human condition by making us all free. This is where I, as a 21st-century reader, part company with the epitaph. Swift did not fight for freedom as we understand it. It could be argued that he only believed in liberty for a select few, the Anglo-Irish Protestants. Yeats's tone is one of admiration for this courageous man, but modern man would not agree with this elitist view of freedom for a select group. Also the confident challenge to the reader to match Swift 'if you dare' comes across to me as arrogance. While I admire Swift's fearlessness, I do not admire his elitism or arrogance.

Examiner's Comment

An original A-grade response to the question. The paragraph raises interesting discussion points about both writers. There is detailed support throughout and a fluent control of language in arguing the case vigorously.

CLASS/HOMEWORK EXERCISES

1. Is Yeats's use of the sailing metaphor effective? Briefly explain your answer.

2. Copy the table below into your own notes and fill in critical comments about the last two quotations.

Key Quotes

Swift has sailed into his rest	Swift has now entered the next life. The tone reflects Yeats's admiration and respect.
Savage indignation there/ Cannot lacerate his breast	He is free from criticism now. Ironically, Swift's own savage criticism is now also at rest.
World-besotted traveller	
he/Served human liberty	

11 AN ACRE OF GRASS

Picture and book remain,
An acre of green grass
For air and exercise,
Now strength and body goes;
Midnight, an old house   5
Where nothing stirs but a mouse.

My temptation is quiet.
Here at life's end
Neither loose imagination,
Nor the mill of the mind   10
Consuming its rag and bone,
Can make the truth known.

Grant me an old man's frenzy,
Myself must I remake
Till I am Timon and Lear   15
Or that William Blake
Who beat upon the wall
Till Truth obeyed his call;

A mind Michael Angelo knew
That can pierce the clouds,   20
Or inspired by frenzy
Shake the dead in their shrouds;
Forgotten else by mankind,
An old man's eagle mind.

'An acre of green grass'

GLOSSARY

(A–Z)

2   *acre*: the secluded garden of Yeats's home, where he spent his final years.
5   *an old house*: the house was in Rathfarnham, Co. Dublin.
9   *loose imagination*: vague, unfocused ideas.
13   *frenzy*: wildly excited state.
15   *Timon and Lear*: two of Shakespeare's elderly tragic heroes, both of whom raged against the world.
16   *William Blake*: English visionary poet and painter (1757–1827).
19   *Michael Angelo*: Michelangelo, Italian Renaissance artist (1475–1564).
22   *shrouds*: burial garments.

EXPLORATIONS

1. How does Yeats create a mood of calm and serenity in the opening stanza?

2. Briefly explain the change of tone in stanza three.

STUDY NOTES

Written in 1936 when Yeats was 71, the poet expresses his resentment towards ageing gracefully. Instead, he will dedicate himself to seeking wisdom through frenzied creativity. People sometimes take a narrow view of the elderly and consider them completely redundant. In Yeats's case, he is determined not to let old age crush his spirit.

Stanza one paints a picture of retirement as a surrender to death. Yeats's life has been reduced to suit his basic needs. 'Picture and book' might refer to the poet's memories. Physically weak, he feels like a prisoner whose enclosed garden area is for 'air and exercise'. There is an underlying **feeling of alienation and inactivity**: 'nothing stirs'.

In **stanza two**, the poet says that it would be easy to give in to the stereotypical image of placid contentment: 'My temptation is quiet', especially since old age ('life's end') has weakened his creative powers. **Yeats admits that his 'loose imagination' is not as sharp as it was when he was in his prime**. He no longer finds immediate inspiration ('truth') in everyday experiences, which he compares to life's 'rag and bone'.

The **third stanza** opens on a much more dramatic and forceful note as the poet confronts his fears: 'Grant me an old man's frenzy'. Yeats's personal prayer is totally lacking in meekness. Instead, he urges himself to focus enthusiastically on his own creative purpose – 'frenzy'. **He pledges to 'remake' himself** in the image of such heroic figures as Timon, Lear and William Blake. The passionate tone and run-on lines add to his sense of commitment to his art.

In **stanza four**, Yeats develops **his spirited pursuit of meaningful old age** by reflecting on 'A mind Michael Angelo knew'. The poet is stimulated and encouraged to follow the great artist's example and 'pierce the clouds'. The image suggests the daring power of imagination to lift the spirit in the search for truth and beauty. The final lines build to a climax as Yeats imagines the joys of 'An old man's eagle mind'. Such intense creativity can 'Shake the dead' and allow the poet to continue experiencing life to its fullest.

ANALYSIS

Based on your reading of the poem, comment on Yeats's response to old age. Refer to the text in your answer.

Sample Paragraph

Yeats takes a highly unusual approach to ageing in 'An Acre of Grass'. He seems to be happy to sit reading in his quiet 'acre of grass'. Everything seems to be very organised, a little too organised for his liking. In the first few lines, we get a picture of someone close to second childhood, with his 'picture and book'. Late at night, he is awake and feels that 'nothing stirs but a mouse'. This is like the mind of a little child and it is what Yeats rebels against. He does not want to fade away. He really wants to keep being a poet and seek truth. To him, it is 'an old man's frenzy'. This suggests that he would prefer to be thought of as mad, but to keep producing his poems rather than fade away quietly. He wants to be like King Lear, the old king in Shakespeare's play who fought to the bitter end. Yeats wants to live life to the full, not fade away quietly. He wants to write his poetry and make use of his active mind until he takes his last breath. I admire his energy even though he seems a grumpy old man. His tone is fierce and defiant throughout most of the poem. He will not fade away on his acre of grass.

Examiner's Comment

There is some very good discussion in this paragraph and a clear sense of individual engagement. The idea of Yeats rejecting second childhood is well supported. The style of writing lacks control at times and there are some awkward expressions and repetition ('fade away'). An average C grade.

CLASS/HOMEWORK EXERCISES

1. How would you describe the structure of this poem? Formal or informal? Regular or irregular? How does the poem's structure and form emphasise Yeats's message about old age?

2. Copy the table below into your own notes and fill in critical comments about the last two quotations.

Key Quotes

Midnight, an old house/ Where nothing stirs but a mouse	Yeats creates an atmosphere of stillness and emptiness associated with lonely old age.
Here at life's end	Central to the poem is Yeats's awareness of death, which makes him determined to make the most of life.
Grant me an old man's frenzy	
An old man's eagle mind	

12   UNDER BEN BULBEN

V
Irish poets, learn your trade,
Sing whatever is well made,
Scorn the sort now growing up
All out of shape from toe to top,
Their unremembering hearts and heads   5
Base-born products of base beds.
Sing the peasantry, and then
Hard-riding country gentlemen,
The holiness of monks, and after
Porter-drinkers' randy laughter;   10
Sing the lords and ladies gay
That were beaten into the clay
Through seven heroic centuries;
Cast your mind on other days
That we in coming days may be   15
Still the indomitable Irishry.

VI
Under bare Ben Bulben's head
In Drumcliff churchyard Yeats is laid,
An ancestor was rector there
Long years ago, a church stands near,   20
By the road an ancient cross.
No marble, no conventional phrase;
On limestone quarried near the spot
By his command these words are cut:
Cast a cold eye   25
On life, on death.
Horseman, pass by!

'Under bare Ben Bulben's head'

GLOSSARY

A-Z

2   *whatever is well made*: great art.
6   *base*: low; unworthy.
16   *indomitable*: invincible; unbeatable.
17   *Under bare Ben Bulben's head*: defiant symbol of the famous mountain.

19   *ancestor*: the poet's greatgrandfather.
27   *Horseman*: possibly a symbolic figure from local folklore; or possibly any passer-by.

EXPLORATIONS

1. Comment on the tone used by Yeats in giving advice to other writers. Refer to the text in your answer.

2. From your reading of the poem, explain the kind of 'Irishry' that Yeats wishes to see celebrated in poetry. Support the points you make with reference or quotation.

3. Describe the mood of Drumcliff churchyard as visualised by the poet. Use close reference to the text to show how Yeats uses language to create this mood.

STUDY NOTES

This was one of Yeats's last poems. Sections V and VI of the elegy sum up his personal views on the future of Irish poetry and also include the enigmatic epitaph he composed for his own gravestone. Using art as a gateway to spiritual fulfilment is characteristic of the poet.

Section V is a hard-hitting address by Yeats to his contemporaries and all the poets who will come after him. He encourages them to set the highest 'well made' standards for their work. His uncompromisingly negative view of contemporary writing ('out of shape from toe to top') is quickly clarified. The reason why modern literature is in such a state of confusion is that the poets' 'unremembering hearts and heads' **have lost touch with tradition**. The formality and discipline of great classic poetry have been replaced by unstructured writing and free verse. The authoritative tone becomes even more scathing as Yeats castigates the inferiority of his peers as 'Base-born products'.

It is not only intellectual artistic tradition that the poet admires; he finds another valuable tradition in the legends and myths of old Ireland. Yeats urges his fellow writers to 'Sing the peasantry'. But he also advises them to **absorb other cultural traditions**. Here he includes the 'Hard-riding country gentlemen' of his own Anglo-Irish class and the 'holiness of monks' – those who seek truth through ascetic or spiritual means. Even the more sensuous 'randy laughter' of 'Porter-drinkers' can be inspirational. For Yeats, the peasant and aristocratic traditions are equally worth celebrating. Irish history is marked by a combination of joy, heroism, defeat and resilience. Yet despite (or perhaps because of) his harsh criticism of the present generation, there is little doubt about the poet's passionate desire to encourage new writing that would reflect the true greatness of 'indomitable Irishry'.

Section VI is a great deal less dogmatic. Writing in the third person, Yeats describes his final resting place in Drumcliff. The voice is **detached and dignified**. Using a series of unadorned images, he takes us to the simple churchyard at the foot of Ben Bulben. The mountain stands as a proud symbol of how our unchanging silent origins outlive human tragedy. It is to his Irish roots that the poet ultimately wants to return. His wishes are modest but curt – 'No marble'. Keen to avoid the well-worn headstone inscriptions, Yeats provides his own incisive epitaph. The three short lines are enigmatic and balance opposing views, typical of so much of his poetry. The poet's last warning ('Cast a cold eye') reminds us to live measured lives based on a realistic understanding of the cycle of life and death. The beautiful Christian setting, subdued tone and measured rhythm all contribute to the quiet dignity of Yeats's final farewell.

ANALYSIS

Some people have criticised this poem as 'a bitter old man's snobbish rant'. Write your response to this comment, supporting your views with reference to the text.

Sample Paragraph

It's easy to see why Yeats could be accused of being elitist and superior. As he nears death, he is clearly not concerned with political correctness. He knows his own worth as the leading Irish writer of his times. He gets straight to the point in advising younger poets – 'learn your trade'. If I was an unpublished writer, I would take him seriously, rather than feeling precious. Yeats does not suffer fools easily and he has no respect for shoddy work that is 'out of shape'. His tone can be harsh, even shrill on occasions, but he is stressing a basic lesson that good writing must be disciplined. Rather than seeing him as someone who is ranting, I appreciate the way Yeats shows his interest in standards. His attitude is actually inclusive. He wants young poets to learn from every source available to them – sacred texts, the Protestant and peasant Catholic traditions, and from the 'Porter-drinkers' of Ireland. I can see no bitterness here. His own funeral instructions are actually humble. He does not demand a hero's courageous tomb, just a simple plot in a country graveyard. To me, Yeats comes across as a man who is neither arrogant nor snobbish, but as a legendary writer concerned about Irish literature.

Examiner's Comment

This is a very spirited and well-sustained personal response that reflects a clear viewpoint. Points are supported robustly with apt quotations and the arguments range over the whole poem. In the main, expression is fluent and controlled. An impressive A-grade standard.

> ## CLASS/HOMEWORK EXERCISES

1. Is Yeats's epitaph in keeping with the views he expresses throughout the rest of the poem? Explain your answer using reference to the text.

2. Copy the table below into your own notes and fill in critical comments about the last two quotations.

Key Quotes

Irish poets, learn your trade	Yeats is enthusiastic about the need for poets to return to the formal, classical tradition that will again celebrate Ireland's heroic and spiritual values.
Base-born products of base beds	The poet is contemptuous of modern poetry, much of which he believed came from inferior writers. Repetition emphasises his disdain.
By the road an ancient cross	
Cast a cold eye/On life, on death	

13 POLITICS

'In our time the destiny of man presents its meanings in political terms.'
Thomas Mann

How can I, that girl standing there,
My attention fix
On Roman or on Russian
Or on Spanish politics,
Yet here's a travelled man that knows   5
What he talks about,
And there's a politician
That has read and thought,
And maybe what they say is true
Of war and war's alarms,   10
But O that I were young again
And held her in my arms!

'But O that I were young again/And held her in my arms'

GLOSSARY

Politics: winning and using power to govern society.
Thomas Mann was a German novelist who argued that the future of man was determined by states and governments.

3–4 *On Roman or on Russian/Or on Spanish politics*: a reference to the political upheavals of Europe in the 1930s.

EXPLORATIONS

1. This poem suggests that politics are not important. Does the poet convince you? Write a paragraph in response, with reference to the text.

2. Where does the language used in the poem convey a sense of deep longing? How effective is this?

STUDY NOTES

'Politics' is a satire written in 1939 when Yeats was 73 in response to a magazine article. He said it was based on 'a moment of meditation'.

A **satire** uses ridicule to expose foolishness. A magazine article praised Yeats for his 'public' work. The poet was delighted with this word, as one of his aims had always been to 'move the common people'. However, the article went on to say that Yeats should have used this 'public' voice to address public issues such as politics. Yeats disagreed, as he had always regarded politics as dishonest and superficial. He thought professional politicians manipulated through 'false news'. This is evident from the ironic comment, 'And maybe what they say is true'. Here we see the poet's indifference to these matters.

This poem addresses **real truths**, the proper material for poems, the universal experience of **human relationships**, not the infinite abstractions that occupied politicians ('war and war's alarms'). Big public events, Yeats is suggesting, are not as important as love. The girl in the poem is more important than all the politics in the world: 'How can I... My attention fix/On Roman or on Russian/Or on Spanish politics'? So Yeats is overthrowing the epigraph at the beginning of the poem where the novelist Thomas Mann is stating that people should be concerned with political matters. Politics is the winning and using of power to govern the state. Yeats is adopting the persona of the distracted lover who is unable to focus on the tangled web of European politics in the 1930s. This poem was to be placed in his last poetry collection, almost like a farewell, as he states again that what he desires is youth and love.

But this poem can also give another view. Is the 'she' in the poem Ireland? Yeats has addressed public issues in poems such as 'Easter, 1916' and 'September 1913' and he was already a senator in the Irish government. As usual, he leaves us with questions as he draws us through this deceptively simple poem with its **ever-changing tones** that range from the questioning opening to mockery, doubt and finally longing. The **steady rhyme** (the second line rhymes with the fourth and so on) drives the poem forward to its emphatic **closing wish**, the cry of an old man who wishes to recapture his youth and lost love.

ANALYSIS

Do you agree with Yeats that only youth and love matter? Discuss, using reference to the poem.

Sample Paragraph

I think Yeats is expressing a deep-seated desire in all of us. We all want to be concerned with our own lives ('My attention fix'), not on the mess that the political world seems to be in, 'Roman or on Russian/Or on Spanish politics'. It is the same today. How often have we turned off the news in disgust or because we just couldn't take any more 'Of war and war's alarms'? And yet I would like to suggest another view on this. We get the governments we deserve. Democracy is fragile when good people are inattentive. So although I agree with Yeats's sentiments and can fully understand his closing wish, 'But O that I were young again/And held her in my arms', I feel that we have to sometimes safeguard the destiny of man. We are the generation that is on watch now for the protection of the environment and the safety of humanity. I think Thomas Mann has a point as he says, 'In our time the destiny of man presents its meanings in political terms'.

Examiner's Comment

The student has engaged personally with the question and has presented a considered argument using relevant quotations effectively. The answer reads well and adjectives (such as 'fragile' and 'inattentive') are well chosen. Grade A.

CLASS/HOMEWORK EXERCISES

1. Comment on the rhythm of the poem, paying particular attention to the use of run-on lines.

2. Copy the table below into your own notes and fill in critical comments about the last two quotations.

Key Quotes

How can I, that girl standing there,/My attention fix	The poet is declaring that his attention is on his personal concerns rather than public concerns such as politics.
On Roman or on Russian	The alliterative 'r' emphasises Yeats's tone of frustration.
And there's a politician/That has read and thought	
But O that I were young again/And held her in my arms	

LEAVING CERT SAMPLE ESSAY

Write an article for a school magazine introducing the poetry of W. B. Yeats to Leaving Certificate students. Tell them what he wrote about and explain what you liked about his writing, suggesting some poems that you think they would enjoy reading. Support your points by reference to the poetry by Yeats that you studied.

Marking Scheme Guidelines

Candidates are free to adopt a register they consider appropriate to the task. The task contains three closely related elements, which may be addressed separately or together. It is not necessary that these elements be given equal treatment.

• What he wrote about (themes, concerns, subject matter).

• What you liked about his writing.

• Suggest enjoyable poems. Reward responses that show clear evidence of engagement with the poems and/or poet.

Some of the following areas might be addressed:

• Political and personal perspective of the poems.

• Variety of the themes.

• Strength of Yeats's vision.

• Depth and range of his feelings.

• Features of style, such as language, imagery, symbolism, sound, etc.

Sample Essay

(Introduction to Yeats)

1. *Allow me to introduce to you a man of passion with a love for art and a great admiration for Ireland's heroes. Seamus Heaney described this man as 'a dreamer, an idealist'. This man, just like many of you, longed for a retreat from all the pressures of civilisation, and I feel we can all identify with him. This man is W. B. Yeats.*

2. *Many of you today may be feeling fed up with school, home, life in general. Yeats felt the same way and longed to escape oppressive city life. This retreat from the irksome routine of the everyday is evoked in Yeats's most well-known poem, 'The Lake Isle of Innisfree'. After you have read these lines, close your eyes and imagine the scene, the colours, 'midnight's all a glimmer, and noon a purple glow'. Imagine the sounds: 'I hear lake water lapping with low sounds by the shore'. The tranquil atmosphere is summoned by 'and peace comes dropping slow'. Suddenly we are in an idyllic paradise as the soothing effect of the lines quietens our frazzled brains. Yeats stored this hypnotic image in his mind and returned to it every time he needed escape, 'While I stand on the roadway, or on the pavements grey'. He heard it in 'the deep heart's core'. We all, like Yeats, have a place or long to have a place, either physical or mental, that we retreat to when the pressure gets too much.*

3. *We are all Celtic Cubs, and if the title was missing from 'September 1913', we could read this poem as a scathing attack on New Ireland, avaricious, selfish and materialistic. But Yeats wrote this poem primarily in response to the 1913 lock-out and the failure to fund the Hugh Lane Gallery with its collection of wonderful modern art. The anger spits off the page as he graphically describes these self-centred people concerned with outward appearances only. The phrase 'fumble in a greasy till' shows their dependence on money. Equally depressing is their attitude to religion which does not sustain them, but 'dries the marrow from the bone'. O'Leary, the Irish Fenian poet, is what an Irishman should be, someone who thought of his country, not himself. The refrain 'It's with O'Leary in the grave' drives this message home, as Yeats gets angrier ('Was it for this?') at the inability of the contemporary Irish to understand the bigger picture. Bitterly he resigns himself to the fact that his contemporaries just don't understand and he warns them not to judge these heroes by their own standards, 'But let them be ... They're with O'Leary in the grave'.*

4. *'Easter, 1916' is, I admit, a difficult poem, but it is worth the struggle. I particularly liked the fact that Yeats was big enough to admit he was wrong. The people he had condemned in the previous poem were capable of great sacrifices and indeed 'A terrible beauty' was born. Even Major MacBride who had married Maud Gonne, the love of Yeats's life, 'A drunken vainglorious lout', was included in 'the song'. The structure of the poem is very clever, four verses, two with 24 lines, two with 16 lines, commemorating the date of the rebellion, the 24th of April 1916. Yeats admires the revolutionary spirit and their dream for independence for Ireland. But his choice of 'the stone' as a symbol of this spirit warns of danger. Sacrifice can turn a heart to stone. When is enough enough? 'O when may it suffice?' We see this every day in current political struggles. The poem ends with a litany, a list of holy names, of the dead: they are 'changed' and will be remembered 'wherever green is worn'.*

5. *My personal favourite is 'Sailing to Byzantium'. Yeats wrote some of his best poetry in his final years, as he raged against old age and death. He writes from an unusual perspective, looking back as he embarks on a journey. He realises he has to go because 'That is no country for old men'. The alliteration shows a fertile land teeming with passionate young life. 'Fish, flesh, or fowl, commend all summer long/ Whatever is begotten, born, and dies'. Pitiful images describe old age, 'A tattered coat upon a stick', something that is only used to scare birds. Again, as in our first poem, Yeats longs to escape. He decides that he will not have a body that is natural*

because then it is subject to age. Instead, he chooses one that is an 'artifice'. But even in Paradise there is a problem. The emperor is 'drowsy' to whom Yeats, in his new form of a golden bird, sings. His heart really wishes to be with 'the young/In one another's arms'. I thought it was very interesting how a man could write so openly about growing old. It has very modern echoes when we see the acres of media space devoted to actually preventing ageing!

6. *Before reading this article, you probably had a stereotypical image of Yeats as a serious young man staring sternly out through old-fashioned glasses. Who would have guessed the spirit and passion that lay beneath the stern exterior? Truly Yeats is a poet who sings to us 'Of what is past, or passing, or to come' and we are wide awake to listen.*

(approx. 880 words)

Examiner's Comment

The candidate fulfilled the task eloquently and displayed a robust personal engagement with the poetry. The answer ranged widely to discuss Yeats's subject matter, what was interesting about the writing and the most enjoyable poems. Excellent use of accurate quotation throughout. A very impressive response.

GRADE: A1

P = 15/15

C = 15/15

L = 15/15

M = 5/5

Total = 50/50

SAMPLE LEAVING CERT QUESTIONS ON YEATS'S POETRY

(45/50 MINUTES)

1. Give your personal estimation of the poetry of W. B. Yeats. Support your answer with reference to the poems on your course.

2. Consider the versions of Ireland that emerge from Yeats's poems. Do these versions form a consistent picture or not? Support your answer with close reference to the poems.

3. If you were asked to give a public reading of some of Yeats's poems, which ones would you choose? Give reasons for your choices, supporting them by reference to the poems by Yeats that you have studied.

Sample Essay Plan (Q1)

Give your personal estimation of the poetry of W. B. Yeats. Support your answer with reference to the poems on your course.

- Intro: A personal response is required; mention both content and style in the response. Public and personal poems are interesting and thought provoking.

- Point 1: 'September 1913' – public poem, accusatory. Note the changing refrain, litany, rhetorical questions, bitter tone, nostalgic view of Irish history.

- Point 2: 'Easter, 1916' – another public poem, an attempt to answer questions about the Rising. All had changed. Yeats admits he was wrong.

- Point 3: 'The Wild Swans at Coole' – autumnal retrospection as he realises how his life had changed in 19 years. Laments loss of youth, passion and love.

- Point 4: 'Sailing to Byzantium' – theme of ageing, use of contrast to convey theme. Declamatory opening, uncertainty a sign of his humanity.

- Conclusion: Yeats – ideal past contrasted with unsatisfactory present, attitude to Irish patriotism, escape, ageing. Raises questions rather than providing answers.

Sample Essay Plan (Q1)

Develop one of the above points into a paragraph.

Sample Paragraph: Point 4

I find the poem 'Sailing to Byzantium' very intriguing. Here was a man who hated the weaknesses brought on by old age: 'An aged man is but a paltry thing'. Yet with passion and fire, he defies time: 'Once out of nature I shall never take/My bodily form from any natural thing'. The rhythmic phrasing of threes conveys the natural harmony of youth and fertility: 'Fish, flesh, or fowl'. This is the world of which Yeats wants to be a part, 'The young in one another's arms'. But that is not life. He presents us with the contrasting truth as he states, 'That is no country for old men'. Again, contrast is used as the beauty of 'artifice', 'the gold mosaic of a wall' is lined up against the brute reality of the soul 'fastened to a dying animal'. Through his clever contrasts, the poet explores the dilemma of ageing, which will come to us all, even though at 17 it seems very remote to me. I was also interested in Yeats's discovery of a flaw in Paradise. Now Yeats is immortal as his soul has taken the bodily form of a golden bird, 'such a form as Grecian goldsmiths make/Of hammered gold and gold enamelling'. However, the audience for his songs/poems, the Emperor, is 'drowsy'. He is not paying attention. Yeats is now raising the question: Is Paradise, 'artifice', all that it is supposed to be? Who will listen as Yeats sings of the great truths, 'Of what is past, or passing, or to come'? All great poets raise questions about life and existence for us to consider. Yeats is no exception.

Examiner's Comment

As part of a full essay answer, this is a competent A-grade paragraph which offers a personal response firmly rooted in the text. The paragraph centres on the use of contrast used by Yeats to explore ageing, and both style and content are examined effectively. Very well supported by suitable quotes.

LAST WORDS ""

'He had this marvellous gift for beating the scrap metal of the day-to-day life into a ringing bell.'

Seamus Heaney

'Yeats's poetry is simple and eloquent to the heart.'

Robert Louis Stevenson

'I have spent my life saying the same thing in different ways.'

W. B. Yeats (writing to his wife)

Glossary of Common Literary Terms

alliteration: the use of the same letter at the beginning of each word or stressed syllable in a line of verse, e.g. 'boilers bursting'.

assonance: the use of the same vowel sound in a group of words, e.g. 'bleared, smeared with toil'.

aubade: a celebratory morning song, sometimes lamenting the parting of lovers.

blank verse: unrhymed iambic pentameter, e.g. 'These waters, rolling from their mountain-springs'.

conceit: an elaborate image or far-fetched comparison, e.g. 'This flea is you and I, and this/Our marriage bed'.

couplet: two successive lines of verse, usually rhymed and of the same metre, e.g. 'So long as men can breathe or eyes can see,/So long lives this, and this gives life to thee'.

elegy: a mournful poem, usually for the dead, e.g. 'Sleep in a world your final sleep has woken'.

emotive language: language designed to arouse an emotional response in the reader, e.g. 'For this that all that blood was shed?'

epiphany: a moment of insight or understanding, e.g. 'Somebody loves us all'.

free verse: unrhymed and unmetred poetry, often used by modern poets, e.g. 'but the words are shadows and you cannot hear me./ You walk away and I cannot follow'.

imagery: descriptive language or word-pictures, especially appealing to the senses, e.g. 'He was speckled with barnacles,/fine rosettes of lime'.

irony: when one thing is said and the opposite is meant, e.g. 'For men were born to pray and save'.

lyric: short musical poem expressing feeling.

metaphor: image that compares two things without using the words 'like' or 'as', e.g. 'I am gall, I am heartburn'.

onomatopoeia: the sound of the word imitates or echoes the sound being described, e.g. 'The murmurous haunt of flies on summer eves'.

paradox: a statement that on the surface appears self-contradictory, e.g. 'I shall have written him one/poem maybe as cold/And passionate as the dawn'.

persona: the speaker or voice in the poem. This is not always the poet, e.g. 'I know that I shall meet my fate/Somewhere among the clouds above'.

personification: where the characteristics of an animate or living being are given to something inanimate, e.g. 'The yellow fog that rubs its back upon the window panes'.

rhyme: identical sound of words, usually at the end of lines of verse, e.g. 'I get down on my knees and do what must be done/And kiss Achilles' hand, the killer of my son'.

rhythm: the beat or movement of words, the arrangement of stressed and unstressed, short and long syllables in a line of poetry, e.g. 'I will arise and go now, and go to Innisfree'.

sestina: a six-stanza, six-line poem with the same six end words occurring throughout. The final stanza contains these six words. 'Time to plant tears, says the almanac:/

The grandmother sings to the marvellous stove/and the child draws another inscrutable house'.

sibilance: the whispering, hissing 's' sound, e.g. 'Singest of summer in full-throated ease'.

sonnet: a 14-line poem. The Petrarchan or Italian sonnet is divided into eight lines (octave) which present a problem or situation. The remaining six lines (sestet) resolve the problem or present another view of the situation. The Shakespearean sonnet is divided into three quatrains and concludes with a rhyming couplet, either summing up what preceded or reversing it.

symbol: a word or phrase representing something other than itself, e.g. 'A tattered coat upon a stick'.

theme: the central idea or message in a poem.

tone: the type of voice or attitude used by the poet towards his or her subject, e.g. 'O but it is dirty'.

villanelle: a five-stanza poem of three lines each, with a concluding quatrain, using only two end rhyming words throughout, e.g. 'I am just going outside and may be some time,/At the heart of the ridiculous, the sublime'.

Acknowledgements

The authors and publisher are grateful to the following for permission to reproduce copyrighted material:

The poems by Emily Dickinson are reprinted by permission of the publishers and the Trustees of Amherst College from *The Poems of Emily Dickinson*, Thomas H. Johnson, ed., Cambridge, Mass: The Belknap Press of Harvard University Press, Copyright © 1951, 1955, 1979, 1983 by the President and Fellows of Harvard College.

The poems 'The Tuft of Flowers', 'Mending Wall', 'After Apple-Picking', 'The Road Not Taken', 'Birches', 'Out, Out—', 'Spring Pools', 'Acquainted with the Night', 'Design' and 'Provide, Provide' by Robert Frost are from *The Poetry of Robert Frost* edited by Edward Connery Lathem. Copyright 1916, 1928, 1930, 1934, 1939, 1969 by Henry Holt and Company, copyright 1936, 1944, 1951, 1956, 1958 by Robert Frost, copyright © 1964, 1967 by Lesley Frost Ballantine.

Poems of John Montague reprinted by kind permission of the author and The Gallery Press, Loughcrew, Oldcastle, County Meath, Ireland, from *New Collected Poems* (2012).

Poems of Eiléan Ní Chuilleanáin reprinted by kind permission of the author and The Gallery Press, Loughcrew, Oldcastle, County Meath, Ireland, from *Selected Poems* (2008) and *The Sun-fish* (2009).

Collected Poems by Sylvia Plath © Sylvia Plath. Reprinted by kind permission of Faber & Faber Ltd.

The authors and publisher have made every effort to trace all copyright holders, but if any has been inadvertently overlooked we would be pleased to make the necessary arrangement at the first opportunity.